# Strategic Planning

## A Practical Guide

Peter J. Rea, Ph.D.
Harold Kerzner, Ph.D.

JOHN WILEY & SONS, INC.
New York Chichester Weinheim Brisbane Singapore Toronto

A NOTE TO THE READER
This book has been electronically reproduced from digital information stored at John Wiley & Sons, Inc. We are pleased that the use of this new technology will enable us to keep works of enduring scholarly value in print as long as there is a reasonable demand for them. The content of this book is identical to previous printings.

This text is printed on acid-free paper. ♾

Copyright © 1997 by John Wiley & Sons, Inc. All rights reserved.

Published simultaneously in Canada.

No part of this publication may be reproduced, stored in a retrieval system or transmitted in any form or by any means, electronic, mechanical, photocopying, recording, scanning or otherwise, except as permitted under Sections 107 or 108 of the 1976 United States Copyright Act, without either the prior written permission of the Publisher, or authorization through payment of the appropriate per-copy fee to the Copyright Clearance Center, 222 Rosewood Drive, Danvers, MA 01923, (978) 750-8400, fax (978) 750-4470. Requests to the Publisher for permission should be addressed to the Permissions Department, John Wiley & Sons, Inc., 111 River Street, Hoboken, NJ 07030, (201) 748-6011, fax (201) 748-6008, E-Mail: PERMREQ@WILEY.COM.

To order books or for customer service please, call 1(800)-CALL-WILEY (225-5945).

This publication is designed to provide accurate and authoritative information in regard to the subject matter covered. It is sold with the understanding that the publisher is not engaged in rendering legal, accounting, or other professional services. If legal advice or other expert assistance is required, the services of a competent professional person should be sought.

**Library of Congress Cataloging-in-Publication Data**

Rea, Peter.
Strategic planning : a practical guide/Peter Rea and Harold Kerzner.
p. cm.
ISBN 0-471-29197-8 (cloth)
1. Strategic planning. I. Kerzner, Harold. II. Title.
HD30.28.R39 1997
658.4'012—dc21 97-14573
CIP

To Our Wives
Julie and Jo Ellyn

# Contents

# Preface

Managers of the future will be under more pressure and will have to meet more challenges than their predecessors. If history has taught us anything, it is that the manager of the future must be an expert planner, specifically with regard to strategic planning and thinking. This textbook is a practical guide to help students and executives apply fundamental strategic concepts to the challenges facing organizations.

Strategic planning has been roundly criticized for being overly intentional and quantitative. In practice, strategic planning can be so intentional that it fails to recognize that plans can also emerge. Strategic planners can also put too much faith in quantitative models that do not take into account how the realities of corporate political life and culture influence strategic decisions. Furthermore, the practice of strategic planning often leads to an endorsement of existing views rather than challenging unquestioned assumptions. Consequently, strategic planning too often hinders rather than promotes strategic thinking.

Clear thinking begins with the formulation of appropriate questions. Yet, the questions and strategic tools that can be used to promote strategic thinking are endless. This text provides fundamental strategic questions that should be raised by all organizations. The text underscores that the way each organization answers fundamental strategic questions will differ according to the organization's circumstances and according to the ability of its executives to resolve strategic questions that are unstructured, ambiguous, and complex.

The text is designed to be a primer for strategic planning, management policy, and strategy. The text covers the "grassroots" principles of strategic planning. The case studies at the end of the chapters are designed to cover only the fundamental issues of strategic planning in selected companies.

The text is designed to be a first course in strategic planning and business policy on the undergraduate and graduate levels. Most faculty members today desire to select their own cases studies from case clearinghouses. Publishers today are providing faculty members with a chance to develop their own case books by selecting from hundreds of available cases. The authors believe that this type of fundamental text, combined with selected case studies, will be the teaching methodology of the future.

PETER REA
HAROLD KERZNER
*Baldwin-Wallace College*

# CHAPTER 1 Strategic Thinking

## The Planet Has Changed and Quickly

In the late 1980s and early 1990s, the Berlin Wall fell, the Warsaw Pact was dissolved, the Soviet Union imploded, and Germany was reunited. In the fall of 1995, Mitterand, Mulrony, Thatcher, Bush, Reagan, Kohl, and Gorbachev attended a conference sponsored by the Bush Library to review events of this unprecedented moment in history. While each head of state differed in opinion about why these events occurred, all agreed that predicting the end of the Cold War was inconceivable at the end of the 1980s (PBS interview, 1995).

Despite all the resources available to them, the leaders of the most powerful nations on earth were unable to predict events two to five years out. If these leaders cannot foresee the future with any clarity, what chance does any organization have?

Corporations face their own set of uncertain events such as rapidly shifting consumer preferences, increased worldwide free trade, privatization, deregulation, and technology transfer. To cope with these issues, organizations can choose from an array of remedies. Popular techniques include total quality management (TQM), continuous improvement, benchmarking, re-engineering, downsizing, learning organizations, groupware, customer focus, core competencies, self-directed teams, just-in-time inventories, scenario planning, activity-based costing, outsourcing, and strategic alliances (Ackoff, 1993).

Ackoff (1993) reported on a survey of 500 executives from manufacturing and service companies conducted by A. D. Little that confirmed that most U.S. companies (93%) have some form of quality-improvement program. Nevertheless, many reported they were not improving fast enough in relation to their competition. Only 36% believed their company's TQM efforts had a significant impact on their competitive position. What prevents these efforts from being successful?

## The Art of Strategy

### THE HISTORY OF STRATEGY

As an academic discipline, strategic management reached its first stage of development in the 1960s with the Business Policy concept at Harvard (Christensen, Andrews, and Bower, 1983). Yet, planning has always been part of civilization.

"The Greeks planned cities; Plato's *Republic* is a plan. The Romans planned, and so did the Chinese in the Han dynasty and the Incas of Peru. Sir Thomas More, John Knox, Diderot, Rousseau, and Jeremy Bentham drew up plans. The *Federalist Papers* are to a considerable extent a planning document. Alexander Hamilton's 1791 Report on the Subject of Manufacturers to the U.S. Congress was a plan to make the new republic less dependent on foreign countries for manufactured goods; it has recently been called 'the most memorable plan for national economic planning that our early history affords.' Thomas Jefferson had a strategic plan for the United States when he negotiated the Louisiana Purchase in 1803, and he devised an educational plan for Virginia and later one for the University of Virginia." (Keller, p. 100)

## STRATEGIC PLANNING—A DEFINITION

Despite a rich and varied history, all this strategic-planning experience has not led to a single school of strategic thought or to a set of concepts that will work well in all circumstances. There are countless ways in which an organization can set direction, conduct an internal and external assessment, identify its stakeholders' needs and evaluate its results. Since no approach fits all sizes, contingency theory rules the day. That is to say, each organizational circumstance is unique and requires a tailored approach.

In general, however, traditional definitions of strategy agree on the following: that it involves formulation of long-term goals followed by the marshaling and allocation of resources to achieve these goals (Chandler, 1962); that it is used to create a "vision of success" and ask how it might be achieved (Mintzberg, 1994); and that free will and intentional design are essential to strategy (Porter, 1987).

Figure 1.1 shows the results when an organization has successfully formulated and implemented strategic initiatives. While these benefits are appealing, there are no guarantees. Each organization's circumstances determine whether the process will bear fruit. Common sense and good judgment are part of the process.

## CRITICISM OF STRATEGIC PLANNING

Despite the obvious benefits of effective strategic planning, it has come under much criticism for a variety of reasons. For example, strategic planning has

- A clear future direction is set for the enterprise
- A clear set of priorities is established
- Coherent decision making is the norm
- Decisions are made across levels and functions
- Significant organizational problems are addressed
- Organizational performance improves
- Teamwork and expertise are built
- Executives think and behave strategically, positioning the firm to respond to changes in the environment

**Figure 1.1**
Results of Successful Strategic Planning and Thinking (Bryson, 1979).

become fragmented and lacks a widely accepted framework. Mintzberg (1994) identified 10 schools of thought concerning strategic planning.

Mintzberg contended that confusion about different schools of thought is further exacerbated by planners who separate thinking and doing. Strategy needs to function beyond an office of well-educated executives who are insulated from those who make the organization work. Planning's failure to transcend the traditional functions of business explains why it has discouraged serious organizational change.

Ackoff (1993) added that leadership and strategy are concerned with effectiveness; management is concerned with efficiency. He contended that leaders emphasize effectiveness—"doing the right thing." Managers emphasize efficiency—"doing things right." While both effectiveness and efficiency are important, Ackoff pointed out that organizations would be better served by doing reasonably well on the right issues rather than performing brilliantly on the wrong issues. Organizations can improve if focused on the "right" issues, but reinforce their mistakes when they remained focused on the "wrong" issues.

According to Mintzberg (1994), "strategic planning" as it is widely practiced is a misnomer because the process simply formalizes strategies that have already been developed. Organizations frequently engage in strategic planning in a way that impairs strategic thinking. The process can lead managers to confuse vision with quantitative analysis. The most successful strategies are visions, not plans.

As illustrated in Figure 1.2, traditionally, strategic planning has advocated

**Figure 1.2** The Traditional Strategic Planning Model.

intentional design. Yet, deliberate strategies are not necessarily good, nor are emergent strategies necessarily bad. Effective strategies have a combination of emergent and deliberate qualities, since all strategies combine some degree of flexible learning with some degree of control.

One of the most common failures of strategies is the failure to recognize the importance of "organizational learning." Organizational learning purports that the strategic formulation and implementation process should continue to teach organizational members about the enterprise and its environment. All employees needed to implement the firm's strategy must think about these factors and modify their behaviors accordingly if there is any hope of realizing success (Mintzberg, 1994).

Mintzberg (1994) contrasted planning, which is about analysis, with strategic thinking, which is about synthesis. The latter involves intuition and creativity that often cannot be developed on schedule. An example of a creative act of synthesis is the development of the Polaroid camera. In 1943, Edwin Land's three-year-old daughter asked why she could not immediately see the picture he had just taken of her. Within an hour, this scientist conceived the camera that fulfilled his daughter's request and changed his company.

# The Gap Between Theory and Practice: Quantitative Approach, Rationality, and Incrementalism

Common criticisms of strategic methods and practices include that they are often overly quantitative, that they assume rationality, and that incrementalism tends to drive the approach adopted by most firms. Dissecting each of these criticisms identifies some common pitfalls to avoid when leaders engage an organization in strategy.

## QUANTITATIVE APPROACH

A significant problem with an overly quantitative approach is the faith placed in forecasts that frequently lack accuracy (Ackoff, 1993). Research that won the Nobel Prize for economics in 1975 revealed that more variables and added complexity can actual reduce the reliability of econometric forecasts. In this instance, more is not better. Several studies showed that forecasts made by experts can perform as well as econometric forecasts (Keller, 1983).

The shortcomings of forecasting were particularly in evidence during the 1973 Arab Oil Embargo. Because oil drives every aspect of the economies of the western world, nothing less than the state of the world economy was at stake. There was a desperate need to estimate the drop in oil production during the embargo. Due to inaccurate forecasting, there was great uncertainty about how much oil was available. Information was contradictory and piecemeal, contributing to the confusion. The actual size of the loss was not learned until after the fact, and though it was large and the disruption of supply channels was real, the loss was not as large as was forecasted. Fanatical behavior compounded the problem; rational forecasts had little impact (Yergin, 1992).

Ackoff (1993) argued that believing we can predict the future is folly. He contends that organizations should start with what they know now about their environment and then, given this knowledge, ask what they should be doing to meet the expectations of their stakeholders.

Numerical analysis clearly has its place in strategic thinking. Yet, highly quantitative management science experts tend to discount human shortcomings and political intrigue (Ackoff, 1993; Mintzberg, 1994). Multiple regression equations cannot include the role of the shrewd, effective leader who builds coalitions in ways that had been previously unimagined. On the other hand, organizations cannot be led effectively by highly political leaders whose actions lack the careful study and rigor proposed by management science (Keller, 1983).

## RATIONALITY

The assumption of rationality is embedded in a heavy quantitative approach, and, for that matter, in traditional strategic management. Adam Smith's notion of the invisible hand of the marketplace assumed everyone was a strategic planner. According to Smith, we all scan our environment, weigh the costs and benefits of our countless alternatives, and make decisions among our options that maximize our investments. As Herbert Simon says, "Economics in fact draws a romantic, almost a heroic picture of the human mind. Classical economics depicts mankind, individually and collectively, as solving immensely complex problems of optimizing the allocation of resources" (Keller, 1983, p. 101). In reality, people make decisions that bring them harm as well as benefit. Despite the best of intentions, organizations inflict damage to themselves due to irrational decisions more often than any care to admit.

Organizations can be viewed as political systems composed of constituencies seeking advantage upon scarce and valued resources (Cyert and March, 1963). Organizational privileges and disadvantages are largely sustained by political forces. Therefore, formulating a strategy requires broad-based support, which is the most difficult and important task of leadership.

Each organization is driven by local knowledge, rules, and culture. The enterprise's culture is based on a set of beliefs, norms, values, and behavioral standards that has served it well in the past. Accordingly, the firm's culture leads managers to maintain the status quo. As Pogo said to his buddies, "We have met the enemy, and he is us."

When an organization confronts a turbulent and confusing environment, a sense of direction and focus will only come about by choosing which issues to address and which to ignore. If the organization lacks strong central direction, the organization will whipsaw from one route to another as competing perspectives are promoted by different groups. The alternative risk is that one perspective may win not because it is superior, but because its advocates are better politicians (Mintzberg, 1990).

## INCREMENTALISM

Some believe that organizational resistance to change blunts abrupt transformations into a new environment. Therefore, patching up an old system is more likely to work than creating a new system. Lots of little changes over a relatively short time can position a firm well. Besides, most change tends to be incremental in nature anyway.

Inherent to incrementalism is the art of making deals, making small changes that depend on the nature of the players and on the political situation. Deals are easier to cut when the pie is growing. The problem is that when the pie shrinks, hard choices and priorities require courage rather than deal making. Since the goal of incrementalism is to focus on the current deal rather than on where the firm should be headed, deal making can contribute to drift and unintended goals that go unexamined.

Because it does not use models, incrementalism falls into the "beagle fallacy." Beagles have an exquisite snout but faulty eyesight, and can miss a rabbit that is under their noses. Incrementalism has no vision or imagination. The most damning comment about incrementalism is that it comes up short in an environment that calls for dramatic change (Keller, 1983).

## THE HUMAN FACTOR: UNCERTAINTY, AMBIGUITY, AND COMPLEXITY

In the 1970s and 1980s more authors began discussing how businesses were facing accelerating rates of change, rising complexity, and more conflicts with stakeholders within and outside the firm. Under these conditions, the traditional strategic-planning framework was called into question because it seemed to underestimate the difficulties of such conditions. Uncertain, complex, and ambiguous strategic problems can simply be more than a leader can handle.

An individual's capacity to process information is limited, so planners/leaders can only construct simplified models of the world, only consider a few alternatives, and usually evaluate them subjectively. Therefore, planners/leaders cannot make an optimal decision, but actually have to accept a "satisficing" outcome (Simon, 1979).

Even when leaders know the "right" strategy, they still face a challenging task to build a consensus among managers who perceive the world differently. One manager might call an emerging issue a strategic threat, a second manager might perceive the threat to be unimportant, and a third might agree about its importance, but see it as an opportunity. If leaders are to encourage significant organizational movement, how can they promote a shared understanding and common agreement?

## WHAT WE KNOW AND HOW WE KNOW IT

William James stated that we always seem to view a new experience in some way compatible to what we already know. He believed that we seem to want to disturb our preexisting thoughts and beliefs as little as possible. An old person who displays these tendencies is referred to as an "old fogy." It is not unusual to discuss with someone the need to change, provide rational ways to do so, force acceptance of the reasons behind the change and the solutions, and a week later find the person holding onto previous habits and beliefs with great comfort (William James, 1892, in Keller, 1983, p. 166).

Executives could be thought of as intuitive scientists who are gifted and generally successful, but whose attempts to understand, predict, and control events are compromised by the way they perceive and make sense of the world. These shortcomings reflect the failure to use a rational, scientific approach. They also reflect a readiness to apply simplistic strategies beyond the strategies' appropriate limits (Kelly, 1967).

The foundation of the scientific method is to control for problems such as sampling bias and measurement error. Yet, these are not problems that we worry about when we try to make sense of the world. Our memory plays a central role in our thought process; preexisting knowledge influences unduly, and often without the individual's awareness, the characterization of a given event. We are at the mercy of events that can be retrieved from memory. Our memory may be clouded and inaccurate. It may only draw from those events that are most vivid. It may also have forgotten events relevant to the decision.

Due to the considerable influence of memory on our views, we are particularly poor at understanding causal relationships. We miscalculate the magnitude between a cause and an effect and draw appropriate inferences poorly. We appear to place more stock in what we already believe than what we actually observed. Even when we manage to detect a causal relationship, we may fail to analyze correctly the possible causes. In some instances, our prior beliefs may override what we observe. In other instances, our conclusions appear to be almost arbitrary or capricious because they are so heavily influenced by our perceptions. We go too far in concluding a past relationship will occur in the future.

Scientists use samples to generalize to a larger population. The central consideration in drawing a sample is whether it is the same as the population. Is the size sufficient to generalize to a larger population? Was the method used to select the sample free from bias? In conducting our daily affairs, the evidence indicates that we ask these questions infrequently and have little understanding of their importance. We seem to have limited appreciation for the idea that increasing the number of observations reduces the problem of sampling bias. We seem to be as willing to draw conclusions from biased samples as we do from those that are not.

Once we make up our minds, our beliefs tend to persist, despite an array of evidence that should invalidate or even reverse them. We tend to remember evidence that confirms our views and ignore evidence that contradicts our views. In sum, "we often look for the wrong data, often see the wrong data, often retain the wrong data, often weight the data improperly, often fail to ask the correct questions of the data, often make the wrong inferences on the basis of our understanding of the data" (Nisbett and Ross, 1980).

"Let us suppose that you wish to buy a new car and have decided that on grounds of economy and longevity you want to purchase one of those solid, stalwart, middle-class Swedish cars—either a Volvo or a Saab. As a prudent and sensible buyer, you go to *Consumer Reports*, which informs you that the consensus of their experts is that the Volvo is mechanically superior, and the consensus of the readership is that the Volvo has the better repair record. Armed with this information, you decide to go and strike a bargain with the Volvo dealer before the week is out. In the interim, however, you go to a cocktail party where you announce this intention to an acquaintance. He reacts with disbelief and alarm: "A Volvo! You've got to be kidding. My brother-in-law had a Volvo. First that fancy fuel injection computer thing went out. 250 bucks. Next he started having trouble with the rear end. Had to replace it. Then the transmission and the clutch. Finally sold it in three years for junk." (in Nisbett and Ross, 1980 p. 129). Reason can be thrown out the window with one emotional and persuasive plea.

Our errors in judgment result from two tendencies: We overutilize our memory to confirm beliefs that we already hold and we underutilize the tenets of scientific inquiry. "It is evident that when the instances on one side of a question are more likely to be remembered and recorded than those on the other, especially if there be any strong motive to preserve the memory of the first, but not of the latter, these last are likely to be overlooked, and escape the observations of the mass of mankind." (John Stuart Mill, p. 90. in Nisbett and Ross, 1980). In short, our outlook seems to be driven by a "don't confuse me with the facts" attitude.

## NEW MODEL

The field of planning is converging. Politics and planning, productivity and vision are coming together in an eclectic school of strategy. Ways of bringing planning and organizational politics together and methods for uniting strategy formulation and implementation have been tested. While unrefined, there is fairly solid evidence about what will and won't work.

A wide range of strategic tools are used to promote strategic thinking. For example, Figure 1.3 lists common strategic processes on the left and their corresponding products on the right. Common processes or strategic tools include analysis of strengths and weaknesses, and opportunities and threats (SWOT), mission and vision statements, strategies and performance measurements. A SWOT analysis helps leaders identify the critical issues confronting the organization. The purpose of a mission statement is to clarify the organization's purpose and who its serves. A vision statement should proclaim what the organization aspires to be. Strategies state how the organization will close the gap between where it is and where it wants to go. To be successful, strategies must successfully match an organization's mission and strength with its opportunities. Lastly, the organization must develop performance measurements so it can assess the degree to which it has been successful.

Continuous, flexible planning, rather than mathematical charts, are what critics call for. Ideally, strategic planning should blend the wisdom of the quantitative and qualitative aspects of leadership. A heavily quantitative plan that ignores human factors is not likely to be implemented. Money, markets, com

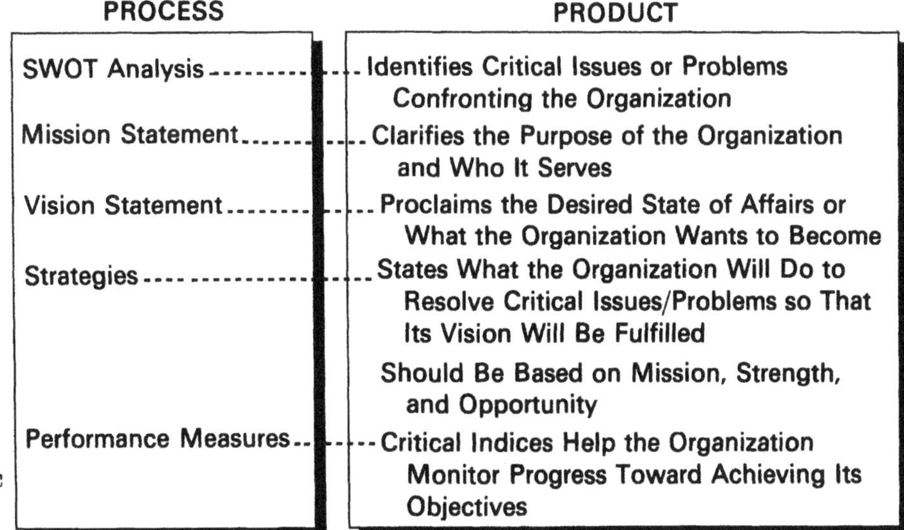


**Figure 1.3** Processes and Products of Strategic Planning.

petitors, and external forces matter as well as traditions, devotion to ideas, and internal preferences. Design is better than drift. Thought is preferable to quarreling (Keller, 1983).

# Getting Started

## IS IT TIME FOR STRATEGY?

In some instances strategic planning may not be prudent. Organizations that lack the skills, resources, or commitment of key decision makers are unlikely to benefit from strategic planning (Bryson, 1979).

Every organization can benefit from a sense of direction. Nevertheless, a grand plan to increase market share is doomed to fail in organizations that have trouble answering customer phone calls. Strategy formulation is not likely to bear fruit for organizations that lack quality leadership and human resources, adequate information to make critical strategic decisions, a sound customer base, an element of comparative advantage, and a commitment to excel. Organizations that are ambitious beyond their resources and abilities would be wise to concentrate on good management.

There is also no sense in promoting a direction for change that no one is willing to follow. Leaders usually serve their organizations best by initially making changes where support for change is greatest and in a way that is traditionally acceptable. After some early success has been achieved, leaders are able to prepare people for the more difficult journey of a serious strategic-planning process (Keller, 1983).

## STRATEGIC INFORMATION, PERCEPTIONS, AND RATIONALITY

The first step to formulating strategy is gathering information vital for sound decision making. Well-managed organizations know their customers, costs, competitors, and environment. Reliable information contributes to rational decision making and promotes strategic decision making (Keller, 1983).

In a perfect world, all decisions would be based on an objective examination of relevant information and the options available. We know, however, that individual perception and memory influence how we make sense of the world. Thus, there may well be as many perceptions of reality as there are decision makers.

Differing perceptions of reality contribute, at least in part, to conflict among decision makers. The way that decision makers perceive the world is a function of what they remember. In other words, the information decision makers use to resolve strategic issues is driven by their perceptions and memory. Inevitably, the information used to understand strategic issues will be perceived differently by decision makers. Therefore, differing perceptions ensure conflict is embedded in every strategic issue. The tension of conflict should be expected and used to promote organizational change.

For example, decision makers may perceive their organization's operations to be weak. Their critical views may overshadow legitimate strengths. Or, perhaps decision makers do not perceive the external environment as an influence in their market. They may then lead the organization to underestimate the competition and/or ignore critical external trends that are reshaping the industry.

Another way in which information promotes rationality is the use of language and numeric data. Initially, organizations use words to express their strategic direction. Inevitably, the language is found to be subjective. A higher degree of objectivity can be achieved if organizations use numbers to operationalize their strategies. Numbers can refine and more precisely communicate the firm's strategic intentions. In addition, if something cannot be counted, it cannot be measured. If a firm is to assess the success of its strategies, it will need to use numbers.

The variables that are used to assess corporate success are often the same even though different organizations use different strategies. For example, regardless of an organization's strategies, all firms are interested in measuring their sales, profits, and market share. Ideally, sales, profits, and market share are all increasing. If sales and profits are up and market share is down, the firm has long-term competitive problems. These findings might indicate the firm is losing its competitive edge in a growing market. Information such as, this can lead decision makers to ask the "right" question. What are competitors offering customers to grab market share?

If sales and market share are up and profits are down, there are problems in raising prices and/or controlling costs. The good news is that customers are satisfied as evidenced by increased sales and market share. The bad news is that this satisfaction may result from low prices that cannot be raised due to competition. Or it may mean the problem is not pricing, but internal cost controls. Either way the firm might be selling its way out of business until it raises prices or lowers costs.

If profit and market share are up and sales are down, there are long-term problems with customer satisfaction. The good news is that the firm is profitable and dominant in in its class. The bad news is that product may be maturing and customers are tiring of the product for some reason.

The use of sales, profit, and market share illustrates how information can be used to identify the "right" issues so that strategy can be adjusted. This type of information does not provide the firm with definitive answers to how an organization should respond to market changes. Instead, the information helps decision makers to formulate clear and important strategic questions. Sound information can help decision makers determine what will help or hinder the organization in accomplishing its mission.

While the need for information about an organization's capabilities and markets is self-evident, perfect knowledge will remain elusive. Even the very best management-information system can be handicapped by inadequate and outdated information. It is generally easier to gather information about the organization—its finances, customer base, and human resources—than about its competitors and potential markets. So, strategic decisions are made with crude insights about an organization's markets.

Emerging markets or markets under significant restructuring present immense assessment problems for analysis. High-tech markets, recently deregulated industries, and markets with numerous and confusing alliances simply move too fast to gather and present information in time to make strategic decisions. In addition, it is nearly impossible to gather accurate information about some foreign markets such as those in India, China, and the Middle East.

Since perfect information is a myth and since a dearth of information blinds decision makers, a balance must be struck. Decision makers who use limited information to make critical strategic decisions can ruin the organization. Decision makers who always need more information can stymie action and miss valuable opportunities. The questions and information that can be gathered to review a firm's strategic options and challenges are endless. With approximate answers to the right questions, a well-managed firm with a core of well-qualified innovative leaders can begin the work of shaping and guiding an organization's future.

# A Strategic Framework

Mintzberg argued that the right questions are central to sound strategic planning (1994). In keeping with this view, the strategic framework that will be presented here is built around six questions. These questions address the most fundamental strategic issues confronting any organization.

There are numerous questions, models, and frameworks that leaders can use to engage an enterprise in strategic planning. However, many of these models are overly complex, attempting to address every conceivable strategic issue. Ironically, by trying to address all issues they seem to cover nothing (Mintzberg, 1994). In addition, given what we know about the limits of human judgment to resolve complex strategic issues—the simpler the model, the better. The questions outlined in Figure 1.4 can be used as a framework to formulate any organization's strategy.

- Strategic issues facing the enterprise
- Competitive advantages
- Match between products/services and customers
- Future direction/innovation and growth
- Stakeholders' satisfaction
- Strategy integration/measurement

**Figure 1.4** Fundamental Strategic Framework.

# What Are the Strategic Issues Facing the Enterprise?

The need to think systematically is central to understanding and responding wisely to the strategic issues facing a firm (Ackoff, 1993). Systems thinking requires that executives see the organization as a whole in relation to its environment.

One way to promote systems thinking is to have decision makers outline the elements of a basic systems model: resources (inputs), present strategy (processes), and performance (outputs)(Bryson, 1979) as seen in Figure 1.5. In other words, what are the sources of the firm's capital, labor, and equipment? How does the firm convert these resources into products and services? Lastly, what outputs does the firm produce and are stakeholders' expectations being met?

Developing a basic systems model can clarify the organization's interactions with its environment as it acquires resources and produces products or services.

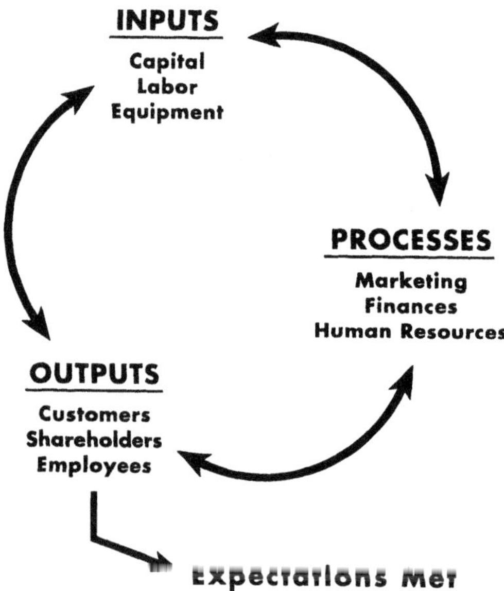


**Figure 1.5** Applied Systems Thinking.

The external trends and issues that influence an organization's supply of labor and capital and its customer base are delineated as leaders answer these questions.

In addition, the systems model can demonstrate the interaction among the organization's internal functional areas such as marketing, finance, and human resources. The problems inherent to the production process rarely present themselves as solely a marketing, finance, or human resource problem. The functional areas are integrally related; each area affects the other. The systems model helps identify the relationships among the various areas.

Most importantly, a simple systems model can clarify who the organization's stakeholders are and what their expectations might be. No corporation can survive for long if it fails to serve the basic needs of customers, shareholders, and employees. By identifying each group of stakeholders, the organization is more likely to consider and include their needs in the strategic planning process.

## IDENTIFYING STRATEGIC ISSUES—SWOT ANALYSIS

To encourage systems thinking, organizations examine their strengths, weaknesses, opportunities, and threats, otherwise known as a SWOT analysis. This fairly straightforward and effective tool can be used to identify an organization's strategic issues. Strengths and weaknesses refer to internal factors such as marketing, finance, human resources, leadership, facilities, equipment, and so on. Opportunities and threats refer to external factors such as social, technical, economic, political, and legal trends and issues.

The fundamental goal of a SWOT analysis is to assess the fit between the organization and its environment. It allows the organization to examine the gap between where the enterprise is today and where it needs to be. In essence, a SWOT analysis formulates the problems confronting an organization before moves are made to resolve these problems.

Again, simpler is usually better. Elaborate, lengthy SWOT analysis procedures are likely to drive out strategic thinking, not promote it. Those involved in formulating an organization's strategy should answer the questions listed in Figure 1.6.

Responses to these questions can then be arranged according to common themes. Usually it is better to start the SWOT analysis by having decision makers consider external rather than internal issues. Decision makers often overemphasize internal issues and limit attention to external issues, leading them to identify strategic issues concerning solutions they have already envisioned rather than be open to changes in their markets (Bryson, 1979).

Gathering and presenting compelling information relevant to specific opportunities/threats and strengths/weaknesses can help to some extent to avoid

- What are major external Opportunities?
- What are major external Threats?
- What are major internal Strengths?
- What are major internal Weaknesses?

**Figure 1.6**
SWOT Analysis

these pitfalls. Useful information will address specifically the strategic decisions to be made. For example, all firms make decisions concerning which customers will be targeted and how products will be distributed, priced, and promoted—with or without adequate information. The absence of sound information means that the organization relies on someone's judgment to make the decisions. Specific, targeted information is vital to the strategic planning process.

Assessing a firm's external threats and opportunities is referred to as "environmental scanning." The goal of environmental scanning is to educate decision makers about external issues that influence the firm's ability to fulfill its mission. The process should identify demographic, economic, political, and technical forces and trends that affect an organization's success or survival. Central to the process is the assessment of the organization's customers and competition. Are the preferences of current and potential customers stable or shifting? What are the firm's competitive advantages? What advantages do competitors possess? In other words, is the firm or its competitors best positioned to serve current and potential customers?

Examining the organization's internal strengths and weaknesses uncovers what the organization does particularly well or where it is vulnerable. In the jargon of strategy, the process should identify the organization's distinctive competencies.

Clearly the strategic issues that have the greatest appeal are combinations of strengths and opportunities. In these instances, the organization is positioned well to take advantage of the opportunities. In contrast, issues that are combinations of weaknesses and threats are obviously disturbing, since the organization will be in a poor position to defend itself against these threats. An organization is also not in a good position to respond to issues that are combinations of weaknesses and opportunities. Finally, issues that combine strengths with threats may not cause problems, assuming the organization is strong enough to respond.

Once issues have been identified, they can be evaluated in terms of the consequences of the failure to address them. Each issue can be placed into one of two categories: (1) issues where no action is required at present, but must be monitored continuously, or (2) issues that require an immediate response (Bryson, 1979).

A SWOT analysis is intended to find the best fit between an organization and its environment based on an intimate understanding of both. To resolve a strategic issue successfully, consideration should be given to the fit between the issue and the organization's mission, stakeholder support, strengths, weaknesses, and financial feasibility. Since identifying an organization's issues is like trying to hit a moving target, follow-up analysis is a given. Strategy is perennial.

## What Are the Firm's Competitive Advantages?

The concept of competitive advantage hails from classic economics. What does the firm do that makes it distinctive and unique in the marketplace? What does it do better than its competitors?

**Figure 1.7**
What Are the Firm's Competitive Advantages?

- What does the firm do that makes it distinctive and unique in the marketplace?
- What does it do better than its competitors?
  1. What is the power of the buyer? seller? (bargaining power of suppliers and buyers)
  2. What is the threat of new entrants?
  3. What are the barriers to exit?
  4. What is the threat of substitute products or services?
  5. What is the rivalry among existing firms?

A competitive analysis is needed to evaluate a firm's comparative advantages. An effective way to do this is by applying Michael Porter's competitive-analysis framework. The framework includes five questions, as seen in Figure 1.7.

An organization that asks these questions about its competitive circumstance can clarify the extent to which it possesses an enduring competitive advantage. If a firm is to endure, it must possess some form of competitive advantage. Clearly the absence of comparative advantage makes a firm vulnerable to superior competition. The application of Porter's model will be discussed in greater detail in Chapter 2 on Marketing Strategy.

## What Is the Match Between the Firm's Products/Services and Customer Needs, Wants, and Values?

If a firm is to define itself around its customers, the most fundamental strategic issue is whether its products and services meet the needs, wants, and values of its customers (Drucker, 1973). The following questions can assess the match between an enterprise's products and its customers:

1. Are there shifts in the customer base that the firm has traditionally served?
2. Are existing products/services satisfying customer's needs, wants, and values?
3. Which products/services should continue as is, which should be modified, which should be eliminated?

Identifying shifts in the customer base helps to focus on whether the firm's traditional markets can be served into the future or whether these markets are eroding. Tracking sales over time and by type of customer is one simple way to answer the question.

Questions regarding customer satisfaction can be answered through indirect measures of customer satisfaction such as sales, market share, and customer retention. Focus groups and customer satisfaction surveys can also be used.

The resolution to the third question—which products or services should be continued, modified, or eliminated—hinges on what was learned in answering the first two questions. It is particularly difficult because it centers on the acquisition and allocation of resources, and because it directly affects employee job security. This is where rationality and partisan politics bump heads.

To minimize partisanship and maximize rationality, there are tools to match markets with products, such as the BCG model and the GE model. These tools provide a rational framework to guide resource acquisition and allocation decisions. Each will be explained within the context of setting the firm's future objectives.

## What Objectives Would Set the Future Direction of the Enterprise so that Innovation and Growth Could Be Achieved?

There are countless ways to set the future direction of an enterprise. A SWOT analysis clarifies the gap between where the firm is and where it should be. A straightforward approach to closing this gap is to ask, Given what we know about our environment today, what should we be doing to meet the expectations of our stakeholders? What would satisfy our customers, shareholders, and employees? Answering these questions can help the organization focus on what it should be doing.

### BCG AND GE MODELS

A SWOT analysis helps focus a firm on the right issues at a broad aggregate level. Portfolio analysis can further refine the firm's strategy. Two widely used portfolio approaches are the BCG and GE models, developed by the Boston Consulting Group and General Electric respectively. Both models are similar conceptually to a financial portfolio in that their primary goal is to encourage a diversity of holdings, or, in this case, products and services.

A portfolio analysis enables a firm to:

1. guide decisions about investment and resource allocation decisions among strategic business units
2. assess the life cycle of key products and balance investments between developing and developed business
3. assess risk and returns

4. identify strategic issues facing the firm, including its present and desired strategic position
5. evaluate the success of past strategies
6. provide executives with shared vocabulary and tools to promote communication of shared judgments and assumptions
7. suggest, with significant executive judgment, possible future strategies (Segev, 1995).

The original BCG model only used two criteria: market growth and market share. The adaptation of the BCG model that will be presented in this text allows firms to rate products as low, medium, or high on two scales using four criteria: (1) quality, (2) centrality, (3) competitive advantage, and (4) growth. Quality and centrality are considered to be internal matters in that they are in a firm's control. Competitive advantage and growth are considered external matters and outside the firm's control. Of course, a corporation would still need to monitor external factors even if they cannot be controlled.

Quality should be defined from the customer's perspective. In other words, would the firm's customers describe its products and services to be of low, medium, or high quality?

Centrality refers to the extent a product is central to a firm's mission. Centrality raises the question, To what extent is a given product central to a firm's mission?

Competitive advantage is a relative measure. In other words, relative to competitors, does the firm have an advantage in the marketplace? A product may be of low quality, but, relative to the competition, is the best offer available to consumers. Therefore, the firm enjoys a competitive advantage. Of course, a firm may offer a high-quality product/service, but may still be at a disadvantage relative to its competition.

Market growth is simply a measure of whether consumer interest in the product industry-wide is declining, flat, or increasing. A common measure of growth potential is the assessment of industry-wide sales plotted over time.

A company can use the BCG model to define each of its products according to these four criteria and then plot the product on two scales. Products are categorized as being stars, problem children, cash cows, or dogs. For example, on a 1 to 10 scale, each product could be rated as being low to high in quality, centrality, competitive advantage, and growth. A product rated as an 8 on competitive advantage and a 9 on growth would be given a score of 17 on the external scale. If the product was rated as a 2 on quality and a 7 on centrality, it would be given a 9 on the internal scale. In this example, the product would be classified as a problem child.

Reviewing a firm's entire product line helps executives sort out opportunity cost issues. In other words, the central question that the BCG model helps answer is, Of all the possible products in which a firm could invest, which will likely generate the best return on investment?

An example of this adapted BCG model is illustrated in Figure 1.8. It outlines characteristics that describe a product and possible strategies for stars, problem children, cash cows, or dogs. Of course, these characterizations and stra-

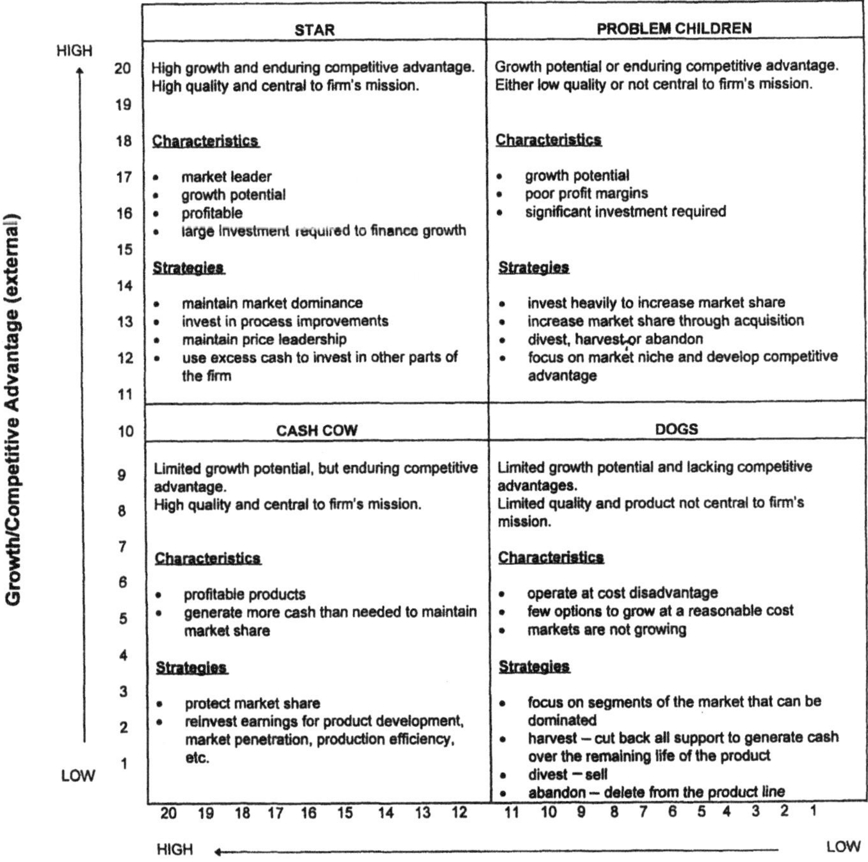


**Figure 1.8**
BCG Model.

tegies are guidelines and not cookbook prescriptions. Nevertheless, the characterizations and proposed strategy can help determine whether each product/service should receive investments to increase market share, should be financed to hold market share, should be harvested to generate cash for investment in other business units, or should be divested.

The GE model categorizes SBUs (strategic business units) into one of nine cells. Its purpose is to compare diverse businesses. It uses both relative objective data (sales, profits, return on investment) and subjective data (employee loyalty, competition position, technology strengths). Different weights can be given to each of these variables according to their importance to the firm's strategy.

Additional criteria could include market share, economies of scale, marketing expertise, structure and culture, organizational leadership, performance, and so on. A SWOT analysis should uncover what it will take to be successful in the firm's industry, thus generating a list of criteria, shown in Figure 1.9, that could be used to evaluate each of the firm's products on a scale of low, medium, and high.

**Attractiveness of Your Business**

**A. Market Factors**
- size (dollars, units)
- size of product market
- market growth rate
- stage in life cycle
- diversity of market (potential for differentiation)
- price elasticity
- bargaining power of customers
- cyclicality/seasonality of demand

**B. Economic and Technical Factors**
- investment intensity
- nature of investments (facilities, working capital, leases)
- ability to pass through effects of inflation
- industry capacity
- level and maturity of technology utilization
- barriers to entry/exit
- access to raw materials

**C. Competitive Forces**
- types of competitors
- structure of competition
- substitution threats
- perceived differentiation among competitors

**D. Environmental Factors**
- regulatory climate
- degree of social acceptance
- human factors such as unionization

**Strength of Your Competitive Position**

**A. Market Position**
- relative share of market
- rate of change of share
- variability of share across segments
- perceived differentiation of quality/price/service
- breadth of product
- company image

**B. Economic and Technical Position**
- relative cost position
- capacity utilization
- technological position
- patented technology, product, or process

**C. Capabilities**
- management strength and depth
- marketing strength
- distribution system
- labor relations
relationships with regulators

**Figure 1.9** Factors Contributing to Market Attractiveness and Business Strength.

Each SBU is then compared against its business strength (relative market dominance) and industry attractiveness (growth potential), as seen in Figure 1.10. The Y axis represents external variables, those not controlled by the firm. The X axis represents controllable internal variables. SBUs that fall into the green cells are considered winners that should receive investment. Yellow cells are profit producers, average businesses, and businesses with questionable futures. Red cells are losers that should be considered for divestment.

Another interpretation of a nine-cell model is shown in Figure 1.11. The product analysis is the same as in the previous model. This model simply provides alternative descriptions and rationales for strategic decisions.

Portfolio analysis is limited by the availability and reliability of data. Internal financial data should be fairly reliable and accessible. Competitor and industry financial data is generally less dependable. Forecasted data is less reliable than historic data. In the end, even "objective" data such as return on investment (ROI) figures require some subjective evaluation.

The GE model presents numerous measurement problems. Accurate placement of a firm's SBUs and markets into one of the GE categories is crucial, yet difficult. Ideally, each SBU should have strategic autonomy, an external market, a distinct customer set, and a distinct competitor set. These definitions are rarely [illegible]

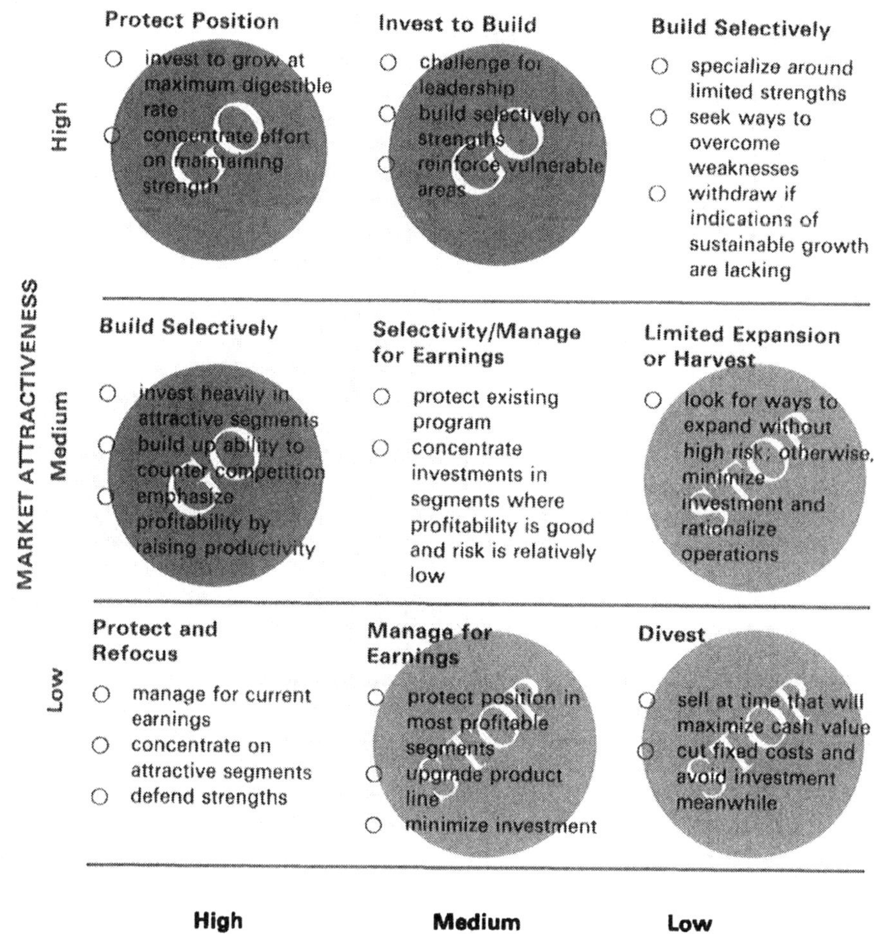


**Figure 1.10**
Strategic Guide to Allocating Resources—Model 1.

Growth rates need to take into account inflation and the business cycle. Growth, of course, is only one measure of business attractiveness. In addition, focus on ROI can result in eliminating risk from consideration. Heavy investments in winners can cause cash-flow problems. Executives can easily manipulate the relevant factors to serve their own agendas. Group decision making tends to result in overuse of the medium classification due to compromise or lack of a clear understanding of strategic issues among executives.

Portfolios are better as descriptive tools than as strategy prescriptions. Generic strategies can be too automatic and simplistic. Sometimes a declining industry can be attractive. As a practical matter, it may be impossible or difficult to sell a dog, given a firm's commitments to a community or a key supplier. Lastly, employees and executives of SBUs defined as dogs or recommended for harvest are not likely to find this designation much help to their morale.

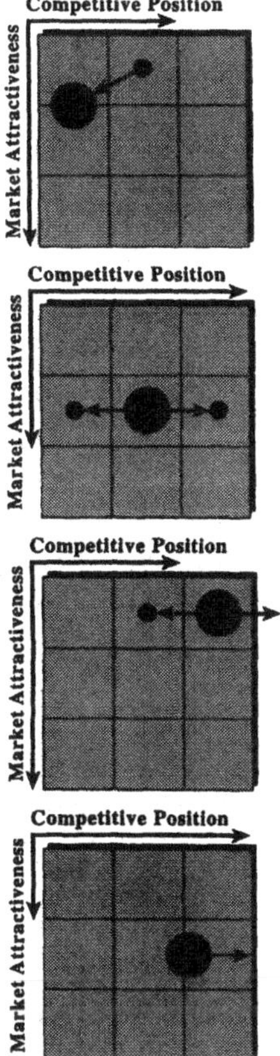


**Invest to Build:** This strategy option is indicated when a highly attractive market offers opportunities for growth that may not be available as the market matures. Significant investments are required to build selectively on strengths and keep up with the rapid growth rates that are typical of these markets.

**Selectivity/Manage for Earnings:** Here, the indicated option is to strengthen the position of the business in segments where profitability is good or barriers to competitive entry can be maintained, while letting the position erode in segments where costs exceed benefits.

**Build Selectivity or Exit:** With a weak position in an attractive market, it is usually desirable to look for protected niches in which to specialize. If this is not feasible or the costs/risks are excessive, then an exit should be considered.

**Harvest:** This involves exchanging the business position for cash, by minimum investment and rationalization of operations. Selective investment may be made with a view to improving the value of the business because it is to be eventually sold.

**Figure 1.11**
Strategic Guide to Allocating Resources—Model 2.

One of the major benefits of a portfolio approach is that it clearly illustrates the problem of opportunity costs. All organizations are limited to some degree by the availability of resources. Therefore, the opportunity to invest in one product must come at the expense of another product or potential product.

The portfolio approach also demonstrates the relationship of each product to the entire firm's profit and growth prospects. Some products need to throw off cash if the organization is to invest in growth opportunities. Unprofitable products drain resources that could be better invested elsewhere.

Perhaps the greatest value of the portfolio approach is its ability to aid decision makers in resolving difficult problems. Making difficult, but the most beneficial, choices among competing interests is what strategy is all about. It is this ability to shed light on complex issues that dictates sensitive handling of this decision-making tool. With the appropriate handling, it allows organizations to base future plans on abilities rather than mere hopes.

Sequentially, the SWOT analysis provides decision makers with a broad understanding of the organization's strategic issues. The use of the BCG and/or GE models can guide resource allocation and acquisition decisions. Wise application of these tools is dependent upon an accurate assessment of the firm's capabilities, its environmental forces, market requirements, and the actions of other firms. The real test of these tools is how well they diagnose a firm's strengths and weaknesses and improve its performance.

# What Is the Mission of the Enterprise?

The mission statement defines the organization's reason for being. It addresses this question, If we were completely successful, what would we look like? Answering this question requires that an enterprise defines the business that it is in; who it serves; and the needs, wants, and values of its stakeholders.

At first glance, a mission statement may seem like the place to begin a strategic-planning process. Depending on an organization's circumstances, this may be true. When there is wide variance among employees about the purpose of the organization, the process of developing a mission statement can help define the firm's core values and identity. Even for a firm whose employees unanimously embrace its purpose, there is benefit in periodically affirming a mission statement.

Johnson & Johnson gave birth to the concept of a mission statement more than 50 years ago by developing "our credo." The statement provided the company's leaders with a set of clear guideposts to navigate the Tylenol poisoning incidents in 1982 and 1986.

On the other hand, missions that are essentially platitudes can waste time, money, and people's patience, especially if the gulf between truth and fiction is wide, or if the statement lacks distinction. Many mission statements claim the organization toils to serve customers well, is committed to enhancing shareholder value, and expects its employees to strive for excellence in everything they do while treating everyone with respect and integrity. These statements may as well include that the organization is against taxes and for lowering crime! If a mission statement fits any and all organizations, then it is not effective.

Louis Gerstner, after assuming the CEO position at IBM, was quoted widely when he said "the last thing IBM needs right now is a vision." At the time, IBM was poised to lose $8 billion, and drastic measures were called for to turn the business around. Since then, Gerstner has led IBM to develop eight principles to guide its employees, including, "the marketplace is the driving force behind everything we do" and "at our core, we are a technology company with an overwhelming commitment to quality" (Boisseau, 1995).

The time to review or affirm a mission statement is usually after a SWOT analysis has been conducted. A thorough environmental scanning process might change the way decision makers define the organization and its clients. Placing the SWOT analysis before the mission statement helps to prevent myopia, a condition in which decision makers become fixed on existing views without considering the environment in which the firm operates. The formulation of a mission statement can be more fruitful after those involved clarify the firm's strategic issues, comparative advantages, and the match between its products and customers. By doing so, the organization can better write a mission statement that clarifies who it serves and demonstrates how it is unique and distinctive.

# How Will the Firm Integrate Its Strategies and Measure Success?

The goal of strategy is to position an enterprise to serve the needs of its stakeholders in a way that integrates its corporate, marketing, financial, and human-resource objectives and strategies. Therefore, a critical measure of success is whether stakeholders' expectations have been met in an integrated way.

## STAKEHOLDERS

Organizations serve multiple stakeholders such as suppliers, government officials, and the community at large. Yet, all for-profit corporations have three principal stakeholders: customers, shareholders, and employees. While other stakeholders may be important, these three are paramount.

Ideally, the expectations of customers, shareholders, and employees can all be met. Yet, if conflict exists, customers come before shareholders who come before employees. Management's interests can only be met if customers are served well at a profit to shareholders. Though the degree to which customers, shareholders, and employees are satisfied is intertwined, customers reign supreme.

## INTEGRATION

One of the most difficult aspects of strategy is to get all employees rowing in roughly the same direction. After a corporate strategy has been formulated, the firm's task is to develop a marketing, financial, and human resource strategy that supports corporate objectives. To this end, the use of performance measures can help fragmented organizations operate better as a whole. Carefully selected performance measures can also help organizations concentrate on serving their stakeholders. Focusing on stakeholder satisfaction by reducing the problem of fragmentation is a central tenet of systems thinking. The problem then becomes deciding which stakeholders should be evaluated and which measuring tools should be used.

## STRATEGIC PERFORMANCE MEASURES

A firm can measure its strengths and weaknesses and those of its competitors by examining customer, shareholder, and employee satisfaction, and its own ability to [illegible] can be used to assess the current state of a firm's affairs as well as to set strategic objectives that define the ideal state of affairs. These measures can determine whether a firm's strategies have been successful.

How can an organization measure the degree to which its stakeholders have been well served? Each organization must measure its success according to its mission and strategy. In addition, consideration needs to be given to the ease with which information can be gathered. What follows are examples of performance measures that assess customer, shareholder, and employee satisfaction (Kaplan and Norton, 1996).

**CUSTOMERS** It seems obvious that an organization should know if its customers are satisfied with its products. Nevertheless, how to secure this deceptively simple piece of feedback is less than clear.

Validity is always a concern to researchers. Validity is the extent to which a research method such as a survey or focus group has measured what it claimed to measure. In other words, did the method really measure customer satisfaction? A survey or focus group may simply measure what customers will say so that they will be left alone. Customers may not be clear in their own minds about what they want. Focus groups and customer surveys, of course, can provide useful feedback to organizations, but they do have their limits.

Indirect measures of customer satisfaction, including sales, customer retention, and market share, provide helpful data. Increased sales are clearly a reasonable measure of customer satisfaction. In particular, customer retention is a useful indirect measure. If they come back for more, the organization must be doing something right. Market share is also a valuable relative measure. When market share rises, customers are selecting the organization's products over competitors' products.

Indirect measures should be considered over time and against the industry, providing time series data to help assess the firm's performance over a three- to 10-year period. For example, time series data would reveal whether sales increased, were flat, or declined in the previous decade. By comparing its sales results against those of its competitors, the organization can determine if it grew, was even with, or declined compared to the market as a whole.

All indirect measures are descriptive in nature. That is to say, while they describe *what* is happening they do not reveal *why* things are going well or poorly. Only qualitative information like that solicited from focus groups or surveys or from causal studies can answer why, for example, sales are up or down. Yet, whatever the research method used, the organization can never be certain why customers are satisfied or dissatisfied with its products and services. Focus group or survey results can be gathered quickly and can provide insightful information. However, these results are always of questionable validity. Causal studies are expensive and time consuming, but they do control more for problems like measurement and sampling errors than an exploratory method such as focus groups. However, to improve its validity a causal study must have a narrow focus, which can result in not seeing the forest for the trees. In addition, no matter how well a study is designed, there will always be errors with which to contend.

The purpose of customer satisfaction measures is not to provide clear answers about what a firm should do. Their purpose is to evaluate the success of the firm's strategies. They can also help the firm formulate the "right" questions to determine why a given strategy succeeded or failed.

**SHAREHOLDERS** Though there are multiple variables to assess shareholder wealth, this task is considerably easier than assessing customer satisfaction. In contrast to meeting customer expectations, return on investment is tangible and quantitative, and so can be measured easily.

Measures that can be used to assess whether shareholder wealth has been enhanced include total return on investment, return on assets, share price appreciation, dividends, and profits. These results need to be judged against other investment options. For example, the ROI achieved by the firm needs to be compared to the industry and to investment options in general over a period of time to assess its performance relative to other opportunities shareholders have to invest their capital.

**EMPLOYEES** Assessing employee satisfaction is similar to assessing customer satisfaction in that the measures available are indirect. With this limit in mind, there are measures of satisfaction and productivity that are relatively easy to obtain. For example, satisfaction can be measured by employee retention, salaries, and benefits and through the use of an employee satisfaction survey. Productivity can be measured by sales and/or profits divided by the number of employees. Again, measures need to be made against competitors and over time to provide some sense of comparison.

## INNOVATION AND GROWTH

The mantra of our times is "innovate or calcify." Corporations must continue to grow and to promote innovation. Customers, shareholders, and employees all have a stake in whether a firm can innovate and grow. Innovation is more difficult to measure than growth, but indirect measures can be used.

Measures of growth are straightforward, including increases in sales and market share. Measures of innovation can include percent of sales coming from new products and new markets. In addition, percent of expenditures devoted to research and development or employee training are indirect measures of innovation.

## EXAMPLES OF STRATEGIC PERFORMANCE MEASURES

Figure 1.12 raises the question, How will the firm measure success? Despite the problems of measuring customer and employee satisfaction in particular, it is critical that leaders attempt to answer this question.

Once selected, measures can evaluate current performance, then project data based on the predicted success of the firm's strategies. Figure 1.13 provides an example of how a firm can use current and projected strategic performance measures to assess whether it satisfied stakeholders and promoted innovation and growth.

**Customers**

(a) may not know what they want
(b) may not want to tell the company what they think
(c) sales/profits easier to measure than customer satisfaction

**Employees**

(a) may not know what will satisfy them
(b) may not want to tell the firm what will satisfy them
(c) productivity easier to measure than satisfaction

**Shareholders**

(a) return on investment
(b) return on assets

**Innovation and Growth**

(a) % of sales coming from products introduced in the past five years
(b) R&D as a % of expenses
(c) training as a % of expenses

**Figure 1.12**
How Will the Firm Measure Its Success?

In this example, sales of $12 million are projected to grow to $14 million while market share and customer retention are improved. ROI is projected to increase from 12% to 14%, while profit margins are increased and overhead is reduced.

Employee productivity is projected to improve from $25,000/employee to $27,000 while retention and satisfaction are improved. Innovation and growth are

| | Current | Projected |
|---|---|---|
| Customer | $12 million - Sales<br>25% - Market Share<br>72% - Customer Retention | $14 million - Sales<br>27% - Market Share<br>75% - Customer Retention |
| Shareholder | 12% - ROI<br>15% - Pre-Tax Profit Margins<br>Overhead - 28% of Expenses | 14% - ROI<br>16% - Pre-Tax Profit Margins<br>Overhead - 26% of Expenses |
| Employee | $25,000 - Per Employee<br>87% - Employee Retention<br>75% - Employee Satisfaction | $27,000 - Per Employee<br>90% - Employee Retention<br>80% - Employee Satisfaction |
| Innovation/Growth | 15% of Sales - New Markets<br><1% of Sales - Employee Training<br>3% of Sales - R&D | 17% of Sales - New Markets<br>2% of Sales - Employee Training<br>4% of Sales - R&D |

**Figure 1.13**
Strategic Performance Measures.

measured by increasing the percent of sales coming from new markets from 15% to 17%, while investments in employee training and R&D are increased. In other words, the assumption is that investment in employee training and R&D results in increased sales.

## INTEGRATING STRATEGY USING PERFORMANCE MEASURES

By focusing attention on hard data, performance measures force decision makers to wrestle with problems of opportunity costs. The competing interests of customers, shareholders, employees, and long-term growth must be balanced. Can the firm serve customers with high-quality products at reasonable prices while it enhances shareholder wealth and employee satisfaction? If so, what would the firm's strategy and performance measures look like?

Engaging decision makers in determining how the organization will define success can bear fruit by itself. A rigorous, disciplined process that selects clear performance measures can minimize the ambiguity inherent in strategic planning. The process can clarify what will meet stakeholder expectations.

Performance measures should be used at all levels of the firm. Measures should be selected by an interdisciplinary team comprised of executives who will be held accountable for these objectives and who will be responsible for implementing strategies to reach these objectives. This approach is intended to promote "buy in" from executives in areas such as marketing, human resources, and finance. Often these areas operate in separate locations and their work is fragmented. Systems thinking among decision makers, who do not work with each other on a daily basis, can be enhanced with a discussion about satisfying stakeholders. For example, when finance executives allocate resources to enhance shareholder wealth, marketing and human resource executives can represent customers and employees, creating a balanced perspective of stakeholder satisfaction.

Strategic measures can be driven further into the company by having these measures direct the organization's performance-evaluation system. Clearly, these measures will take on more meaning for employees if the reward system is driven by them. For example, bonus and merit awards can be linked to reaching or exceeding strategic measures.

As with any strategic tool, there are limits to using performance measures. Reliability, validity, and accessibility of data all need to be taken into account. Relatively objective data can be used to assess strategic goals such as growth, for example, increased sales or units sold. Important, but soft, strategic goals such as customer or employee satisfaction can be measured indirectly. For example, presumably retention measures a behavior that indicates customers are satisfied. Possibly customers are being retained because they are not aware that competing offerings are available. Once they learn about a better offer, they will jump ship posthaste. In addition, there are clear limits in asking customers or employees directly if they are satisfied. They may not know and/or they may not want to tell the company what will satisfy them.

Performance measures are descriptive data. They describe the current and ideal state of stakeholder satisfaction and corporate innovation and growth. These data alone do not identify clearly the cause of distress or success. Of course, this limitation is also true when an analyst reviews a firm's balance sheet and income statement. Similar to performance measures, financial data are descriptive and not causal. Yet, both performance measures and financial statements help executives formulate appropriate questions and focus on critical strategic objectives.

Decision makers should not become captive to these numerical objectives. Yet, data such as these can be helpful guides in allocating resources and setting a firm's direction.

## PROMOTING STRATEGIC THINKING

The challenge to think broadly and across functions, such as having cross-disciplinary teams develop strategic-performance measures, is further complicated by our limited capacity to understand and resolve complex strategic problems. We frequently diagnose the firm's issues incorrectly and then propose inappropriate solutions. The strategic-planning process must uncover ways for participants to break through narrow worlds, and interact with people in different functions so that more people can get a larger sense of the whole (Mintzberg, 1994).

While techniques such as group problem solving can help overcome flawed reasoning, it must be recognized that there are serious barriers to change. Cognitive research shows we cannot easily examine flaws in our thinking. In fact, our most important judgments are particularly prone to resisting our long-held beliefs that may or may not help us to make future decisions. Our capacity for self-delusion appears to be infinite.

The constraints of reasoning ability should not be taken as barriers to action; there is much room for optimism. A colleague who reviewed research on cognitive reasoning asked, How did man make it to the moon if he is so dumb? The answer appears to be that two or more heads are better than one, and thus collective problem solving cancels out the shortcomings of any one person. Decisions of little consequence will and should be guided by our instincts. Important decisions, such as an organization's direction and strategies, must involve multiple perspectives (Nisbett and Ross, 1980).

So, in light of the lessons taught by cognitive psychology, what can firms do to ensure organizational learning and strategic thinking? An important first step is to build initial agreement about the items outlined in Figure 1.14.

Initial agreements can give a process legitimacy that includes providing planners with the authority to pull together cross-functional teams. An initial agreement should outline the general sequence of steps in the strategic planning effort

(1) Introduce the concept of strategic planning and develop an understanding of what it can mean in practice

(2) Think through some of the more important implications of strategic planning concerning the acquisition and allocation of resources

(3) Develop a commitment to strategic planning

**Figure 1.14**
Promoting Strategic Thinking.

STATUS QUO—Widespread commitment to existing plan

REFORMATIVE—Widespread commitment to alternative plan

INDIFFERENT—Low commitment to prevailing and alternative plans

COMPETITIVE—Substantial commitment to two or more plans

**Figure 1.15** Decision Makers (Keller, 1983).

and link the process to key organizational decision points, such as budget decisions (Bryson, 1979).

The degree to which key decision makers are open to change should also be assessed, especially when it comes to resource acquisition and allocation. As a group, decision makers should assess the degree to which there is consensus to change. Typically, decision makers can be categorized into one of the four groups listed in Figure 1.15.

The paradox is that leaders and employees tend to resist change when firms most need flexibility. To survive and prosper, organizations must adapt to changes in the marketplace. Employees at all levels of the organization need to change their behavior and commit to new products, markets, and processes. Accordingly, leaders need to think through how to best communicate strategic issues to employees.

Leaders should communicate facts and avoid communicating values. Values are best communicated through actions and not words. Deeds will best communicate whether senior leaders can be trusted. Trust can either be the glue to sustain a firm through difficult times, or, once violated, erode support for change.

Trust and support can be gained by senior leaders communicating face-to-face with supervisors and employees. Senior leaders should rely on frontline supervisors and avoid dependency on videos, publications, or large meetings to communicate strategic issues. Change happens one person at a time. Each individual needs to understand the strategic issues confronting the firm and what the firm requires of him or her. Individuals will then decide whether they can and want to make a commitment to change.

Since implementing strategy is dependent on the support of middle and frontline supervisors, the firm should seek the support and ideas of these leaders. Senior leaders should clarify the strategic issues confronting the firm to appropriate supervisors and then seek their insights about how to best resolve these issues. Supervisors should understand the position of senior leaders concerning which initiatives will not change and which can be altered. This can be accomplished by senior leaders reporting business facts to supervisors, such as:

1. The company confronts a shift in its customer base, decrease in its profit margins due to entrants of new competitors, erosion of market share due to its inferior products, etc.
2. The firm's strategic response will target new markets, control costs, improve quality, etc.
3. The consequences to employees will be payroll reductions, voluntary leaves, and a process to select involuntary leaves, etc. (Larkin and Larkin, [illegible]).

Supervisors will need this information to help the company implement its strategy. In addition, supervisors are sure to have insights about strategic issues missed by senior leaders.

When strategic planning is done well, it is likely to result in serious disagreements. Creating an atmosphere of free inquiry and discussion focused on strategic issues must be established so that debate is not stifled. In addition, participants must possess good conflict resolution skills if the strategic planning process is to make a difference in the life of the enterprise (Bryson, 1979).

## CONCLUSION

Countless reasons have been proposed to explain the failure of organizations to respond to changes in the environment. Often, the search for solutions to new problems does not extend much beyond already known solutions. The organization is motivated to transform ill-defined problems into a form that can be handled with existing routines (Miles, 1982). This finding is consistent with cognitive psychologists' contention that we are often tenacious in holding onto our existing views.

To minimize the effect of political tensions and to increase the influence of rational decision making, organizational learning at all levels of the firm is required. Strategy is a process that should teach key decision makers about the important issues confronting the firm and how they can best be resolved. The strategic-planning process can inform an organization about its environment, its competitors, its resources, its strengths, its weaknesses, and its purpose. Strategic planning can help executives explore how to better integrate the functions of the business such as marketing, finance, and human resources. At its best, strategic planning can pull the organization together as a unit working toward a common vision of what the enterprise can become.

Historically, strategy has focused mostly on the top of the organization. However, a strategic issue can emerge from anywhere in the organization and initiative to push it forward can be taken by personnel at any level. The problem of implementation and resistance to change demands involvement from all levels of the organization (Kanter, 1989). Those employees responsible for implementing the plan should be involved in its conception.

Yet, the importance of leadership in crafting strategy cannot be overstated. Leadership and strategy are intertwined. Organizations need strategic leadership that promotes systemic thinking and behavior. Leaders need to create organizations that are responsive to their environments and, accordingly, develop structures that promote collaboration and minimize territorial assertions.

Leaders also need to exercise courage to make hard choices that are an inevitable part of strategy. Strategic formulation and implementation provide options that place leaders between rocks and hard places. Nevertheless, when resources are limited, leaders have the opportunity to clarify priorities, eliminate unproductive units, restructure debt, reconsider pricing policies, and reorganize to be more efficient and attractive to customers (Keller, 1983).

Linking strategic planning to retreats and performance reviews heightens its importance and staying power. Strategic-planning efforts must tie the process to key budget decisions to capitalize on strategic visions. Strategic thinking must precede rather than follow budgeting (Bryson, 1979).

The result of strategic planning is that leaders throughout the organization think of problems not only vertically, or top-down, which is done frequently, but also horizontally, which is done infrequently. Incentives need to promote cooperation and the ability to respond rapidly and effectively to the unexpected (Ackoff, 1993).

In the end, ideas matter. They drive a well-led enterprise. Strategic thinking and acting that promote inspiring ideas are more important than any particular approach to strategy formulation and implementation. These ideas must be discussed and evaluated in relation to whether they will satisfy stakeholder expectations. Strategies that are unacceptable to key stakeholders need to be rethought.

Strategy is about numbers and words. It is about leadership and wide-based employee involvement. It is about meeting the expectations of stakeholders. It is about comparative advantage and the firm's environment. Most of all, it is about ideas that inspire and give people a sense of purpose. Strategy can provide stability in a world full of ambiguity and uncertainty.

## REFERENCES


Ackoff, R. "Beyond Total Quality Management." *Journal for Quality and Participation*, March 1993, pp. 66–77.

Boisseau, C. "Mission Statements." *The Plain Dealer*, October 15, 1995, p. 2H.

Bryson, J. M. *Strategic Planning for Public and Nonprofit Organizations*. San Francisco, CA: Jossey-Bass, 1979.

Chandler, A. *Strategy and Structure*. Cambridge, MA: MIT Press, 1962.

Christensen, C. R., Andrews, K. R., and Bower, J. L. *Business Policy: Text and Cases*. Homewood, IL: Richard D. Irwin, 1973.

Cyert, R. M., and March, J. G. *A Behavioral Theory of the Firm*. Englewood Cliffs, NJ: Prentice-Hall, 1963.

Drucker, P. *Management: Tasks, Responsibilities, Practices*. New York: Harper & Row, 1973.

Kanter, R. M. "The New Managerial Work," *Harvard Business Review*, November–December, 1989, p. 92.

Kaplan, R., and Norton, D. "Using the Balanced Scorecard as a Strategic Management System." *Harvard Business Review*, January–February, 1996, p. 75.

Keller, G. *Academic Strategy*. Baltimore, MD: Johns Hopkins Press, 1983.

Kelly, H. "Attribution Theory in Social Psychology." In D. Levine, ed., *Nebraska Symposium on Motivation* (Vol. 15). Lincoln: University of Nebraska Press, 1967.

Larkin, T., and Larkin, S. "Reaching and Changing Frontline Employees," *Harvard Business Review*, May–June, 1996, pp. 95–104.

Miles, R. H. *Coffin Nails and Corporate Strategies*. Englewood Cliffs, NJ: Prentice-Hall, 1982.

Mintzberg, H. "Strategy Formation: Schools of Thought." In J. Frederickson, ed., *Perspectives on Strategic Management.* Boston: Ballinger, 1990.

Mintzberg, H. *The Rise and Fall of Strategic Planning.* New York: The Free Press, 1994.

Nisbett, R., and Ross, L. *Human Inference: Strategies and Shortcomings of Social Judgment.* Englewood Cliffs, NJ: Prentice-Hall, 1980.

Porter, M. *Competitive Strategy: Techniques for Analyzing Industries and Competitors.* New York: The Free Press, 1980.

Porter. M. "Corporate Strategy: the State of Strategic Thinking." *The Economist* 303, 7499 (May 23, 1987), pp. 17–22.

Public Broadcasting System. Interview with Brian Mulrony by Charlie Rose, October 11, 1995.

Segev, E. *Corporate Strategy: Portfolio Models,* International Thomson Publishing, London, 1995.

Simon, H. "Rational Decision Making in Organizations." *American Economic Review* 69, September 1979, pp. 493–513.

Yergin, Daniel. *The Prize.* New York: Touchstone, 1992.

## ESSAY QUESTIONS

Employees can best contribute to an organization's success if they understand and can critique a firm's strategy. To do so, employees must understand the organization's purpose and capabilities and its external trends and issues. Employees can best focus their efforts on the most important issues facing an organization if they can answer the following questions about their current employer or an employer for whom they would like to work:

1. What is happening to long-term growth (demand) in this organization's industry(ies)? In other words, determine which market segments in this industry are growing, stable, or declining. What are the short-term and long-term profit prospects in this industry?
2. Are the number of competitors (supply) increasing or decreasing? What is the rate of new entry by competitors into the industry? Dropout from the industry? What is the relative size of competitors (indicate who the competitors are and their size)?
3. Complete a comprehensive SWOT analysis of this organization. Identify the top three opportunities and threats and explain why you selected these.
4. Describe the history and culture of this organization and speculate on how its past is shaping its future. Include an assessment of the firm's marketing, finance, and human-resource philosophy and the history of its leadership.
5. Is this organization innovative? What are the marketing opportunities available to this organization and is it well-positioned to take advantage of these opportunities? Consider measures such as percent of sales coming from new products and markets in the past three years. Include percent of sales coming from international operations.
6. Provide an overall assessment of this organization's core competencies.
7. Develop a list of strategic options the organization could consider and rank these options according to those that you think present the best probability of success.
8. Select a strategy that you think presents the best probability of success. Assess the extent to which the strategy is consistent with the organization's mission, core competencies, and available opportunities.

9. Develop a list of critical performance measures that can be used to assess customer, employee, and shareholder satisfaction as well as innovation/growth.

## MULTIPLE-CHOICE QUESTIONS

1. An organization's success depends upon its ability to satisfy the needs of:
   a. stockholders
   b. customers
   c. employees
   d. creditors
   e. stakeholders
2. The probability that a firm's strategy will work depends upon:
   a. good fortune and timing
   b. mandates from senior management
   c. employee satisfaction
   d. the match between a firm's mission and core competencies and its external opportunities
   e. regulatory climate
3. Executive capacity to understand and learn about their organization's strategic issues are influenced heavily by:
   a. executive knowledge of sampling, analysis, and decision-making methods
   b. executive memory and ability to resolve complex and unstructured problems
   c. executive knowledge of hypothesis testing, research design, and analysis
   d. executive knowledge of mission statements, internal analysis, and environmental scanning
   e. executive intelligence and logic
4. Strategic direction and vision result from:
   a. executive insight, logic, and intentional behavior
   b. a linear process that flows from the external environment to internal strengths and mission
   c. plans that are some combination of deliberate action and emerging thought that could not have been predicted easily
   d. the insights of charismatic leaders
   e. forecasting the future accurately through the use of quantitative tools and methods
5. The most difficult task of leadership is:
   a. coping with business risk
   b. coping with uncertainty and leading people to work toward a common goal
   c. conducting an environmental scan
   d. developing a mission statement
   e. reaching performance targets
6. The fundamental purpose of strategy is:
   a. increase profits
   b. increase market growth rates
   c. secure customers and respond effectively to competitors
   d. increase market share
   e. enhance shareholder value
7. According to the text, the number of questions that can be raised about an organization's strategies are endless. The fundamental questions that should be addressed by all organizations include all of the following except:
   a. What are the strategic issues facing the enterprise?

**b.** What are the firm's competitive advantages?
**c.** What is the match between the firm's products/services and customer needs, wants, and values?
**d.** How can the firm implement management strategies such as total quality management (TQM)?
**e.** How will strategy be integrated and success be measured?

# CHAPTER 2 Strategic Market Management

The most basic objective of marketing strategy is to retain existing customers and to attract new ones. Often, 20% of a firm's customers account for 80% of its sales. What strategy would a company use if it lost a key account or 10% of its customers? The options are simple: Existing customers must buy more and/or new customers must be attracted. Otherwise, companies fall on hard times, often resulting in downsizing, rightsizing, or whatever euphemism is used to explain that employees will be laid off.

The line that designates the end of corporate strategy and the beginning of marketing strategy is blurred. The central task of corporate strategy is to attract and retain customers (Mintzberg, 1994). An organization's reason for being is to define its business according to the customers that it serves (Levitt, 1975).

Corporate strategy and strategic market management are both meant to help firms serve customers better than the firm's competitors. While there are academic definitions that distinguish between corporate and marketing strategy, for all practical purposes both types of strategy must take into account the firm's internal capabilities and the external trends that affect it.

In fact, strategic thought that fails to integrate marketing and corporate strategy must be considered flawed. Defining an organization as a group of parts—marketing, finance, human resources, and so on—can lead to fragmentation of the firm and create barriers to fulfilling strategic goals. Strategic problems and their solutions can often be found at departmental divisions, the walls inside the organization. The way a firm is organized often restricts its ability to deliver quality service (Kotler, 1994). While strategic issues are interdependent, companies organize and solve problems as if they were not (Kofman and Senge, 1995). Strategic issues never come to executives packaged neatly as marketing, finance, or human-resource problems. Marketing problems are inevitably messy. Marketing both causes and is affected by a firm's human resources and finance efforts in addition to production, R&D, engineering, and so on.

Market-oriented strategic planning is the managerial process of developing and maintaining a viable fit between the organization's objectives, skills, and resources and its changing market opportunities (Kotler, 1994). The aim of strategic-market planning is to retain and/or attract new customers so that the company's businesses and products yield target profits and growth.

As with strategic planning, marketing strategy concepts, tools, and analysis are endless. There are many reasons why strategic planning fails or succeeds. Cer

1. **Customers**: What is the match between the firm's products/services and its current and potential customers?
2. **Competitors**: What is the firm's competitive advantage?
3. **Company**: What are the firm's strengths and weaknesses?
4. **Marketing Strategy**: How can the firm formulate and implement a strategy that retains existing customers and attracts new customers?

**Figure 2.1**
Marketing Strategy Framework.

tainly, one reason strategic market planning approaches misfire is that they fail to aid executives in coping with the ambiguity and uncertainty inherent in marketing problems. To improve the chances that strategic thinking will take hold, the approach outlined in this text will stick to the fundamental objective of marketing strategy—retain and attract new customers. To this end, a well-formulated marketing strategy addresses basic questions, as seen in Figure 2.1.

The use of strategic tools such as SWOT analysis and the BCG and GE models were outlined in Chapter 1. These tools can help a firm better understand its environment and capabilities. This chapter will provide additional tools that can be used to formulate a firm's marketing strategy.

# Marketing Issues and Trends

In order for a firm to retain and/or attract new customers, it must develop an enduring competitive advantage. The word "enduring" can be misleading in that it may imply that a strategy, once set, ensures success for the company. In reality, if the firm is to endure it must remain adaptable to changes in the marketplace.

According to Drucker (1985), a company's winning formula in the last decade will probably be the company's undoing in the next decade. Levitt (1975) put it this way: "To survive, companies with growth products will have to plot the obsolescence of what now produces their livelihood."

In his classic article, "Marketing Myopia," Levitt used the petroleum industry to explain his theory. The oil industry's efforts had focused on improving the *efficiency* of getting and making its product, rather than on improving the generic product or its marketing. Its chief product had continuously been defined in the narrowest possible terms, namely, gasoline, not energy, fuel, or transportation (Levitt, 1975).

Thus, major improvements in gasoline quality have not tended to originate in the oil industry. Development of superior alternative fuels also have come from outside the oil industry. For instance, the petroleum industry owned rights to natural gas, but refused to see natural gas as a replacement for oil heating. Rather than capitalize on the new market, industry executives allowed other investors to organize gas transmission companies (Levitt, 1975).

To survive and prosper, organizations must focus on adapting to their markets in a way that retains and/or attracts customers rather than on myopic devotion to their products. The U.S. consumer market is getting grayer and more ethnically diverse. More women are working and marrying later, are more likely to divorce, and are having smaller families than in previous generations. Corporations demand high-quality products from suppliers, delivered quickly and cheaply. The product life cycle for many firms is shorter than in the past, which requires that products be brought to market faster and with better service. Corporations want improved distribution and promotion methods at lower costs (Kotler, 1994).

In today's world, technology and legislation can rapidly open and close a market. The telecommunications act passed by Congress in 1996 dismantled regulations that separated phone, cable, and computer companies. Technological advances are blurring the uses of telephones, computers, and televisions, and thus the industries that produce them. As a result, mergers and acquisitions similar to Disney's alliance with Cap Cities are likely to continue, thereby creating a fundamentally different way of bringing information, communications, and entertainment to market (*Economist*, 1996).

Over the next several years, public utility companies will continue to deregulate the industry. Consumers will have an increasing number of suppliers from which to choose, forcing local companies to compete with other companies with excess energy to sell. The local company will receive a fee to transfer its competitor's power to the local company's former customers. It is not clear how electric utilities will be deregulated, who will pay for plants and equipment that will become obsolete, or how residential consumers, small businesses, and large corporations can all benefit. Yet, federal legislation has already promoted an independent power generation sector and state governments are now determined to open these markets further (*Harvard Business Review*, 1996).

Corporations increasingly find themselves being held responsible by legislatures and the public for their environmental impact. The central environmental question for the 21st century is whether economic growth can be sustained without harming the planet's ecosystem for future generations. Regulations, media attention, and public pressure are all forcing companies to manage responsibly their effluents, packaging material, waste handling, and other environmental impacts that result from manufacturing and marketing (Kotler, 1994).

Corporations follow markets. If demographics are destiny, the 21st century belongs to Asia. Approximately 40% of the world's population resides in China and India alone. Well-developed eastern economies like Japan are driven by an aging population of 125 million. Emerging eastern economies like Indonesia are driven by a youthful population of over 200 million (U.S. Department of Commerce, 1994).

The global economy has been transformed by international trade liberalization and privatization of public corporations and assets. Advancements in information technology make possible financial connections 24 hours a day around the world. Air transportation, fax machines, the Internet and telephone links, and world television satellite broadcasting advancements have opened markets and supply sources to corporations (Kotler, 1994).

While the U.S. market share of international trade has declined over the past 20 years, American exports still exceed those of any other nation. U.S. corporations are forming strategic alliances with foreign companies who serve as suppliers, distributors, and joint-venture partners. Approximately 22,000 jobs result from every $1 billion of exports (U.S. Department of Commerce, 1984).

International trade agreements such as GATT (General Agreement on Tariffs and Trade) and WTO (World Trade Organization) have been approved at a global level to eliminate trade barriers, set common trade standards and regulations, and provide a form to arbitrate disputes. Regional trade agreements such as the (EU) European Union and NAFTA (North American Free Trade Agreement) are designed to promote trade within a geographic area, giving preferential treatment to goods made in this area.

Domestic and international social, technical, economic, environmental, and political trends shape U.S. consumer aspirations and standard of living. U.S. consumers appear to have raised their expectations at a time when the wages of many have stagnated and feelings of insecurity have increased. A family may have been satisfied with a three-bedroom, $1\frac{1}{2}$ bath house 20 years ago. Today, families want four bedrooms and $2\frac{1}{2}$ baths. Roughly speaking, reports often claim the top 20% of all wage earners continue to get ahead, the middle 60% are treading water, and the bottom 20% are losing ground. That said, between 1979 and 1988, a Treasury study revealed that 86% of those in the lowest income bracket moved to a higher bracket. When income is tracked over time, Americans still appear to be getting ahead. Increased aspirations and insecurities are occurring in an economic climate during the 1990s that is remarkable for its relatively low inflation, interest, and unemployment rates (Federal Reserve Bank, 1995).

# The Marketing Response

The list of marketing trends is not meant to be exhaustive, but it does provide an overview of the broad range of factors that can affect product longevity. As Levitt states, there is, in fact, no guarantee against product obsolescence. If a company's own research does not make its products obsolete, another's will. Unless an industry is especially lucky, it can easily go down in a sea of red figures—just as the railroads have, as the buggy-whip manufacturers have, as the corner grocery chains have, as most of the big movie companies have, and indeed as many other industries have (Levitt, 1975).

In response to continual changes in the marketplace, a truly marketing-minded firm tries to create value-satisfying goods and services that consumers will want to buy. What the firm offers for sale includes not only the generic product or service, but also how it is made available to the customer, in what form, when, under what conditions, and at what terms of trade. Most important, what it offers for sale is determined not by the seller but by the buyer. The seller takes cues from the buyer in such a way that the product becomes a consequence of the marketing effort, not vice versa (Levitt, 1975).

A corporation's profits are dependent on its ability to assess the needs and wants of target markets and then deliver products and services that satisfy consumers more effectively and efficiently than competitors do (Kotler, 1994). Thus, an industry begins with customer needs, not with a patent, a raw material, or a selling skill. Then it develops backwards, first concerning itself with the physical delivery of customer satisfactions, moving backwards further to creating the things by which these satisfactions are in part achieved. How these materials are created makes no difference to the customer.

The organization must learn to think of itself not as producing goods or services but as buying customers, as doing the things that will make people want to do business with it. Management must think of itself not as producing products but as providing customer-creating value satisfactions (Mintzberg, 1994).

## What Is the Match Between the Firm's Products/Services and Current and Potential Customers?

Corporate sales come from either new customers or repeat customers. It is cheaper to keep customers than to attract them. Not surprisingly, the key to customer retention is customer satisfaction (Kotler, 1994).

The benefits of understanding how to best satisfy customers is self-evident. Yet, true understanding is elusive, since customers may not know what will satisfy them, or their desires may change continuously, or they may not wish to share their wants.

Thus, what appears obvious—understanding how to satisfy consumers—proves to be the difficult act of hitting the moving target of customers' changing preferences. The questions listed in Figure 2.2 can focus a firm on market segmentation, understanding its consumers' motivations and identifying unmet needs.

These questions can be answered both empirically and intuitively. The scientific management approach relies heavily on quantitative methods and is the

**1. Segmentation**

- Who are the buyers and users of the product or service?
- Who are the largest buyers?
- What potential customers can be identified who are not now buying from the firm?
- How should the market be segmented?

**2. Customer Motivation**

- What motivates customers to buy and use the products or services?
- What attributes of the offering are important?
- What objectives do the customers seek?
- What changes in customer motivation are occurring or are likely to occur?

**3. Unmet Needs**

- Are the customers satisfied with the product and services they are now buying?
- Do the customers experience problems?
- Are there unmet needs of which customers may not be aware?

**Figure 2.2** Customer Satisfaction (Aaker, 1988).

approach most widely advocated in textbooks. This approach should be understood and considered when appropriate by organizations and will be explained in this text.

The scientific method is limited by its assumption that organizations behave rationally. It assumes executives formulate hypotheses about the firm's markets, design research methods that test their hypotheses, and engage in thoughtful discussions about their findings before strategy is set. In fact, executive memory and impressions are more likely to drive strategy than a cluster analysis of customer segments. The pressure of the marketplace to bring new products to market quickly results in an intuitive and political decision-making process that is far removed from scientific management methods. Even when a company does engage in an exhaustive empirical study, its ability to predict future market demand and consumer behavior is always limited. With or without the benefit of empirical data, at some point executives have to decide who the company will serve and how the firm will satisfy customer needs, wants, and values.

The use of scientific marketing research is further limited by the degree to which consumers know what they want or are willing to share their needs, wants, and values with producers. When asking consumers how they make consumption decisions, a researcher is more likely to learn how consumers think they should make decisions than how they actually make decisions (Ackoff, 1993). Inability to remember actual behaviors and the desire to report "ideal" behaviors limit consumers' capacity to report what they really do.

The degree to which rationality can be assumed by either consumers or by executives who set organizational strategy should be considered. The scientific method still has much to offer organizations when formulating marketing strategies. At the very least, the science of marketing can help firms ask the right questions.

## MARKET SEGMENTATION

Simply stated, the intention of segmentation strategy is to meet the needs of a customer group with appropriate products and services. Market segmentation is the process of identifying distinct groups of buyers who might require separate products and/or marketing mixes, then creating a profile of each group. Market segmentation identifies groups of consumers who respond differently than others to competitive strategies (Aaker, 1988). For example, some consumers choose clothes based primarily on price. Others look for the latest fashion trends. Still others want a classic look with attention to construction.

Companies should focus on whether potential customers seem homogenous in their needs, wants, and values, or more heterogeneous. Companies need to determine whether there are more differences or similarities in customers' preferences for quality, cost, and service. The variables selected to assess this must be measurable, substantial, accessible, differentiable, and actionable (Kotler, 1994).

Segmentation can also uncover unmet needs—needs that are not being met by current products. These segments represent opportunities for a firm to increase market share or to enter a market. Unmet needs may also represent threats to established firms by allowing new market entrants (Aaker, 1988).

There are countless ways to divide a given market. The cost of targeting a segment must, of course, be matched by its benefit in size or potential. A segment also must be open to trying a new product or switching brands (Aaker, 1988).

Market segments are based on either customer characteristics or product characteristics. Some of the most common segment variables are outlined here.

Customer characteristics include:

**geographic segmentation**—countries, region of the country, states, counties, cities, or neighborhoods occupied by potential market life cycles

**demographic segmentation**—socioeconomic status (education, occupation, and income), age, gender, family size, family life cycle, religion, ethnic background of potential market

**psychographic segmentation**—lifestyle and/or personality of potential markets
**behavioral segmentation**—awareness, knowledge, attitude, level of product use (Kotler, 1994).

Product characteristics include:

**application segmentation**—how potential consumers might use a product
**benefits segmentation**—responses of consumers to benefits sought from the product, occasions when and how the product is used, or loyalty to a particular brand; price and quality trade-offs (Aaker, 1988).

The process of segmenting markets to find a good fit can be quite complex. Using the scientific approach, researchers gather data through interviews, focus groups, and questionnaires, and analyze the data to determine where clusters exist. Consumer profiles are then built based on segmentation variables that distinguish the consumption habits of these consumers from others (Kotler, 1994).

After identifying viable customer segments, the next step is to consider the motivations behind the purchase decisions of specific segments. Understanding what affects a consumer's decision to purchase a particular product class, and then which brand among several choices within that class, is important to understanding whether the firm has the assets and skills needed to produce a viable product.

Asking customers to describe their purchase decisions reveals more about how they think decisions should be made than how they actually make them. Asking customers to describe *why* they purchased particular products often produces more realistic answers (Aaker, 1988).

Alternatively, customers can be asked trade-off questions. For example, if forced to make a choice, would an airline passenger choose convenient departure time over price? These difficult judgments ask customers to deal with real-life decisions regarding product choice (Aaker, 1988).

Having identified market segments and discovered customer motivations within those segments, the next step is to target particular markets that the firm is most likely to be able to satisfy either with existing skills and assets, or with those it can develop. The firm may choose to address multiple segments, or may focus on a single segment, much smaller than the market as a whole (Aaker, 1988).

Most firms do not segment their markets this thoroughly. Whether a firm should apply an empirical approach to segmenting its markets is determined by examining the attendant costs and benefits. This more scientific approach is generally cast aside due to time pressures to bring a product to market, political realities, or lack of knowledge among management about the value of empirical research. Executive power and influence is more likely to drive strategy than an empirical analysis. Organizations that rely on marketing research to set strategy can only do so if senior executives support this approach.

If firms are to follow Mintzberg's (1994) advice that strategy should focus on buying customers, then the central purpose of corporate and marketing strategy should be to identify customers' motivations and unmet needs. This knowledge becomes the catalyst that should drive a firm's strategy.

# What Is the Firm's Competitive Circumstance?

The benefit of understanding the competition's performance, objectives, strengths, and weaknesses, and trying to anticipate their motives and strategies is self-evident. Competitive analysis may uncover opportunities that will be the basis of strategic competitive advantage. Competitive advantage is based upon having a position superior to the target competitors on one or more assets or skill areas that are relevant both to the industry and to the strategy employed.

However, the dilemma is how to conduct a competitive analysis. It is rarely easy to answer the question that should be so obvious—Who is our competition? IBM might compete with Apple to sell personal computers and, at the same time, enter a joint alliance with them to conduct R&D of mutual benefit. Does Disney's Epcot Center compete with other theme parks or with a wide range of vacation options?

It is also not clear what information should be gathered to conduct a useful competitive analysis. What quality, service, and price variables should a firm benchmark relative to competitors? In truth, who the firm defines as competitors and what information will be gathered requires executive judgment. There is more art here than science.

Clearly, there are countless ways in which a competitive analysis can be conducted. Michael Porter has developed a framework that is widely accepted. He notes that the roots of competition in an industry are embedded in five competitive forces: threat of new entrants, threat of substitute products, bargaining power of buyers, bargaining power of suppliers, and rivalry among existing firms. The goal of a corporation's competitive strategy is to position the firm to defend or take advantage of these competitive forces (Porter, 1980).

## PORTER'S COMPETITIVE MODEL

**THREAT OF NEW ENTRANTS** When new firms enter a market, they bring new capacity and often substantial resources with the intention of gaining market share. Therefore when analyzing a target market, it is essential to examine barriers to entering the market and the relative strength of those barriers. The six major barriers to entry are:

1. economies of scale, which can leave the new entrant at a price disadvantage
2. product differentiation, which means that products already in the market have brand identification and customer loyalty, making it difficult for new entrants to compete
3. capital requirements, which, if large, can limit the number of firms that can compete

4. switching costs, i.e., costs buyers must pay when they switch from one supplier's products to another's, making it difficult for new entrants to lure current customers
5. access to distribution channels, which can complicate entry to the market if distribution channels are limited or used by current suppliers
6. cost disadvantages independent of scale, advantages that new entrants cannot duplicate, such as proprietary product technology, favorable locations or access to raw materials or government subsidies.

Entry barriers can and do change as market conditions change. Patents expire, product differentiation disappears, economies of scale increase. A firm's strategic decisions can also have a major impact.

A controversial example of how entry barriers affect competition and profits can be found in the tobacco industry. Tobacco companies enjoy virtually no threat of new entrants into their business. Legislation limits cigarette advertising in the hope of reducing the number of smokers, thereby benefitting public health. Paradoxically, restricted advertising and sizable capital expenditures are effective barriers to potential market entrants, thus enhancing existing producers' profits. It certainly may be desirable public health policy to limit the number of tobacco companies to those that exist currently. Yet, increasing barriers to new entrants also enhances the competitive position of existing companies.

**PRESSURE FROM SUBSTITUTE PRODUCTS** Substitute products are those that can meet the same needs as a given industry's product. For example, sugar producers are confronting a loss of market share to producers of high-fructose corn syrup, a substitute sweetener. Marketers must be aware of not only the goals and plans of direct competitors, but of those of producers of substitute products as well. Substitute products that compete favorably on price and performance should be the most carefully monitored. Other substitutes that should be closely watched are those produced by industries that earn high profits (Porter, 1980).

**BARGAINING POWER OF BUYERS** Buyers can influence a firm's decisions about product quality, price, and services. Buyers have particular power when they buy in large volumes, when the product is relatively expensive in relation to buyer income, when the product is standard or undifferentiated, when the cost of changing from one brand or product to another is low, or when the buyer has full information about demand, actual market prices, and supplier costs (Porter, 1980).

These same rules apply to the buying power of wholesalers and retailers, with one exception. When retailers acquire bargaining power over manufacturers they can influence consumers' purchasing decisions. In contrast, wholesalers can acquire bargaining power when they influence the purchase decisions of the retailers. Accordingly, a corporation can improve its strategic position by finding buyers who are least likely to influence it adversely. For example, buyers in isolated geographic areas may not have many products from which to choose, and therefore they do not have much influence on the current product supplier.

The power of Wal-Mart is an example of how a large retailer can force supplier price cuts. The volume of products that Wal-Mart can move through the marketplace is too significant for any large manufacturer to ignore. Wal-Mart was established by serving rural communities that were largely ignored by other retailers. Wal-Mart now serves rural, suburban, and urban communities throughout the United States. Its ability to reach millions of consumers is its source of power to exact price discounts from multi-billion-dollar corporations such as Procter & Gamble and Rubbermaid.

**BARGAINING POWER OF SUPPLIERS** Suppliers can exercise power over buyers by threatening to raise prices or reduce the quality of products and services. Powerful suppliers can thereby decrease a corporation's margins and eliminate its ability to recover from cost increases.

A supplier group is powerful if it is dominated by a few companies, if the buyer is not an important customer, if the suppliers' product is critical to the buyer's business, or if the supplier wants to acquire the buyer's business.

Labor is a supplier that exerts great power over many industries. Highly organized labor, scarce labor, or labor sources that are prevented from growing can be very powerful (Porter, 1980).

The government can have significant influence on an industry as either a buyer or supplier. For example, the defense department influences heavily the strategy of companies such as TRW. In essence, the defense department outsources the manufacturing of satellites to TRW, but influences directly specifications, payment schedule, the degree to which information will be classified, and so on (Porter, 1980).

**INTENSITY OF RIVALRY AMONG EXISTING COMPETITORS** Firms compete against each other on a number of factors: product price and quality, distribution, service, advertising effectiveness, marketing strategies, and so on. Such competition generates a rivalry among existing firms that use tactics like price cutting, advertising battles, product introductions, and increased customer service or warranties to improve their relative positions in the market (Porter, 1980).

The potential intensity of the rivalry depends on the number of competitors, whether the competitors are nearly equal, how rapidly the industry is growing, differentiation of products, relative volume of fixed costs, the importance of product success to each competitor, ease of entry to and exit from the market should that be necessary, the diversity of the competitors, cost to buyers of switching products, and industry elasticity or the ability to cope with increased product supply (Porter, 1980).

## SUMMARY OF COMPETITIVE ANALYSIS

Similar to conducting consumer analysis, completing a competitive analysis requires executive judgment. The methods that can be used and the information that can be collected are endless. This analysis can be more focused by using Porter's five factors to determine which actions will result in competitive advantage. Information can be gathered by using a competitor's communications to suppliers, customers and distributors, security analysts and stockholders, and government legislators and regulators to obtain information needed in the competitive analysis. Trade magazines, trade shows, advertising, speeches, annual reports, technical meetings and journals, and electronic databases also provide useful information (Churchill, 1991).

The conceptualization of strategic groups for a firm can make the process of competitor analysis more manageable. Porter's (1980) definition of a strategic group includes firms with similar competitive strategies (i.e., same distribution and advertising strategy); similar characteristics (i.e., size, aggressiveness); similar assets and skills (i.e., quality, service, and price). Reducing the entire set to a small number of strategic groups makes the analysis compact, feasible, and more usable.

# What Are the Company's Strengths and Weaknesses?

As the phrase implies, "enduring competitive advantage" refers to those qualities of the firm that cannot be easily matched by competitors and that are in demand by customers. While a firm collects information on competitors, it should analyze similar information about itself. In fact, one of the most important results of the industry analysis is the identification of the key success factors for strategic groups in the industry, which the firm should use to measure its own performance. Key success factors are a set of assets and skills that are needed to be successful and perhaps even to survive. Questions to consider include, Which are the most critical skills and assets now, and more importantly, Which will be most critical in the future (Aaker, 1988)?

Any external or customer analysis needs to be directed and purposeful. This analysis should be motivated by a desire to affect strategy, to generate or evaluate strategic options. While the benefit of collecting information to make strategic decisions is self-evident, the process can be endless and lose focus. Time and resources limit how much information should be collected. At some point decisions must be made.

Remember that Levitt's analysis emphasized the need to define the business in terms of the basic customer need rather than in terms of a particular product (Levitt, 1975). In other words, the generic customer need should be described as a means of encouraging creative strategic options and growth directions (Aaker, 1988).

Several methods may be used to uncover unmet needs: interviews or focus groups with consumers in which their experience with the products is discussed; problem research in which priorities are set by asking respondents to rate product problems according to importance and frequency, and deciding whether a solution exists; benefit analysis in which consumers identify what they expect and the extent to which the product fulfills their expectations; and customer satisfaction studies, repeated regularly to identify changes (Aaker, 1988).

Self-analysis often starts with a performance analysis. Information about market share, customer retention, new product development, and so forth, helps assess a firm's strengths and weaknesses. Aaker (1988) notes that self-analysis develops knowledge of organizational strengths, weaknesses, and constraints, and helps build responsive strategies that either exploit strengths, or correct or compensate for weakness.

Porter created the "value chain" concept to identify ways to enhance the product's value to the customer. Using competitors' costs and performances as benchmarks, the firm tries to improve its own costs and performance in each value-added activity. Any time its performance exceeds that of its competitors, the firm has created a competitive advantage (Porter, 1985).

It is especially difficult to anticipate what it will take to remain competitive in markets that are growing rapidly. One way to evaluate competitive response is to examine the relative importance of "key success factors." To do so, a firm determines what element of the product is most likely to add value. For example, at the beginning of the calculator's product life cycle, the integrated circuit was the most significant value added component. As the product matured, keyboard assembly became more important and firms moved operations offshore to remain competitive (Aaker, 1988).

Another consideration is whether experience curve strategies are viable. Can corporations achieve cost advantages through volume? Can significant capital investments achieve economies of scale? (Aaker, 1988).

Systems thinking and cross-functional teams can also be a possible source of adding value. Corporations improve their products and services by creating cross-functional teams that cooperate to improve production and service (Ackoff, 1993).

In fact, many companies today are creating partnerships with suppliers to improve the firm's products and services. Electronic data interchange allows immediate connection to suppliers down the chain, so that they can order what is selling rather than what was forecast to sell. Now, strategic networks are competing against each other, rather than companies (Kotler, 1984).

The distribution system is also a source of potential added value. An analysis of the distribution systems should include three types of strategic questions:

What are the alternative distribution channels?
What are the trends? What channels are growing in importance? What new channels have emerged or are likely to?
Who has the power in the channel and how is that likely to shift? (Aaker, 1988).

New distribution channels can lead to a strategic competitive advantage. A classic example is that of L'eggs hosiery. In the early 1970s, L'eggs began using supermarkets rather than department stores to sell its hosiery line. Because it could solve several problems for the supermarkets, such as using a space-saving vertical display, supplying ordering and stocking functions, and providing a high-quality low cost product supported by national advertising, L'eggs' sales increased from \$9 million to \$290 million in just four years (Bates, 1979).

# Marketing Strategy—What Is the Firm's Enduring Competitive Advantage?

Central to formulating a competitive strategy is ensuring a good fit between the firm and its environment. In general, the environment takes into account social, technical, economic, and political issues and trends. However, the aspect of the environment that has the greatest impact on a corporation is the industry(ies) in which it competes, and which strategies various firms in the industry use to cope in the environment (Porter, 1980).

Review of the firm's customers, competitors, strengths, and weaknesses provides the framework for creating an effective marketing strategy. Managers will have to decide which potential strategy or strategies will lead to the most growth and the strongest competitive advantage.

The goal of competitive strategy is to take offensive or defensive action that creates a defensible position against competitive forces in the industry. Possible strategies include using the firm's capabilities to create the best possible defensive position within the industry. Firms could also try to anticipate changes in the forces and respond, developing new strategies before competitors do (Porter, 1980).

Again, the most basic goal of marketing strategy is to retain existing customers and attract new customers. To this end, there are countless strategic tools. The BCG and GE models, which were described in Chapter 1 on strategic planning, are particularly useful in defining a firm's competitive circumstance. This section will describe the application of the product/market matrix, product life cycle, Porter's generic strategies, and the 4Ps in formulating marketing strategy.

These tools are useful in promoting strategic thinking. Firms comprised of sophisticated executives that serve sophisticated consumers successfully execute and implement complex strategies. Firms comprised of executives who struggle with strategic issues and who serve unsophisticated markets might be advised to keep their strategy simple. A marketing plan should answer the four basic questions outlined in Figure 2.3.

1. Which customers does the firm serve?
2. What are the needs, wants, and values of the firm's current and potential consumers?
3. Relative to competitors, do consumers believe the firm offers a high-quality product? exceptional service? competitive prices?
4. How can the answers to these three questions be used to formulate a strategy that will retain existing customers and attract new customers?

**Figure 2.3**
Strategic Thinking.

Whether the marketing strategy is complex or simple, these are the fundamental questions. The following tools are offered as a way to answer these questions. Most importantly, these tools can help executives think strategically.

## PRODUCT/MARKET MATRIX

The product/market matrix, a tool that has been in use for over 30 years, can help formulate a strategy that can retain existing customers and attract new ones.

Organizations select a marketing strategy from four different options, as shown in Figure 2.4. The selection may be intentionally made with much thought and planning. On the other hand, it may be unintentional, the result of an emerging strategy that proves successful. Lastly, the strategy may reflect organizational drift due to conditioning habit, lack of financing, uninformed leadership, and so on.

The purpose of marketing strategy is to improve continually the ways an organization's products can best serve the needs of existing and potential customers. Accordingly, Figure 2.5 lists three questions that all organizations need to raise to determine whether customer profiles and/or preferences are changing. Once answered, the questions listed in Figure 2.6 can help an organization focus on whether existing and/or potential products will best serve customer needs.

The easiest marketing strategy for an organization to implement is to further penetrate its existing markets with its existing products. As long as the firm's market is growing and its products have a competitive advantage, this strategy is viable. Or sometimes a firm can find an innovative way to bring the old product to an old market. For example, Dell Computers has been very successful selling computers primarily over the telephone. Of course, at some point any firm's market will become saturated and even organizations that offer superior products will eventually lose their competitive advantage if they fail to innovate.

If a firm's products can be used by customers other than those typically served, a market development strategy can be viable. Arm & Hammer baking

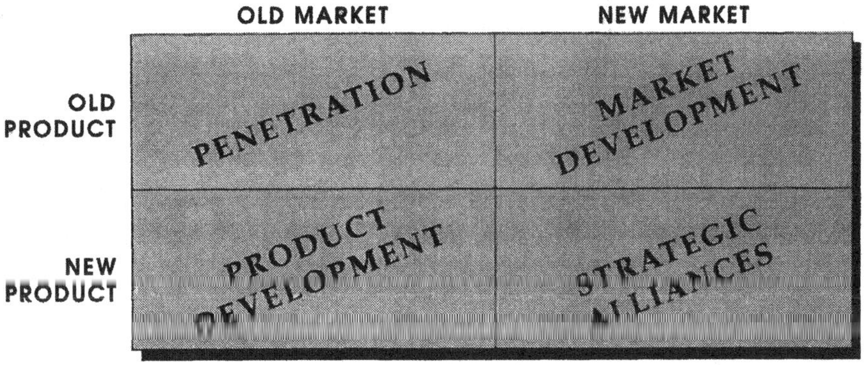

| | OLD MARKET | NEW MARKET |
|---|---|---|
| OLD PRODUCT | PENETRATION | MARKET DEVELOPMENT |
| NEW PRODUCT | PRODUCT DEVELOPMENT | STRATEGIC ALLIANCES |

Figure 2.4 Product/Market Matrix.

- What Is the Size and Mix of Your Current Clientele/Customers?
- Could the Size and Mix of Your Current Clientele/Customers Shift?
- What Do They Want and What Do They Need?

**Figure 2.5**
Clientele/Customers.

soda is an example of a product with a variety of applications, from brushing teeth to controlling odors in refrigerators. Increasing the number of applications without changing the product can result in existing customers buying more of the product for new application or new customers buying the product for applications not used previously. A market-development strategy works for firms that are effective at conducting marketing research and sensing new applications for old products.

A firm can pursue a product development strategy when its traditional market can no longer be served with existing products. Organizations that know their markets well can rely on a product development strategy. For example, in 1995, Hewlett-Packard generated 60% of its revenue from products and services introduced in the previous five years. Gillette and Rubbermaid each generated about one-third of their sales from products developed in the previous five years. These firms reward employees generously for ideas that lead to new products while ensuring that they do not waste resources on ideas that are not commercially viable (*The Economist*, 1996).

When Disney's revenue from its children's movies began to decline, the company successfully created Touchstone Films to produce movies for adults. The result was that parents could send their children to Disney's *Snow White and the Seven Dwarfs*, trusting that the movie would be appropriate for youngsters, while entertaining themselves with Kathleen Turner and Michael Douglas in *Romancing the Stone*.

The most difficult marketing strategy is a joint venture or strategic alliance since the firm may lack experience in knowing the product and the market. Typically, this approach requires a merger or acquisition. Mergers like Pepsi and Pizza Hut can be successful when a product with brand equity (Pepsi) is matched with a well-developed distribution channel (Pizza Hut). Unfortunately, most mergers and acquisitions do not work, as evidenced by the fact that two out of three mergers and acquisitions are later spun off (Forest, Gudridge, Kline, and Zweig, 1995). Apparently, firms are failing to think strategically about the true value added by a merger. Firms with the best acquisition records tend to rely on start-up businesses

- What New Products/Services Should Be Offered?
- What Existing Products/Services Should Be Eliminated?
- What Existing Products/Services Should Be Modified?
- What Existing Products/Services Should Be Left Unchanged?

**Figure 2.6**
Product/Service.

and joint ventures. 3M, Procter & Gamble, and Johnson & Johnson are examples of successful firms which have good records with start-up units. When a firm has the internal strength to start a new unit, it can be safer and less costly to launch a company than to rely on acquisitions (Porter, 1987).

The marketing strategies of penetration, product and market development, and strategic alliances are not mutually exclusive, but do represent the strategic options available to a firm. These seemingly straightforward choices are complicated by whether the firm has adequate information about its markets and competitors and whether it has the resources and talent to successfully execute its strategies.

## PRODUCT LIFE CYCLE

Figure 2.7 illustrates the product life cycle, which describes typical sales and profit patterns that occur over the life of a product. Product sales tend to pass through recognizable stages that require different manufacturing, financial, purchasing, personnel, and marketing strategies. One key concept is that a "life cycle" indicates that product life spans are limited; no product has an endless future (Kotler, 1994). Informed, intentional marketing can, however, maximize profit potential and time spent at each life stage.

A second key concept is that the firm will need to develop new marketing strategies for a product several times over its life span. For example, when a product is introduced, the marketing strategy should be consistent with eventual product positioning. As sales grow, the product may be improved, and new features may be added. When sales growth flattens, products have entered the mature stage. At this point, firms may try to increase usage of the product or find new markets. Finally, sales decline and the firm must decide whether to invest in an attempt to renew the product, or divest in order to reduce losses (Kotler, 1994).

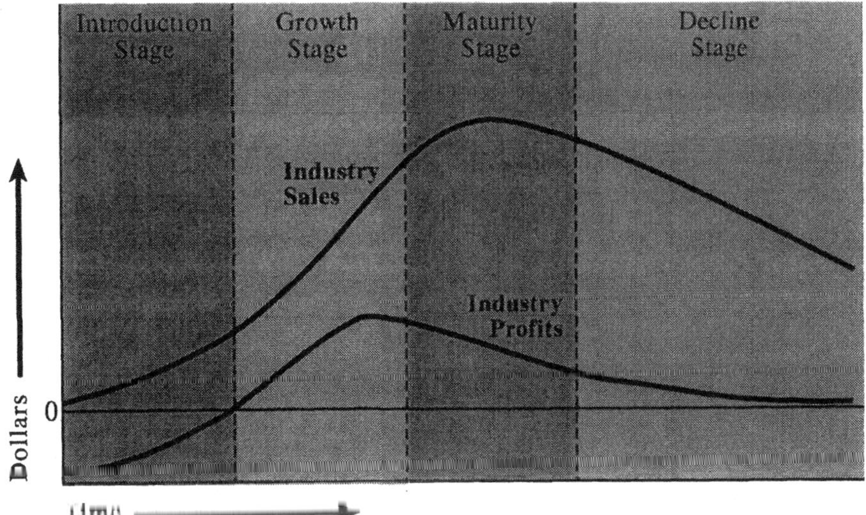


**Figure 2.7**
Four Stages of Product Life Cycle.

Periods of growth, maturity, and decline in industry sales and profits represent different phases of the product life cycle. An economic sector's historic sales and profit patterns can reveal the beginning of maturity or decline. Changes in the level of sales growth are often associated with changes in what it takes for a firm to be successful in an industry.

Price competition frequently occurs when a market matures. Buyers tend to become more aware of product offerings and less willing to pay a premium price. Sales reductions or declines force companies to improve products, downsize, or leave the industry (Aaker, 1988).

As a marketing planning tool, product life cycle helps to outline potential marketing strategies. However, applying product life cycle concepts to forecasting is not particularly useful. Critics claim that sales histories are too diverse, and that stages vary in length for different products. Thus, while it has its purposes, product life cycle concepts must be applied with care (Kotler, 1994).

# Creating Marketing Strategy

A competitive strategy is the glue that holds a business together. Competitive strategy reflects the *ends* (goals) sought by a corporations and the *means* (policies) it will use to achieve those ends (Porter, 1980).

Porter offers three generic strategies that can be identified and used to create an enduring competitive advantage. They are seen in Figure 2.8.

## COST LEADERSHIP

A cost-leadership strategy requires a relentless pursuit to wring out costs, with a premium placed on efficiency. Cost leadership involves containing overhead expenses and reducing unprofitable accounts. Of course, quality and service cannot be ignored. However, gaining cost advantages is what drives corporate strategy (Porter, 1980).

The essence of a cost-leadership strategy is to acquire higher profit margins than competitors, which enables a firm to remain profitable despite price competition. Cost advantages are sought by limiting the power of suppliers and buyers on the firm's operations. In turn, this creates entry barriers to competitors due to cost advantages. Substitute products are also held at bay through a cost position.

- Overall Cost Leadership
- Differentiation
- Focus

**Figure 2.8**
Porter's Generic Strategies.

A well-executed cost-leadership strategy insulates a firm from competitive forces (Porter, 1980).

Cost advantage often requires relatively high market share or advantages such as access to essential raw materials. To this end, the firm may need significant capital investments in state-of-the-art equipment and aggressive pricing or start-up losses to build market share. Reinvestment in new equipment and facilities may be required to sustain a low-cost position (Porter, 1980).

Southwest Airlines successfully executes low-cost, no-frills air transportation and is one of the industry's toughest competitors. While fare reductions reduce profits for other airlines, Southwest's low cost structure traditionally enables the firm to perform well during price wars (Mook, 1996).

## DIFFERENTIATION

The second strategy is to differentiate the product, creating something that is perceived industry wide as being unique. There can be a wide range of unique features such as brand image (Levi Strauss), customer service (Lexus), technology (Intel processors), or distribution (Federal Express).

Differentiation can create brand loyalty and lower sensitivity to price. It can increase profit margins and reduce the need for controlling costs.

Differentiation may result in limited market share since it often requires a perception of exclusivity. Differentiated products are likely to be expensive to produce and probably will preclude a low-cost strategy (Porter, 1980).

Disney successfully executes a differentiation strategy: Its Disney characters products are unique. Disney's synergy among its film, theme parks, and retail chains makes the whole stronger than the sum of the parts. Walt Disney founded the company on the motto, "Everything sells everything else" (*Disney Annual Report*, 1996).

## FOCUS STRATEGY

Focus strategy is the third generic strategy. It calls for focus on a specific market segment. Differentiation and low-cost strategies focus on all segments served by the firm. In contrast, focus strategy targets a particular segment. A focus strategy assumes companies can more effectively and efficiently serve a particular segment than firms that are less refined in who they target. In essence, the firm provides a unique product/service to its target market that best serves the market's needs, possibly at a lower cost. Firms can target markets that are least vulnerable to substitutes or where competitors are vulnerable. A focus strategy often requires a trade-off between profits and sales volume (Porter, 1980).

For example, BMW produces a car that is unique in the speed, power, and status it offers consumers compared to its competitors. Customers are attracted to BMW for its reputation for performance, handling, and being fun to drive. For the first time, in 1995, BMW passed Mercedes in worldwide unit sales. It successfully executed a focus strategy by building a car for a specific market that outperforms others in its class, as evidenced by increased sales (Hadjian 1996).

## SUMMARY OF GENERIC STRATEGIES

Of course, a firm can fail to execute or sustain any of these strategies. In addition, the value of these strategies can be lost if the market changes significantly. Porter identified the risks of each strategy as follows.

### COST LEADERSHIP

- Technological advancements may nullify past investments or corporate core competencies.
- Competitors can imitate or follow a cost advantage when they possess the appropriate core competencies or the ability to invest in the appropriate facilities and equipment.
- Myopic attention to cost control can blind firms from identifying shifting consumer preferences.
- Price differences with competitors narrows due to increased costs.

### DIFFERENTIATION

- Cost difference between differentiated firm and low-cost competitors becomes too great to maintain customer loyalty. Customers become willing to trade off some benefits to save money.
- Need to purchase a differentiated product can decline as consumers become more sophisticated.
- As an industry evolves into a mature stage, imitation often narrows consumers perceptions of differentiation.

### FOCUS

- Market evolves to the point that cost advantages to serving a small market segment narrow.
- Difference between the firm's products or services and its competitors narrows.
- Competitors segment the market in a more focused way than the firm and "outfocus the focuser" (Porter, 1980).

The benefit of Porter's model is its relative simplicity. The model provides executives with a framework to consider their firm's competitive circumstance and the strategies that provide an enduring competitive advantage.

# Vertical Integration

A critical corporate and marketing strategy concerns vertical integration. Vertical integration occurs when a firm moves forward in the value-added chain toward the customer or backward toward the supplier, or both. Backward integration involves the controlling of the raw material input (sources of raw materials, suppliers, etc.). Lack of available resources or sudden surges in the prices charged by suppliers could lead to a strategic disadvantage. Backward integration usually allows for the lowering of costs, thereby putting pressure on competitors who cannot afford the cost associated with vertical integration. These economies of scale lower costs and simultaneously raise capital cost barriers for competitors who wish to enter the industry.

Forward integration involves controlling the channels of distribution for products or services. The advantage of forward integration is that the firm has control over the selection of products sold, their prices, and the choice of promotional activities. Although the firm is eliminating the middlemen and the profit they collect for their value added, the primary advantage is in gaining control over marketing the product directly, rather than any profits that are gained solely from the elimination of middlemen. Sherwin-Williams, which manufactures and sells paints, has gained a strategic competitive strength by developing a distribution channel of 2,000 paint stores.

Forward integration should be considered a marketing strategy for purposes of increasing sales and market share. Forward integration allows the firm more flexibility in differentiation, because the firm can control more successfully the way the product is sold. The salesperson's presentation, physical facilities, and image of the store can help with the product differentiation strategies. Thus, value added is increased by providing a basis for differentiation that was unavailable in the unintegrated state. Forward integration removes the problems of channel access and the bargaining power channels may have. Forward integration may be the only way to reach the market if existing channels are already locked up by competition. The closer to the consumer the firm positions itself, the better access it has to market information. The firm is better able to predict changes in demand and will be able to adjust production processes sooner than if it were not positioned in the forward chain. In industries where final demand is highly cyclical and rapidly changing, there are competitive advantages to timely market information.

Several firms lend themselves to vertical integration because of improved marketing opportunities, technical intelligence, and an improved ability to forecast changes. Furthermore, integration economics can produce large cost savings by eliminating duplication (i.e., overhead) and bypassing time-consuming steps.

## THE RISKS OF VERTICAL INTEGRATION

Successful vertical integration is difficult. Not all firms can be as fully integrated as BP Oil Company, which controls its own oil wells and service stations. Vertical integration is a risky business because of the amount of assets that are exposed. Therefore, a company should consider transferring some of the risk of vertical integration to outside parties. The key to successful use of vertical integration is timing; at a particular point in time, how broadly should the company be integrated?

The benefits of vertical integration are numerous:

- economies of combined operations
- economies of internal control and coordination
- economies of information
- economies of avoiding the market
- economies of stable relationships

- tap into technology
- assure supply and/or demand
- enhance ability for differentiation
- elevate entry and mobility barriers
- enter a higher return business
- defend against foreclosure
- lower procurement costs
- offer value added
- hedge against fluctuation in prices

To achieve the benefits of vertical integration, the firm must maintain sufficient sales so as to support in-house capability or be able to sell the extra output. Unfortunately, this method may result in having to sell the extra output to one's competitor.

Vertical integration may also have its disadvantages, the most common one being cost. Some typical costs include:

- overcoming mobility barriers
- increased operating leverage
- reduced flexibility to change partners
- higher overall exit barriers
- capital investment requirements
- maintaining balance
- dulled incentives
- differing managerial requirements

The disadvantages of vertical integration may very well exceed the advantages. Vertical integration may create exit barriers that make it difficult to exit the business. This depends upon whether the entire vertical chain is affected or just one link. Also, fluctuations in one stage of a process involving vertical integration may have a profound effect if follow-on stages are impacted.

Although vertical integration allows a firm to maintain technological secrecy, it may cut off the supply of technology coming from suppliers, vendors, and customers. Proprietary knowledge is not shared. Also, a technological change in part of the chain may have a serious impact on the other parts of the chain. This is particularly important because if an upstream or downstream unit in the chain is sick, it could simultaneously have an adverse effect on the healthy partners. Not all parts of a value-added chain require the same management skills.

The following questions need to be addressed in considering vertical integration:

- Can the funds to be allocated to vertical integration be invested more prudently elsewhere?
- What happens if internal competition occurs because many managers resent having to purchase goods/services from sister units and pay a profit?
- Will vertical integration make it more difficult to be aware of changing market conditions?

- Does it make sense to vertically integrate into a business where we have no managerial experience?

Because of the costs, vertical integration requires a well-thought-out strategy. Typical vertical integration strategies might include:

- **nonintegrated strategies**—No internal transfers and no ownership is at stake. Customer-designed services may be purchased.
- **quasi-integrated strategies**—Consume or distribute all or none or some of the inputs and outputs.
- **taper-integrated strategies**—Produce or distribute a portion of the requirements internally, but purchase or sell the remainder through specialized suppliers, distributors, or competitors.
- **full integrated strategies**—Firms buy or sell all their materials and/or services internally. Units are normally fully owned subsidiaries, capable of capturing more profit.

The simple fact of going to some form of vertical integration could very well result in a reconstructing of the entire industry. The bargaining power of buyers can be affected as well as the entry and exit barriers.

# How Can a Competitive Advantage Be Sustained Using the 4Ps?

The marketing mix (product, price, promotion, and place) is a marketing framework that a firm can use to pursue its objectives. As outlined in Figure 2.9, the 4Ps can be used as a model to determine on what basis the firm will compete in the marketplace. (Pride and Ferrell, 1993).

**Product**—One approach is to offer products that are unique and meet customer needs, wants, and values such as a Mercedes Benz, Rolex watch, or an Intel computer chip. These three product examples are clearly unique. However, in many instances it is difficult for a company to sustain product uniqueness, since the product can be matched by competitors. Often, a firm simply cannot compete unless the product is of sound quality. Consequently, the company must compete on price, distribution, or promotion.

**Price**—The easiest aspect for a competitor to match is price. For example, gas stations can quickly lower or raise prices in response to competitors. An exception to this would be a firm that has a significant cost advantage and resources that cannot be easily matched. Southwest Airlines' control over its costs provides it with a competitive advantage over other airlines, enabling the company to lower prices below the market and still [illegible]

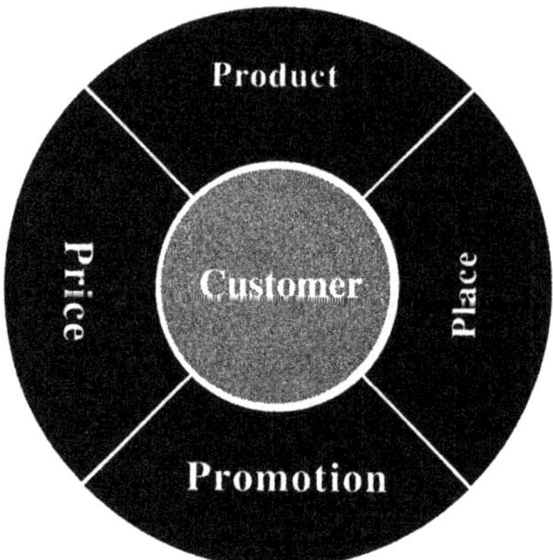


**Figure 2.9** Customers and the 4Ps.

**Promotion**—Differences in resources could result in a firm being able to outspend a competitor in advertisement, point of purchase displays, trade shows, and so on. McDonald's tends to outspend Burger King in advertising 3 to 1 as an example. Of course, this assumes the promotion strategy is effective in increasing sales. Investment in customer service and a well-trained sales force that differentiates a firm from competitors can provide a competitive advantage. Before IBM began to have difficulties for a range of reasons, it was well regarded for the quality of its service and competence of its sales force.

**Place**—Distribution can be a powerful competitive advantage. Wal-Mart has redefined retailing due to its ability to control its distribution channels and suppliers. Land's End redefined the way many people shop through the use of catalogs and phone centers.

## SUMMARY

Formulating and implementing marketing strategy is a task full of ambiguity and uncertainty. Executives vary in their ability to resolve unstructured strategic issues. While the number of strategic tools and the issues they raise can be imposing, answering the four fundamental questions raised in this chapter can help to focus a firm's marketing strategy:

1. **customers**—What is the match between the firm's products/services and its current and potential customers?
2. **competitors**—What is the firm's competitive advantage?
3. **company**—What are the firm's strengths and weaknesses?
4. **marketing strategy**—How can the firm formulate and implement a strategy that retains existing customers and attracts new customers?

These questions help to formulate the strategic options available to a company. The fundamental nature of these questions helps to eliminate some of the confusion inherent in strategy.

Once strategic options are identified, yardsticks are needed to determine which options should be pursued. This chapter will conclude with seven guidelines, as seen in Figure 2.10, that can be used to assess the feasibility of a given strategy.

**1. FOCUS ON THE ENVIRONMENT** One of the most important benefits of strategy is to focus the organization on its environment. The purpose of strategy is to help the organization respond to environmental opportunities/threats. Executives often focus on internal issues and resist change. Yet, the only hope an organization has to sustain itself is to adapt to its environment.

**2. CREATE OR SUSTAIN A COMPETITIVE ADVANTAGE** Sound strategy enables the firm to serve its customers in ways that are difficult for competitors to match. Satisfying customers is central to an organization's mission and success. Effective strategies serve customers well and are consistent with the organization's mission, strengths, capabilities, and resources.

**3. MATCH ORGANIZATIONAL CAPABILITIES/CONSTRAINTS** There must be a "fit" between a strategy and the organization. The firm's structure, systems, people, and culture can be a source of both strengths and weaknesses. Strategies need to be consistent with the firm's culture and talent, for example, goals must be well understood by key implementers, consistent with their values and abilities to

Focus on the environment

Create or sustain a competitive advantage

Match organizational capabilities/constraints

Maintain strategic flexibility

Focus on fundamental strategic questions

Analyze financial resources and constraints

Think systematically

**Figure 2.10**
Strategic Guidelines

ensure commitment and performance. In addition, examining why past strategies have succeeded or failed helps to clarify a firm's options. The reality of organizational life is that strategy based on rationality and good will compete openly with ambition and greed. A sound strategy that promotes systems thinking and teamwork can reduce the failings of human behavior and encourage our better nature.

**4. MAINTAIN STRATEGIC FLEXIBILITY** Flexibility that is built into the strategic plan can help manage the firm's risk. Diversification of markets, technologies, and location can be considered. Investing in underused assets, or maintaining some excess capacity in manufacturing, staffing, or R&D so that the firm can react quickly to opportunities helps.

**5. FOCUS ON FUNDAMENTAL STRATEGIC QUESTIONS** Consider major strategic questions outlined in this text. The ability of executives to resolve strategic issues that are complex, unstructured, and ambiguous is limited. Involving key implementers in resolving fundamental strategic questions increases the chances that strategic thinking and behavior will be promoted.

**6. ANALYZE FINANCIAL RESOURCES AND CONSTRAINTS** Ultimately, judgments need to be made about whether to invest in a business unit or to withdraw cash and return it to shareholders or debt holders. Financial analysis is helpful to determine actual and potential sources and use of funds. Cash-flow analysis projects the cash that will be available from operations, depreciation, and other assets. Growth strategies in particular usually require working capital and other assets, which may exceed the funds available from operations.

**7. THINK SYSTEMICALLY** To understand strategic issues, executives must think systemically. A firm's strategic problems and solutions can often be found in how the company is organized. Departments can fragment a firm's strategy. Sound strategy calls for interdisciplinary teams that focus on the firm's environment. Marketing, finance, and human-resources issues are all intertwined. No one department can resolve a firm's strategic issues.

Following these guidelines increases the chances that marketing strategy will bear fruit. The ultimate objective is to attract existing and new customers so the firm can sustain itself by serving its stakeholders.

## REFERENCES

Aaker, D. *Strategic Market Management*. New York: John Wiley & Sons, 1988.

Ackoff, R. "Beyond Total Quality Management," *Journal for Quality and Participation*, March 1993, pp. 66–77.

Ansoff, H. I. *Corporate Strategy*. New York: McGraw-Hill, 1965.

Bates, A. *Retailing and Its Environment*. New York: Van Nostrand, 1979.

Churchill, G. *Marketing Research*. Chicago: Dryden Press, 1991.

*Disney Annual Report*, 1996.

Drucker, P. "The Discipline of Innovation," *Harvard Business Review*, May–June 1985, pp. 67–68.

*The Economist*. "The Astonishing Microchip," March 23–29, 1996, pp. 19–21.

*The Economist*. "Management Briefs," February 10, 1996, p. 61.

*Federal Reserve Bank of Dallas Annual Report*, 1995.

Forest, A., Gudrige, K., Kline, J., and Zweig, P. "The Case Against Mergers," *Business Week*, October 30, 1995, pp. 122–130.

Hadjian, A. "Speed! Power! Status!" *Fortune*, June 10, 1996, pp. 47–61.

*Harvard Business Review*, "Electric Utility Deregulation Sparks Controversy," May-June, 1996, pp. 150-162.

Kofman, K., and Senge, P. "Communities of Commitment: The Heart of Learning Organizations." In S. Chawla and J. Renesch, eds., *Learning Organizations*. Portland, OR: Productivity Press, 1995.

Kotler, P. *Marketing Management*. Englewood Cliffs, NJ: Prentice Hall, 1994.

Levitt, T. "Marketing Myopia," *Harvard Business Review*, September–October, 1975, pp. 26–38.

Mintzberg, H., *The Rise and Fall of Strategic Planning*. New York: The Free Press, 1994.

Mook, B. "Southwest Air," *Value Line*, March 22, 1996, p. 262.

Porter, M. *Competitive Advantage*. New York: The Free Press, 1985.

Porter, M. *Competitive Strategy*. New York: The Free Press, 1980.

Porter, M. "From Competitive Advantage to Corporate Strategy," *Harvard Business Review*, May–June 1987, pp. 43–59.

Pride, W., and Ferrel, O. C. *Marketing*. Boston: Houghton Mifflin Company, 1993.

U.S. Department of Commerce, Bureau of the Census, 1984.

U.S. Department of Commerce, Bureau of the Census, 1994.

## ESSAY QUESTIONS

Employees can best contribute to the success of their organization and to their career if they understand the marketing challenges and opportunities confronting their employer. The following questions should be applied to your current employer or an organization for whom you would like to work:

1. Apply Porter's model to your organization—power of sellers and buyers, threat of substitutes, barriers to entry and exit, and competitive rivalry.
2. Describe the customers and markets served by this firm. How does this firm segment its markets?
3. What are the strengths and weaknesses of its products? Consider issues such as brand equity, perceived quality, perceived service, market share, sales growth, profitability, etc.
4. What are the strengths and weaknesses of the firm's distribution?
5. What are the strengths and weaknesses of the firm's promotion strategies?
6. What are the strengths and weaknesses of the firm's pricing? Consider the extent to which the firm's pricing strategy is appropriate given competitive factors, organizational strategies, and market forces.
7. Assess the organization's marketing efforts. Develop a chart that summarizes the match between the organization's 4Ps and its environment. Are customers satisfied? Consider graphing over a period of years variables such as sales, market share, customer satisfaction, and [illegible]

8. How can the firm increase sales/profits? Apply the product/market mix to this question.
9. Select a key market for the firm and then design an environmental-scanning/marketing-strategy matrix.
10. Apply the GE model to this firm by assessing industry attractiveness and organizational strengths. Determine where the organization should invest/grow, select/earn, and harvest/divest.

## MULTIPLE-CHOICE QUESTIONS

1. According to Michael Porter, when new firms enter a market, they bring new capacity and resources with the intention to gain market share. Therefore, when analyzing a target market, it is essential to examine barriers to entering the market, and the relative strength of those barriers. Major barriers to entry include all of the following except:
   a. economies of scale
   b. product differentiation
   c. capital requirements
   d. access to distribution channels
   e. all of the above
2. Arm & Hammer baking soda increasing the number of ways customers can use its product without changing the product is an example of:
   a. product development
   b. market development
   c. strategic alliance
   d. penetration
   e. none of the above
3. Portfolio tools such as the BCG and GE models:
   a. guide decisions about investment and resource allocation decisions among strategic business units
   b. assess risk and returns
   c. identify strategic issues facing the firm including its present and desired strategic position
   d. none of the above
   e. all of the above
4. A market opportunity results from:
   a. an increase in market share and profits
   b. an assessment of environmental forces
   c. technological innovation
   d. the right combination of circumstances at the right time so that action can be taken to serve the market
   e. an internal analysis
5. The number of questions that executives can raise about its market strategy are endless. According to the text, fundamental questions that should be addressed by all organizations include the following questions except:
   a. What is the match between the firm's products/services and its current and potential customers?
   b. How can the firm formulate and implement a strategy that retains existing customers and attracts new customers?
   c. Which customers most contribute to the firm's profitability?
   d. What is the firm's competitive advantage?
   e. What are the firm's strengths and weaknesses?

**6.** Coors implemented a growth strategy that involved the acquisition of a can manufacturer. Attempting to grow in this way would be a example of a strategy:
   **a.** conglomerate
   **b.** horizontal
   **c.** forward
   **d.** backward
   **e:** concentric
**7.** Banks often attempt to increase their market share by offering existing services to children. This growth strategy is an example of:
   **a.** backward integration
   **b.** strategic alliance
   **c.** market penetration
   **d.** product development
   **e.** market development

# CASE STUDY: DreamWorks SKG

Imagine getting together with two of your friends and securing financing for $3 billion based on your names alone! Imagine investing 10% of the capital yet retaining two-thirds of the profits. This near impossible task was initiated in October 1994 and appropriately called DreamWorks SKG. The entertainment powerhouses that formed this company are Steven Spielberg, Jeffrey Katzenberg, and David Geffen.

Of the three founders, Steven Spielberg is best known from the movie business. He has acquired a household name through his unprecedented success with movie direction and production of such films as *E.T.* and *Jurassic Park*. Jeffrey Katzenberg is the least known of the three. However, he was instrumental in the revival of Disney during the 1980s. He is also the man behind the most successful animated productions in history—*Beauty and the Beast* and *The Lion King*. David Geffen is the wealthiest of the founders. He brought the public the music of Nirvana and the acting of Tom Cruise. When he sold Geffen Records to MCA, he became an overnight billionaire.

## The Players

In order to make their "dreams" come true, it was necessary to acquire a tremendous amount of financing. From the outset, the DreamTeam had been inundated with offers from sheiks to the Samsung family. However, the founders were not blindly accepting money from just anyone. They sought and found investors that would offer large sums of money for little ownership rights. The success of this ploy was the venture capitalist's nightmare, but the founder's dream.

The first and largest investor was Paul Allen. Mr. Allen was the little-known partner of Bill Gates. Allen became a billionaire from the Microsoft stock that he sold, although he still retains ownerships valued at $4 billion. He relinquished $500 million of pocket change for 18.5% of DreamWorks SKG. The DreamTeam did not choose Paul Allen just for his money. His obvious connections to the software giant forged a relationship between Bill Gates and the DreamTeam. The second major investor was One World Media Corporation. This mass media company contributed $300 million for a 10.8% stake in DreamWorks. The third group of investors was the founders themselves. Spielberg, Katzenberg, and Geffen pooled $33.3 million each for a total investment of $100 million. The amazing part of the deal was that 67% ownership rights were retained by the founders. The remaining 4% of the stock is held by unnamed investors. In addition to the transfer of stock, DreamWorks has secured a line of credit with Chemical Bank for $1 billion. Appendices A, B, and C identify the major players.

## Location, Location, Location

The founders of DreamWorks were interested in creating more than just a new movie studio. They laid out plans for the creation of an entertainment campus that would house all aspects of their company. Instead of the typical warehouse atmosphere of the current industry, the DreamTeam intended to have aesthetically appealing buildings with matching facades. Because of the expertise that each founder brought, to the company the campus would be built to their specifications. In other words, DreamWorks would have "dream" studios. Spielberg would get the movie studio he always wanted, Katzenberg would have the ultimate animation studio, and Geffen would get his recording studio.

Therefore, DreamWorks would need a location relatively close to the homes of executives, employees, and actors. Hollywood, the obvious choice, had high costs and little undeveloped land. Consequently, the leading choice was west of Hollywood in the city of Playa Vista, where there existed property that contained an unused Hughes Aircraft hanger surrounded by plenty of undeveloped land.

## Growth

The company planned to begin with five major divisions: television, movies, animation, music, and interactive software. Because of the maturity of these markets, powerful partnerships were necessary to ensure successful penetration. The following subsections describe these unique alliances.

### Television

The television division of DreamWorks would be managed by Bob Jaquemin, the former head of Disney's Buena Vista Television. DreamWorks developed a partnership with Capital Cities/ABC for network television production. ABC is spending $200 million for the production facilities. The first productions, talk shows and reality-based pieces, were due to be introduced in the fall of 1996. Spielberg eventually wants to produce ABC's entire Saturday morning programming. In addition to network television, HBO is spending $100 million for the licensing of 75–100 movies to be shown on cable television.

### Movies

Steven Spielberg will manage the movie division. A link with IBM has been created to build the digital studio. Current plans are to produce upwards of twelve movies per year; however, Spielberg says that he will not sacrifice quality for quantity. MCA has been signed for the film distribution in the United States and abroad, and HBO will license the features for 10 years. The first movie release for DreamWorks SKG was slated for December of 1996.

### Animation

Jeffrey Katzenberg will manage the animation division that already has a team of 85 animators working on the new feature, *The Prince of Egypt* (a story of the 10 Commandments). This feature is scheduled for Christmas 1998 release. The second feature film is *El Dorado: Cortez and the City of Gold*. The main obstacle to Katzenberg's success is Disney's long-term contractual agreements with the best animators in the world. Katzenberg has begun developing a new team by pairing with Silicon Graphics to establish a digital animation studio. Appropriately, it will be called DreamWorks Digital Studio.

Music

David Geffen will manage the music division. The combination of his talent and the dynamic nature of the music industry offers virtually guaranteed profitability. This division is the only part of DreamWorks that has not paired with a significant force in the related industry.

Interactive Software

DreamWorks SKG has already partnered with Microsoft for interactive software for $30 million. The joint venture is financed equally and entitled DreamWorks Interactive. This company is based in Los Angeles and is expected to have 75 employees by this year's end. The first original releases were due for the holidays in 1996 with future software tie-ins to movies and animation strongly speculated. The interactive products that are likely to be targeted include: cartridges, CD-ROMs, interactive television, and online networks. The company predicts revenues of several hundred million dollars in the first three to five years (based on 12 title releases per year).

## QUESTIONS

1. More than 50 years have passed since a new movie studio has been created. This has given the competition plenty of time to establish a strong foothold. How does DreamWorks SKG expect to overcome this entry barrier?
2. Another major barrier is access to distribution channels for their products. How do they plan to overcome this barrier?
3. DreamWorks is essentially entering into a mature market. Substitute products are innumerable. How do they plan to overcome this problem?
4. Does DreamWorks SKG have a strategic plan?
5. DreamWorks expects to reap a profit of 25%, compounded each year. In three years, the company would double in value at this rate. In 12 years, the company will be worth $40 billion, which is $10 billion more than Disney. Is it conceivable that they will reach their goal? What must happen for the founders to reach their goals?
6. How does one keep a billionaire motivated? What happens if Spielberg and Geffen simply get "bored"?
7. Can DreamWorks grow through vertical integration? If so, how?
8. Could the music division be expanded to include concert promotions, ticket sales, or even a music channel?
9. Could they sign up their own actors, screen writers, and authors?
10. Could they enter the toy market?
11. What threats exist on the horizon for DreamWorks?
12. Although an agreement exists with Microsoft for creating interactive software, the agreement does *not* prevent Microsoft from developing its own interactive software. Can this lead to a problem?
13. What internal strengths are DreamWorks counting on in order to obtain a sustained competitive advantage?
14. Does the diversity of DreamWorks reduce the overall investment risk should one division not have a big hit in two or three years?

## Appendix A PARTNERSHIPS

| *Division* | *Partner* | *Benefit* |
|---|---|---|
| Television | Capital Cities/ABC | Network television |
| | HBO | Films for cable television |
| Movies | IBM | Digital movie studio |
| | MCA | Movie distribution |
| Animation | Silicon Graphics | Digital animation studio |
| Software | Microsoft | Software development |

## Appendix B INVESTORS IN DREAMWORKS SKG (IN MILLIONS)

| | |
|---|---|
| Steven Spielberg | $ 33.3 |
| Jeffrey Katzenberg | 33.3 |
| David Geffen | 33.3 |
| Paul Allen | 500.0 |
| One World Media Corp. | 300.0 |
| Capital Cites/ABC | 200.0 |
| HBO | 100.0 |
| Microsoft | 9.0 |
| Chemical Bank* | 1000.0 |

* Line of credit

## Appendix C STOCKHOLDER'S EQUITY

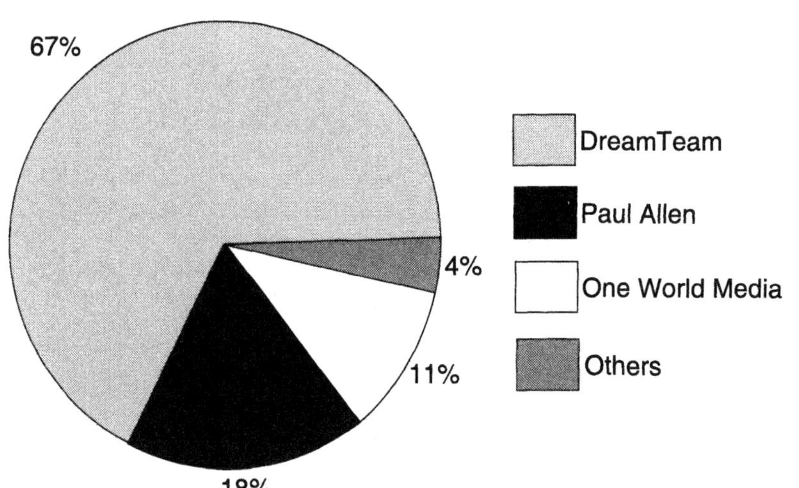

## REFERENCES


Brown, Rich. "HBO's 'Dream' Deal." *Broadcasting & Cable*, v125 (March 13, 1995), p. 10.

Busch, Anita M. "Gates Joins DreamWorks Team." *Variety*, v358 (March 27, 1995), p. 15.

Busch, Anita M. "With $300 Mil, One World Gets 11% of DreamWorks." *Variety*, v359 (May 1, 1995), p. 16.

Caruso, Denise. "Digital Commerce." *New York Times* (April 3, 1995), p. C6.

Corliss, Richard. "Hey, Let's Put on a Show!" *Time*, v145 (March 27, 1995), p. 54.

"DreamWorks/IBM to Link to Build Digital Studio." *New York Times*, v144 (January 16, 1995), p. C1.

"DreamWorks/MCA Strike Deal." *Broadcasting & Cable*, v125 (June 19, 1995), p. 25.

Dunaief, Daniel. "Chemical Wins Starring Role." *American Banker*, v160 (March 31, 1995), p. 1.

"Electronic Arts Shares Rise on Takeover Speculation." *New York Times* (February 10, 1995), p. C3.

Freeman, Michael. "The Newest Dreamworker." *MEDIAWEEK*, v5 (April 3, 1995), p. 12.

Greenman, Catherine. "DreamWorks gets Gates for New Unit." *The Weekly Newspaper for the Home Furnishing Network*, v69 (March 27, 1995), p. 65.

"HBO Does Dreamy Deal." *MEDIAWEEK*, v5 (March 13, 1995), p. 4.

King, Thomas R. "Gates Invests a Byte of Money for Cache of Hollywood Stars." *The Wall Street Journal* (March 23, 1995), p. A3.

Lowry, Brian. "Alphabet Web Ups Ante." *Variety*, v358 (March 13, 1995), p. 29.

Sloan, Allan. "Pennies from Heaven." *Newsweek*, v125 (April 3, 1995), p. 44.

Taninecz, George. "Cinema without Celluloid." *Industry Week*, v244 (June 19, 1995), p. 47.

Weiner, Rex. "DreamWorks Pact Jolts Rivals." *Variety*, v359 (June 5, 1995), p. 31.

Young, Douglas. "DreamWorks Narrows Its List of Possible Studio Locations to Four." *Los Angeles Business Journal*, v17 (April 24, 1995), p. 15A.


# CASE STUDY: Eaton Corporation

## Eaton Corporation's History

In 1911, when Joseph O. Eaton and Viggo V. Torbenson started Eaton Corporation's predecessor company, Torbensen Gear and Axle Company, there was nothing to distinguish this fledgling automotive supplier from thousands of others. Yet, Eaton survived and prospered.

Eaton had a vision of the future of the automotive industry. He foresaw a nation where manufactured products would be transported over the nation's roads. Torbensen Gear and Axle built only seven rear axles, by hand, during 1911. The number jumped to 31 in 1912 and 244 in 1913.

Torbensen Gear and Axle name changed several times during its history, along with many acquisitions, mergers, product diversification, and global expansion.

## Introduction

Eaton Corporation's business is truck parts and controls. Eaton Corporation is a global manufacturer of highly engineered products that serve the automotive, industrial, construction, commercial, aerospace, and marine markets. Principal products include truck transmissions and axles, engine components, hydraulic products, electrical power distribution and control equipment, ion implanters, and a wide variety of controls. Headquartered at Eaton Center in Cleveland, the company has 51,000 employees and 150 manufacturing sites in 18 countries around the world.

### Management

Eaton's executive management team is composed of corporate and operating talent with strong leadership attributes. Eaton's strategic planning is primarily conservative. Many of today's corporate executives have long tenure at the company. Beginning at the plant level, as plant engineers, controllers, and plant managers, they rose through the ranks to vice president and chairman positions.

Eaton has attained the qualities of a stellar performer. Eaton believes "Strategy is leveraging those strengths to realize their remaining goals: sustained, above-average growth in earnings." In 1994, Eaton achieved the highest earnings and sales in its 83-year history, a sign of Eaton's gathering strength. Internal development, global expansion, and acquisitions are Eaton's current strategy to expand its sales and earnings.

### Strategy—Internal Development

Manufacturing companies need to spend a significant percentage of sales in Research and Development (R&D) and engineering to remain competitive in their markets so as to provide highly engineered, high-quality, and safe products. In 1994, R&D and engineering expenses exceeded $250 million. These funds were used to make mechanical products "smart" by applying electronics and to develop assemblies and subsystems instead of components. These strategies mandate complex execution. The strategies rely on multidisciplinary teams, including customers, to bring innovative products to market.

### Strategy—Global Expansion

Eaton's reputation as a market leader in North America and Europe has led Eaton to expand its efforts in Latin America and the Pacific Rim. These regions are expected to have the highest profit growth rates for the foreseeable future. These regions already account for a significant portion of Eaton's business.

### Strategy—Acquisitions

Over the past 10 years, Eaton has acquired and spent $1.7 billion on 26 companies or product lines to strengthen its businesses and assure world-class competitiveness. Eaton's $1.1 billion acquisition of Westinghouse Corporation's Distribution & Control Business Unit (DCBU) on January 31, 1994 was integrated into Eaton's Cutler-Hammer business.

### Strategy—Divestitures

Eaton divested itself of businesses such as lift trucks, locks and hardware items, logging and construction equipment, a foundry, flexible hose, and material-handling systems. These businesses either underperformed or did not fit Eaton's core competencies. During 1994, Eaton closed 23 manufacturing, warehousing, and distribution operations in order to eliminate excess capacity.

### Finance

The company's financial condition remained strong during 1994. The seeds of Eaton's success were planted a decade ago, when company officials began shaping a strategy around a half dozen key businesses. Automotive and appliance controls have grown from $150 million to more than $1 billion in annual sales in the last 10 years, mainly through acquisitions. Since 1986, sales of chip-making equipment have increased from $75 million to nearly $500 million, mainly through internal expansion. Cutler-Hammer sales in 1994 approached $1.5 billion, primarily from industrial controls and power-distribution equipment.

Comparing Eaton's performance in 1993 to 1994, net sales were $6.1 billion, a 38% increase. The increase in sales was a reflection of the contributions of acquired businesses, as well as the improvement in North American transportation and capital goods markets. Return on equity was 23.9%, increase in sales was 37.5%, and increase in profits was 2.5%.

## Strengths, Weaknesses, Opportunities, Threats (SWOT)

A current weakness is that some of Eaton's plants are revealing environmental problems that need to be addressed, resulting in costly cleanup action and possible litigation. The opportunities to expand in Latin America and the Pacific Rim regions are expected to have the highest growth rates for the foreseeable future. Opportunities include internal development of electronic components, improvement in manufacturing processes, and new technologies for improved products and introduction of new products. In the normal course of business, the company is exposed to various financial risks including interest and foreign exchange rates, especially in third-world countries. Eaton has developed systems to continuously measure exposures so appropriate action can be taken to reduce risk. Industry competition and the economy are threats to the company. Eaton's strengths and market leadership are based on continuous improvement in quality and productivity. Market leadership also helps Eaton generate superior rates of return on equity. Large amounts for capital expenditures are committed each year to improve efficiency by providing better tools, equipment, and working environment for 51,000 employees. Another strength is Eaton's brand name and reputation for product quality.

## Conclusion

Eaton believes the future will continue to bring rewards through its leadership in industrial markets. Capital spending in 1995 was projected to be $350 million, the highest in the company's history. Some of these funds will be used to expand capacity in areas where current customer demand requires certain plants to operate at rates well beyond optimum efficiency.

By the end of 1994, Eaton plants had earned more than 800 customers' quality citations and certifications. Nearly 40% of Eaton's plants have already qualified for the International Quality Standard, ISO 9000. Total service is an everyday goal. The focus on customers is at the heart of operational excellence and is the essence of good business. The challenge is to sustain and build on that leadership to steadily improve financial performance.

In 1994, a task force identified 10 countries with exceptional growth prospects as prime markets for Eaton products. Most are in the Far East and Latin America.

William E. Butler, Chairman, has said its customers have benefited from restructurings of the 1980s, resulting in a stronger U.S. manufacturing base, a stronger export market, and a capital-spending boom that has helped drive up manufacturing output 50% more than the general economy.

Overall, Eaton has done a good job in finding opportunities for growth in mature markets by investing in and setting up joint ventures in overseas markets, acquisitions, and introducing new products to maintain market leadership.

**QUESTIONS**

1. Describe Eaton's strategic plan during the past 30 years. Is it a focused strategy?
2. Does Eaton appear to be aggressive or conservative?
3. Describe the nature of the industries in which Eaton competes. Is there opportunity for added growth? If so, where?
4. Perform a SWOT analysis on Eaton.

# CASE STUDY: The Purchase of Midlantic Corp. by PNC Bank Corp.

After surviving the recession and the collapse of the real estate market in 1990, the financial services industry has once again begun to grow. The local, one-state banks that may have only a dozen or so branches are finding it difficult to complete against the growing number of larger super-regional bank holding companies that are entering the small local markets by acquiring local competitors. These super-regional banking companies are looking for areas of growth in the industry and are seeking to acquire the strongest of the local banks in each local marketplace. A focused strategy of growth by acquisition seems to be the norm.

On July 10, 1995, PNC Bank Corp. of Pittsburgh officially announced its agreement to purchase Midlantic Corp. of New Jersey. Upon the completion of this purchase, PNC Bank Corp. will be the eleventh-largest bank-holding company in the country, with assets of $79 billion dollars, serving over three billion households and 140,000 businesses in thirty states.

Midlantic Corp. and its subsidiaries are located throughout New Jersey and southern Pennsylvania. With 328 branches and $13.7 billion in assets, Midlantic has been reborn into an impressive retail franchise servicing the attractive New Jersey market where low-cost depositors abound and profit margins are sizable. In 1990, after suffering losses of $195 million, and with over 10% of its assets classified as unperforming, Midlantic was on the verge of being seized by federal regulators. After signing agreements with regulators that forced restructuring, Garry Scheuring was hired as Chairman of the Board to resurrect Midlantic. Now considered one of the premier banks in New Jersey, Midlantic management has brought the company's stock price per share back from a low $2.87 in 1991 to $41.37 in 1995.

Examining the characteristics of Midlantic Corp. shows that the company's greatest strength is its location. The New Jersey and Philadelphia areas have shown dramatic economic rebirth and appear to be excellent markets for emerging financial services. However, Midlantic's weakness is its inability to provide the vast array of services being provided by the large super-regional banking companies. Though the company shows a strong balance sheet, not having the necessary strength in terms of asset size to make acquisitions on its own, Midlantic's growth has become stagnant. Furthermore, opportunities for Midlantic are limited. In an industry where significant growth is only achieved externally, Midlantic must position itself to be acquired into a situation that is favorable to both companies' customers, employees, and stakeholders. Midlantic is only threatened by possibly negative restructuring after its purchase, or the remote possibility that the company will not be attractive for purchase at all.

In 1995, with $62.1 billion in assets, PNC Bank Corp. of Pittsburgh had grown to become the twelfth-largest bank-holding company in the country. Throughout history PNC maintained a strategy of constant growth through acquisition. Throughout the 1980s its acquisition strategy was particularly strong. The company's asset base grew tenfold as PNC continually made significant acquisitions throughout Pennsylvania. By 1987, the company had surpassed Mellon Bank as the state's largest banking company and was the industry leader in terms of return on assets and return on equity. Having survived the real-estate problems of 1990 through strategic underwriting controls and the selling off of bad loans, PNC restructured to keep costs low and began to concentrate on its core businesses.

Examining PNC shows that the company's greatest strength appears to be its size. Having significant assets and over fifteen subsidiaries covering all aspects of the financial services industry, PNC is able to provide the entire array of services to its customers. Furthermore, due to the company's diversification, PNC is able to reduce its interest rate sensitivity. PNC's weakness revolves around its lack of investment management services. Though the company is strong on the retail side, PNC often cannot provide the incentives to large accounts looking for funds management on the level they receive from the larger financial services firms in New York and Chicago. However, PNC's growth and asset size affords the company additional growth opportunities so that its capital-management presence can be expanded. PNC must remain responsive to developments in its local markets. PNC's competitors threaten the company's market share by entering local markets that have proven to be attractive. PNC must plan strategic acquisitions to maintain its leading positions.

The financial services industry is developing much the same as other industries have: The largest companies grow and are strengthened by buying their smaller and more specialized competition. The significant capital needed and strict new government regulations make entry into the industry difficult, but not unattainable, for some of the largest firms. Though the list is always narrowing through constant acquisitions, the number of substitute products is great. There are thousands of institutions competing for the consumer's dollar. In the financial services industry, technically, the buyers are the suppliers. Both command significant power. A financial services company's livelihood is dependent on the funds the suppliers provide. Therefore, suppliers can capitalize on the competition for their funds and choose the most attractive portfolio offered. Buyers can capitalize on the scale of the industry, rivalry, and heavy competition among competitors. The largest firms spend millions of dollars on advertising. A quick exit from the industry is not easily accomplished either. New government regulations, and the overseeing of the industry by regulatory bodies such as the Securities and Exchange Commission, make exiting the industry a significant task.

The purchase of Midlantic Corp. by PNC Bank Corp. appears to be necessary and prudent for the development of both companies. With cultures that are proclaimed to be complementary by the management of each company, both companies stand to benefit from the purchase. Upon completion of the purchase, PNC will have achieved its strategic objective to become a market leader in New Jersey. Furthermore, PNC will have taken a major step toward the completion of several other strategic objectives, including a balance sheet realignment and a reduction in interest-rate sensitivity. Midlantic with benefit by becoming part of a super-regional financial services leader that has a strategy based on growth, which provides opportunities for both Midlantic's customers and employees. Furthermore, Midlantic's stockholders will benefit by receiving a premium on their shares and stake in a significantly more profitable company.

As super-regional banks continue to look for areas for growth, the strongest local banks will make attractive acquisitions. Relatively small financial companies such as

Midlantic Corp. will only be able to grow for a limited time before their acquisition is inevitable, and relatively large financial companies like PNC Bank Corp. will also be able to grow only to a certain extent before their own further growth will entail an equal merger or an acquisition by a larger firm.

### QUESTIONS

1. What are the differences between the strategies of large banks and small banks?
2. Does it seem right that small banks *want* to be acquired by larger banks? If so, why?
3. Why do large banks prefer to grow externally by acquisitions rather than by internal expansion? What are the advantages of each approach?

## REFERENCES

Associated Press Newswire, July 10, 1995 0181.
Business Wire, April 12, 1995, p4121161.
Dow Jones Newswire, July 10, 1995.
*Hoovers Handbook Database*. Austin, TX: The Reference Press, Inc., 1995.
*Hoovers International Business Database*. Austin, TX: The Reference Press, Inc., 1995.
Reuters Newswire, July 10, 1995.

## CASE STUDY: UNC's Acquisition of Garrett Aviation

UNC Incorporated is a diversified supplier of products and services to the aviation industry. UNC's primary business is an aviation aftermarket, which accounts for approximately 90% of its revenues. These operations include the overhaul and repair of aircraft engines and accessories, the repair and remanufacturing of engine components, and the provision of training and maintenance services to the U.S. and foreign military. Approximately 10% of UNC's revenues in 1995 were derived from manufacturing engine parts for original equipment manufacturers.

UNC has over 8,000 customers including: business aircraft operators; major, national, regional, foreign, charter, and package/cargo airlines; engine and airframe OEMs; and the U.S. and foreign military. UNC operates 16 facilities and performs services at approximately 80 government sites. UNC currently has 5,900 employees. The acquisition of Garrett would expand UNC's range of services, increase the aggregate customer base to over 10,000 customers, and add a total of eight operating locations and approximately 1,000 employees.

### Background

On January 16, 1996, UNC entered into a definitive agreement to acquire Garrett Aviation Services, a leading provider of aviation services to the $2.5 billion business aviation aftermarket. Garrett had been previously sold by AlliedSignal Inc. to a group of investors in June 1994, and they agreed to sell Garrett to UNC. As a result of the acquisition, UNC believes it will be the largest independent aviation services company in the world, with service capabilities for almost all businesses aircraft and engines, combined with their existing broad range of repair, overhaul, and remanufacturing capabilities for the business, commercial, and military markets. For the nine months ending September 30, 1995, on a pro forma basis, UNC and Garrett would have generated approximately $645 million in combined revenues and in excess of $48 million of combined operating cash flow (EBITDA), which includes only a portion of the incremental operating benefits anticipated over the next three years.

The purchase price for the acquisition is approximately $145 million in cash and the assumption of certain Garrett liabilities, including capitalized lease obligations recorded at approximately $5 million. UNC intends to finance the acquisition by (a) issuing $125 million aggregate principal amount of new 10-year senior notes, and (b) issuing 8.5% convertible preferred stock with an issue price of $25 million.

### Garrett

Garrett provides a full range of overhaul services to over 2,000 business aviation customers, including complete engine and airframe repair and overhaul capabilities, full interior-and-exterior refurbishment, new aircraft completions, avionics installation, and spare-parts distribution. Garrett provides its aircraft and engine maintenance and support through six "fly-in" fixed-based operator locations across the United States. For the nine months ending September 30, 1995, Garrett recorded approximately $250.9 million in total revenues and approximately $15.9 million of operating cash flow (EBITDA). Garrett enjoys a 50-year reputation for quality and market leadership in its industry segment.

Garrett currently specializes in providing aircraft, engine, and avionics aftermarket services to aircraft powered by AlliedSignal turbofan engines, which are the leading engine type for the business-jet aviation market. Based on industry data, AlliedSignal engines represent approximately 40% of the turbofan engines in the worldwide market. The leading engine type is the TFE731 turbofan, used to power a variety of business-jet aircraft, including aircraft under the Lear, Falcon, Astra, Citation, Westwind, and Jetstar trade names. Garrett management estimates that it services the AlliedSignal turboprop engines used on business aircraft and certain regional airlines.

Garrett benefits from a 15-year services agreement with AlliedSignal that appoints Garrett as the "Exclusive Factory-Sponsored Service and Support Center" for certain AlliedSignal engines in specified markets. The current AlliedSignal Operating Agreement extends through July 1, 2009. The AlliedSignal Operating Agreement is being assigned to the company as part of the acquisition.

This agreement: (a) specifies the terms on which Garrett purchases engine parts from AlliedSignal; (b) commits Garrett to purchase its engine parts requirements from AlliedSignal or certain approved vendors; (c) commits Garrett to provide aftermarket support to AlliedSignal products in the marketplace; and (d) defines the working relationship between the two companies in a number of areas, including technical training, quality systems and other support, exchange of customer and marketing information, and future programs.

A major advantage to Garrett under the AlliedSignal Operating Agreement is that AlliedSignal provides Garrett with engine parts inventory on a consignment basis. Garrett's customers are also able to access AlliedSignal engines from the AlliedSignal engine rental pool during the period of engine overhauls. The consignment inventory and the engine-pool availability have allowed Garrett to reduce significantly the level of its inventory and fixed asset investment than otherwise would be required.

As a result of the agreement, AlliedSignal is the single largest billing customer of Garrett, due to warranty and other prepaid maintenance programs. AlliedSignal is also the largest single vendor of Garrett, due to the purchase of parts both for engine repair and overhaul, and for the redistribution of spare parts. The AlliedSignal operating agreement may be terminated by AlliedSignal, among other reasons, following a material disruption in AlliedSignal's business resulting from the provision of Garrett's services or following a material downturn in certain of Garrett's businesses. A significant change in, or loss of, the Operating Agreement could have a material adverse effect on Garrett's results of operations.

## Benefits of the Acquisition

UNC's long-term strategy has been to build a leadership position in the aviation aftermarket with a focus on business and military aviation. Additionally, UNC's product focus has been the development of high-value services for its customers such as high technology repair and accessory overhaul processes for aircraft engines and accessories. Garrett provides services in both engine and aircraft maintenance with emphasis on the use of new parts for these services and therefore has not developed extensive capability in parts repair and accessory overhaul. Garrett's strategy is to expand its aircraft maintenance business, which historically has not been emphasized, and to develop more extensive high-value repair and accessory overhaul processes. UNC believes that the acquisition of Garrett is attractive in part because the strategies of each business are complementary and there is no significant overlap in the services provided by each business. UNC also expects that the acquisition will result in substantial other benefits to UNC, including the following:

- **aviation parts and component repair**—Garrett currently has limited in-house capability for the repair of aircraft parts and accessories, and outsources approximately $50 million per year in parts repair and overhaul services to other aviation companies. UNC has substantial capability in this area that should permit increases in consolidated profitability, based on existing levels of revenues.
- **added retail dimension**—The acquisition combines Garrett's front-line "retail" operations with the overhaul and remanufacturing "wholesale" aspects of UNC's operations. As a result, Garrett's direct customer relations should help promote a number of other UNC products and services, including engine overhaul for non-AlliedSignal engines, accessory overhaul, and parts remanufacturing. UNC believes that the availability of these services also should permit Garrett to expand its business with non-AlliedSignal powered aircraft owners and operators.
- **expanded airframe and avionics services**—Garrett has been expanding its airframe and avionics maintenance revenues, building on its established engine repair and overhaul customer base. This market segment is growing faster than the overall business aviation market, due primarily to the large number of business aircraft added to the global fleet between 1977 and 1982. Federal Aviation Administration and Original Equipment Manufacturer mandated service intervals and advances in avionics technology are causing increased demand for retrofit of these older airframes as well as major retrofit of avionics packages. UNC believes this is a major growth opportunity for Garrett. UNC also believes that its current customer base should provide further expansion opportunities in this area.
- **stable base of warranty service**—Garrett is the largest provider of warranty repair services on AlliedSignal engines. Over 55% of AlliedSignal engines are on long-term maintenance service programs and this provides a stable base level of business for Garrett. Garrett also benefits from access to AlliedSignal's detailed market data, which tracks projected maintenance events for the entire engine fleet.

- **increased global presence**—At present, more than 95% of Garrett's revenues are to North American customers. The company's expanding international presence, including its four overseas sales offices, should permit development of Garrett services for overseas locations.
- **military revenues**—Over the past two years, UNC Aviation Services Division has generated approximately $240 million in annual military-related revenues providing contract maintenance and other services to all the U.S. armed services and a variety of foreign military customers. UNC expects Garret's service capabilities will allow the company to pursue a wider range of military contracts that require these additional repair and overhaul services.
- **increased critical mass in the aviation aftermarket**—The acquisition of Garrett will substantially increase the revenue base, approximately 95% of which will be in the aviation aftermarket. UNC believes there are numerous economies of scale that can be achieved in services, marketing, purchasing, administration, and other areas. The aviation aftermarket has tended to be more stable than the OEM segment, because it is not dependent on the level of annual new aircraft deliveries.
- **acquisition expectations**—While UNC believes that it can improve the profitability of the operations of Garret and UNC on a combined basis given the operating synergies UNC expects to achieve, there can be no assurance that they will be able to realize all expected operating and economic efficiencies following the acquisition.

## QUESTIONS

1. Does UNC appear to have a strategic plan? If so, what are the long-term objectives?
2. Why did UNC acquire Garrett Aviation Services rather than expand internally by developing the skills themselves?
3. What opportunities and threats does UNC envision as part of this acquisition?
4. What role does the internal strengths and weaknesses play during this acquisition or any acquisition in general?
5. Is it reasonable to expect that layoffs may occur as part of the acquisition? If so, where will the layoffs come from, and why?

# CASE STUDY: The Wal-Mart Supercenters

Wal-Mart can trace its roots back to the 1940s when Samuel Moore Walton (1918–1992) began his career in retailing with the JCPenney Company. After leaving Penney's and serving a few years in the Army, Mr. Walton opened Walton's 5&10 in Bentonville, Arkansas. Today this original store is the site of the Wal-Mart Visitor's Center.

Wal-Mart, the nation's largest retailer, was founded in 1962 by Sam Walton. Wal-Mart's mission is "Be an agent for consumers, find out what they want, and sell it to them for the lowest possible price." Wal-Mart's objective, "The pursuit of quality, not quantity, through continuous improvement," has made Wal-Mart the market leader with rapid sales growth and better-than-average performance.

Since 1962, Wal-Mart has grown from 18 discount stores to almost 2,000 three decades later. In 1987, it opened its first Hypermart USA in Garland, Texas. The hypermart concept was expected to tap into the $387 billion supermarket business. One year later, it followed with the supercenter, which consisted of the traditional discount store with an attached warehouse-style supermarket.

Based on the success and consumer preference for the supercenter, Wal-Mart decided in 1991 to convert its existing hypermarts into supercenters. Expected average annual sales per unit for the supercenters was $50 million to $60 million.

Wal-Mart presently operates 144 supercenters, and this number is expected to rise to nearly 250 by the end of 1995. Supercenter sales should total about $11 billion by the end of 1995, more than double the sales of 1994. This continued growth should push Wal-Mart ahead of the supermarket leader, Kroger, who has expected 1995 sales of $22 billion.

The supercenter concept is becoming a major portion of Wal-Mart's corporate sales. By the century's end, the supercenter will contribute about 40% of its total revenues. This will add significant market share growth, not only to the discount segment, but it will also allow Wal-Mart to become the major player in the supermarket industry.

Wal-Mart's continued growth into the 21st century will be realized by its expansion into the international market. It presently has supercenters located in Mexico and Brazil with three slated to open in Argentina later this summer. New distribution centers have recently been built in Laredo, Texas and Tuscon, Arizona to supply these stores. In 1991 Wal-Mart acquired 122 Woolco stores in Canada, but does not expect to convert them into supercenters until the necessary expertise is learned for that market. Chile and Europe are speculated as being Wal-Mart's future areas for penetration.

As an industry leader, Wal-Mart's secret to success has been its strict attention to three basic principles. *First* is the concept of providing value and service for customers. Applying advertising to this principle has helped Wal-Mart develop an "Everyday Low Price" philosophy. This allows them to cut costs by advertising less and passing those savings on to customers. Wal-Mart has fought a lawsuit brought against it for selling products below costs. Many states have laws prohibiting such unfair practices. "The company lost a case in Oklahoma state court in 1986, when it was found to have violated a state law that requires retailers to sell products at least 6.75% above cost, unless the store is having a sale or matching a competitor's price." Wal-Mart settled out of court after unsuccessfully lobbying Oklahoma's legislature to repeal the law and agreed to raise prices at all of its stores in the state. Independent retailers in small towns across the country have accused the retailer of selling goods below costs to drive them out of business, then boost prices after it seizes control of the local market. Wal-Mart employees said the company bases its prices on how much competition it faces: more competition, lower prices; less competition, higher prices. The rapid growth experienced by Wal-Mart may have been due to outpricing the competition at any cost. Wal-Mart does not appear to have a change in sales due to this suit.

Wal-Mart has always strived to provide the best service to customers by asking employees to take the Wal-Mart pledge, "I solemnly promise and declare that to every customer that comes within ten feet of me, I will smile, look them in the eye, and greet them, so help me Sam." In addition, Wal-Mart has a unique form of customer service called "The People Greeter." "The People Greeter" has the responsibility of meeting and welcoming customers as they enter Wal-Mart stores. Officially, "The People Greeter" has the job of handing out shopping carts and smiles.

The *second principle* involves a partnership with associates (employees). One of the ways that Wal-Mart stresses the concept of employees as associates is by offering profit-sharing plans to employees who are employed at least one year. Employees are the most valuable asset to Wal-Mart. By continually investing in this asset Wal-Mart can establish a deferential advantage on competitors.

The *third principle* is a commitment to the communities in which stores are located. Each store participates in community-involvement projects, awards annual scholarships to deserving high-school students, and donates large sums of money to such programs as United Way and the Children's Miracle Network. Customer service and community support go hand in hand. By helping to support the community in which Wal-Mart operates, it is ensuring itself a strong base of future support.

Another successful strategy Wal-Mart uses is micromarketing to local needs. For example, the supercenter in Panama City Beach, Florida offers a large selection of subtropical live greenery. Store management has hired local experts who are experienced in plant care to advise customers (Halverson, p. 43). Other supercenters caters to sports, hunting, or fishing needs depending upon the needs of the local community. Tire and Lube Express Centers are big in areas such as Culpepper, Virginia, whereas do-it-yourself automotive accessory departments are popular in the South.

Although Wal-Mart's philosophies and policies have added to its strength in the market, it is not without its soft spots. Most predominant among these is the initial investments needed to open a superstore. Wal-Mart must invest about 40% more to build one of these large structures over the cost of its regular discount store. Even if it is constructing a regular discount store, Wal-Mart invests in additional real estate for each site and expansion plans so that the store can be converted into a superstore in the future.

International expansion is also a concern for Wal-Mart. Huge outlays of cash are necessary to build, with no guarantee of return. Wal-Mart has opened several warehouse clubs in Hong Kong but they are meeting fierce competition from Asian and European competitors. Some of these Wal-Mart stores rarely see a customer. However, Wal-Mart executives look at it as training ground for the future development and penetration into the Asian Market.

On the local front, Wal-Mart is learning how to improve its average grocery return, which accounts for about 40% of its supercenter intake. It has taken significant strides in improving its fresh, frozen, and bakery departments. Meats, however, still tend to be the highest area of customer dissatisfaction.

Another chief weakness in the Wal-Mart strategy is its use of private label, "Great Value." Although these products return a higher profit margin, the perception to the customer is less choice of national-brand products from which to choose. Wal-Mart presently uses 20% private label in its dry-goods department.

Regardless of its few weaknesses, Wal-Mart supercenters are expected to continue to grow well into the 21st century, both domestically and internationally. Wal-Mart will continue to place its "hometown spirit" in many more towns and retain its title as industry leader in doing what it does best: "selling the most for the least."

## QUESTIONS

1. Describe Wal-Mart's overall strategy.
2. What functional strategies are used to implement the overall strategy?
3. Explain the differences between Wal-Mart's domestic and international marketing strategy.
4. Is Wal-Mart's decision to build supercenters a departure from their original strategy? Who was Wal-Mart competing with 10 years ago and who are the supercenters competing with now?

## REFERENCES

"Facts About Wal-Mart Stores" (handout).

Halverson, Richard. "Supercenters Give Hard Lines a Local Twist." *Discount Store News*, April 17, 1995, pp. 32–43.

Hisey, Pete. "Commitment and Excitement Key to Wal-Mart's Merchandising Success." *Discount Store News*, April 17, 1995, p. 5.

Liebeck, Laura. "Wal-Mart Steps upon the Food Chain." *Discount Store News*, April 17, 1995, pp. 23–43.

Longo, Don. "Supercenters Lead Growth into 21st Century." *Discount Store News*, April 17, 1995, pp. 19–43.

Ortega, Bob. "Suit over Wal-Mart's Pricing Practices Goes to Trial Today in Arkansas Court." *Wall Street Journal*, August 23, 1993, p. A3.

## CASE STUDY: Kmart

On March 1, 1962, the first Kmart store was opened in Garden City, Michigan. A year earlier, Gene Sturges, vice-president of S. S. Kresge's personnel, had been sent by Kresge's to study discount retailing. On March 17, 1961, Sturges presented an eight-page report that convinced Harry B. Cunningham, Kresge's head officer, to expand Kresge's into discount retailing. In 1963, Kresge's cut its dividends to put all available resources into the Kmart venture. By 1964, with 93 stores, Kmart had become number one among discounters and retained that position until 1990, when Wal-Mart became number one.[1]

Kmart used the strategy of providing one-stop shopping for consumers by placing its stores in low-rent strip malls as coanchors with supermarkets. Kmart's advantages over other discounters was the strong financial backing of Kresge's and the availability of Kresge's experienced managers and use of its established distribution channels. Cunningham aimed to provide customers with name-brand merchandise at a fair price.[2] Kmart expanded rapidly in the 1960s not only in the United States, but also in foreign countries, such as Canada and Australia. Much of the expansion was done through acquisitions.

In 1972, Robert E. Dewar, former Kresge president, became chairman of the board and CEO. Dewar continued the expansion of Kmart. Then in 1980, Bernard M. Fauber became chairman of the board and CEO.[3] Fauber was experienced in marketing, and his goal was to improve productivity and profits. Kmart had begun to expand into retailing specialties with its acquisitions. For the first time ever, Fauber closed unprofitable stores and slowed Kmart's growth.[4] Wal-Mart and Target began to close in on Kmart for the number-one position. In 1987, Joseph E. Antonini became president, chairman, and CEO. Since 1989, the earnings per share for Kmart have been flat or have dropped.

The entry barriers into the discounting market were not extremely high, as with the airline industry, but they were not extremely low, either. In order to be really successful, it helped to be able to purchase items in bulk and to have a good distribution system. Kmart once had these advantages and could offer products to the consumer at a lower cost than other stores, thus driving the competition out of business.

In 1991, accounting changes were made so that earnings for IRS purposes looked lower, but looked higher for investors.[5] By 1994, there was some question as to whether Kmart would continue to pay dividends. Cutting dividends to conserve cash is usually a bad idea and should be used as a last resort because it conveys a negative message to investors. Moody's had already downgraded Kmart's debt from A3 to Baa1 and Baa2.[6]

What went wrong for Kmart that it lost its lead? Several factors contributed. Probably the biggest factor was that Kmart was so focused on growth that it forgot to look over its shoulder to see what the competition was doing. It also lost contact with the consumer and failed to keep up with technological changes for improving inventory control.

In 1984, Kmart changed the way it advertised and started using a Sunday flier.[7] The problem was that when a consumer went to buy an advertised product, it wasn't on the shelf and the customer would be given a rain check. This became a chronic problem. Customers don't want rain checks, they want the product when they see it advertised on sale. By the time Kmart began to work on its satellite-based communications network in 1986, it had given its competitors, who had the technology for better communications and inventory control, a competitive edge.[8] The competitors were able to give better customer service. In 1994, Kmart's inventory turnover still was only 4.3, compared to the industry average of 6.5.[9]

Kmart needed a way to raise capital to continue expansion. In 1991, Kmart sold preferred equity redemption cumulative stock (PERCS) to raise capital. PERCS pay a higher dividend than common stock and cause less dilution of common stock than a sale of additional common stock would. Kmart did this in order to have cash available to buy discounters that went bankrupt due to the recession.[10] While the strategy for growth through acquisitions and diversification worked to ward off potential takeovers, Kmart should have started using some of its money to upgrade its stores sooner than it did. Now Kmart had to sell off some of its acquisitions to obtain money. In April 1995, arrangements were being made to sell Borders Group[11] and in June 1995, OfficeMax was sold.[12]

Kmart needed to get completely out of specialty retailing and get back to what it did best: discounting. Selling acquisitions provided money needed for internal improvements. This would give Kmart the opportunity to regain the number-one position.

The competition, especially Wal-Mart and Target, are and will continue to be the major threats to Kmart.

Kmart's weakness is its focus. Kmart believes that it needs to concentrate on getting its inventory system upgraded so that it is more efficient. It makes no sense to expand before the inventory system is working smoothly and efficiently. Having more stores will not make the inventory problem go away. The inventory turnover rate needs to be much closer to the 6.5 industry average.

Kmart has one strength that its competitors don't have. The only internal start-up that has not failed has been SuperKmart.[13] Looking closely at SuperKmart, it is very much like the Kmart of 1962: one-stop shopping. The only difference is that it's all under one roof. Its success shows that the original idea still works, more than 30 years later.

Kmart believes it is headed in the right direction if it can get its inventory system straightened out to provide what customers want when they want it, and get management to help cut expenses. It needs to keep a watchful eye on its competitors and watch for new technology that can be used to increase its efficiency, profits, and customer service.

SuperKmart had a very large expansion period in the 1980s, due to a recession. While expansion stopped, the stores were not updated and quality of products and service became poor. Consumer tastes demanded better, even for the less expensive stores such as Kmart.

While consumer tastes were changing to improved quality, Kmart management was resting on its strengths. It had a very large market share, until recently being in the top three discount chains, and had stores conveniently located in most large markets. Management felt the name recognition would keep Kmart strong.

Times changed, and while Kmart management was expecting consumers to remain loyal, along came Wal-Mart and other quality consumer-oriented stores. No longer were customers content with the convenience of Kmart. Consumers became willing to drive a little farther to Wal-Mart or Target.

Management decided to remodel the existing stores at a cost of $3.5 billion while Wal-Mart was opening new "superstores" right under Kmart's nose! This mismanagement cost CEO Joseph Antonini his job.

The 1990s consumer was demanding one-stop shopping and Kmart was ready to make its move into the superstores. Kmart saw the superstore as a more beneficial move for the stockholders than the $3.5 billion proposed to remodel the existing smaller stores. In 1992 the first Super K was opened in Medina, Ohio. The superstore is a general merchandise store with a grocery store on the other side. The average square foot of a Super K is 191,000 feet of space in the general merchandise side, which is double the amount of a regular Kmart.

By the year 2000, Kmart expects to have 450 Super Ks. This breaks down to approximately 1.5 new stores per month. The key to a successful Super K is to be the first Superstore in a given market area.

Why would Kmart, Wal-Mart, and Target want to get involved in the food business? Don Longo, in his article "Supercenters get repackaged for the 1990's one stop shopper," makes several surprising points.

*First*, the discount store business is mature. Most sales growth comes from taking market share away from similar competitors.

*Second*, market share gains are difficult since most of the market is owned by the big three.

*Third*, converting or opening established discount stores is less risky than opening new units in new markets.

*Fourth*, the big three have proven that consumer franchises with established brands and advertising encourage trial and repeat business at the new "supercenter."

*Fifth*, the supermarket industry is a huge ($387 billion) but fragmented market. The largest percentage is owned by Kroger at 6%.

*Sixth*, capturing supermarket share is relatively easy and inexpensive compared with general merchandising market.

*Lastly*, the best reason for stockholders is the addition of food products, which drives up the general merchandise sales for most supercenters by 20% to 30%.[14]

The local grocery-store chains and small "mom and pop" stores do not want to see a Super K or any other superstore open in their area. With the ability to purchase in large quantities, superstore prices will be much lower than in the smaller stores. Market share will be lost to the closing of uncompetitive grocery stores.

It will be the goal of any superstore to have the consumer do all of his or her shopping in one place. Most superstores will offer a dry cleaner, video rental, floral shop, optical shop, and even shoe repair. In addition, to speed you out after you make your purchases will be 30 checkout lines!

With Super K, Kmart is looking to change the image of low-quality stores into high value, high quality. To do this, the Super K will offer fresh-food kiosks, a sit-down deli/café, a bakery with freshly made cookies and breads, top-notch produce, and wider isles for shopper convenience. Compare this to the current Kmart with the specific cheap smell, the tasteless pre-made deli sandwiches and cheap meat, the frozen Coke machine, cramped and cluttered isles, and merchandise in no specific place. Kmart is on the right path and is probably wise to accept the supercenter concept. The old small discount store is a dinosaur. It is time for Kmart to consider closing smaller unprofitable stores and either convert them to Super Ks or build new Super Ks in the same markets. The initial expense of purchasing land will be a large outlay, but can be recouped rather quickly with the profits Super K has shown.

### QUESTIONS

1. Describe Kmart's past and present strategy.
2. What are the barriers to entry into the discount retailing business?
3. What are Kmart's strengths over its competitors?
4. How does one differentiate between management and mismanagement?
5. Does Kmart compete in a mature or immature industry?
6. Do Kmart's internal strengths have to change in order for its new strategy to succeed?

## NOTES


1. "1962–1992: A Historical Overview." *Discount Store News*, Feb. 17, 1992, p. 40.
2. "1962–1992: A Historical Overview." *Discount Store News*, Feb. 17, 1992, p. 40.
3. "A Short History of Kmart." *Discount Store News*, Sept. 26, 1988, p. 75.
4. "1962–1992: A Historical Overview." *Discount Store News*, Feb. 17, 1992, p. 40.
5. Constance Crump, "Accounting Changes Affect Earnings." *Crain's Detroit Business*, May 20, 1991, p. 11.
6. Christina Duff, "Moody's Lowers Rating on Kmart Dept, Citing Chain's 'Further Deterioration'." *Wall Street Journal*, Jan. 30, 1995, p. A18.
7. "1962–1992: A Historical Overview." *Discount Store News*, Feb. 17, 1992, p. 40.
8. "A Short History of Kmart." *Discount Store News*, Sept. 26, 1988, p. 75.
9. David Barkholz, "What Should Kmart Do? Experts Speak." *Crain's Detroit Business*, June 20, 1994, p. 1.
10. "Kmart Taps Stock Exchange for Capital." *Discount Store News*, Aug. 19, 1991, p. 3.
11. "Kmart Corp. Plans IPO for 52% Stake in Borders Group Unit." *Wall Street Journal*, April 5, 1995, p. 10.
12. Donald Sabath, "Kmart to Sell Its OfficeMax Shares." *The Cleveland Plain Dealer*, June 27, 1995, p. C1.
13. "1962–1992: A Historical Overview." *Discount Store News*, Feb. 17, 1992, p. 40.
14. Don Longo, "Supercenters Get Repackaged for the 1990's One Stop Shopper." (Food Merchandising) (editorial). In *Discount Store News*, April 3, 1995, v34, n7, pF3(1).

# CASE STUDY: Viacom's Acquisition of Paramount Communications, Inc. (A Case Study in Vertical Integration)

Life is like a box of chocolates . . . You never know what you're going to get. As Viacom was poised to take control in 1994, Paramount had experienced several years of lackluster performance following a string of film flops. Gross revenues for films such as *Addams Family Values*, *Searching for Bobbie Fischer*, and *Silver* had been discouraging, and Paramount was projected to show a loss for fiscal year 1994. However, the summer hit, *Forrest Gump*, validated Viacom's confidence in Paramount's long-term cash flow potential. Like the title character, Viacom was in the right place at the right time—through May 1995, *Forrest Gump* had realized revenues in excess of $657 million.

## The Players

Viacom, Inc. was in the media and entertainment industry. It owned cable channels such as MTV and VH1, which air music videos; Nickelodeon, which produces children's programming; and the premium movie channel, Showtime.

Viacom is controlled by its Chairman, Sumner Redstone, a 70-year-old billionaire whose temper and tenacity are legendary. Redstone started with a family-owned drive-in movie business and built it into an 800-screen chain. Through shrewd investments, his wealth increased until he was in a position to acquire Viacom in a hostile buyout in 1987 for $3.4 billion. His interest in Viacom was valued at over $5 billion in 1993, making him one of the wealthiest people in the media and entertainment industry.

The 1987 leveraged buyout was through junk bonds, leaving Viacom with a heavy debt and a noninvestment grade credit rating. Viacom's CEO, Frank J. Biondi, Jr., spent the next four years restructuring the debt, selling off assets, and getting Viacom out of the junk-bond market. He is largely credited with fashioning one of the few 1980s leveraged buyouts that worked.

Paramount Communications, Inc. was also in the entertainment industry with varied interests including a movie studio, a large film and television library, Simon & Schuster (the world's largest publisher and information-services company), theme parks, TV stations, and sports teams. The film library includes 900 films from classics such as *Holiday Inn* and *White Christmas* to contemporary films such as *The Firm*, *Indecent Proposal*, and *Raiders of the Lost Ark*. It produced television programs such as *Wings*, *Cheers*, *Frazier*, *Happy Days*, and the cash cow, *Star Trek*, which is still producing spin-offs after more than 25 years.

In early 1994, Viacom agreed to a merger with Blockbuster Entertainment Corporation. Blockbuster is a nationwide retailer specializing in family home entertainment. Its assets including a string of retail outlets for video rentals and music chains. These two specialties are a good fit since they use the same advertising and distribution channels. Historically, Blockbuster has experienced strong earnings growth; gross profit margins for video rentals can be as high as 70%. More recently, Blockbuster has been pursuing diversification strategies since 1992, buying interests in classic film and libraries and Spelling Entertainment Group, the producer of television programs such as *Melrose Place* and *Beverly Hills 90210*.

## Strengths of the Combined Corporations

The primary strengths of the merged companies spring from vertical integration. The films Paramount produces can be distributed through theaters owned by Sumner Redstone. Then, Blockbuster can profit from the video rentals, followed by exclusive showings on Viacom's premium cable channel, Showtime. In addition, Blockbuster's retailing expertise can be utilized for related merchandising from movies and TV shows. Blockbuster has strong brand recognition—its name is familiar to 90% of Americans.

Many cross-promotional activities will benefit various segments of the corporation. Blockbuster's music chains can be advertised on Viacom's MTV and VH1. Simon & Schuster's multimedia educational products can find space on Blockbuster's shelves. MTV's animated characters, Beavis & Butthead, will appear in Paramount films and in Simon & Schuster's books. Nickelodeon's Ren and Stimpy will be featured at Paramount's theme parks.

Along with cash flow of $500 million per year, Blockbuster brought a strong balance sheet to the table. It was nearly debt-free, and therefore had strong borrowing power. Potential cash flow from the combined entity has been estimated at $1.7 billion each year. This amount is three times what will be required to pay the interest on the $10 billion debt assumed to acquire Paramount.

Blockbuster also owns a unique asset—a detailed database of 30 million customers' preferences that would be a useful resource for marketing films. Some have suggested that this database could be used to tailor film projects to known customer preferences by casting actors, choosing directors, or even choosing which movie genre is currently popular.

## Weaknesses of the Combined Corporations

Did Sumner Redstone pay too high a price for Paramount's assets? Many on Wall Street think so. Although he swore he would not raise his original bid, Redstone did—several times. QVC, the Home Shopping network, which was also in the bidding war, pushed the price much higher than was originally anticipated. Viacom had to take on debt in excess of $10 billion, resulting in a debt to equity ration of 38%. In fact, if Paramount's assets were sold piecemeal, its estimated liquidation value ranges from $7.8 to $9.3 billion. Obviously, Redstone had strong faith in Paramount's value as a going concern.

Viacom had to sell assets quickly to reduce the debt. The most likely candidates for divestiture were a $\frac{1}{3}$ interest in the Lifetime cable channel, a $\frac{1}{2}$ interest in USA network, Madison Square Garden arena, sports teams, cable networks, TV stations, and theme parks. Viacom's CEO, Frank Biondi, announced in July 1994 that his first priorities would be to cut the debt load by $2 billion within four years, increase cash flow by $2 billion annually, and operate the studios on a cost-conscious basis. The elimination of duplicate administrative functions would result in lost jobs and higher stress for employees. The uncertainty arising from these diversities and the increased emphasis on profitability had a negative impact on company morale.

Although acknowledged for their strategic and financial skills, Viacom's top executives, Redstone and Biondi, have no expertise managing a creative industry, such as a film studio. Nor do they have experience in managing a publishing business. Simon & Schuster is the world's largest trade publisher but, as a rule, the profit margin in that industry is low. In fact, Viacom has virtually ignored this segment of the acquisition and has not announced any plans to exploit this asset.

Another possible problem was the potential of internal competition between the video rental and cable networks with regard to access to the first releases of hit films.

### Threats

The largest source of Blockbusters' revenue is movie rentals. However, the video-rental market faces potential technological obsolescence. New delivery methods are being tested by both cable and telephone companies. Time Warner is testing a pay-per-view system using the 500-channel capacity of cable. Phone companies, such as Bell Atlantic, are developing a distribution system for movies on demand delivered over telephone lines.

The film studios are concerned about whether Paramount releases will corner all the prime shelf space at Blockbuster stores. Care must be taken not to antagonize the studios excessively, leading to reprisals involving the studios not allowing Blockbuster to distribute their films.

MTV and VH1 will face competition from a new global music channel financed by the four largest record companies led by Time Warner and Sony.

### Opportunities

Although the video-rental market may be shrinking, Blockbuster can maintain its market share through several avenues: (1) buying out small video retailers, (2) expanding into video-game rentals and sales, and (3) overseas expansion. The international market for video rentals is virtually untapped, and the technology that allows movies on demand is much further off overseas.

Video rentals are responsible for half the revenue of a typical film release. Exclusive first-week distribution at Blockbuster outlets would give them a great competitive advantage over other video retailers. Likewise, exclusive or first showings would benefit Showtime and give that premium channel a market advantage at little cost or risk.

With Blockbuster's retailing experience behind it, Viacom could establish studio stores comparable to Warner Brothers and Disney stores. These stores would feature characters from the cable network programs as well as merchandising related to film releases.

### Competitive Environment

There are few exit barriers for Blockbuster's operations. The retail stores are not highly specialized and could be easily sold and converted to other retail use. Paramount, however, has some highly specialized assets, including theme parks, that would be difficult to sell.

The combined operation will become the largest buyer in Hollywood, giving it great influence over its suppliers. Although the global joint venture by Time Warner and Sony will be competition for MTV and VH1, these record companies have promised they will not keep their videos off MTV entirely—it is still too valuable a promotional avenue for the record industry.

Customers, individually, have little power since they are so many and cannot organize. However, substitute products are plentiful. The combined entity competes with a wide range of entertainment alternatives for the consumer's discretionary income.

Capital requirements for entering the video-rental business are relatively low and this market is currently highly attractive. Capital requirements to enter the film-production industry, however, are very high and the industry is very risky. There are moderate legal barriers to enter the cable and television industry.

In consequence, rivalry among competitors is high in this industry, but through vertical integration the combined companies are in a more secure strategic position together than they would be standing alone.

### QUESTIONS

1. Is this really a case of vertical integration?
2. What are the risks of vertical integration in the media and entertainment industry?
3. After the acquisition of Paramount, are Viacom's senior managers managing Viacom or a holding company?
4. What were the internal strengths and weaknesses of Viacom prior to the acquisition?
5. What are the internal strength and weaknesses following the acquisition?
6. What impact could technology have upon the projected opportunities and threats?
7. What impact could technology have upon the internal strengths and weaknesses?
8. Does Viacom actually have a strategic plan?

## REFERENCES


Landro, Laura. "The Drama Ended, Two Stars Get New Scripts." *Wall Street Journal*, February 16, 1994, p. B1.

Landro, Laura. "Grit Bolsters Viacom Chief in Takeover Bid." *Wall Street Journal*, November 16, 1993, p. B1.

Landro, Laura. "Viacom and QVC Debate Who Would Be Better Parent." *Wall Street Journal*, February 9, 1994. p. B1.

Landro, Laura, and Roberts, Johnnie L. "Now the Hard Part: Viacom Is Set to Become Media Colossus—or Burdened Giant." *Wall Street Journal*, February 16, 1994, p. A1.

Roberts, Johnnie L. "Deals Give Hefty Viacom Even More Muscle." *Wall Street Journal*, September 30, 1994, p. B1.

Sharp, Anita. "Blockbuster Deal Is a Smart Move for Its Chief." *Wall Street Journal*, January 10, 1994, p. B1.

Smith, Randall. "Paramount's Fate in the Hands of a Few." *Wall Street Journal*, February 9, 1994, p. B1.

Smith, Randall. "Wall Street's Final Analysis: Might Made Right." *Wall Street Journal*, February 16, 1994, p. B1.


## CASE STUDY: ITT Corporation

### Origins of ITT Corporation

ITT Corporation was founded in 1920 by brothers Sosthenes and Hernand Behn. It began as a telephone operating company. In 1925, the company acquired AT&T's overseas telephone equipment business in addition to miscellaneous overseas manufacturing businesses. The main focus remained on the communication division, leading to the name International Telephone and Telegraph. Although not widely publicized, one of ITT's holdings reportedly was a German aircraft maker, Focke-Wulf, which during World War II built planes that bombed Allied troops. It has also been reported that one of the brothers, Sosthenes, met with Hitler and considered him to be a "gentleman." These were only the beginnings of the scandals that would taint ITT Corporation.

### History under Previous CEOs

In 1959, Harold Geneen took over as President and CEO of the corporation. Under his leadership ITT expanded, diversified, and became one of the world's largest and most unusual conglomerates. Geneen's strategy focused on short-term results rather than long-term benefits for the company. ITT became extremely diversified, with products ranging from military radars to Wonder Bread. Acquisitions included Continental Bakers (makers of Wonder Bread and Hostess products), Levitt & Sons (home builders), Avis Rental Cars, Sheraton Hotels, Hartford Insurance, and numerous financial-service companies (i.e., Thorp Financial Services), just to name a few. During his 18-year reign, Geneen increased sales from $765.6 million to $16.6 billion and increased profits from $29 million to $562 million. To quote Walter Shapiro in his *Washington Post Magazine* (August 8, 1982) article on ITT, "the company, under Geneen, became a controversial symbol of unbridled corporate power." Geneen earned a reputation for being a ruthless leader.

Geneen held monthly meetings with his top managers. These meetings were held either in New York or Brussels and lasted a full week. During the meetings, managers were required to wear gray suits, white shirts, black ties, and laced shoes. Each manager was individually grilled by Geneen regarding his financial results of the previous month.

In 1972, Geneen faced allegations that ITT had made a large contribution to the Republican party in order to get its help in winning a settlement of antitrust charges that arose from the acquisition of Hartford Insurance. ITT executives, including Geneen, were called to testify before Congress regarding the actions taken by their lobbyist, Dita Beard. In 1973, author Anthony Sampson published a book called *The Sovereign State of ITT*, which was a scathing critique of the company's activities. One of the allegations in the book was that Geneen and/or other company officials had met with the CIA to try to bribe them to sabotage the 1970 election of the Marxist leader Salvador Allende Gossens as president of Chile. Gossens was planning to nationalize Chile's telephone company, which was owned by ITT. This would cost ITT millions of dollars. Geneen appeared before the congressional committee to answer these charges. While he admitted meeting with CIA officials, he denied there was any talk of payoffs.

Harold Geneen resigned as President and CEO of ITT on December 31, 1977. He did, however, remain Chairman of the Board. His replacement was Lyman Hamilton. By the time Hamilton took control, ITT had amassed a huge debt load. In an attempt to reduce this debt, Hamilton sold off some of the less profitable ITT properties and began to reduce the size of the staff. These changes were in complete violation of the policies and strategies Geneen had established. To show his displeasure, Geneen orchestrated a boardroom coup that removed Hamilton from his position as President and CEO after just 19 months. The Board of Directors then named Rand V. Araskog as the new President and CEO of ITT Corporation.

## History under Current CEO

Rand V. Araskog took over ITT Corporation in July 1979. At that time, the company had approximately 275 subsidiaries, a mountain of debt, and no clear sense of direction. Taking note of what had happened to his predecessor, Araskog took a firm stand that Harold Geneen would continue to serve as Araskog's adviser and consultant, but Araskog would be the one running the company. With Araskog's position firmly established, Geneen resigned as Chairman of the Board in November 1979 and named Araskog as his successor.

Araskog's agenda was basically to follow the divestiture program started by Hamilton. In his first year, he sold 17 unprofitable companies, stopped construction on a Quebec paper mill, and continued to streamline the company management. By the second quarter of 1981, profits were up 111% and income rose from $64.5 million to $136.1 million from the 1980 figures. While this was encouraging, there was still much work to be done. Araskog continued with his philosophy. In his first five years, he had sold off 69 subsidiaries worth a total of $1.5 billion and reduced the payroll from 368,000 to 278,000.

In 1984, Araskog faced two hostile takeover bids. The first, in May, came on the heels of the announcement of a 64% cut in shareholder dividends due to unexpected profit trouble in several major divisions. Jay Pritzker, chairman of Hyatt Hotels Corp, and Philip Anschutz, a Denver oil man, teamed up to buy ITT stock. They hoped to force a leveraged buyout that would enable them to dismantle the company and sell off its assets. Araskog rejected the bid and rallied the company to fight the takeover. The fight was successful and the takeover threat was avoided. No sooner was this settled than another problem arose. In December 1984, Irwin Jacobs, known as "Irv the Liquidator," began buying large quantities of stock. Araskog's response was to sell of $1.7 billion in assets and persuade the shareholders to reject the takeover bids. His plan was again a success, but the whole issue left him very bitter and feeling betrayed. He vented his anger by writing a book entitled *The ITT Wars: A CEO Speaks Out on Takeovers*.

By 1991, Araskog had sold off about 200 of ITT's 275 subsidiaries and reduced the debt from more than $5 billion to less than $3 billion. He had narrowed the corporate focus to mainly financial services, insurance, and telecommunications. Still, ITT's return on equity had fallen to 11.5% in 1990. Araskog was criticized by the California Public Employees' Retirement System for accepting his compensation of $11.4 million (an increase of 103% over the previous year) while the return on equity was decreasing. Reacting to these accusations, the Board of Directors decided to adopt a pay-for-performance plan, under which bonuses would be directly linked to the company's return on equity. This apparently was a turning point for ITT.

Early 1992 saw ITT's shares trading 20% below book value. This attracted the attention of Wall Street analysts. They predicted ITT had great turnaround potential, and saw increasing gains in most divisions including Hartford Insurance and Sheraton Hotels. On February 26, 1992, Araskog mentioned the possible breakup of ITT. This caused the stock to jump 9% in one day. On March 3, ITT announced it would sell its remaining 37% stake in France's Alcatel, ITT's European communication business. This sale ended ITT's presence in the telecommunications business that was once its core. On May 5, ITT announced plans to buy back 25 million shares of stock, causing stock to jump another 5%. On February 11, 1993, the company announced a major housecleaning with large asset write-downs and restructuring. On May 5, 1993, ITT sold its unsecured loan portfolio for $1.7 billion. On June 28, ITT entered the casino business by purchasing the Desert Inn in Las Vegas. Thus began a new focus for ITT Corporation.

The strategy ITT had followed for most of Araskog's reign had changed. The financial services division fell out of favor with the company and was sold off. In its place was a new focus on the leisure and entertainment industry. In addition to the acquisition of the Desert Inn, ITT has also acquired majority ownership in CIGA SpA, one of Europe's leading luxury hotel groups, the Phoenician Resort and the Cresent Hotel in Arizona, the Park Grand Hotel in Sydney, Australia, half interest in Madison Square Garden in New York City (including partial ownership of the Knicks and the Rangers), and the gaming giant Caesar's World, which includes properties in Las Vegas, Atlantic City, Lake Tahoe, and Windsor, Ontario, Canada.

## Strategy for the Future

Rumors had long been circulating that ITT would restructure the company and divide it into three separate businesses. On June 13, 1995, these plans were confirmed. In a news release, the company announced that the three individual businesses would be

ITT Hartford (insurance services), ITT Industries Inc. (industrial products), and ITT Corporation (hospitality, entertainment, and information services). Each will have its own board of directors, structure, policies, and strategies. Rand Araskog will become Chairman and CEO of the new ITT Corporation. This move may allow Araskog, who faces mandatory retirement in 1996, to continue with the company after he turns 65. The new ITT Corporation includes Sheraton, Caesar's World, Inc., Madison Square Garden, ITT World Directories, the world's largest producer of telephone directories outside the United States, and ITT Educational Services Inc., operating 54 technical institutes in 25 states and serving 20,000 students. The new ITT will employ approximately 30,000 people. Little has been said regarding exactly what Araskog has planned for each of these divisions in the future. He began negotiations to purchase a television network, but withdrew from the negotiations in a short period of time. It is uncertain whether this line of diversification will be pursued again to add to the new ITT Corporation or not.

ITT plans to call the outstanding shares of ITT cumulative preferred stock for redemption prior to the record date for distribution. It has also temporarily suspended dividends on common shares for 1995. Dividend payments are to resume in 1996 and it is expected these dividends will exceed the current dividend 10%. Given the changes ITT has experienced under Araskog's leadership, what the future holds for the company is anyone's guess.

### Recommendations

With limited experience in the leisure and entertainment industry in general and virtually no experience in the gaming industry, ITT may be wise to keep Caesar's World's management team on. Although they have never focused much on growth, they have a niche that has worked well for them. Caesar's has always catered to a more upscale clientele. If changes are made to restructure Caesar's in the mold of Sheraton, many of these clients will be lost, along with the high-roller status and bankrolls they carry. The other properties ITT has acquired should be similarly reviewed and analyzed to focus on their individual strengths.

Many of the recent acquisitions ITT has made could be seen as questionable. Madison Square Garden has made minimal profits for many years, and the gambling industry is finding its way into many more states, which may reduce the attraction of traditional gambling meccas such as Las Vegas and Atlantic City. Additional casino properties for ITT Sheraton are being established in Tunica, Mississippi, Lima, Peru, and Halifax, Nova Scotia. Intense marketing strategies must be put into place to help promote these properties. Additionally, care must be taken not to spread the wealth too thin by acquiring more properties than can effectively be managed. This may turn out to be a learn-as-you-go situation for ITT Corporation. However, they are in too deep now to back out without incurring huge losses for the stockholders.

## REFERENCES

Araskog, Rand V. *Current Biography*, November 1991, p. 3.

Bremner, Brian. "It's a New Day for ITT's Rand Araskog." *Business Week*, July 2, 1990, p. 50.

Grover, Ronald. "Is Rand Araskog Rolling the Right Dice?" *Business Week*, January 16, 1995, p. 34.

Hammonds, Keith H. "Araskog's Big Deal for ITT." *Business Week*, January 9, 1995, p. 47.

"ITT: Finally on Target?" (company profile). *Financial World*, May 10, 1994, p. 16.

Lesly, Elizabeth, "While ITT Lumbers, Its Stock Has Legs." *Business Week*, May 30, 1994, p. 90.

Roberts, Johnnie L. "Goliath Goes Hollywood." *Newsweek*, March 27. 1995, p. 44.
Sherman, Stratford. "Can You Believe What You See At ITT." *Fortune*, April 17, 1995, p. 109.
"The One That Got Away," (company profile). *Forbes*, January 30, 1995, p. 49.
"With Move to Buy Caesar's World, ITT Assumes Major Role in Gaming." *Travel Weekly*, December 26, 1994, p. 1.

# Appendix A

**FOR IMMEDIATE RELEASE**
**ITT World Headquarters**

**June 13, 1995**

**ITT TO SPIN OFF ITS BUSINESSES TO SHAREHOLDERS; CREATES 3 SEPARATE PUBLICLY OWNED COMPANIES**

NEW YORK, NY, June 13, 1995—ITT Corporation said today that its board of directors approved a management plan to spin off its businesses to shareholders to create three separate publicly owned corporations. The transaction, involving sales and revenues of $25 billion, creates three of the largest publicly held independent companies, each with its own board of directors and each listed on the NYSE, respectively in the businesses of insurance services, industrial products, and hospitality, entertainment, and information services.

Created in 1920 as a telephone operating company in the Caribbean, ITT grew into a unique company on the international business scene—International Telephone & Telegraph—later to be known simply as ITT. In the late 1960s and through the 1970s, ITT acquired more than 250 companies, including Avis Rent-a-Car, Continental Baking Company, Canteen, Rayonier, Sheraton, Hartford Fire Insurance Company, and others. In 1986, in one of the most important business transactions of the decade, ITT, then $24 billion in sales and revenues, exited its foundation business with the sale of 63% of its telecommunications operations into a joint venture with Alcatel Alsthom (CGE of France). Today ITT successfully has become a more focused multinational giant with service and manufacturing operations in over 100 countries around the globe. In addition, since the 1986 sale of the telecommunications business, ITT has rebuilt its sales and revenues to the $25 billion level and the market equity value of ITT has nearly tripled from $5 billion to some $13 billion.

ITT's almost equally balanced acquisition and divestiture program since the 1986 telecommunications sale concentrated the company's businesses on three areas that comprise the foundation of today's announcement.

"The creation of three companies represents a natural progression of successful business growth and the creation of value for ITT shareholders today and into the future," said Rand V. Araskog, ITT's chairman, president, and chief executive.

"Throughout its history, ITT has always prided itself on being a company that is right for the times," Mr. Araskog added.

The three independent companies are: ITT Hartford, the current insurance business of ITT; ITT Industries, Inc., the current automotive, defense, and electronics and fluid technology businesses of ITT; and the new ITT Corporation, made up of ITT Sheraton Corporation, ITT's interest in CIGA, Caesars World Inc., ITT's interest in Madison Square Garden, ITT World Directories, Inc., and ITT's interest in ITT Educational Services, Inc.

The distribution plan announced today calls for holders of shares of ITT Common Stock to own one share of Common Stock of each of the three companies for each share of ITT Common Stock owned on the record date.

"After considerable study and detailed analysis, we concluded that our three major businesses would be best positioned as independent, publicly owned companies," Mr. Araskog said. "We firmly believe that this new structure of three separate companies will allow the management of the companies to focus more intensively on their respective businesses and provide the flexibility for each company to grow in a manner best suited for its industry with an expected increase in the availability and decrease in the cost of raising capital," Mr. Araskog said.

"The planned separation will enable the management of each of these businesses to organize their capital structure and design corporate policies and strategies that are based primarily on the business characteristics of the respective companies and to concentrate its financial resources wholly on its own operations. Management will also be able to design incentive compensation programs that relate more directly to its own business characteristics and performance," the chairman said.

"We also believe that as a result of this action, investors will be able to better evaluate the financial performance of each company, each of its businesses and its strategies," Mr. Araskog continued. "We are convinced that this action will increase immediately, and over time, the value of the investment of ITT's shareholders."

"In the last decade our objective was to focus on the creation of three major businesses with leadership positions in their respective industries thereby simplifying and streamlining the corporation. We identified the three business areas we felt had the greatest growth potential and dedicated significant financial resources to them. Today all three of them are financially strong, they are led by innovative and talented management, they have highly skilled and well motivated work forces, and they offer superior quality products and services," Mr. Araskog concluded.

Donald R. Frahm, who is currently chairman and chief executive of ITT Hartford Group, Inc., will become chairman and chief executive officer of ITT Hartford.

D. Travis Engen, who is currently an ITT executive vice president, will become chairman, president, and chief executive of ITT Industries.

Rand V. Araskog, currently chairman, president and chief executive of ITT will become chairman and chief executive of the new ITT Corporation.

The distribution is expected to have little impact on the capital structure of ITT Hartford. The non-ITT Hartford debt will be allocated to ITT Industries and the new ITT Corporation in a manner such that their respective balance sheets will be comparable with their major competitors in their respective industries.

ITT HARTFORD ITT Hartford, founded in 1810 as Hartford Fire Insurance Company, is one of the nation's oldest and most successful multi-line insurance companies with over $82 billion in assets as of March 1995. ITT Hartford generated revenues of $11.1 billion and operating income of $852 million in 1994. The company, with a history steeped in service that has been forged from epochal disasters from the Great Chicago fire to Hurricane Andrew, employs more than 20,000 people and has a presence that reaches around the world.

ITT Hartford's property and casualty operation, headed by Ramani Ayer, is the eighth largest in the U.S. marketplace in terms of written premiums and outperformed the industry in 1994 by growing faster than the industry average. ITT Hartford's life insurance company, headed by Lon Smith and ranked 12th in terms of assets, is the fastest growing life insurer in the United States. The company's growth has been fueled by strong operating profitability and earnings diversity, strategic acquisitions, and joint ventures.

In recent years, ITT Hartford has aggressively pursued international growth opportunities. Much of its international business is written through subsidiaries in Europe, the largest being ITT London and Edinburgh in the United Kingdom and ITT Zwolsche Algemeene in the Netherlands. Earlier this year the company acquired ITT Ercos de Seguros y Reaseguros, a Spanish property/casualty, life and pension provider.

ITT Hartford is expected to sustain its success in 1995 and beyond by continuing its product and distribution flexibility in all its market segments.

ITT INDUSTRIES ITT Industries, comprised of ITT Automotive, ITT Defense & Electronics and ITT Fluid Technology, designs and manufactures a wide range of industrial products. ITT Industries generated 1994 sales totaling $7.6 billion and had an operating income of $418 million.

ITT Automotive, headed by Timothy Leuliette, is one of the largest independent suppliers of systems and components to vehicle manufacturers worldwide. Through operations located in Europe, North America, and South America and joint ventures and licensees in Asia, ITT Automotive designs, engineers, and manufactures a broad range of automotive systems: and components under two major worldwide product groupings: Brake and Chassis Systems and Body and Electrical Systems.

The Brake and Chassis Systems group is the leading global supplier of four-wheel anti-lock brake ("ABS") and traction control ("TCS") systems, chassis systems, foundation brake components, fluid handling products, and Koni shock absorbers.

The Body and Electrical Systems group produces automotive products such as door and window assemblies, wiper module assemblies, seat systems, air management systems, switches, and fractional horsepower DC motors.

The principal customers for products of ITT Automotive are the top vehicle manufacturers worldwide.

ITT Automotive companies have approximately 35,000 employees in 76 facilities located in 18 countries.

ITT Defense & Electronics companies develop, manufacture, and support high-technology electronic systems and components for defense and commercial markets on a worldwide basis, with operations in North America, Europe, and Asia. Defense market products include tactical communications equipment, electronic warfare systems, night vision devices, radar, space payloads, and operations and management services. Commercial products include interconnect products (such as connectors, switches, and cable assemblies) and night vision devices.

ITT Defense & Electronics, headed by Louis Giuliano, sells its products to a wide variety of governmental and nongovernmental entities located throughout the world.

ITT Defense & Electronics companies have approximately 14,700 employees in 74 facilities in 15 countries.

Bertil Nilsson is president of ITT Fluid Technology, a worldwide enterprise engaged in the design, development, production, and sale of systems and services used to move, handle, transfer, control, and contain fluids of all kinds. Operating in more than 100 countries, ITT Fluid Technology is a leading supplier of pumps, valves, heat exchangers, mixers, instruments, and controls for the management of fluids.

ITT Fluid Technology companies have approximately 8,000 employees in 45 facilities located around the world.

"NEW" ITT CORPORATION This new hospitality, entertainment, and information services giant represents several of the world's leading brand names and will provide services to over 100 million people. Robert A. Bowman, currently executive vice president and chief financial officer of ITT, will become president and chief operating officer of the new ITT. Ann N. Reese, currently senior vice president and treasurer, will become chief financial officer.

New ITT combines the world's largest hotel and gaming company with a premier entertainment company and information services businesses to create a dynamic and rapidly growing enterprise. New ITT is expected to generate revenues in excess of $6.5 billion and operating income before interest, taxes, depreciation, and amortization ("EBITDA") of $875 million in 1995, up 35% compared with 1994 on a pro forma basis.

The addition of the world's most recognized gaming company was completed in January 1995 with the acquisition of Caesar's World Inc. (CWI). In March 1995, the world's most famous sports arena and basketball and hockey franchises were added to new ITT through its investment in Madison Square Garden (MSG). Furthermore, CIGA and other key hotel acquisitions were completed in 1994, enhancing new ITT's geographic balance along with its image and profile. These acquisitions have helped to create a formidable hotel, gaming, and entertainment corporation that is a leader in its served markets.

Through the ITT Sheraton brand name, new ITT is represented in most major markets of the world. ITT Sheraton, which has been a wholly owned subsidiary of ITT since 1968, is a worldwide hospitality network of approximately 420 owned, leased, managed, and franchised properties including hotels, casinos, and inns in over 60 countries. John Kapioltas is chairman and chief executive of ITT Sheraton and Daniel Weadock is president and chief operating officer. Gaming operations are marketed under the Caesar's World and ITT Sheraton brand names and are represented in Las Vegas, Atlantic City, Lake Tahoe, and

Tunica County in the United States; Lima in Peru; Halifax and Windsor in Canada; and in Townesville, Australia.

The acquisition of CWI greatly enhanced new ITT's profile in the rapidly growing gaming business. Henry Gluck is chairman and chief executive officer and Peter Boynton is president and chief operating officer of Caesars World. CWI's flagship property is the renowned Caesars Palace in Las Vegas, Nevada and it also owns and operates Caesar's Atlantic City in Atlantic City, New Jersey and Caesar's Tahoe in Stateline, Nevada, both leaders in their served markets. CWI also owns one-third of a management company that operates Casinos Windsor, which was opened in May 1994 in Windsor, Ontario and operates four non-gaming resorts in Pennsylvania's Pocono mountains.

The MSG investment, which was made through a partnership with a subsidiary of Cablevision Systems Corporation, includes the famed Madison Square Garden arena, the paramount special events theater, the New York Knickerbockers and New York Rangers basketball and hockey franchises as well as the Madison Square Garden Network. David Checketts is president of Madison Square Garden.

ITT World Directories, headed by Gerald Crotty, is the world's largest producer of telephone directories outside the United States. ITT World Directories is 20% owned by Bell South Corporation.

ITT Educational Services, operator of 54 ITT Technical Institutes serving 20,000 students in 25 states and run by Rene Champagne, chairman, completes the make-up of the new ITT Corporation. The new ITT will employ approximately 30,000 people.

As part of the separation plan, ITT plans to call all the outstanding shares of ITT Cumulative Preferred Stock, $2.25 Convertible Series N for redemption prior to the record date for the distribution. It is anticipated that holders of the Series N will convert their shares into ITT Common Stock prior to the redemption date in order to participate in the distribution.

The Board of Directors approved ITT's commencement of a tender offer for the outstanding ITT debt in the near future. The Board also approved the temporary suspension of the dividend on common shares for 1995. This will not affect the already Board-approved dividend payment that will be made on the ITT common stock on July 1, 1995. Dividend payments will be resumed in 1996 and the combined dividends are expected to exceed ITT's current dividend by about 10%.

The distribution is subject to the final determination of the record and distribution dates by the Board, following completion of review of filings to be made with the Securities and Exchange Commission and the securing of other necessary approvals. ITT management expects that the record date for the distribution will be in mid-December, 1995. The distribution is anticipated to be completed prior to the end of the year, subject to the receipt of certain favorable tax rulings from the Internal Revenue Service as to the federal income tax consequences of the distribution, the necessary consents of any governmental or regulatory bodies having been obtained, and certain other conditions. Also, the company intends to seek shareholder approval of the distribution at a special meeting of shareholders to be held in September or October of this year.

# CHAPTER 3 Internal Strengths and Weaknesses

All businesses have corporate competencies and resources that distinguish them from their competitors. These competencies and resources are usually identified in terms of a company's strengths and weaknesses. Deciding upon what a company "should do" can only be achieved after assessing the strengths and weaknesses to determine what the company "can do." Strengths support windows of opportunities whereas weaknesses create limitations. Figure 3.1 shows how internal analysis fits into the strategic planning process.

## Understanding Strengths and Weaknesses

Strengths and weaknesses can be identified at all levels of management. Senior management may have a clearer picture of the overall company's position in relation to the external environment, whereas middle management may have a better grasp of the internal strengths and weaknesses. Unfortunately, most managers do not think in terms of strengths and weaknesses and, as a result, worry more about what they should do rather than what they can do.

Although all organizations have strengths and weaknesses, no organization is equally strong in all areas. Procter and Gamble, Budweiser, Coke, and Pepsi are all known for their advertising and marketing. Computer firms are known for technical strengths, whereas General Electric has long been regarded as the training ground for manufacturing executives. Large firms have vast resources with strong technical competency, but react slowly when change is needed. Small firms can react quickly but have limited strengths.

The strengths and weaknesses can change over time and must therefore be closely monitored. In the 1960s IBM's strength was in the service sector, whereas in the 1970s and 1980s, its strength was shifted to the marketing sector. Situations 3.1 and 3.2 illustrate how environmental changes can cause shifts in strengths and weaknesses.

## Situation 3.1: Peco Control Systems*

Between 1960 and 1978, Peco Control Systems (PCS) maintained a strong market

* Disguised name

**Figure 3.1** The Traditional Strategic Planning Model.

share for the control systems used in electric and nuclear power plants. PCS's strength was in the quality of its products and its reputation for customer service.

PCS's technical community was approximately 10% advanced degreed engineers, 20% engineers from four-year institutions, and 70% with associate degrees from two-year technical and vocational institutions. This unusual mixture of educational backgrounds allowed PCS to keep its costs low. Emphasis was on production support rather than new product development.

By 1978, the marketplace was demanding specialty control systems rather than off-the-shelf packages. PCS realized the need to upgrade its technical community. The new president of PCS, realizing that a change was necessary, instructed the human-resources department to hire only engineers with a four-year degree and grade point averages above 3.4. Advanced degreed engineers were also hired.

By 1985, PCS maintained internal strengths in both engineering know-how and quality manufacturing. The overhead rates increased dramatically because of the employment of the higher-salaried workers. PCS's market share dropped significantly by 1985 but increased by 1990 as new process control systems were being developed and available for release.

Had PCS tried to survive simply based upon the internal strength of the quality of its products, it is questionable if the company would still be in existence today.

# Situation 3.2: The Aerospace Dilemma

The firms within the aerospace industry can be subdividing into four categories: R&D, production, R&D and production, and prime contractors. Companies that opted to be production oriented built plants in low-cost areas and kept the overhead relatively low by not hiring high-salaried R&D personnel. One firm that employed over 2,000 people in one plant had only 14 Ph.Ds.

Firms with emphasis on production wanted the R&D firms to design the product. During competitive bidding for production contracts, the production-oriented firms would almost always come in with a low bid since much of the R&D cost did *not* have to be recovered.

By the early 1970s the government changed the evaluation system for proposals. Points were now awarded for various portions of the proposal. Previous knowledge of the system and R&D know-how received significant points. Now, one could be the low bidder but *not* receive the contract because of insufficient points.

What was previously a strength for production-oriented firms had deteriorated into a weakness. The production-orientated firms now had to catch up to the rest of the industry in a short period of time in order to continue receiving contracts. The internal strengths and weaknesses were now changing.

There is a common belief that one can determine a competitor's strategy by how it deploys its resources. The president of a medium-size company commented that he tries to get a look at his competitors' organizational charts every three months or so to see how the resources are being realigned. In one situation, he found that a competitor had added a plastics department to the machine shop that was historically working only with metals. This simple fact provided the president with invaluable information about one of his competitors. Simply stated, the president addressed the competitor as trying to develop a *future* competitive strength in the plastics area.

Determining internal strengths and weaknesses is *not* merely an analytical skill where one can read reports or financial statements and immediately draw conclusions. Good managers must have a keen sense for analyzing the business environment for those less-concrete clues that a potential problem may exist. The macroenvironment of your firm and those of your major competitors should be analyzed for clues (see Figure 3.2). The decisions made by your competitors may not show up in the competitor's financial statements or reports for months and by that time your competitive options to improve internal strengths may be limited. The most crucial managerial skills are perceptual skills that identify problems early enough that corrective action can be taken well before the information is made available through advanced management information systems.

Management must routinely perform an internal analysis of the firm's strengths and weaknesses and then determine the most probable *future* strengths and weaknesses. It is the future strengths and weaknesses that may well be the key

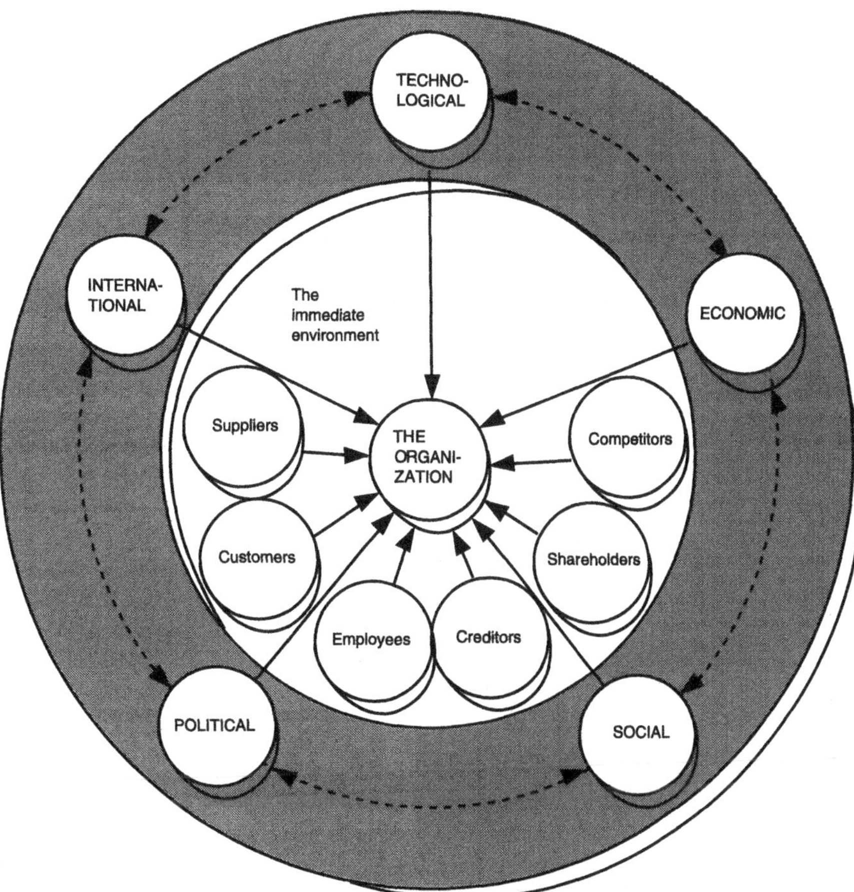


**Figure 3.2** The Macroenvironment of Business. (*Source*: Grover Starling, *The Changing Environment of Business*, International Thomson Publishing, 4th Edition 1996, p 19).

to which strategic option is best. If a gap exists between desired objectives and reality, then management must plan for improving strengths. As an example, in 1994 and 1995 severe cutbacks in government programs (especially DoD) played havoc with government contractors. Companies that relied heavily upon government contracts now had to refocus their efforts to the commercial sector. Government contractors usually employ ex-military and retired government workers in key management positions. This is viewed as a strength when going after government work but may quickly become a weakness when emphasis is placed upon the commercial sector.

For companies to be successful in the long run, they must develop a *sustained* competitive advantage. A sustained competitive advantage is a long-term successful strategy that cannot easily be duplicated by the competition. Time and patience is required to develop a long-term, sustained competitive advantage.

# Classification of Tangible Resources

The strengths and weaknesses of a firm can be described in the terms of its resources. The most common classification for tangible resources is:

- equipment
- facilities
- manpower
- materials
- money
- information/technology

Unfortunately this crude type of classification does not readily lend itself to an accurate determination of internal strengths and weaknesses. A more useful classification would be human resources, nonhuman resources, organizational resources, and financial resources.

## HUMAN RESOURCES

Human resources are the knowledge, skills, capabilities, and talent of the firm's employees. This includes the board of directors, managers at all levels, and employees as a whole. The board of directors provides the company with considerable experience, political astuteness, and connections, and possibly sources of borrowing power. The board of directors is primarily responsible for selecting the CEO and representing the best interest of the diverse stakeholders as a whole.

Top management is responsible for developing the strategic mission and making sure that the strategic mission satisfies the shareholders. All too often, CEOs have singular strengths in one area of business such as marketing, finance, technology, or production. New CEOs often restructure the firm during their first year in office. This could cause a firm to lose some of its internal strengths. Executives are often brought in from outside the firm so as to avoid "inbreeding" and bring to the table new ideas and possibly an entrepreneurial spirit.

The biggest asset of senior management is its decision-making ability, especially during strategic planning. Unfortunately, all too often senior management will delegate strategic planning (and the accompanying decision-making process) to staff personnel. This results in no effective strategic-planning process within the organization.

According to Steiner (1979, p. 294), there are important pitfalls that should be avoided by senior management (see Table 3.1). It should be clear that proper support of senior management is critical and that the support must be visible to all. Invisible or partial support can become a serious weakness not easily overcome.

Another important role of a senior management is to define clearly its own managerial values and the firm's social responsibility (see Figure 3.1). A change in senior management could change the organization's managerial values and social responsibility overnight. An example of this was during the early 1990s when Salomon Brothers was accused of unethical behavior in the way it purchased and sold government bonds. Salomon Brothers hired the well-respected investor Warren Buffett to restore the firm's image.

Lower and middle management are responsible for developing and maintaining the "core" technical competencies of the firm. Every organization maintains a distinct collection of human resources. Middle management must develop

**Table 3.1 The Ten Most Important Pitfalls to Be Avoided as Rated by Respondents (N = 159).**

| Description |
|---|
| 1. Top management's assumption that it can delegate the planning function to a planner. |
| 2. Top management becomes so engrossed in current problems that it spends insufficient time on long-range planning, and the process becomes discredited among other managers and staff. |
| 3. Failure to develop company goals suitable as a basis for formulating long-range plans. |
| 4. Failure to assume the necessary involvement in the planning process of major line personnel. |
| 5. Failing to use plans as standards for measuring managerial performance. |
| 6. Failure to create a climate in the company that is congenial and not resistant to planning. |
| 7. Assuming that corporate comprehensive planning is something separate from the entire management process. |
| 8. Injecting so much formality into the system that it lacks flexibility, looseness, and simplicity, and restrains creativity. |
| 9. Failure of top management to review with departmental and divisional heads the long-range plans that they have developed. |
| 10. Top management's consistently rejecting the formal planning mechanism by making intuitive decisions that conflict with the formal plans. |

*Source*: Steiner, G. A. *Strategic Planning: What Every Manager Must Know* (New York: Free Press; 1979).

some type of cohesive organization such that synergistic effects will follow. It is the synergistic effect that produces the core competencies that lead to sustained competitive advantages.

## NONHUMAN RESOURCES

Nonhuman resources are physical resources that distinguish one organization from another. Boeing and IBM both have sustained competitive advantages but have different physical resources. Physical resources include plant and equipment, distribution networks, proximity of supplies, availability of a raw material, land, and labor.

Companies with superior nonhuman resources may not have a sustained competitive advantage without having superior human resources. Likewise, a company with strong human resources may not be able to take advantage of windows of opportunities without having strong physical resources. An Ohio-based company had a [illegible] year history of sustained competitive advantage in R&D.

Unfortunately, the megaprofits were in production, and in order to acquire physical production resources, the organization diluted some of its technical resources. The firm learned a hard lesson in that the management of human resources is not the same as the management of nonhuman resources.

Firms that endeavor to develop superior manufacturing are faced with two critical issues. First, how reliable are the suppliers? Do the suppliers maintain quality standards? Are the suppliers cost effective? The second concern, and perhaps the more serious of the two, is the ability to cut costs quickly and efficiently to remain competitive. This usually leads to some form of vertical integration.

### ORGANIZATIONAL RESOURCES

Organizational resources is the glue that holds all of the other resources together. Organizational resources include the organizational structure, the formal (and sometimes informal) reporting structure, the planning system, the scheduling system, the control system, and the supporting policies and procedures. Decentralization can create havoc in large firms where each strategic business unit (SBU), functional unit, and operating division can have their own policies, procedures, rules, and guidelines.

### FINANCIAL RESOURCES

Financial resources are the firm's borrowing capability, credit lines, credit rating, ability to generate cash, and relationship with investment bankers. Companies with quality credit ratings can borrow money at a lower rate than companies with nonquality ratings. Companies must maintain a proper balance between equity and credit markets when raising funds. A firm with strong, continuous cash flow may be able to fund growth out of cash flow rather than through borrowing. This is the usual financial-growth strategy for a small firm. The overall risk of maintaining low debt and financing growth through cash flow is that the firm becomes a takeover target.

## Intangible Resources

Human, physical, organizational, and financial resources are regarded as tangible resources. There are also intangible resources that include the organizational culture, reputation, brand name, patents, trademarks, know-how, and relationship with customers and suppliers. Intangible resources do not have the visibility that tangible resources possess, but they can lead to a sustained competitive advantage. When companies develop a "brand name," it is nurtured through advertising and marketing and is often accompanied by a slogan. McDonald's slogan was "What you want is what you get at McDonald's." Wendy's slogan was "Ain't no reason to go anywhere else." Ford's motto was "Quality is job one." Companies with brand name recognition include:

- Gillette: safety razors
- Ford and GM: Lincoln and Cadillac
- Kimberly-Clark: Kleenex
- Microsoft: software
- Intel and Motorola: computer chips
- Mattel: Barbie dolls
- Nike and Reebok: athletic shoes and apparel
- Rubbermaid: Tupperware
- Johnson & Johnson: Tylenol

### SOCIAL RESPONSIBILITY

Social responsibility is also an intangible asset although some consider it both intangible and tangible. Social responsibility is the expectation that the public perceives that a firm will make decisions that are in the best interest of the public as a whole. Social responsibility can include a broad range of topics from environmental protection to consumer safeguards to consumer honesty and employing the disadvantaged. An image of social responsibility can convert a potential disaster into an advantage. Johnson and Johnson earned high marks for social responsibility in the way it handled the two Tylenol tragedies of the 1980s. Nestlé on the other hand, earned low marks for the infant-formula controversy.

## Functional Classification of Resources

Perhaps the most common method for classifying tangible resources (both human and physical) is by functional classification. It is not possible to consider here the depth of the material that would be covered in courses such as marketing or production management. All that is presented here are the most critical internal factors necessary to identify a potential competitive advantage.

Since it is not possible to cover every functional discipline, only the following functions will be discussed:

- R&D factors
- manufacturing factors
- finance and accounting factors
- human-resource management factors
- marketing factors

### R&D FACTORS

Very few companies have sufficient resources to support a large R&D staff. Companies must decide whether their internal strengths will be in offensive or defensive R&D. Offensive R&D requires a firm to maintain a position of market leader with emphasis on a continuous stream of new or improved products. For product lines with short product life cycles, the cost of maintaining such an offensive R&D capability can be exorbitant since the majority of the internal resources may be personnel with advanced degrees.

Another critical problem with pure and applied R&D is that of planning. Market introduction cannot be adequately planned for because one cannot simply prepare a schedule indicating the exact date when a technological breakthrough will appear. Years rather than months are the norm with offensive R&D.

*Defensive R&D*, on the other hand, leads to improvements in materials, design, and manufacturing methods, all of which provide cost advantages through efficiencies. Typical time frames for defensive R&D are weeks or months rather than years, and advanced degrees may not be required. Table 3.2 provides a list of factors that can be used to determine the relative strength or weakness of R&D groups.

Typical R&D budgets are 5–8% of sales for the average company and 8–10% of sales for market leaders. The size of the R&D budget and the type of R&D emphasis is often based upon the marketing strategy. If marketing adopts a "first-to-market" approach, then offensive R&D may very well consume the majority of the R&D budget. If marketing adopts a "me too" or "fast second" approach, the emphasis may be on defensive R&D.

There are several myths involving R&D internal strengths that should be discussed:

- Strength in offensive R&D automatically implies an equal strength in defense in R&D, and vice versa.
- Offensive R&D personnel and defensive R&D personnel can switch positions continuously and still remain highly effective.
- Laying off R&D personnel during a recession is not a problem because the same quality resources can always be rehired later.
- Being the market leader technically implies that a firm always remain as the market leader.
- Making a technological breakthrough is the end of the journey (i.e. the final goal).

Each of these is a myth that generates complacency rather than an ongoing quest for a sustained competitive advantage.

The internal strengths of an R&D group are often based upon two factors:

1. knowing what projects to work on
2. the speed at which technology can be developed

If a company is not "technically astute," the performance gap between what the competitors can achieve and what your firm is doing can be significant enough that previous sustained competitive advantages are lost. This is shown in Figure 3.3.

Since a great deal of time may be required to develop a new product, the ability of the firm to perform *technology forecasting* is critical. The most commonly used techniques for technology forecasting are:

- trend analysis
- expert opinions
- environmental/competitor monitoring
- alternative scenarios

Most companies rely upon some combination of these principles.

Technological innovation takes place in stages, often referred to as life-cycle stages or phases. The benefit of this approach is that an organization can develop some degree of standardization for what should take place in each stage as well as establishing go/no-go decision points. Every company develops its own series of phases or stages. Manufacturing activities can have different stages from engineering or R&D.

**Table 3.2 Internal Factors: R&D.**

1. basic/applied research capability of the firm
2. ability to maintain state-of-the-art knowledge
3. marketing intelligence network
4. manufacturing support for R&D
5. well-equipped laboratories and testing facilities
6. technology forecasting ability
7. managers who can work with and motivate R&D personnel
8. ability to recruit talented specialists
9. creation of an environment that fosters innovation and creativity (and possibly the "freedom" to create)
10. technical managers who also understand the financial aspects of technical decisions
11. proprietary technical knowledge (i.e., patents)
12. rapid reaction capability
13. teamwork
14. compliance with specifications
15. ability to optimize cost with performance
16. offensive R&D capability
    a. previous history
    b. product life cycle
    c. product development time
17. defensive R&D capability
    a. ability to lower manufacturing costs efficiency
    b. low cost product improvements
    [illegible]

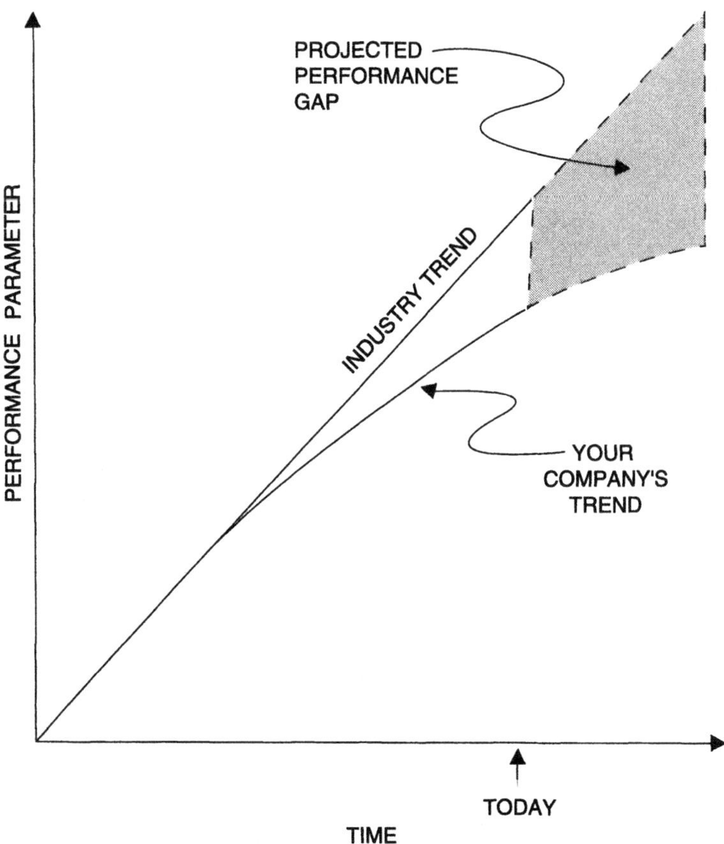


**Figure 3.3**
Projecting
Performance.
(*Source*: Grover Starling, *The Changing Environment of Business*, International Thomson Publishing, 4th Edition 1996, p 91).

The most typical stages for technical innovation are as follows:

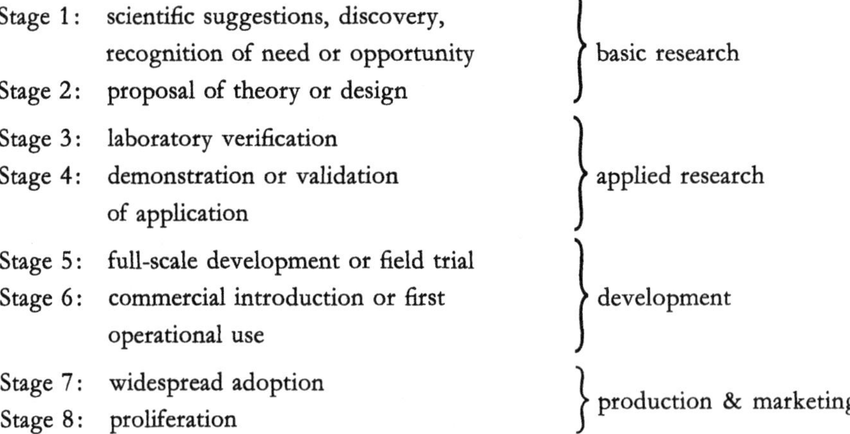

| | | |
|---|---|---|
| Stage 1: | scientific suggestions, discovery, recognition of need or opportunity | basic research |
| Stage 2: | proposal of theory or design | |
| Stage 3: | laboratory verification | applied research |
| Stage 4: | demonstration or validation of application | |
| Stage 5: | full-scale development or field trial | development |
| Stage 6: | commercial introduction or first operational use | |
| Stage 7: | widespread adoption | production & marketing |
| Stage 8: | proliferation | |

Figure 3.4 shows the complexities of trying to maintain a sustained competitive advantage through R&D. As a project goes through basic research, applied

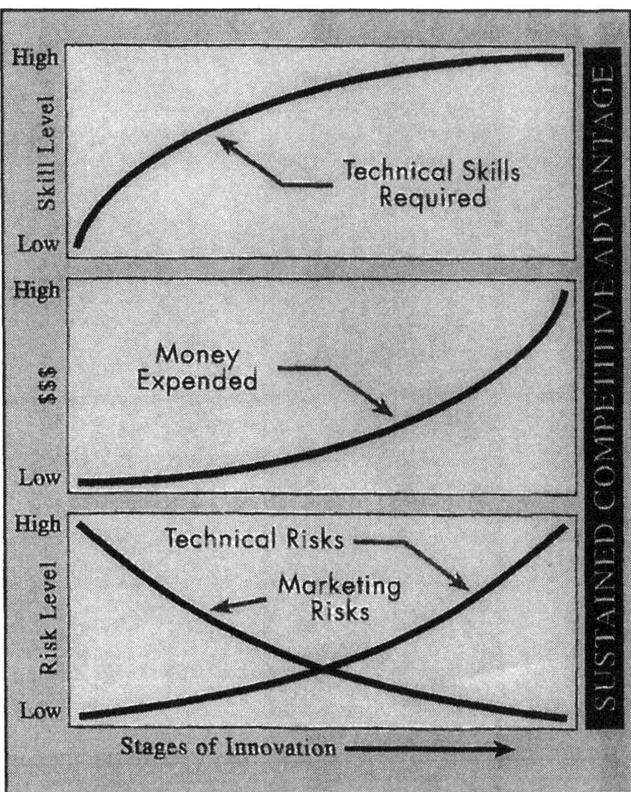


**Figure 3.4** R&D Efforts for a Sustained Competitive Advantage.

research, and development, the technical risks decrease whereas the marketing risks increase. The money committed by the firm increases dramatically.

The technical skills required increase as the project goes from basic research through to development. Although some people may argue this increase in skill levels, the fact remains that what can be developed on a small laboratory bench may never be able to be mass-produced or, even if it can be mass-produced, the quality may have to be degraded. Also, it is in development where one finally obtains hard numbers as to whether the product can be produced at a competitive price.

## MANUFACTURING FACTORS

For years, America's major competitive weapon was its manufacturing capability. Now, the competitive advantage seems to be in Europe, Asia, and Southeast Asia. American plants are becoming obsolete. Capital-improvement budgets are being reduced because of short-term stockholder pressure for profits.

Production facilities require continuous maintenance. The Oil Industry of Venezuela estimated that without continuous maintenance, its refineries would suffer a 20% per year production capacity loss. Its refineries are capable of producing 2.5 million barrels of oil per day even though its OPEC production limit is

**Table 3.3 Internal Factors: Manufacturing.**

1. efficiency of the operation
2. proximity to channels of distribution
3. proximity to other strategic corporate offices
4. raw material availability and cost
5. maintenance capability
6. down time
7. vertical integration abilities
8. flexibility in operations should the need arise (i.e., changeover to other products)
9. inventory-control system
10. quality-assurance system
11. relationship with marketing and R&D
12. magnitude of the capital budgets
13. age of the equipment
14. turnover of personnel
15. relationship with unions
16. precision machinery availability
17. ability to perform trade-offs and lower costs
18. learning-curve applications
19. subsystems integration
20. tight scheduling

1.65 million barrels per day. During the Gulf War, the industry was allowed to increase its production to maximum capacity. Because of its continuous maintenance, the maximum capacity was reached in two weeks.

American workers and their union representatives want job security whereas foreign companies are emphasizing robotics, quality, and efficiency in operations. Fewer plants than ever before are being run at full capacity. Older plants are being replaced by smaller plants that are more efficient and less costly to operate. A classical example is the growth of mini-mills in the steel industry.

The shortening of the product life cycle is also playing havoc with designing the factory of the future. Competition is increasing and buyers are less likely to give suppliers long-term production contracts. Production profits are being squeezed.

More and more companies are relocating manufacturing plants to locations that provide cheaper labor and tax incentives. United Airlines' decision to build a $1.6 billion maintenance facility in Indianapolis rather than at its massive hub at Denver International Airport is a prime example.

Table 3.3 shows the manufacturing internal factors to be considered in developing a sustained competitive advantage. The cost involved to support internal strengths in manufacturing is substantially greater than any other functional area. The overhead rates for manufacturing divisions are almost always greater than overhead rates in the nonmanufacturing divisions.

## FINANCE AND ACCOUNTING FACTORS

Strategies require cash, which in turn requires strengths in accounting and finance. Table 3.4 lists several of the critical factors. Internal strengths in the accounting and finance area can lead to strong competitive positions as well as more strategic flexibility than that of the competition. Financial flexibility allows for more than one strategic option to be undertaken at the same time. More new products can be developed, obsolete plants can be updated, and large-scale vertical integration can be undertaken.

Financial flexibility is based upon numbers but only from a short-term prospective. Accounting methods for tax purposes, depreciation, and goodwill may provide a false sense of short-term security. The book value of the company may be significantly out of date with reality.

Analytically, the analysis of the financial strengths and weaknesses can lead to long-term disaster. During the 1980s, leveraged buyouts were in vogue. Companies borrowed billions of dollars based upon short-term cash flows only to discover that 30% of the companies that financed leveraged buyouts using "junk bonds" during the 1980s went belly-up within the first 10 years.

**Table 3.4 Internal Factors: Finance and Accounting.**

1. dividend policy
2. cash flow (present and future projections)
3. returns on assets
4. debt to equity ratio
5. corporate stock activity
6. corporate credit rating (equity and capital markets)
7. working capital requirements
8. quality of the information system
9. skills in feasibility studies/cost-benefits analyses
10. investment-management skills
11. consumer financing capability
12. size of customer base
13. turnover of customers
14. cyclical or noncyclical business

Cash flow for strategic options must be balanced with working cash-flow needs. Some companies tie up so much of their cash flow into working capital that their strategic options are severely limited. In this case, assets may have to be sold to develop a strategic plan. A classical example of this is the dismantling of Pan American Airways after they filed for bankruptcy.

Companies with strong credit ratings have access to low-cost borrowing as well as a large line of credit. Companies with cash-flow problems have to pay premiums to borrow and may be regulated by restricted covenants.

Wall Street ultimately determines the value of a firm by giving its blessing to the firm's financial strengths and weaknesses. To appease Wall Street, companies usually pay reasonable dividends as well as provide earnings projections based upon hard numbers. When IBM's CEO stated the funds would be used for acquisitions in order to increase the value of the company, Wall Street apparently approved of this strategy. IBM later acquired Lotus as well as buying back a large percentage of its own stock.

# Human-Resource Management Factors

Human-Resource Management (HRM) is the ability to recruit, train, nurture, and retain critical human-resource skills. Table 3.5 lists several of the factors that are critical for a competitive advantage in human resource management. Not all com-

**Table 3.5 Internal Factors: Human-Resource Management.**

1. corporate image
2. turnover rate of key personnel
3. promotion opportunity (multiple career paths)
4. recruitment ability
5. relationship with unions
6. effectiveness of information systems
7. salary structure
8. opportunities for training/education
9. tuition reimbursement plan
10. health and benefit programs
11. relationship with government/regulatory agencies
12. strength of board of directors
13. quality of management at all levels
14. public relations policies
15. social consciousness

panies have strengths in each of these areas. But those that do, usually have 300–400 applicants for every job opening.

Every year, a so-called wish list appears on the bulletin boards of college seniors indicating the top 20 or so companies that are considered as the best for new college graduates. Perennial members on this list include Texas Instruments, Hewlett-Packard, IBM, General Electric, Walt Disney, MMM, Kodak, and Mead Corporation. These companies possess nearly all the characteristics in Table 3.5.

Companies that do not develop *and adhere* to sound salary and promotion policies soon get trapped into salary disparaties. This can lead to poor morale, internal competition, and loss of key personnel. Some companies view the salary structure as a closely guarded secret and even go so far as to threaten people with termination for discussing salaries. Cleveland Electric's acquisition of Toledo Edison faced a major hurdle when salary disparaties in similar positions became apparent.

Unionization is often viewed as a competitive *disadvantage*. However, unionization does not imply inflexibility and lack of creative ability. The key factor is the company's working relationship with its unions. This becomes a critical issue in acquiring, merging, or spinning off a division.

Perhaps the most important factor during mergers or acquisitions is the human-resources management policies. Continental's acquisition of Eastern Airlines showed the disastrous results when a nonunionized company acquires a unionized company. Burrough's acquisition of Sperry and the merger of Federal Express and Tiger International show what happens when two distinctively different corporate cultures try to come together.

From a human-resources point of view, friendly takeovers are less difficult to deal with than unfriendly takeovers. With an unfriendly takeover, corporate cultures must be merged quickly. The easiest way to do this is to replace key managers in the acquired company. Unless this is done effectively, a company can lose its competitive advantage with human-resource management.

Companies like Philip Morris and Pepsico have learned from past mistakes that when a firm's growth is based upon continuous acquisition, it is often best to allow the existing management to remain. The strategy at Philip Morris is acquisition of *well-established*, *market-leader* companies. Most of all, their acquisitions have been unfriendly but have proven to be successful because the existing cultures were not destroyed.

A sound but strategic management information can also be a competitive strength. Mergers and acquisitions can produce a synergistic effect by combining information systems as well as the normal support functions such as payroll, accounting, procurement, and distribution. Because of the necessity for timely but prudent information, many firms have created the position of chief information officer.

To obtain a sustained competitive advantage in human-resource management requires leadership all the way from the board of directors down to the first-line supervisor. Top management must establish a culture that brings out the best in its managers. Jack Welsh, the CEO of General Electric, views all levels of management as being critical in this regard. Employee satisfaction at General Electric permeates the organization, whereas Paul Kazarian, the CEO for Sunbeam, lost his job in January 1993 by placing an excess amount of pressure and expectations on his managers.

All companies are held together by an organizational structure. The structure can be either an asset or a liability in obtaining HRM strength. Although numerous organizational forms exists, the quality of any structure, no matter how poorly it looks on paper, can be made to work effectively and efficiently through communication, cooperation, and trust. It is the responsibility of managers at all levels to foster this atmosphere of cooperation. Companies like General Electric foster a corporate culture where "what's in the best interest of the business" comes before the best interest of a functional unit.

## MARKETING FACTORS

Perhaps the most difficult internal strength to maintain on a continuous basis is marketing. Vast resources are required together with an uncanny business instinct to predict what the customer *wants* and what the competitors will do. Table 3.6 shows the typical factors that must be considered to maintain a sustained competitive advantage in marketing.

The first critical step is to determine what the customers want and need, and then determine whether it can be produced at a profit. This requires extensive market research, consumer testing, working with R&D in product development, working with manufacturing to determine production costs, and then identifying logistic support. After all this has been accomplished, the advertising

**Table 3.6 Internal Factors: Marketing.**

1. competitive position
2. market share
3. sales forecasting ability
4. price-value analysis
5. quality and ability of the sales force
6. budgets allocated for sales, promotions, advertising, and research
7. size and location of sales offices and warehouses
8. size and location of service facilities
9. turnaround time of service facilities
10. completeness of product lines
11. life-cycle phases of each product
12. degree of forward integration
13. brand loyalty
14. patent protection
15. turnover of key people

and promotion policies can be identified. It is easy to understand why companies find it difficult to maintain a competitive advantage in marketing.

Internal marketing strengths can change rapidly. Factors that cause this rapid change include recessions, demographic changes, shifts in brand loyalty, global competition, changes in technology, and deregulation. Any of these factors can instantaneously cause marketing to shift its approach. As an example, during downturns in the economy, emphasis is placed upon "new and improved" versions of existing products rather than risky new products. In this situation, emphasis is on maintaining market share and sales levels.

During economic growth, companies sometimes take risks by using advertisements and promotions well before the product has been developed. A Fortune 100 company's marketing vice president instructed the director of the R&D labs to improve the quality of their product by 20%, and it had to be done within the next 60 days. The lab director insisted that it would take at least six months to a year, at best. The vice president then commented, "But we've already printed the literature telling the customer that you have done it."

Companies that develop competitive marketing strengths find that their strengths come from different areas. Typical areas for strengths may be in product mix, market share, market segmentation, relative market positioning, and channels of distribution. Firms can compete in any or all of these areas. Marketing must decide whether they prefer high versus low price, high versus low quality, general versus specialized products, more or less promotion and advertising, and wide versus segmented markets. And again, all this can change based upon economic conditions.

Some analysts identify internal strengths and weaknesses in marketing/distribution/logistics rather than just marketing. The reason for this is that some products may require maintenance, service, and support after the sale is made (i.e. purchase of a car). This support usually exists throughout the life cycle of the product and is referred to as logistic support. Typical items included under logistic support, and which can lead to a sustained competitive advantage, include:

- maintenance planning: the process of supplying product maintenance
- manpower and personnel: having skilled resources to support the customers
- support equipment: having the necessary nonhuman resources to calibrate the product and detect quickly the cause of failure.
- technical data: having history of product changes.

Companies like IBM maintained superior competitive advantage during the 1970s and 1980s in computer maintenance and repair. Other companies have since copied the IBM approach.

## ESSAY QUESTIONS

1. Under what conditions can an internal strength become an internal weakness, and vice versa? Give examples.
2. When a company is bought out, key individuals usually leave the firm, thus creating a possible weakness. How does the acquiring firm plan to overcome this weakness?

3. What are the advantages and disadvantages of outside members on a firm's board of directors?
4. Why do some mergers fail?
5. Why is human-resources planning important in maintaining a sustained competitive advantage?
6. Explain the relationship between internal strengths and weakness, and external opportunities and threats.
7. What factors influence the *durability* of a sustained competitive advantage?
8. Discuss how "luck" can impact an organization's ability to maintain a sustained competitive advantage through internal strengths and weaknesses.
9. Is it good or bad for an R&D group to design products that are easy to manufacture? Can this be a barrier to entry or an invitation for competition?
10. Explain how a good material-management system such as just-in-time inventory can lead to a competitive advantage. Can it backfire?

## MULTIPLE-CHOICE QUESTIONS

1. Internal strengths indicate what a company:
   a. should so
   b. can do
   c. cannot do
   d. all of the above
   e. a and b only
2. Companies that possess internal strengths usually possess these strengths in all areas of their business.
   a. true
   b. false
   c. cannot be determined
3. A firm can have its internal strength converted into a weakness in approximately what *minimum* time period.
   a. one day
   b. at least six months
   c. minimum of one year
   d. minimum of five years
   e. none of the above
4. A long-term successful strategy is referred to as:
   a. a sustained internal strength
   b. a sustained external strength
   c. a sustained competitive advantage
   d. all of the above
   e. a and b only
5. All too often, executive have ____________ strengths in ____________ area of the business:
   a. multiple; all
   b. no; all
   c. marginal; each
   d. singular; one
   e. all of the above
6. The biggest asset of senior management is its ____________ skills.
   a. marketing
   b. manufacturing

c. strategic-planning
d. decision-making
e. all of the above

7. Which of the following would be considered as intangible resource?
   a. board of directors
   b. management in general
   c. brand name
   d. customer age group
   e. plant and facilities
8. The selection of which R&D project to work on first is often dependent on the firm's ability to perform
   a. an internal technical audit
   b. technology forecasting
   c. market research
   d. competitive analysis
   e. none of the above
9. The life cycle phase approach to innovation provides the company with ___________ and ___________.
   a. standardization; go/no-go decision points
   b. better scheduling; profit maximization
   c. strategic analysis; greater profitability
   d. more opportunities; at lower cost
   e. none of the above
10. The amount of money at stake in new product development ___________ as we go from pure research to prototype development.
    a. increases
    b. decreases
    c. stays the same
    d. cannot be determined
11. Company strengths and weaknesses can be determined at which level of the organization?
    a. board of directors
    b. senior management
    c. middle management
    d. first line supervision
    e. all of the above
12. The position within a firm most frequently filled from outside the company is:
    a. senior management
    b. middle management
    c. first line supervisor
    d. all of the above
    e. b and c only
13. Small companies tend to finance growth from:
    a. bank borrowing
    b. equity markets (i.e. issue stock)
    c. capital markets (i.e. issue bonds)
    d. cash flow
    e. none of the above
14. Most firms relocate manufacturing plants to take advantage of:
    a. cheaper labor
    b. tax incentive

c. tax abatements
d. shorter channels of distribution
e. all of the above

15. All companies are held together by:
a. organizational structure
b. marketing
c. the board of directors
d. financial ratios
e. none of the above

## CASE STUDY: IBM'S $3.3 Billion Gamble

IBM Chairman and CEO Lou Gerstner was the driving force behind Big Blue's push to buy Lotus and its Notes groupware. IBM offered $3.3 billion for Lotus Development. This indicated a drastic shift in IBM's client-server strategy. It is said that "IBM has fired a warning shot at Microsoft." IBM is serious about dominating the groupware market. This is the same type of warning shot IBM fired at Microsoft with its $500 million investment in Warp, the latest version of OS/2, which has so far failed to make a sizable dent in the Windows market.

In May 1995, IBM launched two new incentives aimed at marketing its OS/2 Warp operating system as an integral part of the corporate client-server environment, as well as aiming to head off Microsoft's dual operating-system strategy, Windows NT and Windows 95.

If this is a successful takeover, it would make IBM a significant player in desktop software. Lotus could help IBM with its faltering OS/2 operating system against Microsoft's Windows 95, and for the server, Windows NT. Although some still support OS/2 and IBM's commitment to it, there are others who believe that OS/2 or the server, regardless of the version, is dead. Some people believe "It has nothing to do with technology; just poor marketing." Some experts think that if IBM is looking to buy Lotus primarily to boost OS/2 rather than to leverage Notes, it is about two years too late.

### IBM's History and Philosophy

IBM was founded in 1914 by Thomas J. Watson, Sr. From the onset Watson wanted to reflect his personal values in his company. Reaffirmed by his son Thomas Watson, Jr. in 1956, the company values were easily understood by all.

1. The individual must be respected.
2. The customer must be given the best possible service.
3. Excellence and superior performance must be pursed.

With these values in mind Thomas J. Watson, Sr. grew IBM into a major corporate power, creating and building new markets for accounting machinery. His son assumed the presidency in 1952 and built on his father's success. By 1989, what were once IBM's strengths, style, size, and history, were then becoming its source of vulnerability. Today, IBM has two fundamental missions: "First, we strive to lead in the creation, development and manufacture of the industry's most advanced information technologies, including computer systems, software, networking systems, storage devices, and microelectronics. Second, we translate these advanced technologies into value for our customers worldwide—through our sales and professional services units in North America, Europe/Middle East/Africa, Asia, and Latin America." From this IBM has established six strategic imperatives, as outlined by Louis V. Gerstner, Jr.:

*1.* exploiting our technology
*2.* increasing our share of the client-server computing market
*3.* establishing leadership in the emerging network-centric computing world
*4.* realigning the way we deliver value to customers
*5.* rapidly expanding our position in key emerging geographic markets
*6.* leveraging our size and scale to achieve cost and market advantages

Today IBM's financial data shows a profit for the first time since restructuring.

## IBM Problem Areas

IBM grew into a giant bureaucratic organization in the 1970s. The company became slow-moving and rigid. The 1980s brought about technologies and market conditions that were changing quickly. Flexibility and rapid response would be crucial. The 1990s calls for open, networked computing, and over the last few years, IBM has struggled with this aspect of computing. IBM's flexibility is limited by its installed technology. There is a bond with the customers and IBM has an obligation not to abandon them.

IBM has a scattered collection of incompatible computer families. Although it is trying to do better, in the past it was fairly difficult to link products within the same family let alone those outside, and, even worse yet, networking with non-IBM products.

Arrogance of success was another problem with IBM. A certain mindset was developed at IBM that blinded it to the needs of the customer and the challenges of competition.

To be successful with future endeavors, IBM needs to adhere to its defined strategic imperatives. It needs to get technology out of the labs and into the marketplace, quickly. It needs to continue efforts in the area of global networking. It needs to establish global solutions through a single, worldwide sales and service organization. It needs to move toward common technology and give customers greater interoperability across systems. It needs to expand market share in client-server computing. Finally, it needs to expand in emerging geographic markets: China, Eastern Europe, Northern Asia, South Africa, and India.

Although IBM returned to profitability in 1994, significant challenges remain. The company must continue to focus on productivity improvements, growth industries and emerging markets, costs, and implementation of its long-term strategies. This is especially true with the Personal Computer Company and desktop software.

If the takeover of Lotus is a success, IBM could control the next wave of computing.

## QUESTIONS

1. Does IBM's strategy appear to have changed from what it was in the 1970s and 1980s?
2. Why did IBM buy Lotus?
3. How can the purchase of Lotus affect external opportunities and threats?
4. How can the purchase of Lotus affect internal strengths and weaknesses?

## CASE STUDY: Microsoft Corporation

Microsoft Corporation was founded as a partnership in 1975 and was incorporated in 1981. Microsoft is currently involved in the development, manufacture, licensing, and support of a wide range of software products, including operating systems for personal computers, office machines and personal information devices, application programs and languages, as well as personal computer books, hardware, and multimedia products.

Microsoft's business strategy emphasizes the development of a broad line of microcomputer software products for business and personal use, marketed through multiple channels of distribution. It's Bill Gates's (Microsoft CEO), systematic, business-driven approach to all this that really sets Microsoft apart. Gates is careful not to let some dazzling new technology seduce him into searching for a business in which to apply it. Instead, he uses his knowledge of technology to help identify those choke points in businesses that could give Microsoft new business opportunities.

At the beginning of the decade Microsoft had no formal research-and-development laboratory and fewer consumer products. Today the advanced technology group numbers 600 people and the consumer products division puts out more than 70 products, ranging from CD-ROM encyclopedias to children's word processors. In 1996, Microsoft's research and development budget exceeded $1 billion.

Microsoft has grown by serving the seemingly limitless supply of new customers for PCs and software. But these markets, while not saturated, are fast becoming replacement markets, with the bulk of Microsoft's best customers upgrading their existing software. This upgrading results in a lower profit margin than new business. With this in mind the company seeks new businesses and markets, or, even better, new ways to collect repeat revenues. Gates's real dream for repeat revenues lies in the on-line network business and ultimately the information highway. If Gates plays his hand right, a powerful commercial on-line service, once armed with the technology and band width to provide interactive video service as well, could be the information highway before the cable companies get beyond the living room. What remains in considerable doubt, however, is Microsoft's ability to keep pace technologically with Gates's commercial ambition. Microsoft has experienced the problem of delivering cranky products, behind schedule and often without many of the capabilities initially promised. The latest such debacle was Windows 95, an important revision of the graphic operating system that most PCs now use. The delay wrecked the plans of computer makers and dealers who had hopes that Windows 95's facelift would stir Christmas home-computer sales. Building the software underpinnings for something as vast as the information highway is a more daunting task than the company had faced before.

Somehow, Microsoft has been able to grow and transform itself without the boardroom circuses that hobble other high-profile, high-tech companies. In fact, during its 20-year history, the only thing close to a black eye in governance has been Gates's recurring problems in finding and keeping a company president. In 1982, Gates hired his first president, Jim Towne, then fired him in nine months. Twenty-year IBM veteran Mike Hallman lasted but two years before checking out in 1992. Neither one was passionate enough about PC software to suit Gates. Only Jon Shirley, a former Tandy Corp. executive, worked out. Shirley lasted just seven years before retiring comfortably in 1990 at the age of 52. He remains one of the strongest voices on the board of directors. Gates solved his presidency dilemma by not hiring another president. Instead, he asked his three top executives to join him in what is known around Microsoft as BOOP—Bill and the Office of the President. Even longtime rivals like Steve Jobs, the founder of Apple Computer and now CEO of Next Computer Inc., a competing operating system company, expressed grudging admiration for Gates's managerial acumen: "Bill has done a great job of cloning himself as the company has grown. Now there are all these aggressive 'Little Bills' running the various groups and divisions, and they keep coming at you, just like the Japanese." While they all share Gates's competitiveness and intellect, they aren't merely "Little Bills." They are the team.

## Porter Model

| | | |
|---|---|---|
| Buyer: | Weak | *Industry:* IBM has contracted to pay Microsoft for every computer sold whether MS DOS is loaded or not.<br>*Consumer:* Many consumers. High demand for Windows and Windows compatible software. |
| Supplier: | Weak | Many channels for supplies. Basic product itself is supplied internally by research and development department. The company believes internal development enables them to maintain closer technological control over the products. |
| **Barriers** | | |
| Entry: | High | Capital requirements<br>Access to distribution channels<br>Development of new technology |
| Exit: | Low | Emotional barriers, management fear or pride, corporate image |
| Substitute Products: | Strong | Although Microsoft's agreement with IBM would suggest no threat by substitution (Microsoft is paid by the computer whether MS DOS is loaded or not), the threat of a substitute brought on by new technology is strong. There is also the threat of unlicensed copying. |
| Competition: | Strong | The microcomputer market is intensely competitive and subject to rapid change. The company's competitors include many independent software vendors such as Lotus, Oracle, and Novell. |
| Strengths: | | Strong leadership. Bill Gates and his management style<br>Broad focus in product offering<br>Microsoft name<br>Product reputation |
| Weakness: | | Reputation for delays in release of products |
| Opportunities: | | New technology<br>Commercial on-line service |
| Threats: | | Antitrust allegations<br>Rapid technology change<br>Market saturation<br>Long-term investment cycle |

## Issues and Risks

The Company's 1994 annual report includes discussions of its long-term growth outlook. The following issues and risks, among others, should also be considered in evaluating its outlook.

- *rapid technological change*—The personal computer software industry is characterized by rapid technological change and uncertainty as to the widespread acceptance of new products.
- *long-term investment cycle*—Developing, manufacturing, and licensing software is expensive and the investment in product development often involves a long payback cycle. The Company began investing in the principal products that are significant to its current revenues in the early 1980s. The Company's plans for 1995 include significant investments in software research and development and related opportunities from which significant revenues are not anticipated for a number of years.
- *product ship schedules*—Delays in the release of the new products can cause operational inefficiencies that impact manufacturing capabilities, distribution logistics, and telephone support staffing.
- *Microsoft Office*—Revenues for Microsoft Office may increase as a percentage of total revenues in 1995. The price of Microsoft Office is less than the sum of the prices for the individual application programs included in this product when such programs are sold separately.
- *prices*—Future prices the Company is able to obtain for its products may decrease from historical levels depending upon market or other cost factors.
- *saturation*—Products upgrades, enabling users to upgrade from earlier versions of the Company's products or from competitors' products, have lower prices than new products. As the desktop PC software market becomes saturated, the sales mix shifts from standard products to upgrade products. This trend is expected to continue in 1995.
- *introductory pricing*—The Company has offered certain new products at low introductory prices. This practice may continue with other new product offerings.
- *channel mix*—Average revenue per license is lower from OEM licenses than from retail versions, reflecting the relatively lower direct costs of operations in the OEM channel. An increasingly higher percentage of revenues was achieved through the OEM channel during 1993 and 1994.
- *volume discounts*—In 1994, unit sales increased under Microsoft Select, a large account program designed to permit large organizations to license Microsoft products. Average revenue per copy from select license programs is lower than average per copy from retail versions shipped through the finished goods channels.
- *foreign exchange*—A large percentage of the Company's sales are transacted in local currencies. As a result, the company's revenues are subject to foreign exchange rate fluctuations.
- *Cost of revenues*—Although cost of revenues as a percentage of net revenues was relatively consistent in 1993 and 1994, it varies with channel mix and product mix within channels. Changes in channel and product mix, as well as in the cost of product components, may affect cost of revenues as percentage of net revenues in 1995.
- *sales and marketing and support investments*—The Company's plans for 1995 include continued investments in its sales and marketing and support groups.

Competitors may be able to enter the market without making investments of such magnitude.

- *accounting standards*—Accounting standards promulgated by the Financial Accounting Standards Board change periodically. Changes in such standards, including currently proposed changes in the account for employee stock option plans, may have a negative impact on the Company's future reported earnings.
- *unlicensed copying*—Unlicensed copying of software represents a loss of revenues to the Company. The Company is actively educating consumers and lawmakers on this issue. However, there can be no assurance that continued efforts will affect revenues positively.
- *growth rates*—Management believes the Company's recent revenue growth rates are not sustainable. Operating expenses as a percentage of revenues may increase in 1995 because of the above factors, among others.

## QUESTIONS

1. What are the internal strengths and weaknesses of Microsoft?
2. What role does Bill Gates play in developing the corporate culture?
3. Is the corporate culture strong or weak? Explain your answer.
4. Can a corporate culture be viewed as an internal strength or weakness?
5. Formulate an opinion of what might happen if Bill Gates decided to leave Microsoft.
6. If Bill Gates left Microsoft and you became the CEO, what changes would you consider making? Which functional areas would you change, if any?

# CASE STUDY: American Greetings Corporation

## History

Jacob Sapirstein, an immigrant from Poland, began a business in 1906 selling postcards from the back of a horse-drawn wagon. The business flourished, forcing Sapirstein to expand the business from the house to the garage. This first expansion was in 1917. In 1918 when Sapirstein became ill, his eldest son Irving, then 9, took over the business until his father's health improved. This encouraged the promotion of Irving to become a partner in the business.

In 1932, in response to inferior products, Irving convinced his father to print his own cards. This was achieved with the help of sons Irving, Morris, and Harry, and in 1938 the company known as the Sapirstein Greeting Card Company became American Greetings Publishers. In 1952 the company offered stock to the public totalling 200,000 shares at $12 per share. Every year produced record revenues making American Greetings the largest publicly owned creator, manufacturer, and distributor of greeting cards in the world. This multinational corporation distributes greeting cards and related products in more than 70 countries.

While 66% of its core business is greeting cards, the first of the American Greetings characters was introduced in 1967 with the launch of Holly Hobbie. Consumer response was overwhelming. Other characters have since been created such as

Ziggy, which was lost to Hallmark in 1994 due to a wage dispute, Strawberry Shortcake, and Birthday Bear. The last major product introduced to the public was in 1992 when American Greetings launched CreataCard.

## Major Competition

The greeting-card industry is a textbook oligopoly, with three players controlling 85% of the market. Estimates of what the industry looks like from a market-share perspective can be seen in Figure CS3.1.

## Operating Performance

For the fiscal year ending February 28, 1995, American Greetings reported a net profit of $149 million. Strong sales of the company's core products of everyday, seasonal, and personalized greeting cards resulted in a $99 million or 5.6% growth in sales to $1,869 million. Higher selling prices and a product mix more heavily weighted with lower-cost card products attributed to the company's gross margin improvement to 67.5%. This added $39.0 million to the company's gross profit. Actual gross profits grew $94.9 million to $1,192.8 million. Operating expenses increased by $75.8 million to $958.3 million as higher amortization of deferred costs related to agreements with certain retail customers caused selling, distribution, and marketing expenses to grow by $71.3 million. Despite the rise in operating expenses, the higher gross profit allowed the company's operating income to increase by $19.1 million to $234.5 million. Interest of $16.9 million and taxes of $78.4 million, offset slightly by $9.5 million in other income, brought the bottom line down to $148.8 million.

## Financial Condition

At fiscal year end February 28, 1995, American Greetings had an operating shortfall of $45.8 million. Internal cash flow of $217.2 million, an increase in other liabilities of $91.0 million, and an expanded reliance on trade credit of $12.9 million were not sufficient to support a $152.2 million increase in prepaids and deferred costs, $39.4 million in dividend payments, a $35.9 million rise in inventory, and current maturities of $19.1 million. The company extended its average payment period by eight days to 84 days, resulting in the growth in accounts payable to $140.7 million. The growth in other liabilities and the expansion in prepaids and deferred costs, primarily deferred costs, related to payment agreements with certain customers. The higher inventory

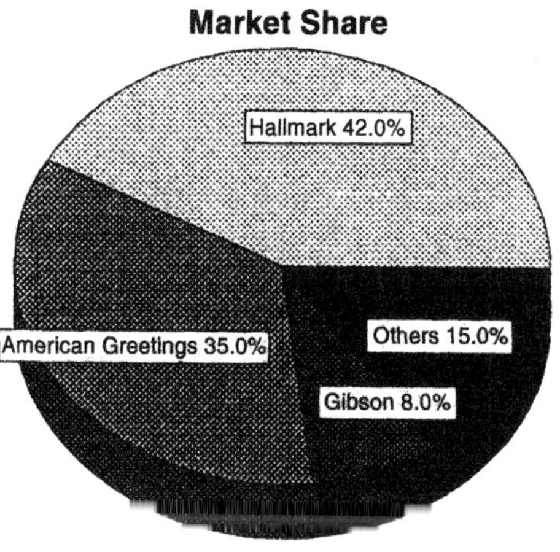


**Figure CS3.1** Greeting Card Induotry.

balances were due primarily to increases in finished goods inventory in the United States to meet forecasted requirements, particularly for new programs. The increase also reflected advance purchases of paper for gift-wrap production.

American Greetings primarily relied on $21.1 million in additional long-term debt from the company's revolving credit facility, $9.6 million in additional short-term debt, and $13.9 million from its cash account to support its operating shortfall of $45.8 million and capital expenditures of $88.3 million for equipment and fixtures. During 1995, American Greetings replaced its $250 million revolving credit agreement with a $400 million revolving credit agreement to support its commercial paper borrowing arrangement and provide a six-year option for up to $200 million. Despite the increase in long-term debt, the company's working capital increased to $531.2 million from $473.3 million in 1994. Its leverage ratio declined slightly to 0.52 : 1 compared to 0.49 : 1 in the prior year.

## Management

Many view the management philosophy of this company similar to the growth of its core business—stable, predictable, yet unexciting. In 1990, when Ed Fruchtenbaum was promoted to President of American Greetings, he became the first non-family member to run this company. During his tenure as President, he has done things a bit differently than his predecessors. Under his management strategy, CreataCard was launched. This was the industry's first computerized system, enabling consumers to write and design their own greeting cards. Although CreataCard encountered a somewhat disappointing start, it was an aggressive, forward-thinking idea that could prove to be successful and profitable in the long run. This was *not* the product of a predictable, unexciting management team.

## Growth Opportunities

There is a low elasticity of demand for greeting cards. The bulk of the cards are purchased for special occasions (i.e., birthdays, holidays) that require consumers to purchase a card. Demographic trends in the United States will benefit the card industry in the coming years as the aging of America should bolster sales. Part of the growth success of American Greetings core product has been the fact that its primary channel of distribution (mass merchandise, drugstores, grocers) has experienced a tremendous amount of growth.

## What's Next

A threefold corporate strategy for American Greetings will include acquisitions, internal development, and interrelated expansion. In the area of acquisition, American Greetings is considering a unit of Gibson Greetings. American Greetings continues to focus on consumer research, which results in a continued expansion of its product line.

On May 10, 1995 American Greetings announced an agreement with Microsoft Corp. to offer greeting cards to the growing base of consumers shopping on on-line computer networks. American Greetings will offer cards that can be personalized, ordered on-line, and mailed by American Greetings to the recipient. Also available will be electronic greetings that can be personalized and delivered via electronic mail (e-mail) from one computer user to another, thus eliminating paper.

## QUESTIONS

1. Apply a SWOT analysis on American Greetings.
2. Apply Porter's Model to American Greetings.
3. Develop a strategy for American Greetings' continued success.

4. Compare the strategy you selected in Question 3 with its past strategy. Is it consistent?
5. Does American Greetings' strategy from 1980 to 1995 seem to be aggressive or conservative?
6. Are they competing in a mature industry? If so, what strategic options exist for growth in a mature industry?
7. How important is the American Greetings' culture, past and present, in setting strategic direction?

## REFERENCES

"Acquisition of Custom Expressions." *Plain Dealer*, July 29, 1992, p. F-1.
*Annual Report*. American Greeting, 1995.
"Cards on Internet." *Wall Street Journal*, May 2, 1995, p. B6.
"Changing Society." *Plain Dealer*, May 31, 1992, p. E-1.
"CreataCard." *Plain Dealer*, August 3, 1993, p. F-2.
"CreataCard." *Plain Dealer*, October 12, 1992, p. G-2.
"Sell cards via computer." *Crains Cleveland*, May 1, 1995, p. 3.
"Ziggy Creator, Tom Wilson Zags to Hallmark." *Plain Dealer*, October 7, 1994, P. C-1.

## CASE STUDY: Figgie International, Inc.

Figgie International, Inc. was founded on December 31, 1963, by Harry E. Figgie, Jr. Holding a Bachelor of Science in Metallurgical Engineering, a Masters of Science in Industrial Engineering, a Masters of Business Administration from Harvard Business School, and a Law Degree, he initiated the building of his empire through a leveraged buyout of Automatic Sprinkler Corp. of America. Known for his strategy in acquiring struggling companies, by 1989 Harry E. Figgie, Jr. grew the corporation to a healthy $1.3 billion in sales with little or no capital investments, and strict cash control. Figgie International, Inc. consisted of more than 30 divisions. Although some business analysts would criticize the lack of core competency, Figgie International was a diversified corporation manufacturing everything from fire-fighting gear to sporting goods to insurance and lease holdings.

Positioned with a strong healthy corporation, Harry E. Figgie Jr., embarked on his vision to become the primary world class manufacturer in each of his diverse divisions. Contrary to his prior strategy of growth in the marketplace, attempts to implement world class manufacturing were initiated in selected divisions. There was, among other strategies, the influx of capital expenditures in training, computerization, and automated equipment. However, failure to gain consensus of the divisions' senior management in backing this program sowed the seeds of failure. By 1989 Figgie's vision was only that, a vision.

A new strategy had to be implemented and had to be implemented quickly because Figgie International was losing market share across the board. The emphasis was to force the implementation of world class onto the divisions with a strong "nudge" from the corporate level. Plans of consolidation of plants, automated equipment, state-of-the-art computerization, and use of consulting firms were obtained.

In 1992 Harry Figgie, III assumed the responsibilities of implementing this plan. Soon thereafter he assumed control of the corporation from his ailing father. The original blueprint of a five-year plan for implementation of World Class was soon compressed to a 6-month plan, then to an excruciating 18-month plan. These timetables were driven by Harry Figgie, Jr., due to his fears of the economy, as reflected in his views outlined in his book *Bankruptcy 1995*.

Spending over $200 million in consolidations, automation, and consulting fees, the corporation's debt quickly rose in 1993 from $82 million to $536 million. Poor management, bad luck, and heavy debt sent the company into a tailspin, nearly driving it into bankruptcy. The vision of world class was still only a vision and the corporation was now in a free fall. This was the start of the demise of the Figgie family's control of the corporation. By early 1994, the board of directors and the shareholders forced the resignation of Harry Figgie, III and the corporation's Chief Financial Officer. Soon thereafter, Harry Figgie Jr. (the founder of Figgie International) resigned. Walter M. Vannoy, a senior board member, was voted to become temporary chief executive officer and chairman of the board.

Figgie's banks were unwilling to roll over its loans. "Out of cash and out of credit" was the word on the street. On the verge of bankruptcy, a class action suit was filed by a former executive and shareholder, alleging the Figgies had diverted company funds for private use and inflated financial results. Within the courts, a class action suit allows the board of directors to formally respond and implement corrective action to those charges if the charges were not formally introduced to the board prior to the suit. Thus, the suit may have been a blessing in disguise to buy time for the failing corporation.

Vannoy's first step in correcting the ailing corporation was to emphasize strategic planning. He recognized a critical link was missing in the strategic plan, i.e., Figgie International was operating without a permanent chief executive officer. This also was recognized by many investors who had serious doubts about the direction of the company as share values were plummeting. The corporation needed to show it had a long-term strategy if it wanted to regain the market's confidence.

The first building block of that long-term strategy was a strategic plan for the downsizing and selling of valuable assets to pay down debt. The high-profile Rawling's Sporting Goods Co. was one of the first divisions sold. The initial success of this plan made it possible for the short-term financing to prevent Figgie International from entering bankruptcy.

By August 1994, Figgie International realized its need to revise its corporate strategy. Strategic teams consisting of board members and senior corporate officers evaluated the current situation, identifying Figgie International's strengths and weaknesses. From this reevaluation, a three-phase plan was derived: (1) recovery, (2) consolidation, and (3) resumption of growth. The greatest emphasis was placed on the recovery period. Consolidation and resumption of growth were established to identify plans necessary to permit ultimate success in the near future. The importance of the recovery period was to assure a rapid transition from survival mode to an orderly recovery plan. The movement was toward a more cohesive organization, and to be in less diverse markets and technology. The strategy was also to express due concern and courtesy to customers, employees, suppliers, lenders, and shareholders, and to assure that all future plans specifically addressed the needs of each of these groups.

In September 1994 Figgie International requested all the divisions to prepare a 1995 business plan according to specific guidelines. The approach was for each division to prepare a plan that had a 95% probability of success. They were then instructed to prepare a backup plan with a more difficult task level of 75%. This meant at least a 20% growth in sales and several cost reductions. The strategy of this particular business plan outline was to identify profit-producing [illegible] each division in relationship to its importance to the survival and growth of the corporation. This approach confirmed corporate strategic plans on the identification of "keepers" versus divestitures.

In January 1995, Figgie International named John P. "Jack" Reilly the president and chief executive officer of the corporation. He was also voted to fill a vacancy on the board of directors and be a member of the Executive and Finance, Strategic Planning, and Management Development and Compensation Committees. He currently stands as the chairman of the board along with the above noted titles.

Reilly and the board developed drastic plans for the restructuring of the company. Their goal was to pare Figgie International down to less than a quarter of its former size and use the proceeds from the divestitures to pay off the crushing $536 million debt in bank loans and leases. Soon after Reilly's inauguration, his first objective was to take the action necessary to meet the bank plan requirements and to return the corporation to the point of generating cash. Reilly announced plans to divest at least 15 of Figgie International's 22 businesses, including Automatic Sprinkler, the founding division. He estimated that Figgie would reap $300 million from the divestitures, which would pay down leases and bank loans, cutting total debt to $236 million. Reilly's objective was to return Figgie to profitability by the third quarter of 1995.

In addition, Reilly planned to slash the bloated overhead left behind by Harry Figgie, Jr., and his son. Reilly would also ax many perks, decentralize the divisions, cut corporate staff in half, and slash outside professional fees. He was projecting an estimated savings of $22 million annually by taking these measures.

Figgie International also believed that the creation of a "Mission Statement" for the corporation was critical in the restructuring. The corporation devised the following preliminary outline of a Mission Statement:

> Figgie International's mission is (1) to provide marketing leadership, to understand all markets in which they participate as well as or better than the operating units with the objective of pursuing a strategy of low-cost producer, or niche and/or differentiated product to be a leader in all their markets; (2) to provide general management services and leadership to achieve across-the-board productivity improvements of 10% during the consolidation phase and twice inflation thereafter; and (3) to provide financial services to the operating units at a lower cost than they could obtain on their own.

The objective of the corporation was restructured to have three basic market areas: electronics, health/safety, and industrial products. This was the start of core competency within the corporation. The need to have the corporate staff fully qualified to understand these markets and have the necessary analytical and managerial skills to recognize opportunities for synergy and growth in these markets is a necessity. In addition, the corporate managerial staff must provide guidance and assistance, not force, to divisional management. The goal is to complete the consolidation phase by January 1, 1997, then move to the completion phase of the strategic plan that involves a return to growth phase and obtaining a stock price of $20 per share.

Figgie International corporate management acknowledged that recent actions had left the corporation with excessive debt and liabilities, numerous high-risk situations, and a very diminished corporate image. It also recognized that neither customers, subsidiaries, employees, lenders, nor shareholders were responsible for creating these problems, and accepted responsibility for taking corrective action.

## QUESTIONS

1. How important is it to convince creditors and stockholders that a company does, in fact, have a strategic plan?
2. How different is a strategic plan prepared during a time of crisis (i.e. a failing corporation) from when a corporation is highly profitable?
3. How does one prepare integration strategies for a firm that is highly diversified yet possibly short of cash?
4. How frequently should a strategic plan be updated?
5. How frequently should functional strategies and integration strategies be updated?

CHAPTER 4

# Strategic Market Planning Using Learning Curves

Competitive pricing has become an integral part of the marketing and sales responsibility in many industries. A multitude of estimating techniques are available to assist managers in arriving at a competitive price. If the final price is too high, the company may not be competitive. If the price is too low, the company may have to incur the cost of the overrun out of its own pocket. For a small firm, this overrun could lead to financial disaster.

Perhaps some of the most difficult activities to estimate are those that involve the development and ultimate manufacturing of a large quantity of units. As an example, a company is asked to price out the development and manufacturing of 15,000 components. The company is able to develop a cost for the manufacturing of its first unit, but what will be the cost for the 10th, 100th, 1,000th, or 10,000th unit? Obviously, the production cost of each successive unit should be less than the previous unit, but by how much? Fortunately for managers there exist highly accurate estimating techniques for these types of activities. These estimating techniques are referred to as "learning" or "experience" curves and assist management in performing strategic market planning.

## GENERAL THEORY

Experience curves are based upon the old adage that practice makes perfect. A product can always be manufactured better and in a shorter time period not only the second time, but each succeeding time. This concept is highly applicable to labor-intensive projects such as those in manufacturing where labor forecasting has been a tedious and time-consuming effort.

The experience-curve concept dates back to 1860 when Chauncey Jerome, a pioneer in clock manufacturing, wrote, "The business of manufacture of them has become so systematized of late that it has brought the prices exceedingly low and it has long been the astonishment of the whole world how they could be made so cheap and yet so good."[1] Perhaps the earliest quantifiable effect of experience curves occurred in 1925 when the commander of Wright-Patterson Air Force Base found that the total hours required to assemble an aircraft decreased as the number of aircraft assembled increased. Not only did this fact result in a lower aircraft cost, but it also implied that, in time of war, more aircraft could be produced with the same resources and in a shorter period of time. Because of the high cost of building an aircraft, the effects of learning curves became more conspicuous in the aircraft industry than in any other industry.

It wasn't until the 1960s that the true implications of experience curves became evident. Personnel from the Boston Consulting Group showed that each time that cumulative production doubled, the total manufacturing time and cost fell by a *constant* and *predictable* amount. Furthermore, the Boston Consulting Group showed that this curve effect was not limited to just the aircraft industry, but extended to other industries such as chemicals, metals, and electronic components.

Today's executives often measure the profitability of a corporation as a function of market share. As market share increases, profitability will increase more because of lower production costs than because of increased margins. This is the experience-curve effect. Large market shares allow companies to build large manufacturing plants so that the fixed capital costs are spread out over more units, thus lowering the unit cost. This increase in efficiency is referred to as "economies of scale" and may be the main reason why large manufacturing organizations may be more efficient than smaller ones.

In certain industries, such as chemicals, mathematical expressions exist that clearly show the cost implications of economies of scale and learning curves.

Capital equipment costs follow the rule of six-tenths power of capacity. As an example, consider a plant that has the capacity to produce 35,000 units each year. The plant's construction cost was $10 million. If the company wishes to build a new plant with a capacity of 70,000 units, what will the construction cost be?

$$\frac{\$\ \text{new}}{\$\ \text{old}} = \left(\frac{70{,}000}{35{,}000}\right)^{0.6}$$

Solving for $ new, we find that the new plant will cost approximately $15 million, or one and one-half times the cost of the old plant. (For a more accurate determination, the costs must be adjusted for inflation.)

# The Learning Curve Concept

Learning curves stipulate that manufacturing man-hours (specifically direct labor) will decline each time a company doubles its output. Typically, learning curves produce a cost and time savings of 10% to 30% each time a company's experience at producing a product doubles. As an example, consider the data shown in Table 4.1, which represents a company operating on a 75% learning curve. The time for the second unit is 75% of the time of the first unit. The time for the 40th unit is 75% of the time for the 20th unit. The time for the 800th unit is 75% of the time for the 400th unit. Likewise, we can *forecast* the time for the 1,000th unit as being 75% of the time for the 500th unit. In this example, the time decreased by a fixed amount of 25%. Theoretically, this decrease could occur indefinitely.

In Table 4.1, we could have replaced the man-hours per production unit with the cost per production unit. It is more common to use man-hours because exact costs are either not always known or not publicly disclosed by the firm. Also, the use of costs implies the added complexity of considering escalation factors on salary, cost of living adjustments, and possibly the time value of money.

**Table 4.1 Cumulative Production and Labor Hour Data.**

| Cumulative production | Hours this unit | Cumulative total hours |
|---|---|---|
| 1 | 812 | 812 |
| 2 | 609 | 1421 |
| 10 | 312 | 4538 |
| 12 | 289 | 5127 |
| 15 | 264 | 5943 |
| 20 | 234 | 7169 |
| 40 | 176 | 11142 |
| 60 | 148 | 14343 |
| 75 | 135 | 16459 |
| 100 | 120 | 19631 |
| 150 | 101 | 25116 |
| 200 | 90 | 29880 |
| 250 | 82 | 34170 |
| 300 | 76 | 38117 |
| 400 | 68 | 45267 |
| 500 | 62 | 51704 |
| 600 | 57 | 57622 |
| 700 | 54 | 63147 |
| 800 | 51 | 68349 |
| 840 | 50 | 70354 |

For manufacturing runs under a year or two, costs are often used instead of man-hours.

These types of costs are often referred to as "value-added costs," and can also appear in the form of lower freight and procurement costs through bulk quantities. The value-added costs are actually cost savings for both the customer and the contractor.

The learning curve was adapted from the historical observation that individuals performing repetitive tasks exhibit an improvement in performance as the task is repeated a number of times. Empirical studies of this phenomenon yielded three conclusions on which the current theory and practice is based:

- The time required to perform a task reduces as the task is repeated.
- The amount of improvement decreases as more units are produced.
- The rate of improvement has sufficient consistency to allow its use as a prediction tool.

The consistency in improvement has been found to exist in the form of a constant percentage reduction in time required over successive doubled quantities of units produced.

It's important to recognize the significance of using the learning curve for manufacturing projects. Consider a project where 75% of the total direct labor is in assembly (such as aircraft assembly) and the remaining 25% is in machine work. With direct labor, learning improvements are possible, whereas with machine work, output may be restricted due to the performance of the machine. In the above example, with 75% direct labor and 25% machine work, a company may find itself performing on an 80% learning curve. But, if the direct labor were 25% and the machine work were 75%, then the company may find itself on a 90% learning curve.

## GRAPHIC REPRESENTATION

Figure 4.1 shows the learning curve plotted from the data in Table 4.1. The horizontal axis represents the total number of units produced. The vertical axis represents the total labor hours (or cost) for each unit. The labor-hour graph in Figure 4.1 represents a hyperbola when drawn on ordinary graph paper (i.e., rectangular coordinates). The curve shows that the difference or amount of labor-hour reduction is *not* consistent. Rather, it declines by a continuously diminishing amount as the quantities are doubled. But the rate of change or decline has been found to be a constant percentage of the prior cost, because the decline in the base figure is proportionate to the decline in the amount of change. To illustrate this, we can use the data in Table 4.1, which was used to construct Figure 4.1. In doubling production from the first to the second unit, a reduction of 203 hours occurs. In doubling from 100 to 200 units, a reduction of 30 hours occurs. However in both cases, the percentage decrease was 25%. Again, in going from 400 to 800 units, a 25% reduction of 17 hours results. We can therefore conclude that, as more units are produced, the rate of change remains constant but the magnitude of the change diminishes.

When the data from Figure 4.1 is plotted on log-log paper, the result is a straight line which represents the learning curve as shown in Figure 4.2.

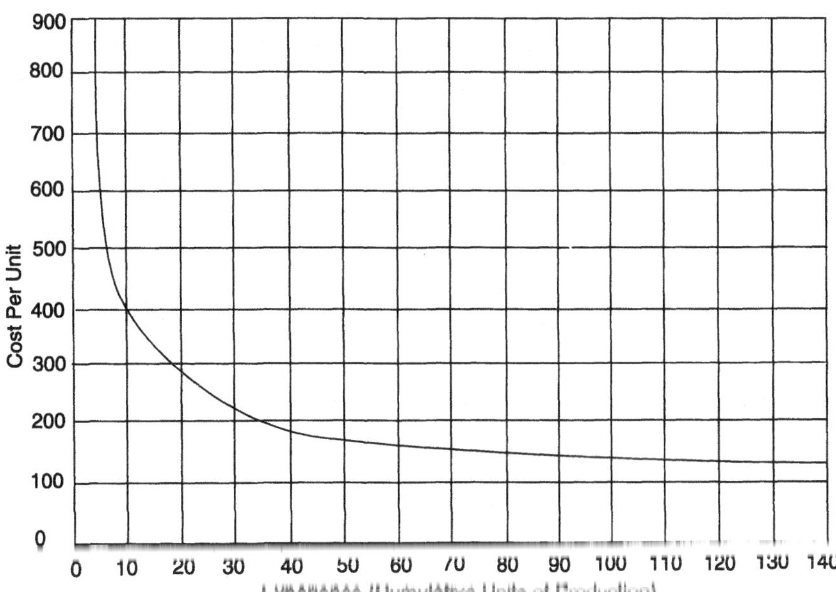


**Figure 4.1**
A 75% Learning Curve.

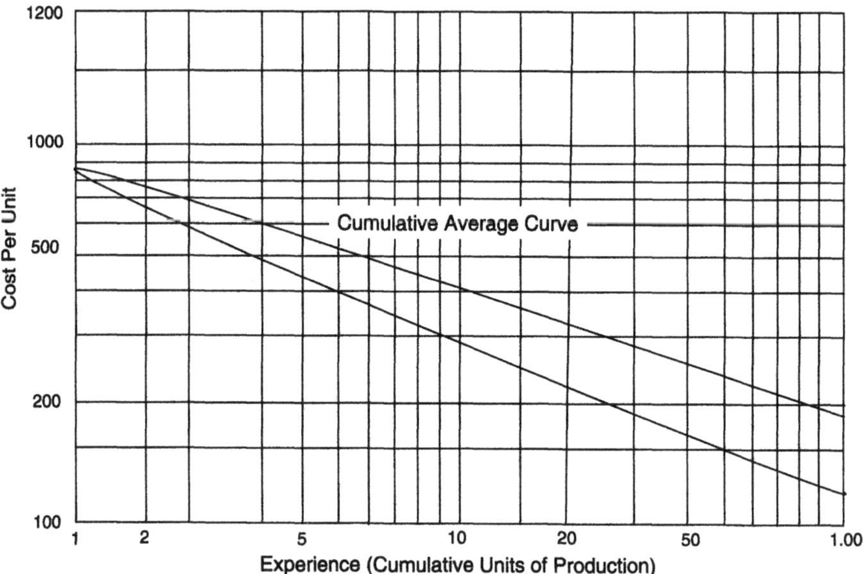


**Figure 4.2**
A 75% Learning Curve.

There are two fundamental models of the learning curve in general use: the unit curve and the cumulative average curve. Both are shown in Figure 4.2. The unit curve focuses on the hours or cost involved in specific units of production. The theory can be stated as follows: As the total quantity of units produced doubles, the cost per unit decreases by some constant percentage. The constant percentage by which the costs of doubled quantities decrease is called the rate of learning.

The "slope" of the learning curve is related to the rate of learning. It is the difference between 100% and the rate of learning. For example, if the hours between doubled quantities are reduced by 20% (rate of learning), it would be described as a curve with an 80% slope.

To plot a straight line, one must know either two points or one point and the slope of the line. Generally speaking, the latter is more common. The question is whether the company knows the man-hours for the first unit or uses a projected number of man-hours for a target or standard unit to be used for pricing purposes.

The cumulative average curve in Figure 4.2 can be obtained from columns 1 and 3 in Table 4.1. Dividing column 3 by column 1, we find that the average hours for the first 100 units is 196 hours. For 200 units, the average is 149 hours. This becomes important in determining the cost for a manufacturing project.

## KEY WORDS ASSOCIATED WITH LEARNING CURVES

To utilize learning-curve theory, certain key phrases listed below are of importance:

- **Slope of the curve**—A percentage figure that represents the steepness (constant rate of improvement) of the curve. Using the unit-curve theory, this percentage represents the value (e.g., hours or cost) at a doubled production quantity in relation to the previous quantity. For example, with an experience curve having 80% slope, the value of unit two is 80% of the value of unit one, the value of unit four is 80% of the value at unit two, the value at unit 1,000 is 80% of the value of unit 500, and so on.

- **Unit one**—the first unit of product actually completed during a production run. This is not to be confused with a unit produced in any reproduction phase of the overall acquisition program.
- **Cumulative average hours**—the average hours expended per unit for all units produced through any given unit. When illustrated on a graph by a line drawn through each successive unit, the values form a cumulative average curve.
- **Unit hours**—the total direct labor hours expended to complete any specific unit. When a line is drawn on a graph through the values for each successive unit, the values form a unit curve.
- **Cumulative total hours**—the total hours expended for all units produced through any given unit. The data plotted on a graph with each point connected by a line form a cumulative total curve.

The greatest benefit of learning curves lies in the story they tell when plotted on log-log paper.

Typical relationships can be seen in Figure 4.3.

## THE CUMULATIVE AVERAGE CURVE

It is common practice to plot the learning curve on log-log paper but to calculate the cumulative average from the following formula:

$$T_x = T_1 X^{-K}$$

where $T_x$ = direct labor hours for unit $n$
$T_1$ = the direct labor hours for the first unit, (unit one)
$X$ = the cumulative unit produced
$-K$ = a factor derived from the slope of the experience curve

Typical values for the exponent $K$ are:

| Learning Curve % | $K$ |
|---|---|
| 100 | 0.0 |
| 95 | 0.074 |
| 90 | 0.152 |
| 85 | 0.235 |
| 80 | 0.322 |
| 75 | 0.415 |
| 70 | 0.515 |

As an example, consider a situation where the first unit requires 812 hours and the company is performing on a 75% learning curve. The man-hours required for the 250th unit would be:

$$T_{250} = (812)(250)^{0.415}$$
$$= 82 \text{ HOURS}$$

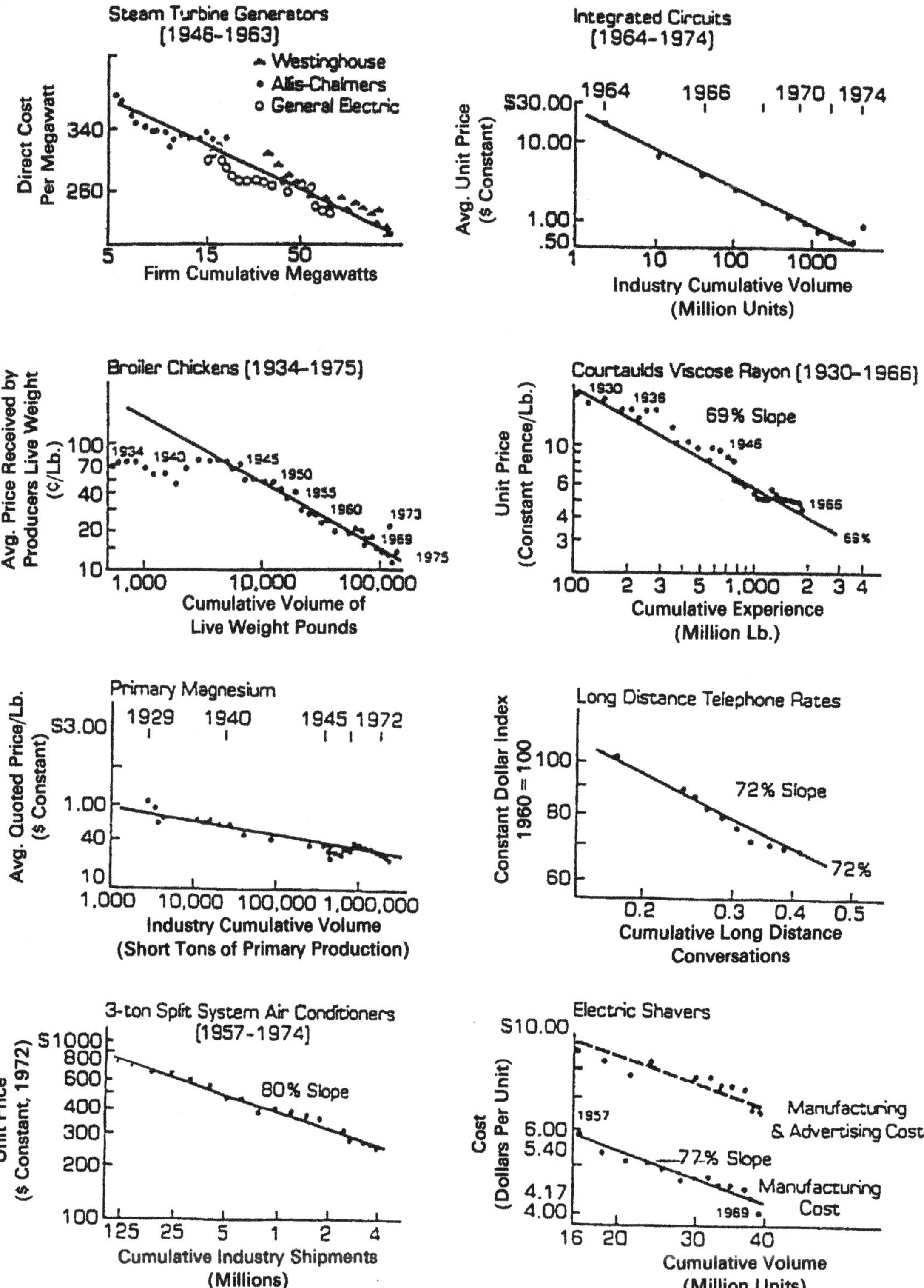


**Figure 4.3** Some Sample Experience Curves.

This agrees with the data in Table 4.1.

Sometimes companies do not know the time for the first unit. Instead, they assume a target unit and accompanying target man-hours. As an example, consider a company that assumes that the standard for performance will be the 100th unit, which is targeted for 120 man-hours, and performs on a 75% learning curve. Solving for $T_1$, we have:

$$T_1 = T_x X^K$$
$$= (120)(100)^{0.415}$$
$$= 811 \text{ HOURS}$$

This is in approximate agreement with the data in Table 4.1.

The cumulative average number of labor hours can be *approximated* from the expression

$$T_c = \frac{T_1(X)^{-K}}{1 - K}$$

where $T_c$ = cumulative average labor hours for the $X_{th}$ unit
$X$ = cumulative units produced
$T_1$ = direct labor hours for 1st unit

for the 250th unit,

$$T_c = \frac{(812)(250)^{-0.415}}{1 - 0.415}$$
$$= 135 \text{ HOURS}$$

From Table 4.1, the cumulative average for the 250th unit is 34,170 man-hours divided by 250, or 137 hours. We must remember that the above expression is merely an approximation. Significant errors can occur using this expression for less than 100 units. For large values of $X$, the error becomes insignificant.

It is possible to use the learning curve equation to develop Table 4.2, which shows typical cost reductions due to increased experience. Suppose that the production level is quadrupled and you are performing on an 80% learning curve. Using Table 4.2, the costs will be reduced by 36%.

## SOURCES OF EXPERIENCE

There are several factors that contribute to the learning curve phenomenon. None of the factors performs entirely independently, but are interrelated through a complex network. However, for simplicity sake, these factors will be sorted out for discussion purposes.

**LABOR EFFICIENCY** The first factor is labor efficiency. This is the most common factor, which says that we learn more and more each time we repeat a task. As we learn, the time and cost of performing the task should diminish. As the employee learns the task, less managerial supervision is required, waste and inefficiency can be reduced or even eliminated, and productivity will increase.

Unfortunately, labor efficiency does not occur automatically. Personnel management policies in the area of *work force stability* and *worker compensation* are of vital

**Table 4.2 Sample Cost Reductions due to Increased Experience.**

| Ratio of Old Experience to New Experience | EXPERIENCE CURVE 70% | 75% | 80% | 85% | 90% | 95% |
|---|---|---|---|---|---|---|
| 1.1 | 5% | 4% | 3% | 2% | 1% | 1% |
| 1.25 | 11 | 9 | 7 | 5 | 4 | 2 |
| 1.5 | 19 | 15 | 12 | 9 | 6 | 3 |
| 1.75 | 25 | 21 | 16 | 12 | 8 | 4 |
| 2.0 | 30 | 25 | 20 | 15 | 10 | 5 |
| 2.5 | 38 | 32 | 26 | 19 | 13 | 7 |
| 3.0 | 43 | 37 | 30 | 23 | 15 | 8 |
| 4.0 | 51 | 44 | 36 | 28 | 19 | 10 |
| 6.0 | 60 | 52 | 44 | 34 | 24 | 12 |
| 8.0 | 66 | 58 | 49 | 39 | 27 | 14 |
| 16.0 | 76 | 68 | 59 | 48 | 34 | 19 |

*Source:* Derek F. Abell and John S. Hammond, *Stragtic Market Planning*, Prentice-Hall, 1979, p. 109.

Example:
If experience is quadrupled and the product is on an 85% experience curve, then costs will be reduced by 28%.

importance. As workers mature and become more efficient, it becomes increasingly important to maintain this pool of skilled labor. Loss of a contract or interruption between contracts could force employees to seek employment elsewhere. In certain industries, like aerospace and defense, engineers are often regarded as migratory workers, moving from contract to contract and from company to company.

Upturns and downturns in the economy can have a serious impact on maintaining experience curves. During downturns in the economy, people work slower, trying to preserve their job. Eventually the company is forced into a position of having to reassign people to other activities or to lay people off. During upturns in the economy, massive training programs may be needed in order to accelerate the rate of learning.

If an employee is expected to get the job done in a shorter period of time, then the employee expects to be adequately compensated. Wage incentives can produce either a positive or negative effect based upon how they are applied. Learning curves and productivity can become a "bargaining" tool by labor as it negotiates for greater pay.

Fixed compensation plans generally do not motivate workers to produce more. If an employee is expected to produce more at a lower cost, then the employee expects to receive part of the cost savings as either added compensation or fringe benefits.

The learning effect goes beyond the labor directly involved in manufacturing. Maintenance personnel, supervisors, and people in other line and staff manufacturing positions also increase their productivity, as do people in marketing, sales, administration, and other functions.

Ways to improve learning curve efficiencies include:[2]

**WORK SPECIALIZATION AND METHODS IMPROVEMENT** Specialization increases worker proficiency at a given task. Consider what happens when two workers, who formerly did both parts of a two-stage operation, each specialize in a single stage. Each worker now handles twice as many items and accumulates experience twice as fast on the more specialized task. Redesign of work operations (methods) can also result in greater efficiency.

**NEW PRODUCTION PROCESSES** Process innovations and improvements can be an important source of cost reductions, especially in capital-intensive industries. The low-labor-content semiconductor industry, for instance, achieves experience curves at 70% to 80% from improved production technology by devoting a large percentage of its research and development to process improvements. Similar process improvements have been observed in refineries, nuclear power plants, and steel mills, to mention a few.

**GETTING BETTER PERFORMANCE FROM PRODUCTION EQUIPMENT** When first designed, a piece of production equipment may have conservatively rated output. Experience may reveal innovative ways of increasing its output. For instance, capacity of a fluid catalytic cracking unit typically "grows" by about 50% over a 10-year period.

**CHANGES IN THE RESOURCE MIX** As experience accumulates, a producer can often incorporate different or less-expensive resources in operation. For instance, less-skilled workers can replace skilled workers or automation can replace labor.

**PRODUCT STANDARDIZATION** Standardization allows the replication of tasks necessary for worker learning. Production of the Ford Model T, for example, followed a strategy of deliberate standardization; as a result, from 1909 to 1923 its price was repeatedly reduced, following an 85% experience curve. Even when flexibility and/or wider product line are important marketing considerations, standardization can be achieved by modularization. For example, by making just a few types of engines, transmissions, chassis, seats, body styles, and soon, an auto manufacturer can achieve experience effects due to specialization in each part. These in turn can be assembled into a wide variety of models.

**PRODUCT REDESIGN** As experience is gained with a product, both the manufacturer and customers gain a clearer understanding of its performance requirements. This understanding allows the product to be redesigned to conserve material, allow greater efficiency in manufacture, and substitute less costly materials and resources, while at the same time improving performance on relevant dimensions. The change from wooden to brass clockworks in the early 1800s is a good example; so are the new designs and substitutions of plastic, synthetic fiber, and rubber for leather in ski boots.

**INCENTIVES AND DISINCENTIVES** Compensation plans and other sources of experience can be both incentives and disincentives. Incentives can change the slope of the learning curve as shown in Figure 4.4. This is referred to as a "toe-down" learning curve where a more favorable learning process can occur. In Figure 4.5, we have a "toe-up" or "scallop" learning curve, which is the result of disincentives. After the toe-up occurs, the learning curve may have a new slope that was not as favorable as the original slope. According to Hirschmann,[3]

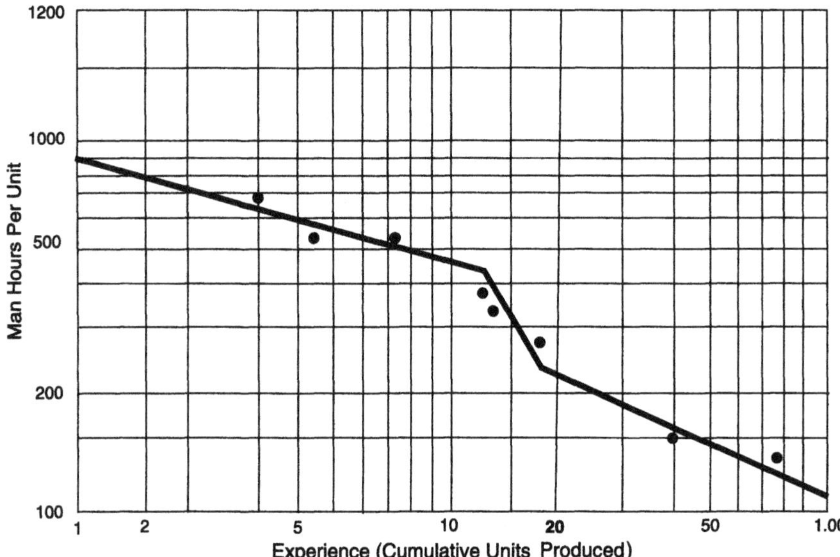


**Figure 4.4**
A "Toe-Down" Learning Curve.

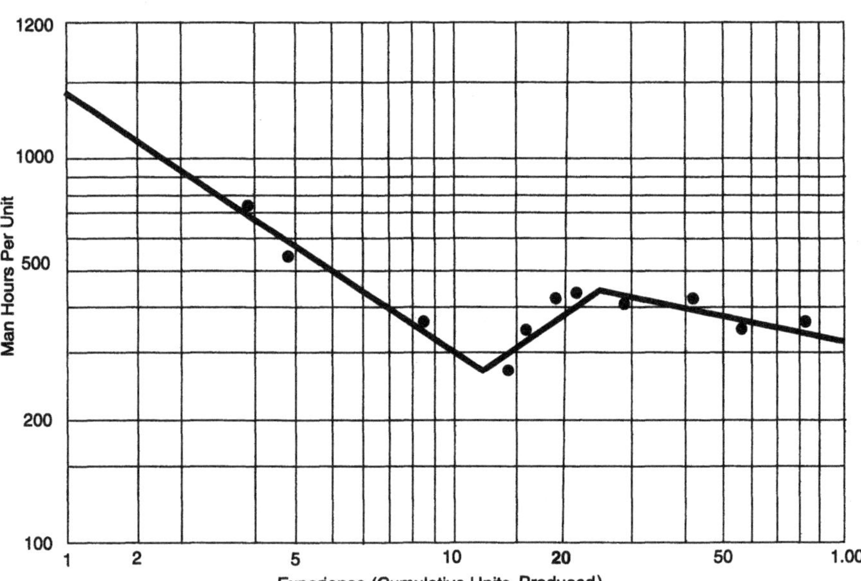


**Figure 4.5**
A "Toe-Up" Learning Curve.

A rise in the curve can occur in the middle of a contract, too, owing to a substantial interruption (such as that caused by introducing changes in a model, by moving operations to a new building, or by halting operations for a while so that forgetting occurs). Shortly after operations recommence and skill in handling changes is acquired, the curve declines rapidly to approach the old slope. Such a break in the curve occurs frequently enough to have acquired the descriptive term "scallop." In fact, if, instead of merely a change being made, a new model is introduced, or a new type of item is put into production, the scallop occurs initially and the curve essentially starts again. Thus, the direct labor input reverts back to what it had been when the first item of the preceding type was put into production (assuming that the two items were of similar type and configuration).

Worker dissatisfaction can also create a leveling off of the learning curve as shown in Figure 4.6. This leveling off can also occur as a result of inefficiencies due to closing out of a production line or transferring workers to other activities at the end of a contract.

# DEVELOPING SLOPE MEASURES

Research by the Stanford Research Institute revealed that many different slopes were experienced by different manufacturers, sometimes on similar manufacturing programs. In fact, manufacturing data collected from World War II aircraft manufacturing industry had slopes ranging from 69.7% to almost 100%. These slopes averaged 80%, giving rise to an industry average curve of 80%. Other research has developed measures for other industries such as 95.6% for a sample of 162 electronics programs. Unfortunately, this industry average curve is frequently misapplied by practitioners who use it as a standard or norm. When estimating slopes without the benefit of data on the item being manufactured from the plant of the

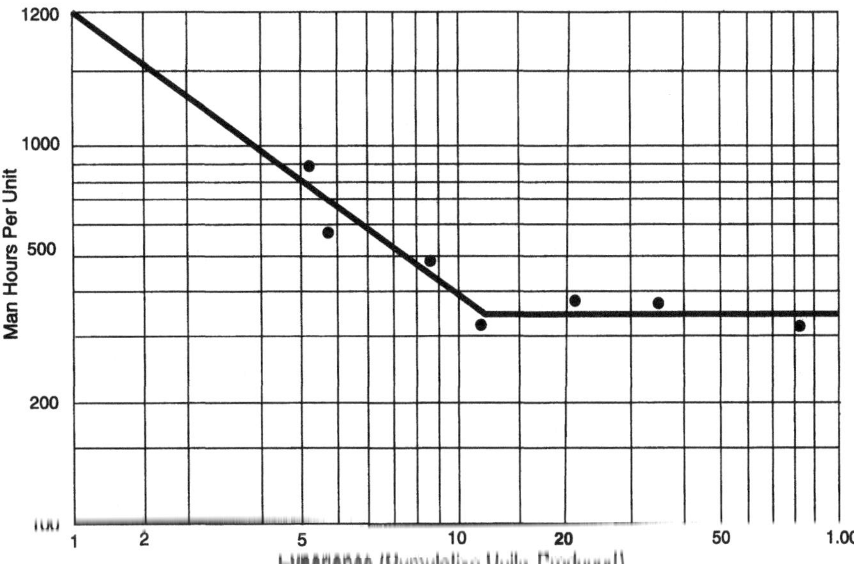


**Figure 4.6**
A Levelling Off of the Learning Curve

manufacturer, it is better to use learning curve slopes from similar items at the manufacturer's plant rather than the industry average.

The analyst needs to know the slope of the learning curve for a number of reasons. One is to facilitate communication, because it is part of the language of the learning-curve theory. The steeper the slope (lower the percent), the more rapidly the resource requirements (hours) will decline as production increases. Accordingly, the slope of the learning curve is usually an issue in production contract negotiation. The slope of the learning curve is also needed to project follow-on costs, using either the learning tables or computational assistance. Another need for a slope is in many production situations where a given slope may be established as a standard based on reliable historical experience. Learning curves developed from actual experience on current production can then be compared against this standard slope to determine whether the improvement on a particular contract is or is not reasonable.

## UNIT COSTS AND USE OF MIDPOINTS

The use of the learning curve is dependent on the methods of recording costs that companies employ. An accounting or statistical record system must be devised by a company so that data is available for learning-curve purposes. Otherwise, it may be impossible to construct a learning curve. Costs, such as labor hours per unit or dollars per unit, must be identified with the unit of product. It is preferable to use labor hours rather than dollars, because the latter contain an additional variable, the effect of inflation or deflation (both wage-rate and material cost changes), which the former does not contain. In any event, the record system must have definite cutoff points for such costs, permitting identification of the costs with the units involved. Most companies use a lot-release system, whereby costs are accumulated on a job order in which the number of units completed are specified and the costs are cut off at the completion of the number of units. In this case, however, the costs are usually equated with equivalent units rather than actual units. Because the job-order system is commonly used, the unit cost is not the actual cost per unit in the lot. This means that when lots are plotted on graph paper, the unit value corresponding with the average cost value must be found.

## SELECTION OF LEARNING CURVES

Existing experience curves, by definition, reflect past experience. "Trend lines" are developed from accumulated data plotted on logarithmic paper (preferably) and "smoothed out" to portray the curve. The type of curve may represent one of several concepts. The data may have been accumulated by product, process, department, or by other functional or organizational segregations, depending on the needs of the user. But whichever experience curve concept or method of data accumulation is selected for use, based on suitability to the experience pattern, the data should be applied consistently in order to render meaningful information to management. Consistency in curve concept and data accumulation cannot be overemphasized, because existing experience curves play a major role in determining the projected experience curve for a new item or product.

When selecting the proper curve for a new production item when only one point of data is available and the slope is unknown, the following, in decreasing order of magnitude, should be considered.

- similarity between the new item and an item or items previously produced
- physical comparisons
  - addition or deletion of processes and components
  - differences in material, if any
  - effect of engineering changes in items previously produced
- duration of time since a similar item was produced
  - condition of tooling and equipment
  - personnel turnover
  - changes in working conditions or morale
- Other comparable factors between similar items
  - delivery schedules
  - availability of material and components
  - personnel turnover during production cycle of item previously produced
  - comparison of actual production data with previously extrapolated or theoretical curves to identify deviations

It is feasible to assign weights to these factors as well as to any other factors that are of comparable nature in an attempt to quantify differences between items. These factors are again historical in nature and only comparison of several existing curves and their actuals would reveal the importance of these factors.

If at least two points of data are available, the slope of the curve may be determined. Naturally, the distance between these two points must be considered when evaluating the reliability of the slope. The availability of additional points of data will enhance the reliability of the curve. Regardless of the number of points and the assumed reliability of the slope, comparisons with similar items are considered the most desirable approach and should be made whenever possible.

A value for unit one may be arrived at either by accumulation of data or statistical derivation. When production is under way, available data can be readily plotted, and the curve may be extrapolated to a desired unit. However, if production has yet to be started, actual unit one data would not be available, and a theoretical unit one value would have to be developed. This may be accomplished in one of three ways:

- A statistically derived relationship between the preproduction unit hours and first unit hours can be applied to the actual hours from the preproduction phase.
- A cost estimating relationship (CER) for first unit cost based upon physical or performance parameters can be used to develop a first unit cost estimate.
- The slope and the point at which the curve and the labor standard value converge are known. In this case, a unit one value can be determined. This is accomplished by dividing the labor standard by the appropriate unit value.

## FOLLOW-ON ORDERS

Once the initial experience curve has been developed for either the initial order or production run, the values through the last unit on the cumulative average and unit curves can be determined. Follow-on orders and continuations of production runs, which are considered extensions of the original orders or runs, are plotted as extensions on the appropriate curve. However, the cumulative average value through the final point of the extended curve is not the cumulative average for the follow-on portion of that curve. It is the cumulative average for both portions of the curve, assuming no break in production. Thus, estimating the cost for the follow-on effort only requires evaluation of the difference between cumulative average costs for the initial run and the follow-on. Likewise, the last unit value for both portions of the unit curve would represent the last unit value for the combined curve.

## MANUFACTURING BREAKS

The "manufacturing break" is the time lapse between the completion of an order or manufacturing run of certain units of equipment and the commencement of a follow-on order or restart of a manufacturing run for identical units. This time lapse disrupts the continuous flow of manufacturing and constitutes a definite cost impact. The time lapse under discussion here pertains to significant periods of time (weeks and months) as opposed to the minutes or hours for personnel allowances, machine delays, power failures, and the like.

It is logical to assume that because the experience curve has time/cost relationship, a break will affect both time and cost. Therefore, the length of the break becomes as significant as the length of the initial order or manufacturing run. Because the break is quantifiable, the remaining factor to be determined is the cost of this lapse in manufacturing (that is, the additional cost incurred over and above that which would have been incurred had either the initial order or the run continued through the duration of the follow-on order or the restarted run).

When a manufacturer relies on experience curves as management information tools, it can be assumed that the necessary, accurate data for determining the initial curves have been accumulated, recorded, and properly validated. Therefore, if the manufacturer has experienced breaks, the experience curve data for the orders (lots) or runs involved should be available in such form that appropriate curves can be developed.

George Anderlohr, in the September 1969 issue of *Industrial Engineering*, suggests a method that assumes loss of learning is dependent on five factors:[4]

- **Manufacturing personnel learning**—In this area, the physical loss of personnel, either through regular movement or layoff, must be determined. The company's personnel records can usually furnish evidence on which to establish this learning loss. The percentage of learning lost by the personnel retained on other plant projects should also be ascertained. These people will lose their physical dexterity and familiarity with the product, and the momentum of repetition.

- **Supervisory learning**—Once again, a percentage of supervisory personnel will be lost as a result of the break in repetition. Management will make a greater effort to retain this higher caliber of personnel, so the physical loss, in the majority of cases, will be far less than in the area of production personnel. However, the supervisory personnel retained will lose their overall familiarity with the job, so that the guidance they can furnish will be reduced. In addition, because of the loss of production personnel, the supervisor will have no knowledge of the new hires and their individual personalities and capabilities.
- **Continuity of productivity**—This relates to the physical positioning of the line, the relationship of one workstation to another, and the location of lighting, bins, parts, and tools within the workstation. It also included the position adjustment to optimize the individual needs. In addition, a major factor affecting this area is the balanced line or the work-in-process buildup. Of all the elements of learning, the greatest initial loss is suffered in this area.
- **Methods**—This area is least affected by a break. As long as the method sheets are kept on file, learning can never be completely lost. However, drastic revisions to the method sheets may be required as a result of a change from soft to hard tooling.
- **Special tooling**—New and better tooling is a major contributor to learning. In relating loss in tooling area to learning, the major factors are wear, physical misplacement, and breakage. An additional consideration must be the comparison of short-run or so-called soft tooling to long-run or hard tooling, and the effect of the transition from soft to hard tooling.

## LEARNING CURVE LIMITATIONS

There are limitations to the use of learning curves, and care must be taken that erroneous conclusions do not result from their use. Typical limitations include:

- The learning curve does not continue forever. The percentage decline in hours/dollars diminishes over time.
- The learning-curve knowledge gained on one product may not be extendable to other products unless there exist shared experiences.
- Cost data may not be readily available in order to construct a meaningful learning curve. Other problems can occur if overhead costs are included with the direct labor cost, or if the accounting codes cannot separate work packages sufficiently in order to identify those elements that truly demonstrate experience effects.
- Quantity discounts can distort the costs and the perceived benefits of learning curves.
- Inflation must be expressed in constant dollars. Otherwise, the gains realized from experience may be neutralized.
- Learning curves are most useful on long-term horizons (i.e., years). On short-term horizons, benefits perceived may not be the result of learning [illegible]

- External influences, such as limitations on materials, patents, or even government regulations, can restrict the benefits of learning curves.
- Constant annual production (i.e., no growth) may have a limiting experience effect after a few years.

## PRICES AND EXPERIENCE

If the competitive marketplace is stable, then as cost decreases as a function of the learning-curve experience, prices will decrease similarly. This assumes that profit margins are expressed as a percentage of price rather than in absolute dollar terms. Therefore, the gap between selling price and cost will remain a constant, as shown in Figure 4.7.

Unfortunately, price and cost will most likely follow the relationship shown in Figure 4.8. Companies that use learning curves develop pricing policies based on either an industry average cost or an average cost based on a target production volume. In *phase A*, new product prices are less than the company cost, because the market would probably be reluctant to purchase the first few items at the actual production cost. As the company enters *phase B*, profits begin to materialize as the experience curve takes hold. Fixed costs are recovered. Prices may remain firm because of market strategies adopted by the market leader.

The longer one remains in phase B, the greater and profits. Unfortunately, phase B is relatively unstable. One or more competitors will quickly drop their prices, because if the profit potential were too large, new entrants into the highly profitable marketplace would soon occur. In *phase C*, prices drop faster than costs, thus forcing a shakeout of the marketplace where marginal producers exit the market. The shakeout phase ends when prices begin to follow industry costs down

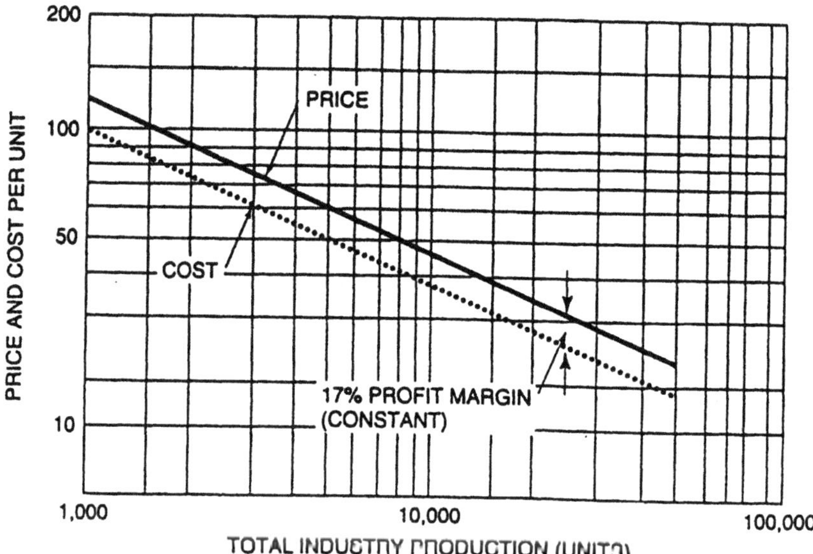


**Figure 4.7**
An Idealized Price-Cost Relationship when Profit Margin Is Constant.
*Source:* Derek F. Abell and John S. Hammond, *Strategic Market Planning*, Prentice Hall, 1979, p. 115

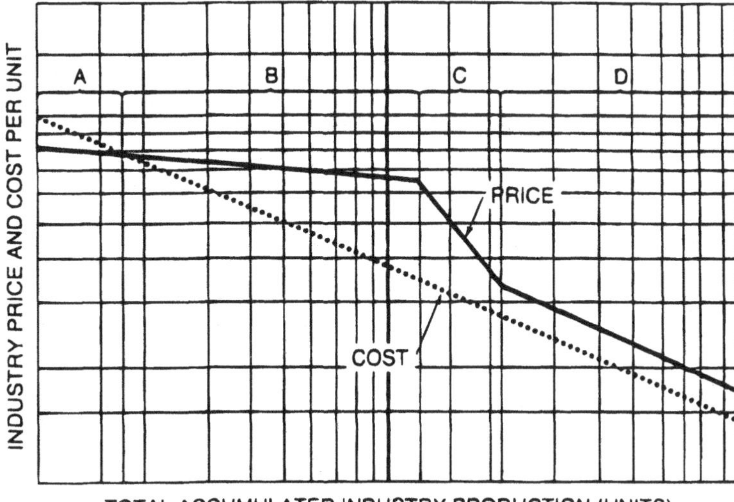


**Figure 4.8**
Typical Price-Cost Relationships.
*Source:* Derek F. Abell and John S. Hammond, *Strategic Market Planning,* Prentice Hall, 1979, p. 116. Adapted from *Perspectives on Experience,* The Boston Consulting Group, 1972, p. 21.

the experience curve. This is *phase D,* which represents a stable market condition. Figure 4.9 shows examples for the semiconductor and chemical industries.

The average cost of the dominant market producers virtually regulates the industry. Whatever learning curve the industry leader uses, then so must the competitors. If the competitors' costs or volume cannot match the industry leader, then the slower rate of cost reductions will force profits to decrease or disappear, thus eliminating these competitors from the marketplace.

## COMPETITIVE WEAPON

Learning curves are a strong competitive weapon, especially in developing a pricing strategy. The actual pricing strategy depends upon the product life-cycle stage, the firm's market position, the competitor's available resources and market position, the time horizon, and the firm's financial position. To illustrate corporate philosophy toward pricing, although companies such as Texas Instruments (TI) and Digital Equipment (DEC) have used "experience curve pricing" to achieve an early market share and a subsequent strong competitive position, companies such as Hewlett-Packard Co. (HP) have used completely different approaches to achieve a commanding portion in the market. The focal point of TI's and DEC's strategy has been to price a new product in relation to the manufacturing costs that they expect to achieve when the product is mature. In contrast, HP, instead of competing on price, concentrates on developing products so advanced that customers are willing to pay a premium for them. David Packard, chairman of HP, drives the point home by saying,

> The main determinant of our growth is the effectiveness of our new product programs . . . Anyone can build market share, and if you set your price low enough, you can get the whole damn market. But I will tell you it won't get you anywhere around [illegible]

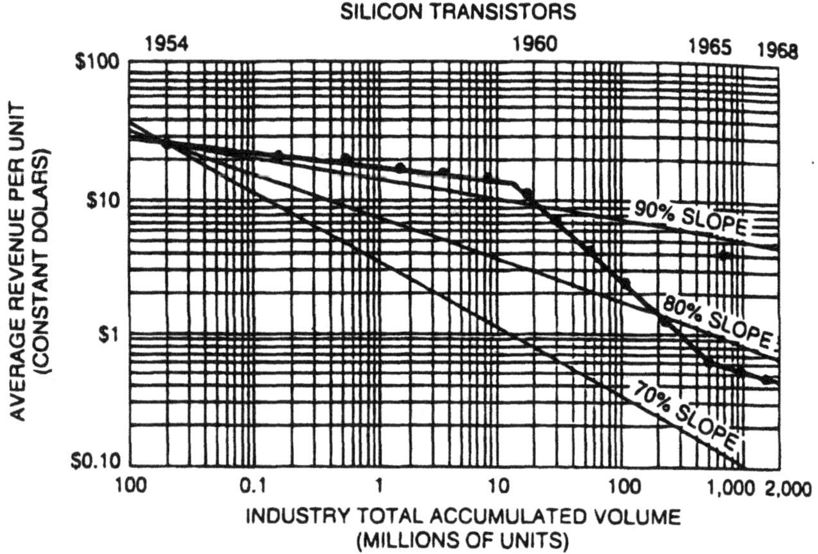


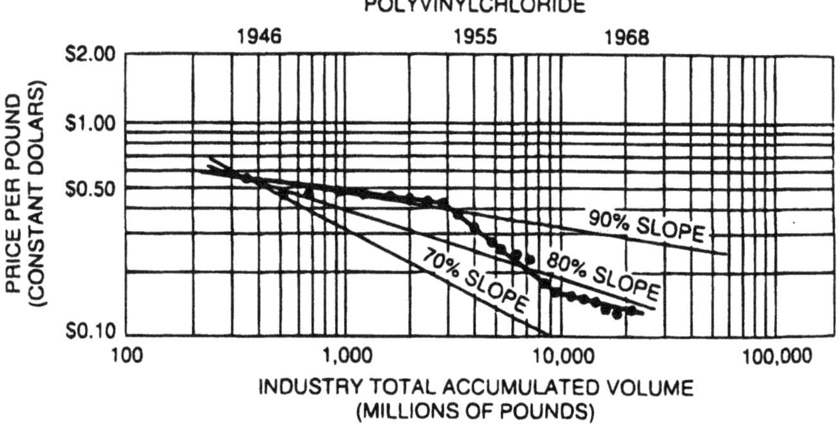


**Figure 4.9** Representative Price-Experience Curves (Each Dot Represents One Year). *Source: Perspectives on Experience*, The Boston Consulting Group, Boston, Massachusetts, 1968, pp. 72, 85.

From a project management perspective, learning-curve pricing can be a competitive weapon. As an example, consider a company that is burdened at $60/hour and is bidding on a job to produce 500 units. Let us assume that the data in Table 4.1 applies. For 500 units of production, the cumulative total hours are 51704, giving us an average rate of 103.4 hours per unit. The cost for the job would be 51704 hours × $60/hour, or $3,102,240. If the target profit is 10%, then the final bid should be $3,412,464. This includes a profit of $310,224.

Even though a 10% profit is projected, the *actual* profit may be substantially less. Each product is priced out an average of 103.4 hours/unit. The first unit, however, will require 812 hours. The company will *lose* 708.6 hours × $60/hour, or $42,516, on the first unit produced. The 100th unit will require 120 hours, giving us a loss of $996 (i.e., [120 hours-103.4 hours] × $60/hour). Profit will

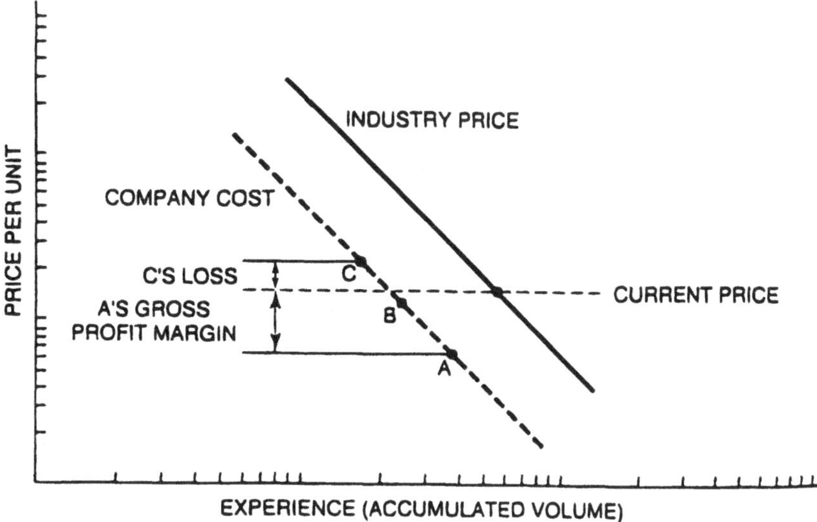


**Figure 4.10** Profitability Advantages of Greater Experience (Market Share).
*Source:* Adapted from "The Experience Curve Revisited: I. The Concept," The Boston Consulting Group, 1974, *Perspectives*, no. 124.

begin when the 150th unit is produced, because the hours required to produce the 150th unit are less than the average hour per unit of 103.4.

Simply stated, the first 150 units are a drain on cash flow. This can be seen graphically in Figure 4.8. The cash-flow drain may require the company to "borrow" money to finance operations until the 150th unit is produced, thus lowering the target profit.

During competitive bidding, it is important to know where the competitors sit on the learning curve. Consider the situation shown in Figure 4.10 where three firms are competing for a new production contract. All three firms are performing on the same experience curve. Firm A has an advantage over Firm B and a superior advantage over Firm C. Firm C is also performing at a higher cost than the current market price. If Firm C submits a bid at the current market price, then a substantial loss will occur. Therefore, it is not advisable for Firm C to bid the job.

Both Firms A and B could bid the job and make a profit, with Firm A making more profit. However, if Firm A lowers its price to a point *below* Firm B's cost per unit, then Firm A could drastically improve their chances of winning the contract, but at a lower profit.

## NOTES

1. Chauncey, Jerome, *History of the American Clock Business For the Past Sixty Years: Life of Chauncey Jerome, Written by himself*, New Haven, F. C. Dayton Jr., 1860.
2. The next six elements are from Derek F. Abell and John S. Hammond, *Strategic Market Planning*, Prentice-Hall, 1979, pp. 112–113.
3. Winfred B. Hirschmann, "Profit from the Learning Curve," *Harvard Business Review*, January–February, 1964, p. [illegible]

4. George Anderlohr, "What Product Breaks Cost," *Industrial Engineering*, September 1969, p. 35.
5. "Hewlett-Packard: When Slower Growth Is Smarter Management," *Business Week*, June 9, 1975, pp. 50–58.

## ESSAY QUESTIONS

1. When a learning curve is plotted on ordinary graph paper, the curve appears to level off. But when the curve is plotted on log-log paper, it appears that the improvements can go on forever. How do you account for the difference? Can the improvements occur indefinitely? If not, what factors could limit continuous improvements?
2. A company is performing on an 85% learning curve. If the first unit requires 620 hours, how much time will be required for the 300th unit?
3. A company working on a 75% learning curve has decided that the production standard should be 85 hours of production for the 100th unit. How much time should be required for the first unit? If the first unit requires more hours than you anticipated, does this mean that the learning curve is wrong?
4. A company has just received a contract for 700 units of a certain product. The pricing department has predicted that the first unit should require 2,250 hours. The pricing department believes that a 75% learning curve is justified. If the actual learning curve is 77%, how much money has the company lost? Assume that a fully burdened hour is $65. What percentage error in total hours results from a 2% increase in learning-curve percentage?
5. If the first unit of production requires 1,200 hours and the 150th unit requires 315 hours, then what learning curve is the company performing at?
6. A company has decided to bid on a follow-on contract for 500 units of a product. The company has already produced 2000 units on a 75% learning curve. The 2,000th unit required 80 hours of production time. If a fully burdened hour is $80 and the company wishes to generate a 12% profit, how much should be bid?
7. Referring to Question 6, how many units of the follow-on contract must be produced before a profit is realized?
8. A manufacturing company wishes to enter a new market. By the end of next year, the market leader will have produced 16,000 units on an 80% learning curve, and the year-end price is expected to be $475/unit. Your manufacturing personnel tell you that the first unit will require $7,150 to produce and, with the new technology you have developed, you should be able to perform at a 75% learning curve. How many units must you produce and sell over the next year in order to compete with the leader at $475/unit at year end? Is your answer realistic, and what assumptions have you made?
9. Rylon Corporation is an assembler of electrical components. The company estimates that for the next year, the demand will be 800 units. The company is performing on an 80% learning curve. The company is considering purchasing some assembly machinery to accelerate the assembly time. Most assembly activities are 85–90% labor intensive. However, with the new machinery, the assembly activities will be only 25–45% labor intensive. If the company purchases and installs the new equipment, it will occur after the 200th unit is produced. Therefore, the remaining 600 units will be produced with the new equipment. The 200th unit will require 620 hours of assembly. However, the 201st unit will require only 400 hours of assembly but on a 90% learning curve.
   a. Will the new machine shorten product assembly time for all 800 units and, if so, by how many hours?
   b. If the company is burdened at $70 per hour, and the new equipment is depreciated over five years, what is the most money that the company should pay for the new equipment? What assumptions have you made?

## MULTIPLE-CHOICE QUESTIONS

1. Learning curves are used for:
   a. competitive bidding
   b. product pricing
   c. cost estimating
   d. labor planning
   e. all the above
2. Learning curve theory states that every time the production levels ————, learning takes place at a ———— rate.
   a. increase, higher than normal
   b. quadruple, fixed
   c. double, fixed
   d. double, higher
   e. increase, lower than normal
3. Ten years ago, your company built a plant capable of producing 100,000 units per year. The cost to build the plan was $30 million. The cost of producing a plant today with a production capacity of 400,000 units per year will be:
   a. $60 million
   b. $69 million
   c. $85 million
   d. $120 million
   e. cannot de determined from data provided
4. On a 90% learning curve, the 100th unit requires 80 hours. The 400th unit should require:
   a. 72 hours
   b. 64.8 hours
   c. 55 hours
   d. 43.6 hours
   e. none of the above
5. If the 20th unit requires 60 hours and the 40th unit requires 48 hours, then the learning curve is ———— %.
   a. 90
   b. 85
   c. 80
   d. 75
   e. 70
6. If the first unit requires 600 hours on a 75% learning curve, then the *average* time required for the first two units will be ———— hours.
   a. 400
   b. 450
   c. 525
   d. 600
   e. 1,050
7. Learning curves appear as a straight line when plotted:
   a. on cartesian coordinates
   b. on polar coordinates
   c. on semilog paper
   d. on log-log paper
   e. as a percentage of total cost
8. To plot a learning curve requires:
   a. two data points

   b. one data point and the learning curve percentage
   c. the learning curve percentage
   d. all the above
   e. a and b only
9. Sources of learning curve experience can include:
   a. new production processes
   b. product redesign
   c. incentives and disincentives
   d. changes in the resource mix
   e. all the above
10. Which of the following is/are limitations to the learning curve?
   a. The learning curve are ideal for short term planning.
   b. Cost data may not be readily available.
   c. The learning curve applies only to quantity discounts.
   d. all the above
   e. a and c only

## CASE STUDY: Saber Engineering, Inc.

Saber Engineering, Inc. (SEI) is a high-technology company with expertise in laser engineering. SEI's R&D group had world-class recognition. All its product lines are for commercial customers, including the medical profession, manufacturing, and automotive.

By 1992, the recession was beginning to take its toll on SEI. The company was forced to downsize, reorganize, lay off 12% of its labor force, and reduce its employee benefits packages. Sales had decreased by 10–15% each year since the recession began in 1989. New sources of revenue had to be found or deep cuts would have to be made in the core resource base.

Marketing identified a window of opportunity for laser research (and possibly production) in the government sector. SEI had avoided government work in the past due to fear of restructuring their accounting and cost-reporting systems to adhere to government requirements. Senior management reluctantly agreed to allow marketing to compete for government contracts.

SEI submitted an unsolicited proposal to Department of Defense (DoD) for R&D on a pulsating laser cannon. The laser cannon could easily become the weapon of the future. Every military aircraft could eventually require such weaponry. Laser weaponry would require less weight than conventional weaponry, thus extending the range of the aircraft. The problem would be to keep the cost at a level acceptable to the government. In the fall of 1992, SEI was awarded an 18-month R&D contract at a firm, fixed price. SEI knew that DoD had funded concurrently two other competitors to conduct similar R&D. SEI had faith in the quality of its R&D group and believed that it could beat out the competition, at least technically. The cost issue posed another problem. In July 1994, SEI successfully completed the R&D contract with the development of an operational prototype. The project was deemed a major success by DoD and showed tremendous promise for future DoD contracts. SEI had entered a new market.

By mid August 1994 DoD wanted an immediate production contract for 800 laser cannons. DoD allowed the bidders to determine the period of performance. The contract would be a fixed-price effort, but the production cost estimating had to be based upon learning curves. SEI had virtually no experience with learning curves. Conversations with companies experienced in learning curves indicated that estimating mistakes could be very costly.

SEI would be one of three companies invited to bid on the DoD contract. Although SEI was considered to be the favorite technically, it might not be very competitive cost-wise. Since the contract would be fixed price, SEI would have to become experienced in the use of learning curves and have divisions dedicated to government programs.

SEI had 60 days to submit its bid. With virtually no learning-curve experience, SEI established a high-level task force that included several senior managers. The task force's mission was to learn as much as possible about learning curves within the next two weeks and come to some type of consensus as to the pricing methodology. A consultant experienced in learning curves was hired to function as an adviser to the task force. The consultant reported directly to the president.

Interviews by the adviser provided the following comments:

### Helene Sardi, Vice President for Accounting and Finance

"The R&D project may have been a technical success, but financially it was a disaster. We ended up with a cost overrun of almost 40%. I'm not sure we want to risk any more funds. Simply preparing a proposal will be a costly effort. The economy seems to be turning around and I would prefer to take the conservative approach and cultivate our bread-and-butter product lines. We don't need the headaches that go along with government contracts, especially with the low profit margins."

### Mike Conneau, Vice President for Production

"We estimated 430 hours to build the operational prototype during the R&D contract. The actual time was 616 hours. This should help us adjust our future estimating since we now have a small database to work with. The first production unit should require the same 616 hours. Material cost will be $2,250 per cannon. We will need a scrap factor of 10%. Our people learn quickly. I'm just a little concerned about how steep our learning curve should be. Perhaps 85–90% seems reasonable. Our workers are not going to be happy being measured against a learning curve unless we offer them incentive pay. This could pose a problem because the workers on the standard products production lines will receive no incentive pay.

"As you know, manufacturing works very little overtime at SEI. I expect this program to require massive overtime and the added pay will be a bonus for the workers. I may have to give all the employees a chance to work overtime and this means that very few people will be full time for the duration of the project. Conservatively, I can provide 6,350 hours of labor each month for the duration of the project if we win it. The problem, of course, is what to do if our standard products require an increase in production? Where will I get the people to support both programs? Are we willing to let the government contract slip? Who will make that decision?"

### Paul Savoy, Project Manager

"This project will be a challenge. We have learned quite a lot from the R&D contract. Our cost overrun was due to poor estimating for direct labor. We can correct this problem by selecting the proper learning curve. Our forward pricing rates indicate that the overhead rate should remain fixed and that a full, burdened hour should be priced out at $103. In addition, project management and

## Exhibit 4.1 75% Learning Curve

| Cumulative Production | Hours This Unit | Cumulative Total Hours |
|---|---|---|
| 1 | 616 | 616 |
| 2 | 462 | 1078 |
| 10 | 237 | 3445 |
| 12 | 220 | 3893 |
| 15 | 201 | 4512 |
| 20 | 178 | 5444 |
| 40 | 134 | 8467 |
| 60 | 113 | 10903 |
| 75 | 103 | 12515 |
| 100 | 92 | 14932 |
| 150 | 77 | 19115 |
| 200 | 69 | 22751 |
| 250 | 63 | 26027 |
| 300 | 58 | 29043 |
| 400 | 52 | 34513 |
| 500 | 47 | 39442 |
| 600 | 44 | 43980 |
| 700 | 41 | 48217 |
| 800 | 39 | 52212 |
| 840 | 38 | 53752 |

management support should be a fixed 740 hours per month for the duration of the project."

### Dr. Peter Weltman, Vice President for R&D

"Bidding and winning the R&D contract, even at a loss, was acceptable last year because it kept our people employed mainly at the government's expense. But for a long-term effort, do we really want to be in this business? I would prefer doing 'offensive R&D' to penetrate new markets to maintain our market share. This project is a risk and will consume valuable resources in my area.

"Technically, I believe that SEI has superior knowledge compared to our competitors even though the competition has been doing government work longer than we have. We could probably win this project if we really want to be in this business."

### Ellen Burke, Vice President for Marketing

"It is absolutely foolish to turn away work. This project could open up new markets and diversify our business base. Our reputation is at stake here, and I want this project. This could end up being a 20-year project if we consider all of the potential follow-on work and long-term scope changes.

"My marketing intelligence personnel tell me that the government wants learning-curve pricing because they expect to have follow-on work. And even if we do not win the project, we might later get a smaller project as a second source supplier. The government likes to do this not only to keep costs down, but to maintain a second source supplier. It sounds a little like spreading around the wealth.

"My marketing group has reliable contacts in both of the competitors. Both competitors appear to be working on an 80% learning curve. We should price out our effort using a 75% learning curve. This will give us a competitive advantage.

"We are currently checking out a comment that was made by one of the competitors that their standard is 74 hours for the 250th unit. I'm not sure this is correct. We'll have to substantiate it. Perhaps 123 hours per cannon is closer to the truth.

"To win the contract, we may wish to forego the profit. I would like to go with a 75% learning curve and a very conservative 4% profit margin. I think that I can sell this to our president."

The consultant met with the president to discuss his interviews with members of the task force. The consultant believed that learning curves were applicable because the majority of the manufacturing and assembly operations were labor intensive. Selecting the true learning curve would be difficult. The consultant also expressed his concern that some standard would have to be set.

The president instructed the consultant to compare the results of an 80% learning curve versus a 75% learning curve. Furthermore, the president declared that this project will not be bid unless SEI receives at least a 10% profit.

The consultant pulled out his laptop computer and calculated both the 75% and 80% learning curves, assuming that the 1st production unit would require 616 hours. (The results appear in Exhibits 4.1 and 4.2.)

## QUESTIONS

1. What is the time for the 800th unit of 75% learning curve?

## Exhibit 4.2 80% Learning Curve

| Cumulative Production | Hours This Unit | Cumulative Total Hours |
|---|---|---|
| 1 | 616 | 616 |
| 2 | 493 | 1109 |
| 10 | 294 | 3892 |
| 12 | 277 | 4454 |
| 15 | 258 | 5246 |
| 20 | 235 | 6463 |
| 40 | 188 | 10603 |
| 60 | 165 | 14105 |
| 75 | 154 | 16488 |
| 100 | 140 | 20147 |
| 150 | 123 | 26685 |
| 200 | 112 | 32549 |
| 250 | 105 | 37957 |
| 300 | 99 | 43028 |
| 400 | 90 | 52424 |
| 500 | 84 | 61090 |
| 600 | 79 | 69216 |
| 700 | 75 | 76917 |
| 800 | 72 | [illegible] |
| 840 | 71 | 87133 |

2. What is the average time per laser cannon for all 800 units on the 75% learning curve?
3. Using the 75% learning curve, how much time (in months) will be needed for the 800-unit production contract?
4. Using the 75% learning curve, what should be the value of SEI's bid and how much profit can they expect if everything goes according to plan?
5. What assumptions, if any, have you made in arriving at your answers to Question 4?
6. What is the time for the 800th unit of the 80% learning curve?
7. What is the average time per cannon for all 800 units on the 80% learning curve?
8. Using the 80% learning curve, calculate the schedule slippage (in months) if the company bids on a 75% learning curve and actual learning is 80%?
9. How much profit or loss will SEI experience if the actual learning is 80%, and SEI submits their bid based upon a 75% learning curve?
10. Exhibits 1 and 2 used 616 hours as the time for the first production run. Is it realistic to assume that if the working prototype requires 616 hours, then the first production unit would require the same 616 hours, or close to it?
11. The consultant decided that manufacturing's estimate of 616 hours for the first production run may be an error. Using 676 hours for the first production run, and assuming an 80% learning curve, the consultant generated the results shown in Exhibit 4.3. Compare Exhibits 4.2 and 4.3. What are your conclusions?
12. The consultant had trouble believing that marketing's competitive intelligence sources may be correct in assuming that the competitors had a standard of 74

## Exhibit 4.3 80% Learning Curve (1st Unit at 676 Hours)

| Cumulative Production | Hours This Unit | Cumulative Total Hours |
|---|---|---|
| 1 | 676 | 676 |
| 2 | 541 | 1217 |
| 10 | 322 | 4271 |
| 12 | 304 | 4888 |
| 15 | 283 | 5756 |
| 20 | 258 | 7093 |
| 40 | 207 | 11634 |
| 60 | 181 | 15477 |
| 75 | 169 | 18092 |
| 100 | 154 | 22106 |
| 150 | 135 | 29279 |
| 200 | 123 | 35712 |
| 250 | 115 | 41645 |
| 300 | 108 | 47208 |
| 400 | 99 | 57515 |
| 500 | 92 | 67021 |
| 600 | 87 | 75934 |
| 700 | 82 | 84381 |
| 800 | 79 | 92450 |
| 840 | 78 | 95586 |

hours for the 250th unit. Exhibit 4.4 shows an 80% learning curve where the 250th unit is at 74 hours. What conclusions can you reach? (i.e., compare Exhibit 4.2 with Exhibit 4.4). Does a standard of 74 hours for the 250th unit seem correct?

**13.** After extensive research, the consultant concluded that on an 80% learning curve (Exhibit 4.2), the standard of performance would be reached after the 300th unit. This equates to 99 hours per unit. However, the workers would probably "peg" their output to 118% of the standard, and then level off their output. (i.e., If the standard is 99 hours and performance is pegged at 118% of standard, then

$$\frac{99\text{ hours}}{118\%} = 84\text{ hours}$$

In other words, once the workers achieve 84 hours per cannon, all remaining cannons will require 84 hours per cannon.) How many units must be produced before we reach 118% of standard?

**14.** Using your answer to Question 13, what is the new average hour per unit for all 800 units?

**15.** Using your answers to Questions 13 and 14, what are the total hours and cost for the job if performance is pegged? By how much time will the project be late?

**16.** Compare your answer to Question 15 with Question 4. Will the company make more or less money, and by how much if work is pegged at 118% of standard?

**17.** Should SEI bid on the job? If so, what should be the bid price? Identify all assumptions made.

**18.** Analyze the comments of each of the people interviewed. Do they appear to have "hidden agendas"? Do they understand project management?

**Exhibit 4.4 80% Learning Curve (Standard at 74 Hours for 250th Unit)**

| Cumulative Production | Hours This Unit | Cumulative Total Hours |
|---|---|---|
| 1 | 433 | 433 |
| 2 | 346 | 779 |
| 10 | 206 | 2735 |
| 12 | 195 | 3130 |
| 15 | 181 | 3687 |
| 20 | 165 | 4543 |
| 40 | 132 | 7453 |
| 60 | 116 | 9916 |
| 75 | 108 | 11592 |
| 100 | 99 | 14165 |
| 150 | 87 | 18765 |
| 200 | 79 | 22891 |
| 250 | 74 | 26697 |
| 300 | 69 | 30266 |
| 400 | 63 | 36880 |
| 500 | 59 | 42982 |
| 600 | 56 | 48704 |
| 700 | 53 | 51100 |

# CASE STUDY: Microtech Devices

Microtech Devices (MTD), a small division of Monroe Electronics, was now at a critical junction. With limited resources, a decision had to be made as to which market they wished to compete in. During the past five years, MTD tried unsuccessfully to compete in the watch market, calculator market, and microchip market at the same time. With limited resources, the best MTD could do was to be a follower in all three markets, surviving on the "table crumbs" left by the market leaders. Breakeven was generally the best that MTD could expect.

MTD's management had to decide where to complete. Technically, the microchip market was lost. MTD could not compete with Motorola, Intel, or the partnerships formed by the major PC manufacturers. The watch market was also lost. The Swiss, Japanese, and Germans were providing low-cost, quality competition. The only feasible approach was to compete in the low- to medium-priced calculator market.

MTD maintained a small 5% share of the market. This market share would not be enough to support MTD even if downsizing were to occur. To compete successfully in the low- to medium-priced calculator market, MTD would require at least a 25% share of the market as well as have to match the competitors' selling prices.

The president of MTD realized that funding from the parent Monroe Electronics would be required. A plan had to be developed in order to convince Monroe that MTD could compete successfully in the low- to medium-priced calculator market. Funding would be required not only to support daily operations, but for massive marketing and advertising. There were rumors circulating that Monroe wanted to sell the MTD Division. The president realized that the best he could hope for would be three years to turn the division around and make it profitable.

Certain facts were available to help MTD's management develop a plan:

- **a.** All the major competitors perform on the same learning curve.
- **b.** At present, calculators are selling at $38 apiece. Three years from now, the selling price is expected to drop to $31 per calculator according to the learning-curve data of the market leader.
- **c.** The market leader has a 20% share of the market and expects sales to be flat at 1 million units per year for each of the next three years.
- **d.** MTD has produced almost 1 million calculators to date. However, more than 800,000 of these were for one of their military clients.

The stockholder's report for the market leader indicated that they had produced 5 million calculators thus far. Using this information, MTD constructed the learning curve shown in Exhibit 4A.1.

## QUESTIONS

1. How did MTD construct Exhibit 4A.1? What data were used?
2. What learning curve percentage is shown in Exhibit 4A.1?
3. MTD's marketing personnel believe that with an all-out campaign, 1 million units can be sold next year. However, this will require an extensive marketing and advertising campaign of at least $10 million per year for each of the next three years. Assume MTD successfully sells 1 million units next year. What *constant*

## Exhibit 4A.1 Learning Curve

| Cumulative Production | Cost This Unit | Cumulative Total Hours |
|---|---|---|
| 200,000 | 174 | 5714 |
| 400,000 | 125 | 8602 |
| 600,000 | 104 | 10,860 |
| 750,000 | 93 | 12,327 |
| 1,000,000 | 81 | 14,493 |
| 1,500,000 | 67 | 18,168 |
| 2,000,000 | 59 | 21,300 |
| 2,500,000 | 53 | 24,081 |
| 3,000,000 | 49 | 26,611 |
| 4,000,000 | 42 | 31,137 |
| 5,000,000 | 38 | 35,158 |
| 6,000,000 | 35 | 38,817 |
| 7,000,000 | 33 | 42,200 |
| 8,000,000 | 31 | 45,365 |

growth rate will be required the second and third years in order to catch the market leader by the end of the third year? Is this realistic?

4. Assume that the market leader sets the selling price each year in accordance with Exhibit 4A.1, and that the selling price is fixed for 12 months. What will be the selling price for each of the next three years?
5. Neglecting the profit that is included in the selling price, how much funding will MTD require from Monroe in order to catch up to the market leader by the end of the third year? Assume that an advertising budget of $10 million per year will be needed.
6. Suppose that at the end of the third year, the selling levels off at $31 per calculator and remains the same for five more years. If MTD were able to sell 4 million units per year, beginning in year 4, what would be the payback period for the funding provided by Monroe? Use $5 million as a yearly advertising expense beginning in year 4 and assume that a selling price of $31 per calculator will include a 12% profit margin. (Neglect the value of money implication.)
7. Does MTD's plan have a chance of success? If so, what must happen for success to be viable?

# CHAPTER 5 The Role of R&D

## Role of R&D in Strategic Planning

Strategic planning and R&D are similar in that both deal with the future profits and growth of the organization. Without a continuous stream of new products, the company's strategic-planning options may be limited. Today, advances in technology and growing competitive pressure are forcing companies to develop new and innovative products while the life cycle of existing products appears to be decreasing at an alarming rate. Yet, at the same time, executives may keep research groups in a vacuum and fail to take advantage of the potential profit contribution of R&D strategic planning.

There are three primary reasons why corporations conduct research and development:

- to produce new products or services for profitable growth
- to produce profitable improvements to existing products and services
- to produce scientific knowledge that can assist in identifying new opportunities or in "fighting fires"

Successful R&D programs are targeted, but targeting requires a good information system and this, unfortunately, is the weakest link in most companies. Information systems are needed for optimum R&D targeting efforts and this includes assessing customer and market needs, economic evaluation, and project selection.

Assessing customer and market needs involves opportunity-seeking and commercial intelligence functions. Most companies delegate these responsibilities to the marketing group, and this may result in a detrimental effort because marketing groups appear to be overwhelmed with today's products and near-term profitability. They simply do not have the time or resources to adequately analyze other R&D activities that have long-term implications. Also, marketing groups do not have technically trained personnel who can communicate effectively with the R&D groups of the customers and suppliers.

The implications of a corporate strategic plan may be dependent solely upon that point in time where marketing tests the new products in the marketplace. Quite often, senior management will attempt to shorten the R&D time in order to increase earnings at a faster rate. The problem here is that the legality of product liability may be overlooked in the executives' haste to produce results due to stockholder pressure. In time of trouble, executives cut R&D funding in the mistaken belief that cost reductions will occur. In either event, the long-term impact on the organization may prove unhealthy.

Another major problem in industry today is budgeting amounts for new product development. Research is a costly process and is so uncertain that it is difficult to use normal investment criteria for budgeting. This problem is further compounded by the fact that the success ratio from the idea screening stage to a successful new product is 1 : 64, according to one author.[1]

High-tech industries such as aerospace, defense, computers, electronics, and transportation have strategic plans that include billions of dollars for R&D. These industries spend between 5% and 10% of their sales dollars for R&D. At the lower end of the scale are found such industries as wood products, paper, and textiles.

Budgeting for R&D, and for that matter, budgeting for any aspect of a modern business, must begin with a solid foundation of effective corporate planning. Only when there are adequate strategic plans that establish well-defined goals and objectives for the enterprise can R&D managers formulate, prioritize, and implement the needed R&D projects. These projects, once approved, generate the need for an effective method of budgeting, feedback, and control to verify that the work is progressing according to the strategic direction. Every R&D project can be viewed as part of the executive's strategic plan.

The R&D function, regardless of its position within the organizational structure of the firm, can be viewed as a strategic-planning system where an input of money results in an output of products. Furthermore, as with most systems, there must exist a feedback mechanism such that the flow of money can be diverted from less promising projects to those with the greater potential. This implies that the R&D systems must be continuously monitored, perhaps more so than other systems. This leads to considering the following topics (at a minimum) in discussing the R&D budgeting process:

- **new product innovation**—An understanding of this process helps identify the cost/benefits of R&D and the chances of success.
- **corporate objectives and strategic plans**—This provides the framework of setting technical objectives and decisions regarding the funding of a new product, program, or project.
- **project evaluation and selection**—This provides a method for screening and relating the potential of projects to others under consideration for funding.
- **budgeting approaches**—This provides a method for screening and relating the potential of projects to others under consideration for funding

# Innovation Background

A host of environmental forces, including changes in industrial customer needs, competitor behavior, technology, and government policy, combine to make R&D and new-product innovation a vital element in corporate planning. The future of many industrial companies are closely tied to their ability to develop and successfully market new products. In addition, companies with highly sophisticated industrial products are the most prone to technological obsolescence. As a result, most successful industrial firms must pursue product innovation in addition to maintaining current product lines or risk obsolescence. One of the best ways for an industrial company to stay competitive is through active participation in the development of the latest technologies. These technologies can then be used to develop new products to satisfy changing customer needs.

An appreciation of the innovation process requires an understanding of the various types and stages of innovation. Three distinct types have been distinguished by Marquis, as follows:[2]

First, there is the *complex system*, such as communication networks, moon missions, and energy systems, that takes many years and many millions of dollars to accomplish. This type of innovation is characterized by thorough long-range planning that assures the required technologies will be available and fit together at the proper time in the final development stage. This type of innovation also requires large amounts of resources and effective budgeting techniques.

Second, there is the kind of innovation represented by major radical breakthroughs in technology that change the whole character of an industry. The jet engine and xerography are typical examples. Such innovations are quite rare and unpredictable and are predominantly developed by independent inventors outside the affected industry.

Last, there is the modest type of innovation characterized by product improvement, cost cutting, quality-control improvements, and so on. This is the ordinary, everyday, within-the-firm kind of technological change. Without this type of innovation, industrial firms can, and do, perish.

# New-Product Evolution

In a study of the new-product activities of several hundred companies in all industries, Booz, Allen, and Hamilton[3] defined the new-product evolution process as the time it takes to bring a product to commercial existence. This process begins with company objectives, which include fields of product interest, goals, and growth plans, and ends with, hopefully, a successful product. The more specifically these objectives are defined, the greater guidance will be given to the new-product program. This process can be broken down into six manageable, fairly clear sequential stages:

- **exploration**—the search for product ideas to meet company objectives
- **screening**—a quick analysis to determine which ideas are pertinent and merit more detailed study

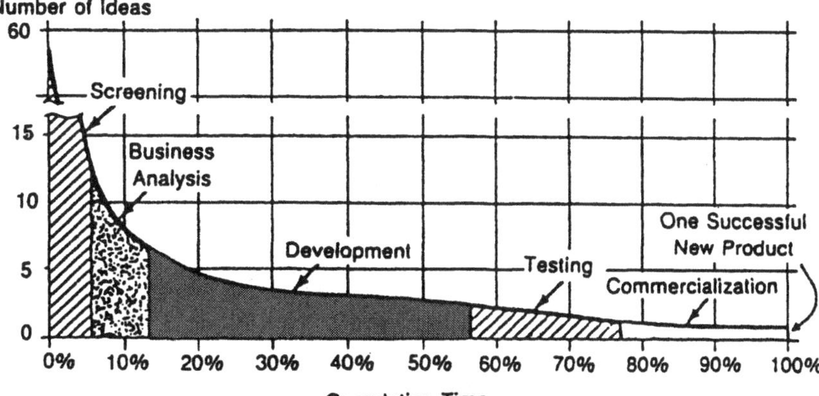


**Figure 5.1**
Mortality of New Product Ideas.
*Source: Management of New Products,* Booz, Allen & Hamilton, Inc., 1984, p. 180.

- **business analysis**—the expansion of the idea, through creative analysis, into a concrete business recommendation including product features, financial analysis, risk analysis, market assessment, and a program for the product
- **development**—turning the idea-on-paper into a product-in-hand, demonstrable and producible. This stage focuses on R&D and the inventive capacity of the firm. Unanticipated problems usually arise, and new solutions and trade-offs are sought. In many instances, the obstacles are so great that a solution cannot be found, and work is terminated or deferred.
- **testing**—the technical and commercial experiments necessary to verify earlier technical and business judgments
- **commercialization**—launching the product in full-scale production and sale; committing the company's reputation and resources

The new-product process can be characterized by a decay curve for ideas as shown in Figure 5.1. This shows a progressive rejection of idea or projects by stages in the product-evolution process. Although the rate of rejection varies between industries and companies, the general shape of the decay curve is typical. It generally takes close to 60 ideas to yield just one successful new product.

The process of new-product evolution involves a series of management decisions. Each stage is progressively more expensive, as measured in expenditures of both time and money. Figure 5.2 shows the rate at which expense dollars are spent as time accumulates for the average project within a sample of leading companies. This information was based on an all-industry average and should, therefore, be useful in understanding the typical industrial new-product process. It is significant to note that the majority of capital expenditures is concentrated in the last three stages of evolution. It is, therefore, very important to do a better job of screening for business and financial analysis. This will help eliminate ideas of limited potential before they reach the more expensive stages of evolution.

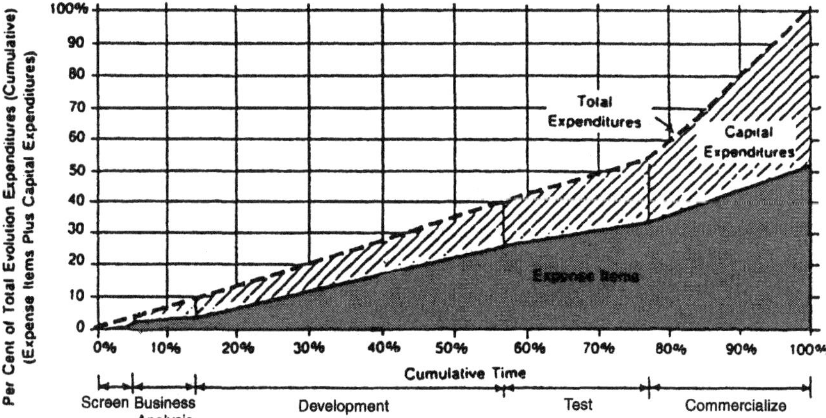


**Figure 5.2** Cumulative Expenditures and Time.
*Source*: *Management of New Products*, Booz, Allen & Hamilton, Inc., 1984, p. 181.

# New Product Success

Mansfield and Wagner[4] investigated the success probabilities of new industrial products in different stages of their development cycles and reported a 57% success rate of technical completion based on the development of a working product prototype; a 65% success rate of commercialization (bringing the product to market) following successful technical completion; and a 74% probability of economic success after commercialization.

This leads to a 27% ccommercial success rate for industrial product development projects by compounding these success rates through the cycle. Although this number should be interpreted carefully because of sample size considerations and lack of agreement on the definition of commercial success, it provides a gross estimate of the risks associated with new-product development activities.

The high cost of product innovation together with the high mortality rate of products makes it imperative that R&D be properly targeted through the strategic plan. This targeting includes.

- establishing the overall company objectives in light of expected future economic and technological forecasts and development
- clearly communicating these objectives to the R&D organization
- defining the R&D mission
- periodic reassessment of R&D progress in light of current economic and technological developments (i.e., balancing R&D projects against environmental [internal and external] threats and opportunities)

# Portfolio Management

When a corporation develops its strategic plan for R&D, the plan must be aligned with the corporation's strategic business unit and product portfolio. A corporation should have a balanced mix of products. This mix consists of stars, cash cows, dogs, and question marks. Some products generate cash, while others use cash.

Obviously, in order to run the company in the short term, cash cows are required. On the other hand, in both the short and long term, a company needs stars coming into the marketplace and in development for future growth. It is doubtful that a company would want to invest very heavily in R&D for the development of new products in a declining mature market. In this example, a company may choose to have R&D work on a cost-reduction program for existing products.

A company must develop product-line strategies that are linked to its R&D strategies. Is marketing interested in investment and growth, thus establishing an offensive posture and building market share? Do they want to maintain position by having a defensive posture and maintaining market share? Another strategy is to harvest a product by maximizing profits and reinvesting the profits in better opportunities. The last strategy is to divest or abandon a product. By understanding this delicate balance, one can then plan future product development implications on product life cycles.

A balanced product portfolio means new products must be under development or in their growth phase to replace those in maturity or already in decline. A continued product improvement program is necessary to remain ahead of the competition. The development of new markets for existing products prolongs the growth phase of that product. "Me-too" products require another set of capabilities, depending on the lead product's position in its product life cycle.

# Patents

A company must decide what type of strategy it wishes to pursue regarding the protection of its technology. One course of action is to patent the technology. There are advantages and disadvantages to obtaining a patent. Some of these are as follows:

| **Advantages** | **Disadvantages** |
| --- | --- |
| • easier to license technology | • additional demands on R&D staff |
| • permits 17 years of use | • increases costs |
| • allows for the development of and access to a technological base | • provides competition with information |

It is important to note that the evolving doctrine of "absolute novelty" states that any public disclosure prior to filing for a patent may foreclose on your company's opportunity to obtain patent coverage.

# Nondisclosure Agreements, Secrecy Agreements, and Confidentiality Agreements

In the course of doing business, few companies can develop and market a new product without some help from outside their company. When it is necessary to secure outside help, it is essential to protect the proprietary nature of the information being transmitted to the outside party. In order to do this, an agreement is drawn up between the two parties and signed by a corporate officer from each firm.

Top management must develop a policy on how to handle the transfer of confidential information regarding technological developments to outside sources. Generally speaking, there are two types of agreements: one-way and mutual. The one-way agreement is exactly what the name implies in that the company with the confidential information is transferring that information to the second party with nothing coming back. The mutual agreement calls for the transfer of confidential information between both parties.

# Government Influence

Foreign and domestic governments play a significant role in the strategic-planning process for R&D. The laws and policies set forth by government can encourage or discourage R&D. This effect can be direct or indirect. The government may have tax incentives that will foster a climate for R&D to flourish. Government can also impose regulations or standards that will encourage the development of new products to meet those standards. The behavior and posture of foreign governments can influence licensing agreements, the competitive edge on new products, the ability to market new products, and so on.

The Japanese robotics industry developed quickly because there was a labor shortage in some rapidly growing industries such as automobiles. A receptive atmosphere for new technology and important assistance from the government in the form of accelerated depreciation allowances and subsidized research and development were instrumental in allowing for quick success. The role of government is a subject much too broad to be covered in this book. The following list is but a sampling of how government can control and influence industrial research and development.

- fiscal and monetary policies
- international operations and control
- technology transfer restrictions
- patents
- policy impact on technological corporations
- taxes; monetary flow restrictions
- labor/management relations
- risk
- regulation
- sponsor of technological advance, with corporate involvement

# Research and Development Ratio

A company must determine the balance or ratio of basic research, applied research, and product development. Basic research may or may not respond directly to a specific problem or need, but it is selected and directed into those fields where advances will have a major impact on the company's future core businesses.

Applied research is the next step in using a technology to accomplish business objectives that may include processes, cost reduction, and so on. Product development uses all technologies available to it to develop a product that is consistent with the direction of the company.

An industrial company needs to determine the ratio of the above-mentioned areas when determining its strategy for short- and long-term decisions. Basic research is generally a long-term commitment that must be made and driven by top management. Marketing, sales, and manufacturing do not have the incentive to sponsor applied research and more product-development research for short-term programs. Therefore, it is the responsibility of top management to provide direction to the research and development effort within the corporation.

# Manufacturing and Sales

These two groups must be included in the strategic-planning process for research and development. This is particularly true in the development of new products and technologies. It is essential to know if manufacturing has the capability to make the product using existing manufacturing facilities and equipment. Will the existing manufacturing plants have sufficient capacity to meet demand? Will they be able to manufacture the product and be cost effective? If new equipment and plants are needed, this information needs to be factored into the overall plan so they will be ready when the new product is ready to be launched. Just as important is the sales force. Is the present sales force adequate? Adequacy must be evaluated in terms of numbers, training, location, and so on. Will the new product require different selling skills than the company's present product line? Another factor that must be evaluated is the possible reduction in sales force due to a new product. What adverse effect might that have on the morale of the sales group? What are the behavioral ramifications of such a move?

# Human Behavior

One of the key factors in strategic planning is the ability to communicate effectively with a great deal of emphasis placed on teamwork, interaction between groups, and knowing your customer. Obviously, the more top management understands human behavior, the more they can control productivity and the management of limited human resources.

One of the many problems associated with R&D is ownership. Top management may feel that they have the need and the right to constantly control a project. Management must relinquish control in order to allow R&D to inject the degree of creativity needed to make the project successful. On the other hand, the individual or team within R&D who is working on the project also needs to relinquish control once the project is ready to be released to manufacturing and marketing.

Recently, there is a greater emphasis within R&D organizations to hire behavioral psychologists to work with their staff. The driving force for this is to improve communication and increase productivity. There is also a growing trend to use behavioral psychologists to analyze the consumer and determine how to develop and position industrial products both present and future.

# Research versus Development

Although most people consider R&D as a total entity, there are critical differences between research and development.

- **specifications**—Researchers generally function with weak specifications because of the freedom to invent, whereas development personnel are paid not to create new alternatives but to reduce available alternatives to one hopefully simple solution available for implementation.
- **resources**—Generally, more resources are needed for development work rather than pure research. This generates a greater need for structured supervision, whereas research is often conducted in a campuslike work environment.
- **scheduling**—Researchers prefer very loose schedules with the freedom to go off on tangents, whereas developmental schedules are more rigid. Research schedules identify parallel activities whereas in development, scheduled activities are sequential.
- **engineering changes**—In the research stages of a project, engineering changes, specification changes, and engineering redirection (even if simply caused by the personal whims of management) may have a minor cost impact compared to these same changes occurring in the development stage.

For simplicity's sake, however, we will assume that R&D is a single entity.

# R&D Benefits

For the past seven years, the percent of Gross National Product (GNP) spent on R&D has decreased substantially in the United States, England, and France, but increased in Russia, Japan, and West Germany. This concern over the decline in R&D expenditures has caused observers to believe that this indicates the demise of U.S. innovation and, ultimately, economic decline. Some go beyond the economists' effort to link faltering R&D with faltering productivity. In the near term, a company's ability to produce innovative results may be directly related, but in the long term, the results may not be directly measurable.

- How do we measure the R&D spillover effects across industries? (medical benefits derived from the space program)
- How do we measure progress if the productivity gains are not anticipated until 10 or more years from now? (SOHIO's massive investment to

improve production efficiency for the mining/processing of copper was not expected to yield profitable results until 10 years later.)

- How do we evaluate R&D expenditures on socially valuable activities such as health and environment? (How many companies have benefited from the work of OSHA and EPA?)

If the benefits of R&D are to be measured solely by financial achievements such as return on investment (ROI), then the innovation process will undergo severe restraints because executives will consider R&D planning as too costly a process, will not be able to establish projected revenue benefits from basic research, and will be unable to see future economic dividends as a result of a project that failed, even though the negative results indicate that the company should direct their efforts in a different direction.

Among the ills that plague modern management, Hayes and Abernathy identify several that bias decision making against innovation and technological aggressiveness.[5] All are reasonably construed as undermining R&D. They are interwoven to represent what is wrong about R&D planning now. Consider:

- **financial control**—The prevailing profit-center concept necessitates greater dependence on short-term financial measurements for evaluating managerial performance. Do tight, short-term controls stifle R&D creativity and innovation?
- **corporate portfolio management**—The analytical formulas of portfolio theory push managers even further toward extreme caution in allocating resources. Is this cautious management mode directing behavior away from assuming responsibility for reasonable risk and closing the door on resource allocations for R&D?
- **market-driven behavior**—Exclusive reliance on customer-driven resource allocation for product development is untenable. Customers define their needs in terms of existing products, processes, markets, and prices. So the market-driven strategy opts for customer satisfaction and lower risk at the expense of superior products in the future. Is market-driven behavior a question for lagging commitment to new technology and new capital equipment through R&D?
- **backward integration**—In deciding to integrate backward because of apparent short-term rewards, managers often restrict their ability to strike out in innovative directions in the future. Are American managers subjugating R&D-based innovative products and market development to "results now" ROI-based integration? Are they paralyzing the company's long-term ability to stay abreast of technological change? Or are their near-term-based decisions locking the company into long-term outdated technology?
- **limited process development**—Many American managers—especially in mature industries—are reluctant to invest heavily in the development of new manufacturing processes. They tend to restrict investments in process development to only those items likely to return short-run costs. Has management lost sight of the reality that users, not producers, are the usual source of individual process innovations and that R&D-based

proprietary process can be as much a competitive edge as proprietary products?

- **"professional" managers**—Modern senior managers are less informed about their industry because there is an increasing propensity for executives to have interests in financial or legal areas, not production. The business community has developed an acceptance of the notion that an individual having no expertise in any particular industry or technology can nevertheless step into an unfamiliar company and run it successfully through strict application of financial controls, portfolio concepts, and a market-driven strategy. In the meantime, what becomes of the unglamorous, arduous process of maintaining R&D strength so that at the strategic level the business remains vigorous and competitive?

# Modeling the R&D Strategic Planning Function

Schematic modeling of the R&D function requires an understanding of how R&D fits into the total strategic plan and the R&D functional strategy. Figure 5.3 illustrates the integration of R&D into the total strategic-planning function. Once the business is defined, together with an environmental analysis of strengths, weaknesses, opportunities, and threats, the corporate goals and objectives are defined. Unfortunately, the definition of the strategic goals and objectives is usually made in financial terms or through the product/market element. This type of definition implies a critical assumption: R&D can and will develop the new products or product improvements within the required specifications in order to meet target goals and objectives.

Unfortunately, many companies have not realized the importance of soliciting R&D input into the objective-setting stage and, therefore, treat R&D simply as a service organization.

Once the objectives are set, marketing will identify the products and approach (tactics) to achieve the strategies. Here again, R&D may be treated as a service organization.

The corporate culture will dictate the selection process for R&D projects. It is not uncommon for either the entire R&D selection process to be controlled by marketing or for the entire R&D budget to be part of the marketing budget. The reason for this is because marketing wants to be sure that it can sell successfully what R&D products.

In mature organizations, however, R&D personnel are allowed to express their concerns over the feasibility of the goals and objectives and of the probability of successfully achieving the R&D objectives. In such a case, there exists a feedback loop from project selection to objective-setting as show in Figure 5.3.

The box in Figure 5.3 entitled "Support for new Products" requires that the R&D strategy account for the management of innovation and entrepreneurship and can be modeled as shown in Figure 5.4. Not all companies have entrepreneurship strategies like 3M or Texas Instruments because of a slow and tedious

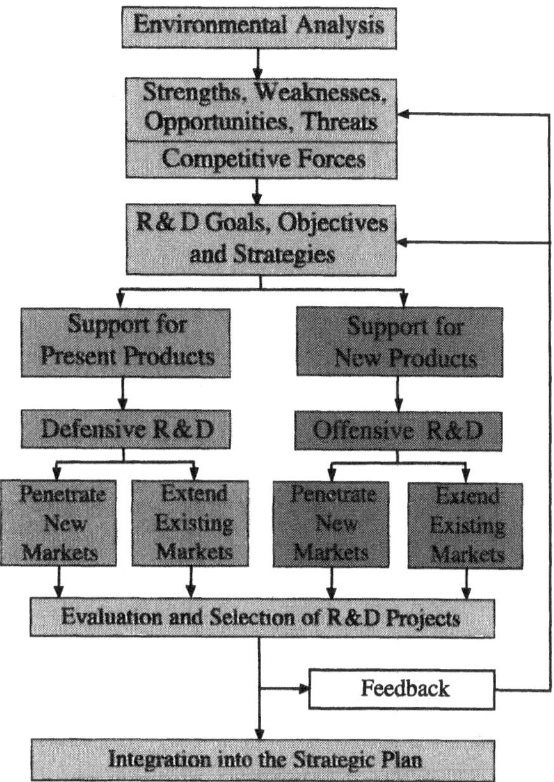


**Figure 5.3**
The R&D Strategic-Planning Process.

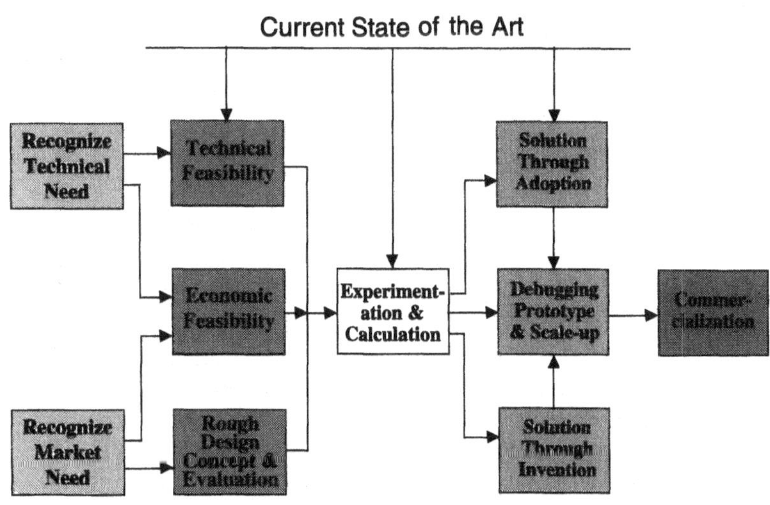


Problem | Problem | Solution/ | Commer-

**Figure 5.4**
Modelling the Innovation Process

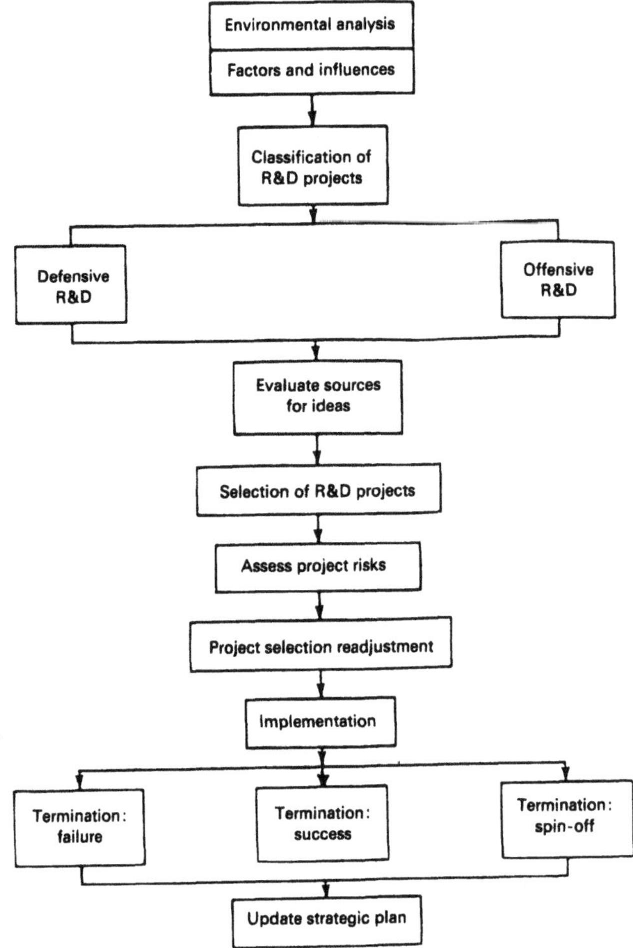


**Figure 5.5**
**Offensive versus Defensive R&D.**

permeation process into the corporate culture. The successful companies consider entrepreneurship as "business" in itself and marry it to the mainstream of the company.

Figure 5.3 also shows that successful integration of R&D into the strategic plan requires that R&D understand the firm's production process, distribution process market research, and market distribution channels. This requires that R&D understand marketing's decision to introduce a new product by being either first to market, second to market, application engineering, or "me too."

When a company has perceived a strategic need to enter a new market, increase growth, or improve an existing product, the company is faced with the problem of how to acquire the technical skills necessary for integration into the strategic plan. The alternatives are:

- R&D with existing resources that have the technical capability
- R&D with existing resources through internal technical training
- R&D through newly hired employees

- R&D through consultants
- acquisition of a company with the required technology
- joint ventures
- buying technology through licensing

As described previously, functional strategies may be performed independently up to the point of integration into the total plan. The functional R&D strategy is shown in Figure 5.5. Each of the steps in Figure 5.5 will be discussed in the following sections. The environmental analysis box in Figure 5.5 is somewhat different from the environmental analysis box in Figure 5.3. The box in Figure 5.5 is accomplished entirely by R&D to stay abreast of the state of the art and what the competition is doing. It is also important to note that the termination of each project should result in an updating of the strategic plan.

It is extremely difficult to uncouple R&D from other functions. Figure 5.6 illustrates the role of key functional units within the R&D functional strategy process. Several interesting points exist in Figure 5.6. They include:

- Marketing and R&D are strongly coupled.
- Executives generally express more of an interest in offensive rather than defensive R&D because of the impact on the strategic plan.
- Manufacturing involvement should exist in the implementation of the R&D project because what R&D can develop on a bench may require a different approach during full-scale production runs.
- Financial involvement is limited to selection and risk assessment of R&D projects.

Functional Decisions

| Function | Environmental analysis | Classification of projects | Defensive R&D | Offensive R&D | Evaluate sources of ideas | Selection of R&D projects | Assess project risks | Project selection readjustment | Implementation | Termination | Update strategic plan |
|---|---|---|---|---|---|---|---|---|---|---|---|
| Executives | ○ | ◓ | ○ | ◓ | ○ | ◓ | ○ | ○ | ○ | ◓ | ● |
| Marketing | ◓ | ◓ | ● | ● | ◓ | ● | ○ | ◓ | ○ | ● | ◓ |
| Finance | ○ | ○ | ○ | ○ | ○ | ◓ | ◓ | ○ | ○ | ○ | ○ |
| Manufacturing | ○ | ○ | ◓ | ◓ | ○ | ○ | ○ | ○ | ◓ | ○ | ○ |
| R&D | ● | ● | ● | ● | ● | ● | ● | ● | ● | ● | ○ |

○ = Little or no involvement ◓ = Some involvement ● = Large amount of involvement

**Figure 5.6**
The Involvement Mix.

The models shown in Figures 5.3, 5.5, and 5.6 are very sensitive to the length of the product life cycle and the size of the company. Table 5.1 shows the basic differences in strategic planning as a result of short and long product life cycles. For short product life cycles, management must be willing to respond rapidly, especially if the environment is ever-changing. Adaptability to short product life cycles are characteristic of short organizational structures with a wide span of control. Because decision making must be quick in short product life cycles, organizational coupling must be high between marketing, R&D, and manufacturing. Weak coupling can result in the late introduction of new products into the marketplace.

The shorter the product life cycle, the greater the involvement of senior management. Strategic planning at the strategic business unit (SBU) level may be cumbersome with short product life cycles. The shorter the product life cycle, the greater the amount of new products needed to sustain a reasonable growth. As a result, shorter product life cycles have a greater need for superior R&D talent.

As a final note, the strategic-marketing approach to the product life cycle can vary based upon the size of company. Small companies that compete in short product life cycle markets must be first to market to reap profits. In short product life cycles, large companies can commit vast resources to take advantage of experience curves, thus creating a barrier to entry for smaller companies that try to employe a follow-the-leader approach.

The process of model building for R&D is essential in order to develop a systematic framework for decision making.

- Business managers regularly face many technological issues and decisions, such as what the key performance parameters are in the eyes of the customer. In the absence of a systematic framework, the business context for these decisions is more difficult to establish and communicate in a company. When technology is the lifeblood of a firm, decision makers cannot permit technological resources to be allocated suboptimally, nor

**Table 5.1 R&D Impact Due to Length of Product Life Cycle.**

| Variable | Short Product Life Cycle | Long Product Life Cycle |
|---|---|---|
| • Management Reaction | • Quick Response | • Slow Response |
| • Environmental Adaptability | • Quick | • Slow |
| • Organizational Coupling | • High | • Moderate |
| • Organizational Planning | • Parallel Activities | • Serial Activities |
| • Strategic Decision-Making Level | • Executive-Level | • SBU Level |
| • Technical Talent | • Strong | • Moderate |

can they afford a business strategy that fails to recognize the implications of their technological assets.[6]

- In the market-oriented era of the future, this technological push process of research that has characterized the past will further be replaced by market-pull innovations. Research functions will emphasize the development of entirely new products rather than products to replace existing ones. To avoid tying the research department to the goals of specific departments, a planning process must be developed that is tuned to overall corporate objectives. Fluent communication will be necessary between the research director and other top management members. Career development patterns will have to be changed in order that research departments can take advantage of the skills to be obtained form other sectors of the corporation.[7]

# Factors Influencing R&D Strategies

The development of a technical strategy is a complex process requiring the identification of numerous factors, most of which are beyond the immediate access of R&D personnel. The identification of these factors requires strong executive leadership focused on joint participation of marketing, engineering, R&D, and manufacturing. A typical list of seed questions to identify the key factors might include:[8]

**technology objectives**—Is it our objective to apply technology for product innovation, for process innovation, for product performance improvement, or for cost reduction? Do we need to replenish our technology (i.e., advance and/or catch up) with the state of art?

**technology selection**—What technology(ies) to invest in for current products? What future technology(ies) to invest in to provide opportunities for future growth? How to exploit existing technological capability for maximum return and/or new products for new markets?

**technology investment level**—How much to invest in each technology? How stable to maintain R&D investment?

**external intelligence**—How much effort to expend obtaining knowledge of competitive and external direction? How to organize the technological surveillance effort?

**technological posture**—How close to state of the art should the firm's technology be? Should we be the leader or just maintain an awareness? What should the balance be between basic approach, applied approach, development, and applications engineering?

**technology acquisition**—To what extent should interval versus external sources of technology be relied on? (Licensing, joint venture, acquisition, other division, central research organization, contract research [government and outside companies], and internal development are possible options.)

**technology organization and policies**—How to organize technology in the business (e.g., centralized vs. decentralized)? Should a project functional, or matrix, organization be used? Is a "dual ladder" necessary? Should R&D facilities be established in other countries? Are the hiring and reward practices consistent with the strategy?

Additional questions that executives can ask include:

- What is the company's attitude toward risk taking, stability, and growth?
- Can we identify the company's strengths, weaknesses, opportunities, and threats?
- How confident are we with the capabilities of our R&D personnel?
- Do we fully understand the product life cycle and the competition?
- How well do we make decisions, especially for trade-offs?
- Is the R&D function successfully coupled to other operations units, and how receptive are these other units toward R&D?
- Have we properly identified the costs attributed to research and development?
- Have we identified the market and financial return benefits (sales volume, sales dollars, profits, market share, ROI)?
- Have we identified the market and financial contributions (cost-reduction impacts, sales facilitation of other products, reduced raw material costs to other products)?
- Have we identified the technical contributions (contribution to other products, contribution to science, contribution to know-how)?
- Have we identified our regret-avoidance contributions (maintenance of our current position, reduction of losses, avoidance of lost opportunity)?

# Marketing Involvement

Marketing often provides the largest input in identifying the critical variables. Marketing involvement includes identification of:

- market attractiveness for each product/product line
- relative market share (and trend)
- sales growth rate (and trend)
- current business strength
- forecasted market-share trend
- recommended investment strategy

Additional factors include marketing's policy toward first-to-market, follow-the-leader, applications engineering, and "me-too." Ansoff and Stewart[9] have identified the R&D impact of each of the following policies.

## FIRST-TO-MARKET

This risky but potential rewarding strategy has a number of important ramifications throughout the business:

1. a research-intensive effort, supported by major development resources
2. close downstream coupling in product planning and moderately close coupling thereafter
3. high proximity to the state of the art
4. high R&D investment ratio
5. a high risk of failure for individual products

The implications of these have been discussed earlier. Taken together, they outline a clear philosophy of business. The company must recruit and retain outstanding technical personnel who can win leadership in the industry. It must see that these technical people are in close and useful communication with marketing planners to identify potentially profitable markets. It must often risk large investments of time and money in technical and market development without any immediate return. It must be able to absorb mistakes, withdraw, and recoup without losing its position in other product lines. As the nature of the market clarifies, initial plans must quickly be modified and approximation refined into precision.

Perhaps most important, top management must be able to make important judgments of timing, balancing the improved product development stemming from a delayed introduction against the risk of being second into the market. Such a company must have more than its share of long-range thinkers who can confidently assess market and competitive trends in their earliest stages and plan with both confidence and flexibility.

## FOLLOW THE LEADER

This marketing strategy implies:

1. development-intensive technical effort
2. moderate competence across the spectrum of relevant technologies
3. exceptionally rapid response time in product development and marketing on the basis of finished research
4. high downstream coupling of R&D with marketing and manufacturing
5. superior competitive intelligence

The company that follows this strategy is—or should be—an organization that gets things done. It uses many interfunctional techniques, responds rapidly to change, and often seems to be in a perpetual fire drill. It has few scientists on its payroll, but some of the best development engineers available. Its senior executives are constantly concerned with maintaining the right balance of strengths among the technical, marketing, and manufacturing functions so that the company can respond effectively to the leader's moves in any of these three areas.

## APPLICATION ENGINEERING

This strategy requires:

1. substantial product design and engineering resources, but no research and little real development
2. ready access to product users within customer companies

3. technically perceptive salesmen and sales engineers who work closely with product designers
4. good product-line control to prevent costly proliferation
5. considerable cost consciousness in deciding what applications to develop
6. an efficiency-oriented manufacturing organization
7. a flair for minimizing development and manufacturing cost by using the same parts or elements in many different applications.

The applications-engineering strategy tends to avoid innovative efforts in the interest of economy. Planning is precise, assignments are clear, and new technology is introduced cautiously, well behind the economic state of the art. Return-on-investment and cash-flow calculations are standard practice, and the entire management is profit-oriented.

### "ME-TOO"

This strategy, which has flourished in the past decade as never before, is distinguished by:

1. no research or development
2. strong manufacturing function, dominating product design
3. strong price and delivery performance
4. ability to copy new designs quickly, modifying them only to reduce production costs

Competing on price, taking a low margin, but avoiding all development expense, a company that has adopted this strategy can wreak havoc with competitors following the first-to-market or follow-the-leader strategies. This is because the "me-too" strategy, effectively pursued, shortens the profitable period after market introduction when the leaders' margins are most substantial. The me-too strategy requires a low-overhead approach to manufacturing and administration and a direct hard sell on price and delivery to the customer. It does not require any technical enthusiasm, nor does it aim to generate any.

## R&D Involvement

In addition to the questions identified previously, R&D must address two key questions: How costly is the process of innovation? And how easy will it be for the competition to successfully imitate our product?

High innovation costs are generally well worth the risk if the company is first to market and can reap the large profits associated with the leadership position. If the innovation process can be duplicated quickly by a large number of competitors, however, even if there exists a large market share, the company may not want to take the risk.

# Fragmented Markets

Fragmented markets have a tendency to discourage innovation because of high cost. In such cases, government agencies provide funding in order to stimulate innovation. Even in partially fragmented industries, such as aerospace/electronics, the government cannot expect companies to finance all innovations out of retained earnings.

# Product Life Cycle

The length of the product life cycle has a bearing on how much risk the company should take. Long product life cycles may generate sufficient cash flow and lead time for new product introduction. Unfortunately, many companies put the emphasis in the wrong place. As the product life cycle grows, emphasis shifts from a competitive position, based on product performance, to product variations and ultimately lower costs due to learning curve effects.

Many companies prefer taking the low risk (cost-wise) of developing "line extension" or "flanker" products, which are simply the same product in a different form. Needless to say, bringing out something new is a risky business, and some companies simply prefer to develop cheap imitations. During the recession, Procter and Gamble had introduced several supposedly new products that looked quite similar to existing products.[10]

Many small companies thrive on short product life cycles, even in fragmented markets. As an example, consider that if the top executive of a small engineering company is also the founding genius and top scientist, new products are developed quickly and move rapidly from R&D to the marketplace. This company has learned to cope well with short product life cycles.

# The Corporate Image

Regardless of how well we define the variables for technical strategy formulation, the executive's perception of the desired corporate image will overrule all else. Some companies have a stabilized image of progressiveness and emphasize their ability to:

- attract talented technical personnel
- allow technical personnel the opportunity to be creative
- increase public confidence in the quality of the product

Well-managed companies can generally make the following statements:

"We can predict with some confidence that next year we will have one major new capital-absorbing development as a result of our past fundamental research. We don't know what the development will be, but we do know we can expect it."

"We figure on one major money-making discovery for roughly every 'x Ph.D. year' we invest. It is very difficult to draw a definite line between 'major' or 'minor'; we do have a fair idea of the expected impact of research in a given area."[11]

The above examples stress the long-term corporate image. Quinn and Mueller have provided another excellent example of the long-term view:

> The chairman of the operating board of a multiproduct company said: "Any damn fool can make a profit for a month—or even a year—by gutting the organization's future. Top management's job is to keep the company 'future oriented.' We try to do this by using a complex of long-term management controls. We play down the use of current profit and return standards in any rigid sense. Instead we purposely use intuitive judgments concerning how well each operating unit is building its organization and technology to meet future demands. So far, we have resisted taking on board members from banks and financial houses because we feel they overemphasize current profits, often at the expense of future strength."[12]

Quinn and Mueller have also given an example of the short-term view and the disastrous effects that can follow:

> A consumer products company, every time it spotted a poor fiscal period ahead, would defer or cut R&D expenditures in order to make periodic financial statements "look good" to stockholders and investment groups. Each such cut eventually lowered the company's competitive margin and seriously affected the research division's capacity to attract topflight people.[13]

# R&D Position

The placement of the R&D group within the organization may have an impact on the expected role of the R&D. Foster[14] poses three stages through which organizations might pass as they mature:

- The "lab-in-woods stage" where R&D is an isolated organizational unit that is expected to produce significant technological advances, but otherwise has little need to be connected to the main stream.
- The "marketing-is-the-answer" stage in which the R&D function is viewed as a potentially valuable contributor to ongoing business activity and is expected to market its product to various users in the corporation.
- The "strategic-management-of-technology" stage in which the R&D function is an integral part of corporate strategy and is positioned both to assist in formulating strategy and to help with its implementation in both the domestic and international context.

# Planning according to Market Share

Whenever market-share analysis is combined with market-growth analysis, the executive is provided with an excellent tool to determine whether there exists an investment opportunity, a source of cash, or an item that should be removed from service. The general terminology for these elements of the market-share/market-growth matrix are cash cows, stars, dogs, and either question marks or problem children. In portfolio planning, each of these has a bearing upon the direction of the R&D thrust to either maintain market share, build market share, harvest, or simply withdraw.

**maintain market share**—This strategy represents a stable market and is ideal for stars or cash cows. In this case, the accompanying R&D strategy should stress defensive R&D and applications engineering rather than diversification.

**build market share**—This strategy is ideal for selected stars and problem children. The R&D strategy to support this would include methods for lowering production costs, improving quality, and applications engineering. This build-market-share strategy can also be used for dogs, provided that the company sees a technological breakthrough that will drastically increase market share and perhaps some degree of patent protection that will guarantee a profitable life cycle.

**harvest market share**—This strategy is used for a cash cow, where the funds are needed for other activities as R&D. A reasonable R&D strategy here would be to improve the quality or lower the cost.

**withdraw market share**—This strategy is used with dogs, where the troublesome product has a very low market share and is marginally profitable or operating at a loss. The R&D strategy, if employed at all, should be to look for spin-offs, specialized applications if profitable, or minimal defensive R&D to support future activities that may need this technology as a base.

# The External Environment

Every executive is paid to make decisions and take risk. In technological companies, executives are required to make rational decisions about the extent of its R&D activities, and these decisions must be made within the framework of the internal and external environments.

Many of the factors influencing the internal environment were presented in the previous section. Internally, executives may have some degree of environment control, but externally the environment is ever-changing and turbulent.

For R&D executives, increased regulation of technological change has proved to be a burden. The general public has become extremely critical of the safety of new products. Consequently, government agencies such as the Food and Drug Administration have expanded their powers to investigate and ban those products that may be unsafe. The result of this increased regulation has been higher R&D costs, a lengthening of the product life cycle from R&D to market introduction, the funding of fewer R&D projects, and much more overseas research in countries with few health and safety regulations.

The industries impacted most by regulations appear to be pharmaceutical, food, construction, transportation, and electrical appliances. These industries must conduct a "technological assessment" of all new products/concepts before commercialization because of potentially strong opposition groups toward the construction of waste treatment plants, nuclear products, skyscrapers, projects affecting wildlife and conservation, and birth control.

# Life-Cycle Management

Analysis of the external environment must include life-cycle management of existing products. Life-cycle management is often the guiding light for directing new products and product mixes. Clifford has given several examples of how keen external environmental analysis can lead toward success.[15]

- Spurred by rapid technological change and by the trend toward packaging everything—a consequence of our self-service way of life—packaging has been a growth industry for well over a decade. One of the industry leaders has been E. I. Du Pont de Nemours & Co. Du Pont has been strongest in cellophane, a product so well known it has become almost a synonym for transparent packaging.

  With the end of World War II, flexible packaging, and cellophane in particular, entered a period of accelerated growth, but in the 1950s new products—notably polyethylene—began to meet certain packaging needs more effectively. Polyethylene film, for example, was less easily ruptured in cold weather—and in time it also became lower in price. Consequently, cellophane began losing its share of the flexible packaging market. It became clear that sales volume would soon begin falling unless strong corrective action was taken.

  Faced with the immediate threat of obsolescence in a highly profitable product, Du Pont—followed by the two other cellophane manufacturers—introduced a series of modifications designed to maintain cellophane's growth and prolong its maturity. These included special coatings, new types, and lighter grades at prices more competitive with the newer packaging materials. In all, the customers' choice of cellophane types grew from a handful to well over 100.

  The cumulative effect of these improvements had an impressive impact on cellophane sales. Contrary to widespread predictions of dramatic decline, cellophane maintained the bulk of its sales volume—of which the traditional grades now represent a relatively small fraction. With more than half of a $300 million market, Du Pont has been the primary beneficiary of this reversal of fortunes.

  Further testimony to Du Pont's effectiveness in life-cycle management can be found in its control over the life-cycle mix of its flexible packaging products. Recognizing the maturity of cellophane, Du Pont developed a strong position in polyethylene and in other new packaging materials. While maintaining its leadership in flexible packaging by reshaping the life cycle of cellophane, the company also provided for growth by adding new products to strengthen its product mix.

- During the mid-1950s, Procter & Gamble's Gleem had attained a strong position in the toothpaste market. But the total market was growing at a slow rate, and P&G wanted to grow faster. Having introduced Crest as the first decay-preventive dentifrice, P&G found the way to explosive growth by obtaining endorsement of the new toothpaste by the American Dental Association—an achievement that had evaded other manufacturers for years. P&G thus reshaped the life cycle of the new dentifrice. Crest's share of the toothpaste market quadrupled between 1958 and 1963, while the sales curves of other brands of toothpaste showed strong signs of obsolescence, declining on the average more than 15%.
- Decades after the introduction of Jell-O, General Foods succeeded in converting it from a mature to a growth product by a revamping of marketing strategy. GF changed the Jello-O formula, repackaged the product, and repriced it, found a host of new uses for Jello-O, and publicized them to the housewife through stepped-up advertising. Today, Jello-O remains one of GF's biggest selling and most profitable products.
- Aggressive life-cycle management was also demonstrated when International Business Machines introduced its "Series 360" computers early in 1964. By the early 1960s, competition in this field had rapidly become severe. IBM controlled three-quarters of the computer business, but intensified competition was shortening the life cycles of its computer line. Management foresaw that the rapid growth it had enjoyed in the 1950s would soon slow down unless the company undertook a major shift in product and marketing strategy.

  The solution adopted by IBM was to rapidly obsolete its own equipment—much of which had been on the market for less than four years. At the same time, the company moved to secure its entrenched position in computers by providing an expandable system that would make it uneconomic or inefficient for customers to switch to competing systems as their computer needs grew.

These examples clearly indicate that executives must be willing to search for "opportunities." This is a much more common strategy for small companies that must continuously examine changing consumer behavior in order to maintain a competitive advantage. Small companies generally look for a short-term product plan based upon opportunism and within the constraints of available dedicated resources.

Another objective of a small company is to develop a "customer-efficiency" strategy by offering products or services that can improve the efficiency of the customer's operations. As described by Curtis:[16]

> The greatest success is achieved when the product or service brings about a structural improvement in the customer's businesses, not just an increase in manufacturing efficiency. Structural improvements can be achieved by offering a product or service that reduces the amount of inventory a company must carry, or that reduces or eliminates complex scheduling of the sort that occurs on a production line, which makes products with different sets of custom features. This strategy is similar to opportunism since it requires a detailed understanding of the customers

needs. However, it does not require the rapid response that the opportunism strategy does.

# External Influences

Robert A. Linn, in his article "A Sectoral Approach to Strategic Planning for R&D,"[17] has identified four major external influences on R&D:

## STABILITY AND THE NEED FOR CHANGE

This includes the stability of the external environment, the ability to reach a goal by more than one competitive means, and the perceived need for stability or change. Consider first a market that is stable or static because of some prior action taken by the firm. Such stable situations, in which the firm has gained appreciable control over the market, can be highly profitable, and a rational strategy may be to preserve or enhance the situation.

An R&D program effectuating this strategy may comprise the following:

- a search to uncover possible substitutes for the technology that confers the leadership position. The goal is to discover and patent such substitutes before the competition.
- a program to lower costs and thereby increase margins
- evaluation of competitors' innovations as they become known to determine whether they threaten the firm's leadership position
- a technical service program to further develop the firm's relationships with its customers
- a search for new ways to capitalize on the firm's proprietary position

The program should be designed to reflect the product life cycle, product-process life cycle, and experience curve. For example, during the life-cycle growth phase, product quality improvement may be stressed. Later on, cost cutting and technical service may be employed.

To implement the first case, R&D should use structures and procedures designed for thoroughness. The technical service program would be designed for speed, a quick, satisfactory response to customer needs being the goal. The intensity of the program will reflect the firm's interest in the particular market. Furthermore, the program can be modified if the firm perceives a need for change. For example, if a price change will require substitution of a new raw material, additional process and product research may be required.

For a second case, consider a static market caused by a patent owned by a competitor that refuses to license. If the firm wishes to compete, it must either develop technology that circumvents the patent coverage or wait until the patent expires. Usually, learning-curve experience will grant the patent owner lower costs over time, and this poses a threat of price competition should the firm enter the market. Hence the firm may not adopt either strategy without one or two signals: knowledge that the market perceives a change to be desirable (e.g., customer companies would welcome a second supplier to guarantee supply), and/or an acceptable probability that the firm can develop technology that will allow it to remain competitive even if the patent owner lowers its price.

In the first case, the firm may have already qualified raw materials from several suppliers or guaranteed delivery by a long-term contract with one of them. Alternatively, research may be undertaken to develop an internal source of critical raw materials. Further, the firm in the second case may consider such research in an attempt to have a cheaper source of such materials so it can better meet any price competition by the patent owner. In stable, mature product lines, vertical integration helps profitability, but in changing (growing or declining) markets, the opposite is true.

Today, most business climates are changing rather than static. The more unstable the external environment, the more innovative the firm must be. Hence, each company must position itself to meet the level of change posed by external technical or market requirements. This has deep-seated ramifications, because such positioning requires suitable strategies and internal structures.

If there is a market shift from a stable to an unstable environment, then the firm must radically change its internal environment to meet the challenge. For example, Table 5.2 illustrates the contrasting requirements for the commodity and specialty chemical businesses. As shown, a specialty chemical company cannot enter the commodity chemical business without undergoing many important changes. The same holds true for commodity chemical companies that want to enter the specialty chemical business. This point is currently important, because commodity chemical companies are being lured by higher profits in specialty chemical businesses.

## THE PRIOR ART

Before imitating a research project, technical and patent literature must be reviewed to prevent "re-inventing the wheel" or working within claims of a blocking patent for which a license is unavailable. Frequently, the patent situation uncovered falls within one of the following categories, or a combination thereof:

- Much prior art is uncovered, most of which falls short of present commercial requirements. In many instances, commercial exploitation stemming from this art will depend on finding a heretofore unobvious solution to what made the art commercially unacceptable in the first place. This means the firm will be unable to remedy the deficiencies of the prior art without making an invention or discovery, perhaps through application of its own proprietary technology. If the firm views the probability of invention or discovery as slim, the uncovered prior art should not be replowed, but another approach should be taken.
- A fair amount of prior art is uncovered, much of which pertains to commercialized technology. This situation can arise when a firm wishes to apply its superior development or engineering skills to enter a market presently being served by others with patented technology. There are two possibilities:
  1. The patents belong to one party. When more than one patent is directed to commercially used technology and variations thereof, this coverage may be difficult to design around. When researchers spend too much time conducting experiments within the scope of patent coverage presently in force this could indicate that the researchers lack

**Table 5.2 Contrasting Requirements for the Commodity and Specialty Chemical Businesses.**

| | Commodity Chemicals | Specialty Chemicals |
|---|---|---|
| Definition | Sold on the basis of chemical composition or physical properties e.g., monomers and solvents. | Sold on the basis of performance, e.g., detergents, antioxidants, stabilizers. |
| Composition | Usually a pure or near-pure chemical compound. Competitors may make identical products. | Often the combination of several materials. Composition can vary among suppliers. |
| Growth | Generally markets are growing slower than specialties markets. | Generally faster growing than commodity chemicals. |
| Life Span | Can be long, 10 or more years. | Generally shorter life cycles, perhaps five or fewer years. |
| Markets | Relatively stable, many markets are mature. Customers consider different brands interchangeable. | Opportunities for market segmentation and targeted market mix. Customers develop loyalty toward reliable supplier. |
| Price Competition | Much competition on price. | Market changes seldom on price alone. |
| Capital Requirements | High, e.g., one dollar of capital for each dollar of annual sales. | Should be kept low, e.g., 50¢ of capital per each dollar of annual sales. |
| Processes | Automated, continuous. Little flexibility. | Batch, specialty operations. Much flexibility. |
| Operating Margins | Low | High |
| Sales Expenses | Low; service component is low. | Very high, cut deeply into margins. A high service committment is required. |
| Strategies for Success | A product and technology orientation. Thorough, careful research. Emphasis on low-cost product volume and product standardization. | Entrepreneurial spirit. Ability to act quickly. A market-focused orientation. Emphasis on good service and high-quality products. |
| Research | Diminished synthesis effort Much engineering development. Look for a cheaper process to make a product of reliably, uniform quality. | Considerable chemical synthesis effort required. Look for a unique product. |
| Protection of Know-how | Frequently no protection on products is obtainable. For processes, trade secrets or patents can be relied upon depending on the state of the art and patent enforceability. | Product composition and process frequently protected by trade secrets. |

meaningful ideas on how to circumvent the coverage, or else that management has not defined the project broadly enough to allow probes at alternative technology. In either case, a collegial review of the program, including its goals, key problems, and progress to date should be conducted to see if alternative approaches can be identified. If not, the program should be terminated.

2. The patents belong to several firms. In this situation, the patents may be easier to design around, especially if the program has the benefit of advice from skilled patent counsel. Each firm owning patents is trying to protect its own technology, and in a crowded art, gaps will be left between patents when distinguishing what is claimed from what is old in the art.

   When the firm tries to thread its way between the patents, the developed technology may have different engineering requirements than the art being designed around. Hence, the development process must have close coupling with engineering to keep the project focused toward a commercially viable innovation.

   If the firm is entering into a market late, but before expiration of important adverse patents, the "best" technology may already be covered by patents issued to unwilling licensers. In such a situation, a project objective to improve over the prior art may be unrealistic, and a realistic goal may be to discover infringement-free technology that is "just as good" as the competition. For such a project, the profit potential may be low. This is especially true if the technology being developed will require more expensive engineering to put it into commercial practice, or if the involved engineering is outside the scope of the firm's prior experience. Therefore, the firm should not undertake too many "me-too" or applications-engineering development projects unless content to settle for relatively low profit levels.

- Little prior art is found. If the uncovered art is old enough to be in the public domain, it can be used free of any infringement question. Sometimes, however, very recent prior art is uncovered, and this prompts research utilizing the technology reported. Researchers will feel they can confidently use the reported technology if it is not directly covered by claims within the disclosing document. However, caution is advised. The document itself shows that someone with a head start is working in the area and troublesome patents may be forthcoming, or the other party will beat the firm to commercialization.
- No prior art is uncovered. In this event, the firm should consider a redundant search using a different data bank to make sure nothing of consequence was missed. Also, if there is no prior art to guide researchers, the research project may be lengthy (and the introductory phase of the product life cycle may also be lengthy if the research is successful).

## THE EFFECT OF MARKET SHARE

A firm must understand its position in the market. Being first has many advantages. It confers the greatest relative benefits of the experience curve and thereby allows pricing to be used as a competitive weapon. Usually, companies with leading market shares have the highest profits and return on investment. Moreover, market share is fundamental to superior accomplishments during a substantial future period.

If the company is first in market share, then its strategy should be to maintain that position. If it is second or third, then the strategy is to get out of that position, or if that is impossible, to minimize the disadvantages. Usually, the latter is accomplished by segmenting the market to find a niche in which the firm can assume a leadership position. Winning market share from the leader is a lengthy, expensive proposition unless the leader is asleep. On the other hand, share can be lost quite rapidly to a firm that knowingly applies share-building strategies. Market share is so important that the portfolio of R&D projects and the motivation of employees from the highest level down must focus on performance relative to it.

## CURRENT BUSINESS AND POLITICAL FACTORS

Current external factors such as high cost, push inflation, slow economic growth, greater worldwide competition, low predictability, and high turbulence will continue to increase the obsolescence rate of present products, and operating and investment costs, and decrease productivity and real profitability. In light of these factors, management has a lessened margin for error and an enhanced need to plan.

Increasingly, formulation of corporate strategy is of major importance to shareholders. Institutional investors play a major ownership role in leading technological companies; hence, the degree of company appeal to the institutional investor has a significant impact on the market price of a share of stock. Also, the goal of management is to maximize shareholder wealth. This goal in quantified in two ways. First, management must seek to maximize the return and the cost of capital to be as large as possible. Second, management needs to maximize the value of a share of common stock. The immediate market value of a share is of importance to management because it bears on the ability to arrange beneficial mergers, or to raise new equity through issuing new shares.

# Executive Involvement in R&D

In order for product innovation to be successful, the implementation of R&D policy and funding should be based on the overall long-range corporate strategy and objectives. Without a clear company position and direction, a company defeats itself. Warner and Strong[18] estimated that about 80% of all industrial products fail to meet company objectives and thus are considered failures by their firms. This rate appears to be rather high and may be due to the particular definition of a product failure as one that does not achieve its objectives. Before technical objectives can be established, corporate objectives must be set and communicated downward. Unspecified objectives can result in technological failure.

The following list identifies the basic criteria for choosing an objective.

- specific, not general
- not overly complex
- measurable, tangible, and verifiable
- realistic and attainable
- established within resource bounds
- consistent with resources available or anticipated
- consistent with organization plans, policies, procedures

For projects that are definable and well-structured, almost all these criteria can be met. For R&D projects, however, only a small portion may be appropriate, and prioritization of the criteria may be necessary. Because the prioritization may be different at each level of management, senior management must take an active role so that corporate position is known to all.

Understanding the corporate position, its finances, technological level, and current condition leads to setting realistic long-term objectives. With these objectives and long-term growth goals, the level of technological spending can be set. This level considers all or some of the following:

- the long-range company position in the industry
- overtaking specific competitors
- maintaining market share
- a lead or lag position technologically
- growth in specific market segments
- quality or value relative to competition
- technological diversification plans
- new markets for existing technology

Hanson and Nason[19] reported the following three recommendations for budgeting and control of R&D expenditures related to firm objectives and planning:

- Budgeting and control of expenditures can only be effective if based on sound planning. Even if prepared on an annual basis, plans should look forward over the period for which resources are already largely committed; a rolling five-year plan is recommended.
- Long-term and exploratory research programs should not be exclusively originated by the research staff. If such work is funded on a corporate basis, its origin and review must be at corporate level, research direction taking its due part in these processes. Funds for such corporate research should be protected from short-term fluctuations.
- R&D funded by operating divisions of the company, and directed to their objectives, must be reported and reviewed against these targets, but the divisions should be encouraged not to take too short-term a view.

Unfortunately, many executives have found that there are other strategic objectives that compete for the same resources. According to Hanson and Nason:[20]

> It should be noted that most companies have had to direct more and more of their already scarce resources to problems resulting from legislation and regulation with respect to such items as

- product liability
- environmental matters
- health
- safety
- energy supplies

The end result is a very small residual for investment in innovation, growth, and productivity.

There are two critical questions that companies must ask: In what direction should we grow? Should we change our image and, if so, what should it be?

If a company decides to grow vertically, then growth can be directed toward either markets or raw-material sources. Horizontal growth is normally directed to new markets or new applications for existing markets. The methods for growth in either direction will be based upon acquisition, merger, licensing, and internal R&D.

In each method for growth, the company's image must be considered. If a company wishes to be considered as progressive, then the company's image may be to attract top technical talent or to increase public acceptance of its products. Today, many companies advertise an image of compliance with government policies on pollution, health, safety, equal employment opportunity (EEO), and minority group hirings. Years ago, companies were less concerned about their social values and more concerned with maximizing stockholder wealth. Today, there appears to be a changing trend.

Obviously, there are other objectives that must be considered, such as:

- geographic markets
- market size
- market share
- company size
- dependence on suppliers
- dependence on limited customer base
- profitability
- return on investment
- bond market rating

# Aligning Goals and Objectives

The chief executive officer must make sure that the R&D goals and objectives are in line with the corporate goals and objectives. The first step in aligning the goals and objectives is to define the types of businesses. There are essentially four types of businesses:

- selling technical products
- selling technical services
- selling materials
- a combination of the above

When a company sells technical products, the customer owns, rents, or operates the products. Corporations that sell technical products must maintain a strong

R&D group capable of introducing a continuous stream of new products. Such companies usually stress advanced state-of-the-art achievements rather than applications engineering or customer service. Technical products companies measure success by how many new customers abandoned their current but still serviceable products to buy ours, and by how many of our existing customers wanted to be upgraded to better equipment. Such companies would include IBM, Control Data, Digital Equipment, Unisys, Polaroid, and the automotive industry.

Companies that sell technical services include AT&T, Bechtel, and hospital administration companies. These companies own and operate the systems themselves. In such organizations, the target for the R&D groups may be to improve the value of the service sold by upgrading rather than to seek out new products. In these organizations, executives should continuously ask, "How can our technical services be improved?"

Companies that sell materials are in the most volatile position because they must rely heavily upon extensive market analysis to see if a continuous need exists. Chemical companies are an example. Such companies emphasize patent protection or patent dodging and may stress all-purpose material to take advantage of learning curves rather than specialty products. These types of companies stress long life cycles and encourage new-product development. The number of patents that an individual or group has is a strong motivational force.

# Priority Setting

Priorities create colossal management headaches for the R&D project manager because R&D projects are usually prioritized on a different list from all other projects. Functional managers must now supply resources according to two priority lists. Unfortunately, the R&D priority list is usually not given proper attention.

As an example of this, the director of R&D of a Fortune 25 corporation made the following remarks:

> Each of our operating divisions have their own R&D projects and priorities. Last year, corporate R&D had a very high R&D project geared toward cost improvement in the manufacturing areas. Our priorities were based upon the short-run requirements. Unfortunately, the operating division that had to supply resources to our project felt that the benefits would not be received until the long run and, therefore, placed support for our project low on their priority list.

Communication of priorities is often a problem in the R&D area. Setting of priorities on the divisional level may not be passed down to the departmental level, and vice versa. We must have early feedback of priorities so that functional managers can make their own plans.

# Working with Marketing

In most organizations, either R&D drives marketing or marketing drives R&D. The latter is more common. Well managed organizations maintain a proper balance between marketing and R&D. Marketing-driven organizations can create havoc, especially if marketing continuously requests information faster than R&D can deliver it and if bootleg R&D is eliminated. In this case, all R&D activities must be approved by marketing. In some organizations, R&D funding comes out of the marketing budget.

In order to stimulate creativity, R&D should have control over at least a portion of its own budget. This is a necessity, because not all R&D activities are designed to benefit marketing. Some activities are simply to improve technology or create a new way of doing business.

Marketing support, if needed, should be available to all R&D projects regardless of whether they originate in marketing or R&D. An R&D project manager at a major food manufacturer made the following remarks:

> A few years ago, one of our R&D people came up with an idea and I was assigned as the project manager. When the project was completed, we had developed a new product, ready for market introduction and testing. Unfortunately, R&D does not maintain funds for the market testing of a new product. The funds come out of marketing. Our marketing people did not understand the product and placed it low on their priority list. We in R&D tried to talk to them. They were reluctant to test the new product because the project was our idea. Marketing lives in their own little world. To make a long story short, last year one of our competitors introduced the same product into the marketplace. Now, instead of being the leader, we are playing catch-up. I know R&D project managers are not trained in market testing, but what if marketing refuses to support R&D-conceived projects? What can we do?

Several organizations today have R&D project managers reporting directly to a new business group, business development group, or marketing. Engineering-oriented R&D project managers continuously voice displeasure at being evaluated for promotion by someone in marketing who really may not understand the technical difficulties in managing an R&D project. Yet, executives have valid arguments for this arrangement, asserting that these high technology R&D project managers are so in love with their projects that they don't know how and when to cancel a project. Marketing executives contend that projects should be canceled when:

- costs become excessive, causing product cost to be noncompetitive
- return on investment will occur too late
- competition is too stiff and not worth the risk

Of course, the question arises, "Should marketing have a vote in the cancellation of each R&D project or only those that are marketing-driven?" Some organizations cancel projects upon consensus of the project team.

The role of an executive may change because of his or her working relationship with other executives. Items such as decision making, authority, and power can be changed. Kotler[21] has elaborated on the working relationship between marketing and R&D:

> The company's desire for successful new projects is often thwarted by poor working relations between R&D and marketing. In many ways, these groups represent two different cultures in the organization. The R&D department is staffed with scientists and technicians who pride themselves on scientific curiosity and detachment, like to

work on challenging technical problems without much concern for immediate sales payoffs, and like to work without much supervision or accountability for research costs. The marketing/sales department is staffed with business-oriented persons who pride themselves on a practical understanding of the world, like to see many new products with sales features that can be promoted to customers, and feel compelled to pay attention to costs. Each group often carries negative stereotypes of the other group. Marketers see the R&D people as impractical, longhaired, mad-scientist types who don't understand business, while R&D people see marketers as gimmick-oriented hucksters who are more interested in sales than in the technical features of the product. These stereotypes get in the way of productive teamwork.

Companies turn out to be either R&D dominated, marketing dominated, or balanced. In R&D-dominated companies, the R&D staff researches fundamental problems, looks for major breakthroughs, and strives for technical perfection in product development. R&D expenditures are high, and the new-product success rate tends to be low, although R&D occasionally comes up with major new products.

In marketing-dominated companies, the R&D staff designs products for specific market needs, much of it involving product modification and the application of existing technologies. A higher ratio of new products succeed, but they represent mainly product modifications with relatively short product lives.

A balanced R&D/marketing company is one in which effective organizational relationships have been worked out between R&D and marketing to share responsibility for successful market-orientation innovations. The R&D staff takes responsibility not for invention alone but for successful innovation. The marketing staff takes responsibility not for new sales features alone but also for helping identify new ways to satisfy needs. R&D/marketing cooperation is facilitated in several ways:

1. Joint seminars are sponsored to build understanding and respect for each other's goals, working styles, and problems.
2. Each new project is assigned to an R&D person and a marketing person who work together through the life of the project.
3. R&D and marketing personnel are interchanged so that they have a chance to experience each other's work situations (some R&D people may travel with the sales force, while some marketing people might hang around the lab for a short time).
4. Conflicts are worked out by higher management, following a clear procedure.

# Planning for R&D

Planning for R&D in today's economy presents many problems. When resources become more scarce, vision tends to become shorter. Senior management must communicate with R&D managers in order to develop the proper balance between the many trade-offs. The tendency to give up on strategic planning and resort to operational-type planning must be resisted. Good planners still practice good strategic planning while [illegible] today's economy. The tool that will permit this is effective scheduling coupled with short-range milestones, carefully designed to permit aborting, if that alternative is in the best interest for the company.

One approach to the formulation and construction of a corporate R&D activity is to use a procedure that requires participative involvement of both corporate executives and the R&D staff. Corporate executives from Marketing/Sales, Manufacturing/Production, and Corporate Planning are invited to a series of informal meetings carefully designed to obtain their input into the R&D budget. At the same time, the R&D staff is given an opportunity to participate in the formulation of R&D programs. This is accomplished through a series of meetings involving successively lower levels of supervision, including the first level, which would involve the individual bench chemist or engineer. Subordinates are requested to cost out a suggested budget in a three-level format:

- Level 1—assume that the total resources available for R&D will be at the "current level."
- Level 2—very desirable projects that could require the displacement of certain Level 1 projects.
- Level 3—projects that identify the backlog of quality R&D investment opportunity projects.

This overall approach has several important strengths, such as:

- providing for participative involvement of corporate departments
- developing a better understanding within R&D of other departments
- establishing a sound foundation for effective management by objectives

There are, however, some weaknesses, such as:

- creating personal conflict and misunderstandings
- awakening some "sleeping dogs"
- creating conflicts in the event that the management style is highly authoritarian[22]

The chemical group of a large corporation uses two principal documents in its R&D project-planning format. The first of these is the R&D project plan and authorization that summarizes the proposed project activities and its costs, increments, and incentives and provides informational linkages to other planning and budgeting documents. The second document is an incremental impact summary that provides more detail on the specific tasks and other resources required for each increment.

Prioritizing of R&D projects is essential to the process. One method used by the chemical group is as follows:

- support required for existing business
- expansion programs of the existing budget base
- deferrable programs

After prioritization, R&D management should meet with operating division/unit management until agreement is reached on details. Next, group and corporate management review and evaluate the proposed budgets leading to final approval.[23]

Several attempts have been made to identify effective planning practices for R&D. Perhaps the best document known to the authors was prepared by Hughes Aircraft Company[24] and includes:

- Ensure that all affected organizations and individuals are involved in the planning.
- Quantize plans whenever possible.
- Examine all pertinent trade-offs.
- Eliminate all unnecessary items and avoid excessive detail.
- Ensure realistic cost and schedule parameters.
- Optimally time-phase all important elements of a plan—delays at any part of an effort may adversely impact the remaining.
- Examine ("debug") plans critically before implementing them.
- Develop contingency plans well in advance of potential events that may have a negative effect on the effort.
- Recognize that plans can succeed only if they are communicated effectively, are understood, and are properly carried out.
- Orient budgets to the future, not the past—base them on future needs, not on past actuals.
- Assure that planned budgets adequately represent the realities of effective operations. (Unfortunately, in practice, budgets are often increased for organizations that traditionally overrun and decreased for organizations that consistently underrun).
- Assign specific responsibilities for adhering to budgets—stress accountability.
- Make potential return-on-investment a major consideration in selecting and planning R&D projects.
- Optimize cash flow in financial planning.
- Plan major capital investments well in advance of actual need.
- Have managers annually prepare plans for the overall improvement of their organizations in the coming year and review progress against their plans at the end of the year.
- Maintain an ongoing program/plan for replacement or updating of obsolete plant and facilities.
- Plan for proper maintenance of plant and facilities.
- Make optimum use of computers as an aid to planning.
- Avoid overplanning.

# Location of the R&D Function

R&D project management in small organizations is generally easier than similar functions in large organizations. In small companies, there usually exists a single R&D group responsible for all R&D activities. In large companies, each division may have its own R&D function. The giant corporations try to encourage decentralized R&D under the supervision of a central research (or corporate research) group. The following problems were identified by a central research group project manager.

- parallel projects going on at the same time
- duplication of effort because each division its own R&D and quality-control functions; poor passing of information between divisions
- "central research originally developed to perform research functions which could not be effectively handled by the division. Although we are supposed to be a service group, we still bill each division for the work we do for them. Some pay us and some don't. Last year, several divisions stopped using us because they felt that it was cheaper to do the work themselves. Now, we are funded entirely by corporate and have more work than we can handle. Everyone can think of work for us to do when it is free."
- "I know that there is planning going on now for activities which I will be doing three months from now. How should I plan for this? I don't have any formal or informal data on planning as yet. What should I tell my boss?"

Executives should not try to understaff the R&D function. Forcing R&D personnel and project managers to work on too many projects at once can drastically reduce creativity. This does not imply that personnel should be used on only one project at a time. Most companies do not have this luxury, but this situation of multiproject management should be carefully monitored.

As a final note, executives must be very careful about how they wish to maintain control over the R&D project managers. Too much control can drastically reduce bootleg research and, in the long run, the company may suffer.

# Scheduling

Overall, scheduling of R&D projects becomes a must at this point in the budgeting for R&D projects. Prior to this point, the R&D manager will have assembled a package of continuing and new projects. Each will have been evaluated and prioritized, but only by assembling a master schedule of all proposed projects will it be possible to have the necessary information on hand for the reviews with senior management that will lead to the ultimate funding.

Master scheduling, together with the next step, funding, becomes an iterative process. One of senior management's roles is to examine the trade-offs between available resources, current economic conditions, and corporate goals and objectives. Conceivably, the package of R&D projects could exceed the availability of internal R&D manpower. In this event, senior management would be faced with considering contract R&D as opposed to dropping the lowest priority projects.

There are basically two types of R&D projects that have to be placed in the master schedule: non-well-defined projects and well-defined projects.

The non-well-defined projects are the most difficult to schedule because they are simply ideas that required "seed money" to explore. If the results are positive, then the project may become a well-defined effort and combined with other projects as part of the R&D selection portfolio. "Seed money" projects can occur at any time and can easily cause major shifts in the master schedule.

Scheduling activities for R&D projects is extremely difficult because of the previously mentioned problems. Many R&D people believe that if you know how long it will take to complete the objective, you do not need R&D. Most R&D schedules are not detailed, but are composed of major milestones where executives can decide whether additional money or resources should be committed. Some executives and R&D managers believe in the philosophy that, "I'll give you 'so much time' to answer." In R&D project management, failure is often construed as an acceptable answer.

There are two schools of thought on R&D scheduling, depending of course upon the type of project, the time duration, and resources required. The first school of thought involves the tight R&D schedule. This may occur if the project is a one-person activity. R&D personnel are generally highly optimistic and believe that they can do anything. They, therefore, have the tendency to lay out rather tight, optimistic schedules. This type of optimism is actually a good trait. Where would we be without it? How many projects would be prematurely canceled without optimistic R&D personnel?

Tight schedules occur mostly on limited-resource projects. Project managers tend to avoid tight schedules if they feel that there exists a poor window in the functional organization for a timely commitment of resources. Another reason is that R&D personnel know that in time of crisis or fire fighting on manufacturing lines (which are yielding immediate profits), they may lose their key functional project employees, perhaps for an extended period of time.

The second school of thought believes that R&D project management is not as mechanical as other forms of project management and, therefore, all schedules must be loose. Scientists do not like or want tight structuring because they feel that they cannot be creative without having sufficient freedom to do their job. Many good results have been obtained from spin-offs and other activities where R&D project managers have deviated from predetermined schedules. Of course, too much freedom can prove to be disastrous, because the individual might try to be overly creative and "reinvent the wheel."

The second school says that R&D project managers should not focus on limited objectives. Rather, the project manager should be able to realize that other possible objectives can be achieved with further exploration of some of the activities.

An interesting problem facing executives is how much of an input the bench researcher should have in selecting R&D projects. This does not imply that researchers should have complete freedom in selecting projects. Well-planned R&D strategic planning programs hire researchers because of their abilities in specific technical disciplines. Some organizations boast of one new moneymaking effort or one new product each year.

Researchers may already be predisposed with the technical problems of new product development, and to burden the researcher further with project selection committees may distract from their usefulness. Thus, the interrelationship between executives (specifically R&D executives) takes on paramount importance. According to Quinn and Cavanaugh,[25] the researchers' input to project selection should be between the researcher and the research executive:

> We expect the individual researcher to come up with proposals within his specialty. He discusses any major new approach with his director. Normally, the director encourages the researcher to perform some exploratory investigations and come back in about a month to discuss the areas again. If the approach then looks scientifically promising to the researcher and his director, he goes ahead for another three months. His progress and the promise of the field are then checked again by a small group of research directors. If things are still encouraging, he is given a commitment for another six months. If the project continues after this checkpoint, it is looked at annually by the research committee in the regular review cycle. This system only works because we are a research-oriented company, and there is strong mutual respect between the researchers, our research executives, and our top management.

The authors have also commented on the individual relationship with the scientist himself:[26]

> One of our biggest problems is that our scientists become 'organization men' too rapidly. We hire them for their brilliance, objectivity, and willingness to try things no one has done before. Within two or three years, they begin second-guessing 'what we want' from them in the way of science and start worrying about organizational status and the like. Sure, we want a man to know the company's needs so he doesn't feel frustrated by not seeing his work applied. But we don't want him to lose the very creativity we hired him for just because he is trying to 'make a mark' for himself in the organization and please everybody in sight.

Because each R&D project is part of an executives' strategic plan, executives are expected to be actively involved in R&D activities. As an example as one vice president of research said:[27]

> A new product is like a baby. You don't just bring it into the world and expect it to grow up and be a success. It needs a mother (enthusiasm) to love it and keep it going when things are tough. It needs a pediatrician (expert information and technical skills) to solve the problems the mother can't cope with alone. And it needs a father (authority with resources) to feed it and house it. Without any one of these, the baby may still turn out all right, but its chances of survival are a lot lower.

The following situations affect interfacing with R&D personnel:

*Isolating R&D*—The vice president for R&D did not understand the necessity for developing a good liaison with marketing personnel and decided to shield his group from "commercial pressures." The result of this sheltering was that the operations group did not hear about technical achievements until the very last moment and, consequently, technology transfer from R&D to manufacturing required years.

*Integrating Research with Development*—A chemical company maintains a pure research group. Unfortunately, although a large expense was incurred in supporting the group, only "lip service" was given to achievements, and many promising results were simply shelved because of weak development activities. As a result of this frustration, there was a large turnover in personnel, many of whom opened their own companies.

*The R&D Vacuum-Suppliers*—A medium-size electrical equipment manufacturer prided itself on its ability to develop new products for its customers. Unfortunately, what was proven valid with bench testing could not be mass-produced in manufacturing because suppliers could not keep up with the company's rapidly changing needs. As a result, the company found it necessary to develop a better liaison with its suppliers during R&D activities.

*Organizational Aging*—An industrial products company appointed a 62-year-old executive in charge of new-product development. He immediately set up a project-selection committee composed of senior company managers. During his four-year tenure, only short-term R&D projects were selected. It appeared that the selection committee was reluctant to accept new technology projects that would yield profits only after they retired.

*Organizational Approval Process*—An electrical equipment manufacturer was forced to cut back on R&D expenditures during the 1979–1982 downturn in the economy. As a result, numerous approval committees were established to approve each R&D project depending, of course, upon the size of the requested budgets. In many cases, by the time the projects were approved, many of the key individuals had been reassigned to other activities and interest in the project dissipated.

*The Integration Vacuum*—A small appliance company maintained an aggressive approach toward R&D, quite often as the industry leader. Unfortunately, the manufacturing personnel preferred the status quo, and worker resistance to new technologies was very strong. Management alleviated the problem by allowing manufacturing to participate in the R&D strategic-planning process. As a result, strategic R&D planning helped smooth the way for anticipated technological changes in manufacturing.

*The Central Research Vacuum*—A Fortune 500 food company established a central research group to keep all nontechnical managers abreast of all corporate R&D. However, the objectives of corporate R&D appeared to be quite different from divisional objectives. As a result, the liaison between the divisions and R&D dissipated to such a degree that central research is now reduced to the status of a separate division.

# Classification of R&D Projects

R&D projects can be classified into seven major categories.

## GRASS ROOTS PROJECTS

The first category is the *grass roots* project. This type of project can be simply an idea with as few as one or two good data points. Grass roots projects are funded with "seed money," which is a small sum of money usually under the control of the R&D manager. The purpose of the seed money is to see if the grass roots project is feasible enough to be developed into a full-blown, well-funded R&D project to be further incorporated into the strategic plan.

## BOOTLEGGED PROJECTS

The second category is the *bootlegged project*. This type of project is one in which funding does not exist either because the selection team did not consider this project worthy of funding or because funding had been terminated (or ran out) and funding renewal was not considered appropriate. In either event, a bootlegged project is done on the sly, using another project's budgeted charge numbers. Bootlegged projects run the complete spectrum for conceptual ideas to terminated, well-defined activities.

## BASIC RESEARCH PROJECTS

The third category is the *basic research project* and may include the grass roots and bootlegged project. Basic research activities are designed to expand knowledge in a specific scientific area or to improve the state of the art. These types of projects do not generally result in products that can be directly sold by marketing and, as a result, require special handling.

## APPLIED RESEARCH PROJECTS

The fourth category is the *applied-research project*. The applied-research project is an extension or follow-on to the basic research project and explores direct application of a given body of knowledge. These types of projects hopefully result in marketable products, product improvements, or new applications for existing products.

## ADVANCED DEVELOPMENT PROJECTS

The fifth category is the *advanced development project*. These types of activities follow the applied research or exploratory development projects with the intent of producing full-scale prototypes supported by experimental testing.

## FULL-SCALE ENGINEERING DEVELOPMENT PROJECTS

The sixth category is the *full-scale engineering development project*. This activity includes, complete, working, drawing design of the product together with a detailed bill of materials, exact vendor quotes, and specification development. This type of R&D activity requires strong manufacturing involvement.

## PRODUCTION SUPPORT R&D PROJECTS

The seventh and final category is the *production support R&D project*. This category can include either applications engineering to find better uses of this product for a customer or internal-operations support to investigate limitations and feasibility of a given system with hopes of modification or redesign. Projects designed to find ways of lowering production costs or improving product quality are examples of internal production support projects.

# Contract R&D

Contract R&D is another form of strategic planning that can be used with any of the seven classifications for projects. There are different reasons for conducting contract R&D, depending on whether you are the customer or the contractor. Customers subcontract out R&D because they may not have the necessary in-house technical skills; have in-house skills, but the resources are committed to higher-priority activities; and/or may have the available talent, but external sources have superior talent and may be able to product the desired results in less time and for less money.

From a subcontractor's point of view, contract R&D is a way to develop new technologies at someone else's expense. Subcontractors view contract R&D as a way to:

- minimize the internal cost of supporting R&D personnel
- develop new technologies to penetrate new markets/products
- develop new technologies to support existing market/products
- maintain technical leadership
- improve resource utilization by balancing workloads
- maintain customer goodwill
- look for spin-offs on existing products

There also exist disadvantages to contract R&D from the customer's point of view:

- How dependent should I become on a subcontractor to produce the desired results within time and cost?
- What criteria are used to evaluate subcontractors?
- What type of communication network should be established?
- How do I know if the subcontractor is being honest with me?
- If trade-offs are needed, how will decisions be made?
- Who controls patent rights resulting from the research under contract?
- Will project failures impact strategic planning process?

From the subcontractor's point of view:

- What influence will the customer try to exercise over my personnel?
- Will project success generate follow-on work?
- Will project success enhance goodwill image?
- Will project failure damage goodwill image?
- Based upon the type of contract, are there risks that we will have to finance part of the project with our own money?
- Can this contract generate legal headaches?

Contract research, licensing, joint ventures, acquisitions, and the luxury of hiring additional personnel are taken for granted in the United States. Foreign countries may not have these luxuries, and additional classifications are needed, usually by the level of technology. According to one foreign country, the following levels are used:

- Level I—Technology exists within the company.
- Level II—Technology can be purchased from companies within the country.
- Level III—Technology can be purchased from outside the country.
- Level IV—Technology must be researched in other countries and brought back into the parent country.

Because a great many foreign countries fall into Levels III and IV, several foreign corporations have established employee sabbatical funds. Each month the company withholds 3% of the employee's salary and matches this with 7% of company funds. Every five or six years, each participating employee is allowed to study abroad to bring technical expertise back into the country. The employee draws his or her full salary while on sabbatical in addition to the sabbatical fund.

For strategic R&D planning, this type of sabbatical leave creates a gap in the organization. Management can delay a sabbatical leave for an employee for one year only. What happens if the employee is in a strategic position? What if the employee is working on a critical project? What if the employee is the only person with the needed skills in a specific discipline? Who replaces the employee? Where do we put the employee upon his or her return to the organization? What happens if the employee's previous management slot is no longer vacant? Obviously, these questions have serious impact on the strategic-planning process.

# Offensive versus Defensive R&D

Should a company direct its resources toward offensive or defensive R&D? Offensive R&D is product R&D, whereas defensive R&D is process R&D. In offensive R&D, the intent is to penetrate a new market as quickly as possible, replace an existing product, or simply satisfy a particular customer's need. Offensive R&D stresses a first-to-market approach.

Defensive R&D, on the other hand, is used to either lengthen the product life cycle or to protect existing product lines from serious competitive pressures. Defensive R&D is also employed in situations where the company has a successful product line and fears that the introduction of a new technology at this time may jeopardize existing profits. Defensive R&D concentrates on minor improvements rather than major discoveries and, as a result, requires less funding. Today, with the high cost of money, companies are concentrating on minor product improvements, such as style, and introduce the product into the marketplace as a new, improved version when, in fact, it is simply the original product slightly changed. This approach has been used successfully by the Japanese in copying someone else's successful product, improving the quality, changing the style, and introducing it into the marketplace. A big advantage to the Japanese approach is that the product can be sold at a lower cost, because the selling price does not have to include recovery of expensive R&D costs.

Defensive R&D is a necessity for those organizations that must support existing products and hopefully extend the product's life span. According to Goldring,[28] properly managed defensive research can provide six operational improvements:

- improved coordination between R&D personnel and operational groups
- improved contact with the marketplace
- better judgment in corporate and R&D planning
- better acceptance by operating personnel, especially decision-making personnel in operating divisions
- better access to varied sources of technological innovation
- greater emotional satisfaction for R&D personnel through improved perception of the value of their contributions

Goldring concludes his argument by stating that:

> Payoffs from defensive research performed by the corporate R&D group will occur through the application of lower cost materials, design and manufacturing improvements, higher speed machinery, reduced defect rate in manufactured goods, and so forth. These payoffs should be clearly visible and directly demonstrable. When this defensive research is consistently sustained over long periods of time, the cumulative effect can product technological innovation with relatively little scientific discovery. These innovations develop almost without planning and with little extra expense.
>
> Although defensive research lacks the glamour of technological breakthrough, it is a pragmatic approach for maintaining technological innovation in the firm. Properly directed, it can maintain the firm's competitive position, broaden markets, and give timely warning when technological developments threaten a product or process with obsolescence. It is a powerful tool for stimulating technological innovation by bringing needs and technical ability together.[29]

A firm's strategic posture in the marketplace is, therefore, not restricted solely to new-product introduction. Companies must find the proper technological balance between offensive and defensive R&D.

# Sources of Ideas

Unlike other types of planning, strategic R&D planning must be willing to solicit ideas from the depths of the organization. Successful companies with a reputation for continuous new-product introduction have new-product development teams that operate in a relatively unstructured environment to obtain the best possible ideas. Some companies go so far as to develop idea inventories, idea banks, and idea clearinghouses.

These idea sessions are brainstorming sessions and not intended for problem solving. If properly structured, the meeting will have an atmosphere of free expression and creative thinking, an ideal technique for stimulating ideas. Arguments against brainstorming sessions include no rewards for creators, attack of only superficial problems, possibility of potentially good ideas coming out prematurely and being disregarded, and lack of consideration for those individuals who are more creative by themselves.

Principles that can be used in brainstorming sessions include:

- Select personnel from a variety of levels; avoid those responsible for implementation.
- Allow people to decline assignments.
- Avoid evaluation and criticism of ideas.
- Provide credit recognition and/or rewards for contributors.
- Limit session to 60 minutes.

Ideas are not merely limited to internal sources. There are several external sources of new product ideas[30] such as:

- customers
- competitors
- suppliers
- purchase of technologies
- licensing of technologies
- unsolicited ideas from customers or others
- private inventors
- acquisitions
- trade fairs
- technology fairs
- private data banks
- technical journals
- trade journals
- government-funded research programs
- government innovation/technology transfer programs
- government agencies

Perhaps the best method for idea generation is to monitor the competition for information on new products.[31] This includes:

- **current product information**
  - product quality and performance
  - breadth of line
  - product costs
  - new-product developments
- **technological information**
  - R&D activities
  - patent and licensing activities
  - technical capabilities
- **financial information**
  - sales
  - profits and losses
  - operating expenditures

- **production information**
  - production capacity
  - facility location
  - capital investment
  - volume
- **market information**
  - pricing, discounts, volume
  - market share
  - distribution methods
  - advertising
  - customer relations
  - new-market potentials and plans

# Strategic Selection of R&D Projects

The selection of R&D projects must, in the final analysis, be the responsibility of top management. Unfortunately, too many executives wait for the following symptoms[32] to occur before considering some type of systematic process for project selection:

- the executives who want new products, but do not know or cannot agree on what kinds of projects in which to be interested
- the laboratory crowded with development products, but with few new products coming out, and too many of these not paying off
- the "orphan" project that goes on and on because nobody has given it much thought or had the heart to kill it
- the "bottomless hole" product that took three times as long and cost five times as much as expected, and finally got to market behind all other competitors
- the product with "bugs" that were hidden until 10,000 units came back from consumers
- the "me-too" product that has no competitive reason for existence
- the scientific triumph that turned out to have no market value when someone thought to investigate it

It is no wonder that companies waste large sums of money on projects that are not justified for commercial usefulness (excluding basic research). If the R&D project-selection process is not aligned to the corporate posture, there will undoubtedly be a dissipation of critical resources.

The ideal situation is for a company to select a low-risk project with a high payout. Unfortunately, this seldom happens because most projects do not fall within these limits. Therefore, it is imperative for companies to develop some type of selection criteria.

Roussel[33] suggests that what is needed is a common language between management and R&D technical staff. He acknowledges that managers in American industry often lack a research background. He suggests that R&D and management learn to communicate comprehensibly and credibly by employing a series of simple tasks in project evaluation:

1. Define the research objective in commercial and technical terms. The definition must specify all the successful technical steps required for commercialization.
2. By a series of approximations, estimate the potential of real commercial reward.
3. Redefine all the major technical steps in terms of assumptions, postulates, or theories that must be found valid for each to succeed.
4. Determine whether the validity of these assumptions, postulates, or theories can be tested within the state of the art. Redefine any that are found untestable.
5. Estimate the probability of conducting a conclusive test of each assumption, postulate, or theory with the desired level of research resources.
6. Put the various tests in a logical and chronological sequence.
7. Forecast the cost and time required for completion of crucial tests.
8. Decide whether the risk-reward-time strategic relationships justify the project.

Roussel suggests that employing the eight-step process will make it possible to convert R&D uncertainties to risks, thus providing managers a rational basis for decision making.

There are numerous approaches that companies can use for project selection. Figure 5.7 illustrates one such approach by asking a logical sequence of questions:[34]

- Is this a good business for anyone to be in?
  1. What is the probability of commercial success?
  2. What is the sales/profit potential?

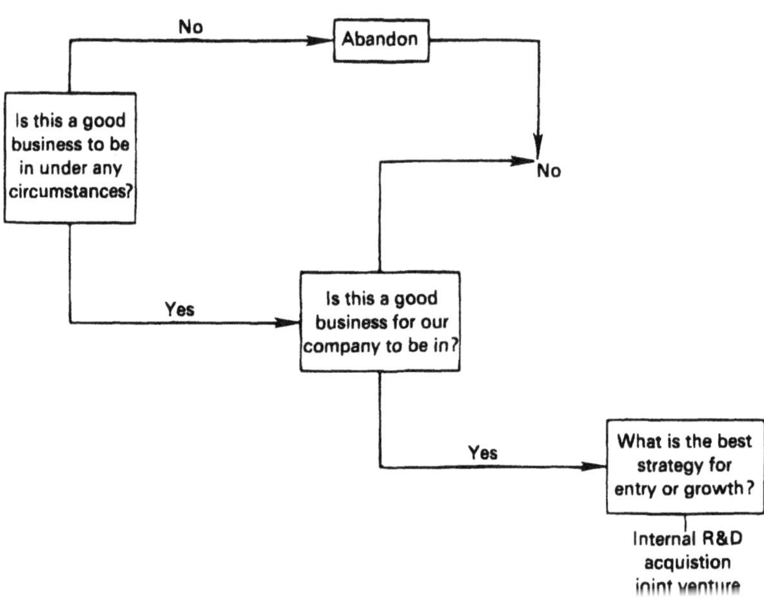


**Figure 5.7**
Logical Approach to Project Selection.

3. What is the yearly growth potential?
4. How strong is the competition?
5. Is the market easy or difficult for competitors to enter?
6. How might competition react?
7. What socio-political factors must be considered?
8. Is there a value added by manufacturing?

- Is this a good business for us to be in?
  1. What are the risks to the company?
  2. What capital needs must be considered?
  3. Is our cash flow compatible with capital needs?
  4. Do we have the marketing/sales force to support the product?
  5. Is in-house manufacturing capability strong enough to support production?
  6. How strong is our technical capability?
  7. How strong is our management capability?
  8. Is raw material availability a problem?

These last eight questions require further comment. Some companies may not be willing to accept the risks of developing a new product (even if considered to be profitable) because it may be *too good* of a fit with the other products (all our eggs in one basket). In other words, if capital is limited, it may be best to undertake these projects that can lead to diversification.

Although a product that requires a small amount of capital may be a low financial risk to the company, the overall risk to the company may be quite high if it invites competition. On the other hand, a capital-intensive project may serve as a barrier to entry for the competition but requires a better understanding of the potential risks. High-capital-intensive projects require reasonably good cash flows.

All too often, companies forecast a market need or an untapped market niche and proceed "full speed ahead" without giving serious thought to the availability of an adequate marketing/sales force. Training a new sales force or developing a new marketing approach may take years. By the time the training is completed, the life cycle of the product could be expired, the product could be obsolete, the market niche could disappear, or a new technology could have been developed. In any case, if training is necessary, it should be done concurrently with product development if at all possible.

Manufacturing capability is a decisive factor in project selection. Simply because the R&D personnel have the capability to develop the product and the associated pilot plant and prototype, does not imply that full commercial production capability exists. Developing manufacturing capability concurrently with development may not be possible until the design and performance specifications are frozen. One alternative to this would be to delay commercial production until the prototype is complete. This may result in late market entry and a large loss in profits. A second alternative may be to subcontract the manufacturing, but this places the company at the mercy of the subcontractors. An untimely increase in the subcontractor's costs could eliminate all profits if the margins are already tight.

Technical capability strength is measured in four areas: R&D, production, customer service, and patent protection. Simply maintaining a strong R&D group does not mean that the company can respond quickly to changes in the state of the art, customer application engineering, or customer service. To compete effectively, a company's technical base should be at least at the same strength as that of the competition.

The most frequently documented cause of failure of potentially good products is due to the fact that the company does not know how to manage a newly acquired product line. As an example, Company A buys out Company B in order to diversify. Company B has several new products, many of which have solid potential. However, the executives in Company A believe that both companies should be managed the same. The moral is to diversify into areas in which you possess the managerial skills.

Full-scale commercialization of a new product requires accessibility to raw materials. It is not uncommon for a company to select those projects for development that fit their suppliers, even though other higher-profit-potential projects are available. Obviously the best situation and least risk would be to select high-profit-potential projects that fit a backwards integration strategy.

For the R&D selection process to be meaningful, there must exist a systematic approach based upon a well-defined criteria. For military application, the following approach may be useful:

- **cost-benefit ratio**—This criterion involved comparing the cost required to complete the research project with the advantages to be received by the Air Force because of its successful completion. Formal procedures existed for performing such comparisons.
- **technical merit**—This criterion involved arriving at a judgment regarding the extent to which the research project provided a new or better technical capability to the Air Force. This process was administratively formalized but subjective in nature as estimates of the future were involved.
- **resource availability**—This criterion involved a decision about the availability of the appropriate personnel, equipment, facilities, and other resources needed to complete the research project. In general, this factor was concerned with the capability to perform the required research involved in the proposed project.
- **likelihood of success**—This criterion was concerned with the likelihood that the proposed research project would achieve technical success, given its planned time and resource constraints. The likelihood involved resulted from subjective probability estimates.
- **time period**—This criterion involved the length of time that was required to complete the proposed research project. In general, with all other things equal, relatively short research projects were favored over relatively long research projects. It was generally agreed that extremely long research projects have almost no chance of being selected, given the resource constraints that existed at the time of the study.
- **Air Force need**—This criterion involved examining the extent to which it had been established that an actual need existed within the Air Force for the technical capability to be provided by a particular research project.

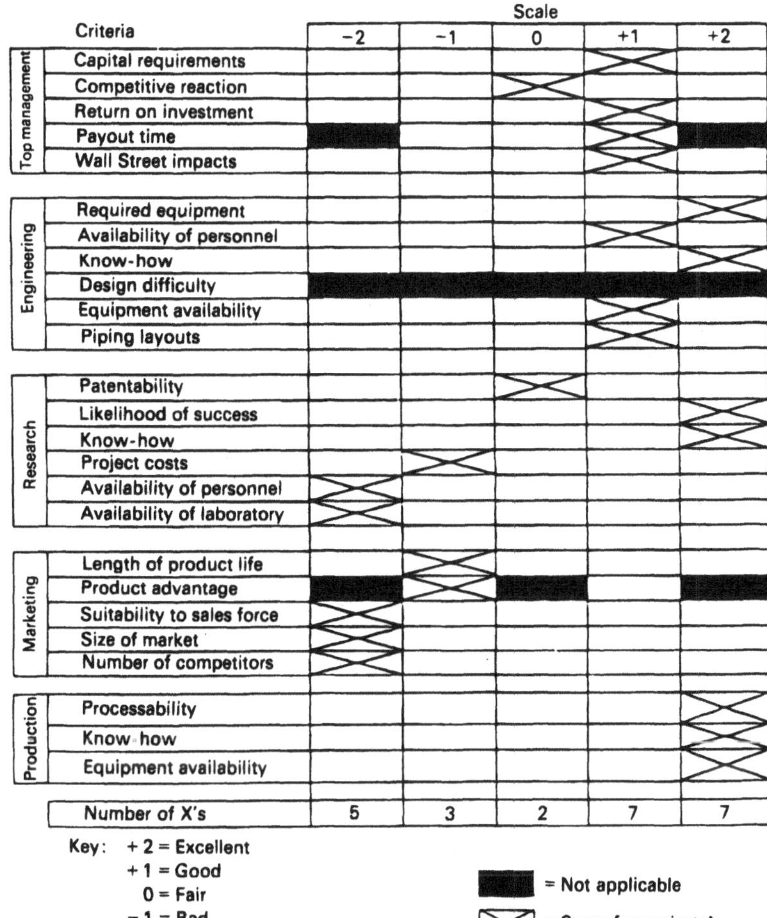


**Figure 5.8** Illustration of a Scaling Model for One Project, Project A. *Source*: William E. Souder, *Project Selection and Economic Appraisal*, Van Nostrand, 1984, p. 66.

For industrial applications, the criteria list must be subdivided into two parts: a business criteria list[35] and an R&D criteria list.[36]

- **business enterprise R&D criteria**
  - ratio of research costs to profits
  - percentage of total earnings due to new products
  - share of market due to new products
  - research costs related to increases in sales
  - research costs to ratio of new and old sales
  - research costs per employee
  - research costs as a ratio of administrative and selling costs
  - cash flows
  - research audits
  - weighted averages of costs and objectives
  - project profiles

- **some suitability criteria**
  - similar in technology
  - similar marketing methods are used
  - similar distribution channels are used
  - can be sold by current sales force
  - will be purchased by same customers as current products
  - fits the company philosophy or image
  - uses existing know-how or expertise
  - fits current production facilities
  - both research and marketing personnel enthusiastic
  - fits the company long-range plan
  - fits current profit goals

The need for two lists should be obvious. Regardless how well a new-product idea fits the business criteria list, the organization must have adequate resources for support.

The criteria list can be transformed into rating models as shown in Figs 5.8, 5.9, and 5.10. Fortunately, these criteria must be further elaborated, such as in Table 5.3, so that a clear understanding of the criteria is available to all evaluators.[37]

| Criteria | Profitability | Patentability | Marketability | Produceability |
|---|---|---|---|---|
| Criterion Weights | 4 | 3 | 2 | 1 |

| Projects | Criterion scores* | | | | Total Weighted Score |
|---|---|---|---|---|---|
| Project D | 10 | 6 | 4 | 3 | 69 |
| Project E | 5 | 10 | 10 | 5 | 75 |
| Project F | 3 | 7 | 10 | 10 | 63 |

Total weighted Score = Σ Criterion score X Criterion Weight

* Scale: 10 = excellent; 1 = unacceptable

**Figure 5.9** Illustration of a Scoring Model.
*Source*: William Souder, *Project Selection and Economic Appraisal*, Van Nostrand, 1984, p. 69.

## Table 5.3 Factor and Subfactor Ratings for a New Product.

| | Very Good | Good | Average | Poor | Very Poor |
|---|---|---|---|---|---|
| *1. Marketability* | | | | | |
| A. Relation to present distribution channels | Can reach major markets by distributing through present channels. | Can reach major markets by distributing mostly through present channels, partly through new channels. | Will have to distribute equally between new and present channels, in order to reach major markets. | Will have to distribute mostly through new channels in order to reach major markets. | Will have to distribute entirely through new channels in order to reach major markets. |
| B. Relation to present product lines | Complements a present line that needs more products to fill it. | Complements a present line that does not need, but can handle, another product. | Can be fitted into a present line. | Can be fitted into a present line but does not fit entirely. | Does not fit in with any present product line. |
| C. Quality/price relationship | Price below all competing products of similar quality. | Priced below most competing products of similar quality. | Approximately the same price as competing products of similar quality. | Priced above many competing products of similar quality. | Priced above all competing products of similar quality. |
| D. Number of sizes and grades | Few staple sizes and grades. | Several sizes and grades, but customers will be satisfied with few staples. | Several sizes and grades, but can satisfy customer wants with small inventory of nonstaples. | Several sizes and grades, each of which will have to be stocked in equal amounts. | Many sizes and grades, which will necessitate heavy inventories. |
| E. Merchandisability | Has product characteristics over and above those of competing products that lend themselves to the kind of promotion, advertising, and display that the given company does best. | Has promotable characteristics that will compare favorably with the characteristics of competing products. | Has promotable characteristics that are equal to those of other products. | Has a few characteristics that are promotable, but generally does not measure up to characteristics of competing products. | Has no characteristics at all that are equal to competitors' or that lend themselves to imaginative promotion. |
| F. Effects on sales of present products | Should aid in sales of present products. | May help sales of present products; definitely will not be harmful to present sales. | Should have no effect on present sales. | May hinder present sales some; definitely will not aid present sales. | Will reduce sales of presently profitable. |
| *2. Durability* | | | | | |
| A. Stability | Basic product that can always expect to have uses. | Product that will have uses long enough to earn back initial investment, plus at least 10 years of additional profits. | Product that will have uses long enough to earn back initial investment, plus several (from 5 to 10) years of additional profits. | Products that will have uses long enough to earn back initial investment, plus 1 to 5 years of additional profits. | Product that will probably be obsolete in near future. |
| B. Breadth of market | A national market, a wide variety of consumers, and a potential foreign market. | A national market and a wide variety of consumers. | Either a national market or a wide variety of consumers. | A regional market and a restricted variety of consumers. | A specialized market in a small marketing area. |
| C. Resistance to cyclical fluctuations | Will sell readily inflation or depression. | Effects of cyclical changes will be moderate, and will be felt after changes in economic outlook. | Sales will rise and fall with the economy. | Effects of cyclical changes will be heavy, and will be felt before changes in economic outlook. | Cyclical changes will cause extreme fluctuations in demand. |

**Table 5.3 (continued)**

| | Very Good | Good | Average | Poor | Very Poor |
|---|---|---|---|---|---|
| D. Resistance to seasonal fluctuations | Steady sales throughout the year. | Steady sales—except under unusual circumstances. | Seasonal fluctuations, but inventory and personnel problems can be absorbed. | Heavy seasonal fluctuations that will cause considerable inventory and personnel problems. | Severe seasonal fluctuations that will necessitate layoffs and heavey inventories. |
| E. Exclusiveness of design | Can be protected by a patent with no loopholes. | Can be patented, but the patent might be circumvented. | Cannot be patented, but has certain salient characteristics that cannot be copied very well. | Cannot be patented, and can be copied by larger, more knowledgeable companies. | Cannot be patented, and and can be copied by anyone. |
| *III. Productive Ability* | | | | | |
| A. Equipment necessary | Can be produced with equipment that is presently idle. | Can be produced with present equipment, but production will have to be scheduled with other products. | Can be produced largely with present equipment but the company will have to purchase some additional equipment. | Company will have to buy a good deal of new equipment, but some present equipment can be used. | Company will have to buy all new equipment. |
| B. Production knowledge and personnel necessary | Present knowledge and personnel will be able to produce new product. | With very few minor exceptions, present knowledge and personnel will be able to produce new product. | With some exceptions, present knowledge and personnel will be able to produce new product. | A ratio of approximately 50–50 will prevail between the needs for new knowledge and personnel and for present knowledge and personnel. | Mostly new knowledge and personnel are needed to produce the new product. |
| C. Raw materials' availability | Company has purchase raw materials from its best supplier(s) exclusively. | Company can purchase major portion of raw materials from its best supplier(s), and remainder from any of a number of companies. | Company can purchase approximately half of raw materials from its best supplier(s), and other half from any one of a number of companies. | Company must purchase most of raw materials from any one of a number of companies other than its best supplier(s). | Company must purchase most or all of raw materials from a certain few companies other than its best supplier(s). |
| *IV. Growth Potential* | | | | | |
| A. Place in market | New type of product that will fill a need presently not being filled. | Product that will substantially improve on products presently on the market. | Product that will have certain new characteristics that will appeal to a substantial segment of the market. | Product that will have minor improvements over products presently on the market. | Product similar to those presently on the market and adds nothing new. |
| B. Expected competitive situation—value added | Very high value added so as to substantially restrict number of competitors. | High enough value added so that, unless product is extremely well suited to other firms, they will not want to invest in additional facilities. | High enough value added so that, unless other companies are as strong in market as this firm, it will not be profitable for them to compete. | Lower value added so as to allow large, medium, and some smaller companies to compete. | Very low value added so that all companies can profitably enter. |
| C. Expected availability of end users | Number of end users will increase substantially. | Number of end users will increase moderately. | Number of end users will increase slightly, if at all. | Number of end users will decrease moderately. | Number of end users will decrease substantially. |

*Source*: Robert R. Rothberg, *Corporate Strategy and Product Innovation*, 2nd Edition, The Free Press, Addison and Macmillan Publishing Co., Inc., 1981, p. 316, 317, 318.

|  | Profitability |  |  | Marketability |  |  | Success likelihood |  |  |  |
|---|---|---|---|---|---|---|---|---|---|---|
| Projects | 3 | 2 | 1 | 3 | 2 | 1 | 3 | 2 | 1 | Total score |
| Project A | ✓ |  |  |  | ✓ |  |  | ✓ |  | 7 |
| Project B |  | ✓ |  | ✓ |  |  |  |  | ✓ | 6 |
| Project C |  |  | ✓ |  |  | ✓ |  |  | ✓ | 3 |

Criteria

**Figure 5.10** Illustration of a Checklist for Three Projects.
*Source*: Willam Souder, *Project Selection and Economic Appraisal*, Van Nostrand, 1984, p. 68.

# Strategy Readjustment

Many R&D projects are managed by overly optimistic prima donnas who truly believe that they can develop any type of product if left alone and provided with sufficient funding. Unfortunately, such projects never end because the R&D managers either do not know when the project is over (poor understanding of the objectives) or do not want the project to end (exceeding objectives). In either event, periodic project review and readjustment action must be considered.

The primary reason for periodic review is to reassess the risks based upon current strategic thinking and project performance. Souder has identified several types of project risks:[38]

- technical failure
- market failure
- failure to perform
- failure to finish on time
- research failure
- development failure
- engineering failure
- production failure
- user acceptance failure
- unforeseen events
- insurmountable technical obstacles
- unexpected outcomes
- inadequate know-how
- legal/regulatory uncertainties

Project risks generally result in project-selection readjustment. Souder has also provided a list of readjustment actions:[39]

- replanning project
- readjusting portfolio of projects
- reallocating funds
- rescheduling project
- backlogging project
- reprioritizing projects
- terminating project
- replacement with backlogged project
- replacement with new project

# Project Termination

Previously, we stated that R&D projects should be periodically reviewed so that readjustment actions can be taken. One technique for readjustment is to terminate the project. The following are the most common reasons and indications that termination is necessary:

- final achievement of the objectives—This is obviously the best of all possible reasons.
- poor initial planning and market prognosis—This could be caused by a loss of interest in the project by the marketing personnel or an overly optimistic initial strategy.
- a better alternative has been found—This could be caused by finding a new approach that has a higher likelihood of success.
- a change in the company interest and strategy—This could be caused by a loss of the market, major changes in the market, development of a new strategy, or simply a lack of commitment and enthusiasm of project personnel.
- allocated time has been exceeded.
- budget costs have been exceeded.
- key people have left the organization—This could be caused by a major change in the technical difficulty of the project with the departure of key scientists who had the specialized knowledge.
- personal whims of management—This could be caused by the loss of interest by senior management.
- problem too complex for the resources available—This could be caused by an optimistic initial view when, in fact, the project has insurmountable technological hurdles that did not appear until well into the project.

Executives normally employ one or more of the following methods to terminate the R&D projects:

- orderly planned termination
- the hatchet (withdrawal of funds and cutting of personnel)

- reassignment of people to higher-priority projects
- redirection of efforts toward different objectives or strategies
- bury it or let it die on the vine

R&D personnel are highly motivated and hate to see projects terminate in midstream. Executives must carefully assess the risks and morale effects of project termination.

# Strategic Budgeting for R&D

Formulation of the R&D budget is a complex mechanism involving feedback loops and decision methodologies. As was the case with project screening and planning, several questions must be considered in analyzing the environment:

- **common strategy**
  - first in with new product
  - close follower to industry leader
  - produce a "me-too" product
- **technological effort**
  - present size of R&D effort
  - level of morale of R&D staff that, in part, is due to freedom to choose interesting and challenging projects
  - state of the art of the technology utilized now and required in the future
- **financial considerations**
  - availability of money from internal or external sources to fund both the technical segment as well as the commercial segment of the innovation
  - return on investment in R&D projects versus investment in other projects such as purchasing new product machinery or building a new warehouse
  - requirements for stable financial support for R&D
- **production capability**
  - availability or ability of the production facilities to produce the new innovation at a competitive cost
- **market conditions**
  - highly competitive versus stable market environment
  - length of the product life cycle
  - profit opportunities or market niches

Unfortunately, many of the environmental questions identified above do not carry equal weight. The authors have found that, most often, financial considerations may dominate. The following list further expands the financial considerations:

- **What are the risks?**
  - Technical risk is often quite modest.
  - Commercial risk is often substantial.

- **What makes for success**?
  - Economic success is the product of three separate factors: the probability of technical success, the probability of commercialization, and/or the probability of economic success.
- **What is the right portfolio**?
  - The right proportion of low-risk R&D activity and technically more ambitious projects whose probability of economic success is higher is needed.
  - A good mix of both long-term and shor-term projects is important.
  - Economic evaluation of both project proposals and continuing projects using rate of return on discounted cash flow methods is necessary.
- **What is the rate of return**?
  - The rate is different for products than for processes.
  - There is both a private rate and a social rate.
  - A generous time horizon is needed by senior management because short-term fluctuations in returns do occur.[40]

Budgeting methodologies range from "what the chief executive wants" to some very analytical models that are organized in highly logical and consistent steps. These steps, which may use the above questions as a basis, are necessary to determine the level of the R&D budget so that requirements can be specified for:

- manpower/management-planning activities
- facilities/services
- capital equipment expenditures
- documentation

Also, the budgeting environmental activities attempt to identify the following major elements of the financial plan:

- source of funds (Where?)
- allocation of costs (To whom?)
- funding decision makers (By Whom?)
- schedules and milestones (When and How?)

A major consideration in any budgeting process is the ability to identify those features that distinguish an effective budget from an ineffective one. According to Bunge,[41] there are seven major considerations involving high-risk ventures:

1. **The budget is built around people.** R&D budgets must be built around and controlled through the human and nonhuman resources, not by the reports, account classifications, or computer printouts.
2. **The budget must have the support of top management.** Continuous support by top management should create enthusiasm for lower-level managers. Likewise, if top management simply provides lip service, lack of enthusiasm will appear down the entire line and budgeting control may be disregarded.
3. **The budget must be realistic.** Unrealistic budgets cause people to lose respect for the project. Unfortunately, many managers and executives set

unrealistic budgets on the assumption that the budget will eventually be overrun. Enthusiastic executives normally set a budget slightly more than what is needed in hopes that R&D managers will be motivated enough to exceed performance requirements.

4. **The budget is flexible.** Because the R&D environment is extremely turbulent and uncertain, flexible budgets are a must in R&D. Inflexible budgets are merely a series of appropriations and are appropriate to static rather than dynamic operations.
5. **The budget is comprehensive and complete.** A good budget includes all types of income and all types of expenditures. Good budgets include every area and every level of responsibility from the president's office on down.
6. **The budget is based upon information, communication, and participation.** A good budget is a synthesis, not an analysis. It is developed through participation of all who have a hand in spending the company's money and upon whom management has placed the responsibility of some measure of authority.
7. **There is an effective program of follow-up.** Good planning alone does not assure success. There must exist a method for follow-up such that trade-offs on time, cost, and performance can be made. Follow-up is usually accomplished with reports that identify the slippages or variations from the target, as well as an explanation of the corrective action to be taken and the impact on the constraints of time, cost, and performance.

# Controlling Costs

Top management must retain a fair amount of cost control for these types of projects. As stated earlier, resources are becoming more scarce and R&D, by its very nature, is a high-risk operation. Simply monitoring a project is not adequate. There must be a cost-and-control system in place.

Controlling is a three-step process of measuring progress toward an objective, evaluating what needs to be done, and taking the necessary corrective action to achieve or exceed the objectives.

The project manager is basically responsible for ensuring the accomplishment of group and organizational goals and objectives.

Effective management of a program during the operating cycle requires that a well-organized cost-and-control system be designed, developed, and implemented so that immediate feedback can be obtained in order that the up-to-date usage of resources can be compared to those that were established as target objectives during the planning cycle. The requirements for an effective control system (for both cost and schedule/performance) should include:

- thorough planning of work to be performed to complete project
- good estimating of time, labor, and costs
- clear communication of scope and required tasks
- disciplined budget and authorization of expenditures

- timely accounting of physical progress and cost expenditures
- periodic, re-estimation of time and cost to completion
- frequent, periodic comparison of actual progress and expenditures to schedules and budgets, both at the time of comparison and at project completion

This periodic appraisal allows for tracking and reporting, as well as reapportionment of committed funds. After initiation of most R&D programs, they quickly fall into the following categories:

1. Project is right on stream.
2. Project is ahead of progress plans.
3. Project has encountered unforeseen problems.
4. Project is in real trouble.
5. Project requires major enlargement and/or acceleration.

Projects falling into the first two categories are not major problems and, fortunately, comprise the majority of R&D programs. The latter three categories can cause major revisions to both the budget and funding exercises. The "unforeseen problem" project may result in being a fund contributor to other projects if the problem is identified as not being able to utilize appropriate funds effectively. The "real trouble" project must be watched closely, and continuance of the project may result in disaster because the project manager is not prone to killing his or her own project.

The fifth project may result when technological breakthroughs or new vistas are gained during the original project. Additional funds required may necessitate reductions or elimination of other projects. This may require a totally new process of budgeting and funding and may also hold the greatest future rewards for the company.

# Life-Cycle Costing (LCC)

For years, many R&D organizations have operated in a vacuum where technical decisions made during R&D were based entirely upon the R&D portion of the plan with little regard for what happens after production begins. Today, industrial firms are adopting the *life-cycle costing* approach that has been developed and used by military organizations. Simply stated, LCC requires that decisions made during the R&D process be evaluated against the total life-cycle cost of the system. As an example, the R&D group has two possible design configurations for a new product. Both design configurations will require the same budget for R&D and the same costs for manufacturing. However, the maintenance and support costs may be substantially greater for one of the products. If these downstream costs are not considered in the R&D phase, large unanticipated expenses may result.

Life-cycle costs are the total cost to the organization for the ownership and acquisition of the product over its full life. This includes the cost of R&D

production, operation, support, and, where applicable, disposal. A typical breakdown description might include:

**R&D costs**—the cost of feasibility studies; cost/benefit analyses; system analyses; detail design and development; fabrication, assembly, and test of engineering models; initial product evaluation; and associated documentation

**production cost**—the cost of fabrication, assembly, and testing of production models; operation and maintenance of the production capability; and associated internal logistic support requirements, including test and support equipment development, spare/repair parts provisioning, technical data development, training, and entry of items into inventory

**construction cost**—the cost of manufacturing facilities or upgrading existing structures to accommodate production and operation of support requirements

**operation and maintenance cost**—the cost of sustaining operational personnel and maintenance support, spare/repair parts and related inventories, test and support equipment maintenance, transportation and handling, facilities, modifications and technical data changes, and so on

**product retirement and phaseout cost**—the cost of phasing the product out of inventory due to obsolescence or wearout, and subsequent equipment item recycling and reclamation as appropriate.

Life-cycle cost analysis is the systematic analytical process of evaluating various alternative courses of action early on in a project with the objective of choosing the best way to employ scarce resources. Life-cycle cost is employed in the evaluation of alternative design configurations, alternative manufacturing methods, alternative support schemes, and so on. This process includes:

- defining the problem (what information is needed)
- defining the requirements of cost model being used
- college historical data/cost relationships
- developing estimate and test results

Successful application of LCC will:

- provide downstream resource impact visibility
- provide life-cycle cost management
- influence R&D decision making
- support downstream strategic budgeting

There are also several limitations to life-cycle cost analyses. They include the assumption that the product has a known, finite life cycle, that it has a high cost to produce and may not be appropriate for low-cost/low-volume production, and that it has a high sensitivity to changing requirements.

Life-cycle costing requires estimates to be made. The estimating method selected is based upon the problem context (decisions to be made, required accuracy, complexity of the product, and the development status of the product), and

**Table 5.4 Advantages and Disadvantages of Informal and Formal Estimating Methods.**

| Estimating Technique | Application | Advantages | Disadvantages |
|---|---|---|---|
| Engineering Estimates | Reprocurement | • Most detailed technique | • Requires detailed program and product definition |
| | Production | • Best inherent accuracy | • Time consuming and may be expensive |
| Empirical | Development | • Provides best estimating base for future program change estimates | • Subject to engineering bias<br>• May overlook system integration costs |
| Parametric Estimates and Scaling | Production and Low-Cost Development | • Application is simple<br>• Statistical database can provide expected values and prediction intervals | • Requires parametric cost relationships to be established<br>• Limited frequently to specific subsystems or functional hardware of systems |
| Statistical | | • Can be used for equipment or systems prior to detail design or program planning | • Depends on quantity and quality of the database<br>• Limited by data and number of independent variables |
| Equipment/Subsystems Analogy Estimates | Reprocurement | • Relatively simple | • Require analogous product and program data |
| | Production | • Low cost | • Limited to stable technology |
| Comparative | Development | • Emphasizes incremental program and product changes | • Narrow range of electronic applications |
| | Program Planning | • Good accuracy for similar systems | • May be limited to systems and equipment built by the same firm |
| Expert Opinion | All Program Phases | • Available when there are insufficient data, paramametric cost relationships, or program/product definition | • Subject to bias<br>• Increased product or program complexity can degrade estimates<br>• Estimate substantiation is not quantifiable |

the operational considerations (market introduction date, time available for analysis, and available resources).

The estimating methods available can be classified as follows:

- **informal estimating methods**
  - judgment based on experience
  - analogy
  - SWAG method
  - ROM method
  - rule of thumb method
- **formal estimating methods**
  - detailed (from Industrial Engineering Standards)
  - parametric

Table 5.4 shows the advantages/disadvantages of each method.

Figure 5.11 shows the various life-cycle phases for Department of Defense projects. At the end of the demonstration and validation phase (which is at the completion of R&D), 85% of the decisions affecting the total life-cycle cost will have been made, and the cost-reduction opportunity is limited to a maximum of 22% (excluding the effects of learning curve experiences). Figure 5.12 shows that, at the end of the R&D phase, 95% of the cumulative life-cycle cost is committed by the government. Figure 5.13 shows that for every $12 that DOD puts into R&D, $28 are needed downstream for production and $60 for operation and support.

Life-cycle cost analysis is an integral part of strategic planning because today's decisions will affect tomorrow's actions. Yet, there are common errors made during life-cycle cost analyses:

- loss or omission of data
- lack of systematic structure
- misinterpretation of data
- wrong or misused technique
- concentration on insignificant facts
- failure to assess uncertainty
- failure to check work
- estimating wrong items

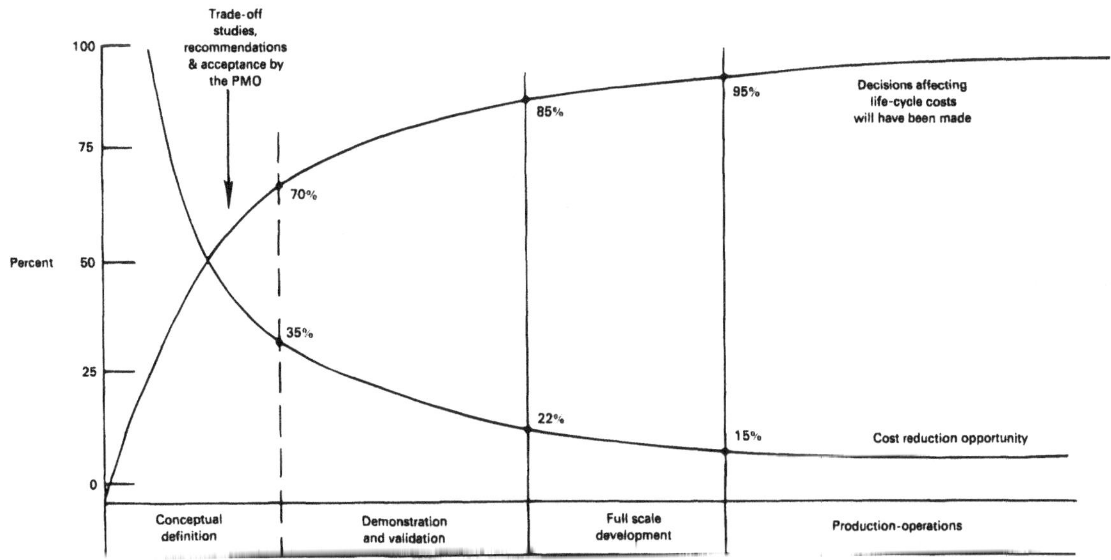


Figure 5.11 Life-cycle Phases for Department of Defense Projects

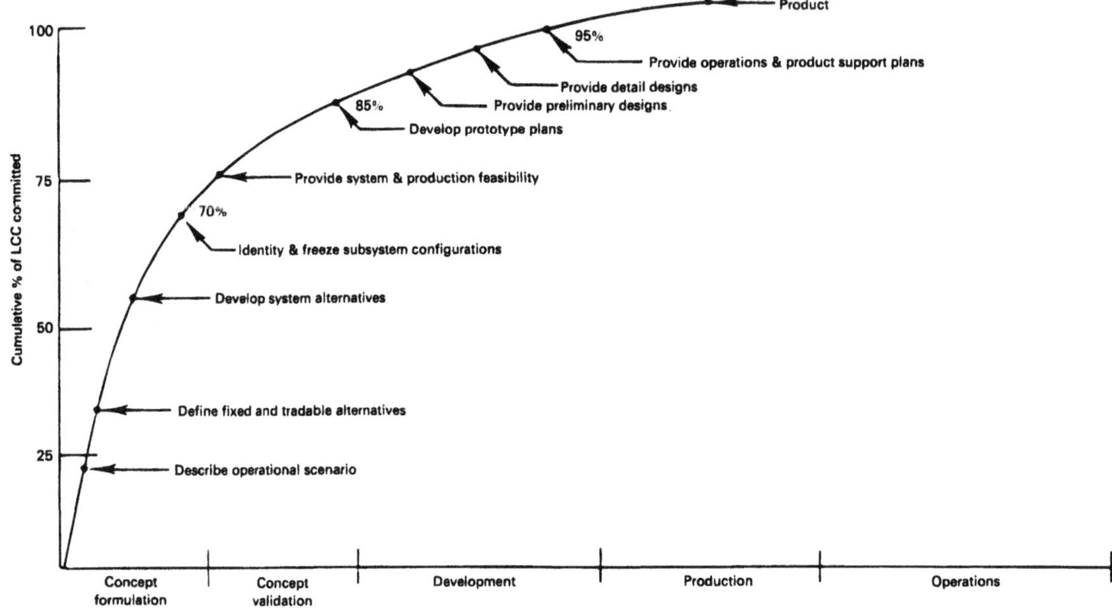


**Figure 5.12** Actions Affecting Life-cycle Cost (LCC).

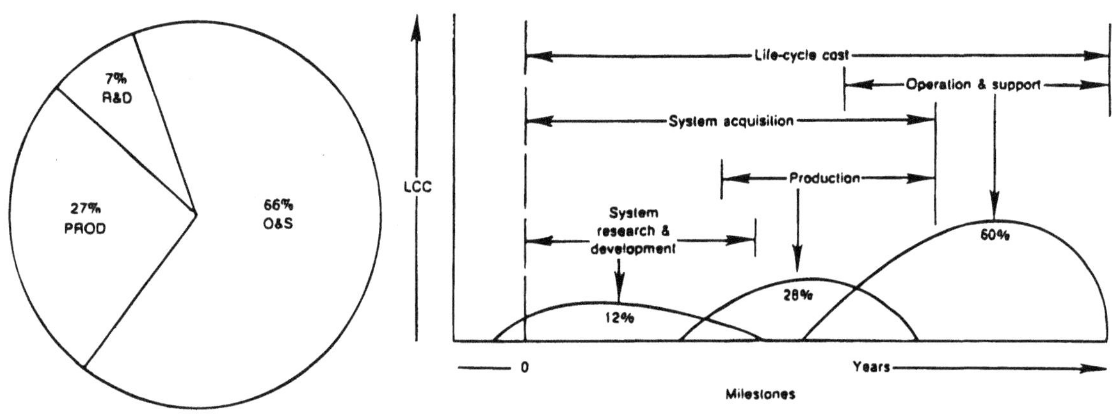


**Figure 5.13** Downstream Production and Operations Costs.

# Integrating R&D into the Strategic Plan

In the previous sections we indicated that proper coupling of R&D to marketing and manufacturing is a necessity to integrate R&D into the strategic plan. Figure

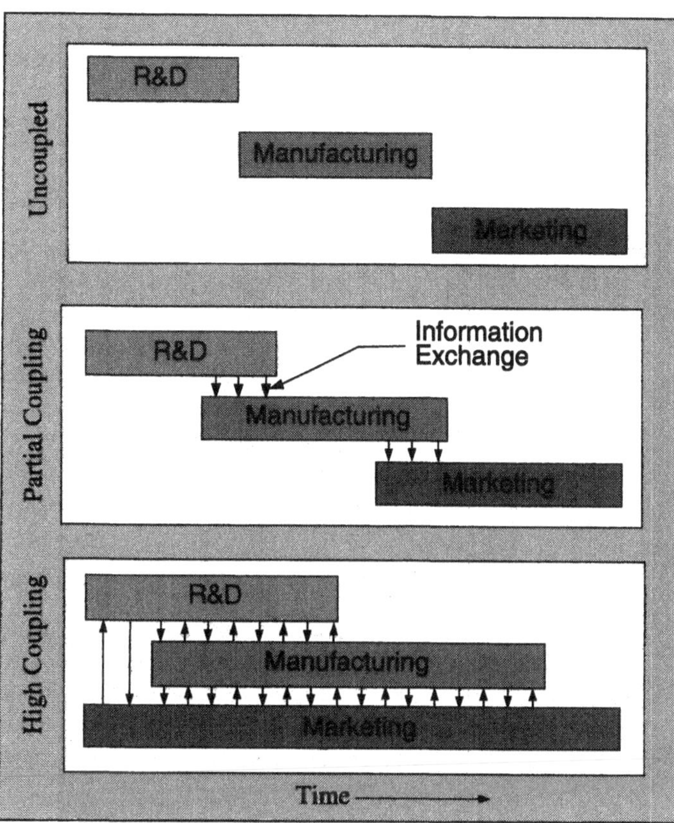


**Figure 5.14** Degrees of Downstream Coupling.

5.14 illustrates the degrees of downstream coupling. There are several reasons why companies prefer strong downstream coupling. First, as described previously under life-cycle costing, downstream costs such as service engineering must be considered during R&D trade-offs. Second, R&D planning and decision making must attempt to minimize the disruptive effects on manufacturing, Third, R&D must be planned for with consideration for the quality-control efforts needed in manufacturing.

Highly coupled systems are generally dynamic rather than static and respond better to changes in the strategic-planning system. Figure 5.15 shows the matrix that couples R&D plans to the business objectives. For a highly dynamic, highly coupled system, there exists a continuous reassessment of the technical efforts necessary to support the business-technical portfolio.

Quinn and Mueller[42] have developed a four-step program to improve the flow of technical information from research into operations.

**Step I. Examine technological transfer points.**

- Analyze the critical points across which technology must flow if it is to be successfully exploited.
- Recognize the potential resistances to the flow at each of these interfaces.

**Step II. Provide information to target research.**

- Generate adequate information so that research can be targeted toward company goals and needs.
- Develop a comprehensive long-range planning program to determine what technology is relevant to the company's future and to serve as a focal point for information flows.
- Establish special organizations, where needed, to seek specific new technological opportunities for the company, to provide commercial intelligence information about competitive activities and to make careful economic evaluations of technologically based new ventures.

**Step III. Foster a positive motivational environment.**

- Establish a motivational environment that actively stimulates technological progress and its associated organizational change.
- Develop tough-minded, top-management attitudes, policies, and long-range term controls that foster—rather than hinder—the production and use of new technologies.

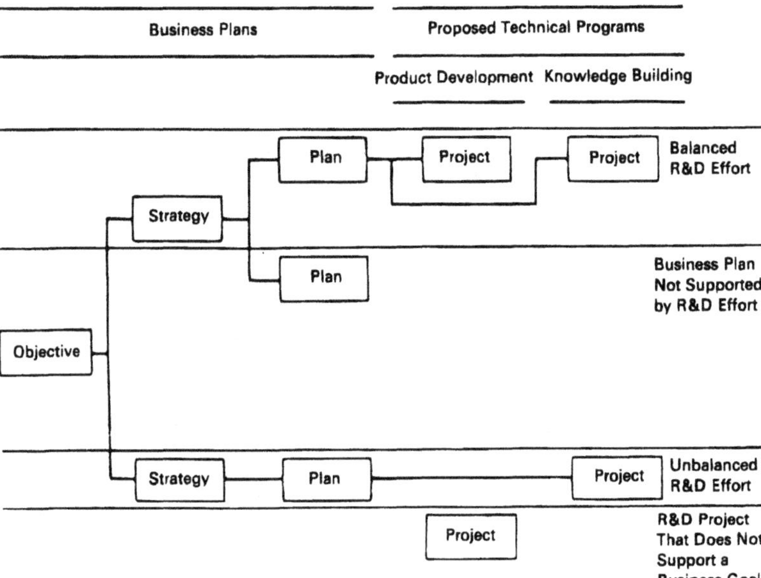


**Figure 5.15** Matrix That Couples R&D Plans and Business Objectives. *Source*: James F. Lyons, "Strategic Management and Strategic Planning in the 1980's," *The Strategic Management Handbook*, Kenneth J. Albert, Editor-in-Chief, McGraw-Hill, 1983, p. 3.

**Step IV. Plan and control exploitation of R&D results.**

- Design special exploitation organizations and procedures to ensure (a) that competent groups have both the authority and the obligation to develop new technologies at each of their critical stages; (b) that each major technological transfer is planned and monitored to control effort expenditures, cash flows, and timing; and (c) that the entire transfer system implements the critical strategy—which determines success or failure—at each major technological transfer point.

Quinn and Mueller also provide an example of a company that has knitted all of the pieces together into one well-developed plan:[43]

- A large chemical company regularly follows this planning procedure. It prepares its long-range plan semiannually, in conjunction with its operating and capital budgets—each of which extends five years into the future. The executive committee—acting on information from a central long-range planning staff—establishes overall company objectives for the next five years. These objectives—specifying "what" should be done and "when" it should be done—are fed down to operating and service groups who then draw up specific programs to meet them.

Each program tells "how" the organization will effect its part of the company's objectives and estimates the financial implications (both capital and expense) of the program. The central staff group and a long-range planning committee work with each group to see that each program is coordinated with other phases of the total corporate plan. Special subcommittees then review each of the final budgets before they go to the long-range planning committee and executive committee for final recommendations and approval.

Here is how research needs and aspirations are fitted into the long-range plan. Working from technological forecasts and past program information, research draws up a tentative program. It checks this with each major operating division and with the key corporate executives individuals. It then draws up a modified program (and budgets) and submits this to a formal review by the research subcommittee, which looks for issues of balance, project priorities, and program scope. The long-range planning committee makes a few final recommendations, sees that operating division plans adequately anticipate research technology, and then sends the final plans to the executive committee for approval. Of course, throughout the entire process there is a constant modification of objectives and plans as mutual interaction dictates.

The coupling of R&D to marketing is extremely critical, especially in organizations with short product life cycle. Figure 5.16 shows the two-dimensional characteristics of products classified by product objectives. Figure 5.16 can be transformed into Figure 5.17 to show the relationship of new-product responsibilities by department. Regions where there exist joint responsibilities indicates the need for highly coupled downstream integration of people and activities.

| | INCREASING TECHNOLOGICAL NEWNESS → | | |
|---|---|---|---|
| PRODUCT OBJECTIVES | NO TECHNOLOGICAL CHANGE | IMPROVED TECHNOLOGY<br>To utilize more fully the company's present scientific knowledge and production skills. | NEW TECHNOLOGY<br>To acquire scientific knowledge and production skills new to the company. |
| NO MARKET CHANGE | | *Reformulation*<br>To maintain an optimum balance of cost, quality, and availability in the formulas of present company products.<br>Example: use of oxidized microcrystaline waxes in Glo-Coat (1946). | *Replacement*<br>To seek new and better ingredients or formulation for present company products in technology not now employed by the cpmpany.<br>Example: development of synthetic resin as a replacement for shellac in Glo-Coat (1950). |
| STRENGTHENED MARKET<br>To exploit more fully the existing markets for the present company products. | *Remerchandising*<br>To increase sales to consumers of types now served by the company.<br>Example: use of dripless spout can for emulsion waxes (1955). | *Improved Product*<br>To improve present products for greater utility and merchandisability to consumers.<br>Example: combination of auto paste wax and cleaner into one-step "J. Wax" (1956). | *Product Line Extension*<br>To broaden the line of products offered to present consumers through new technology<br>Example: development of a general purpose floor cleaner "Emerel" in maintenance product line (1953). |
| NEW MARKET<br>To increase the number of types of consumers served by the company. | *New Use*<br>To find new classes of consumers that can utilize present company products.<br>Example: sale of paste wax to furniture manufacturers for Caul Board wax (1946). | *Market Extension*<br>To reach new classes of consumers by modifying present products.<br>Example: wax-based coolants and drawing compounds for industrial machining operations (1951). | *Diversification*<br>To add to the classes of consumers served by developing new technical knowledge.<br>Example: development of "Raid" – dual purpose insecticide (1955). |

↓ INCREASING MARKET NEWNESS

**Figure 5.16** Classification of New Products by Product Objective. *Source*: Robert R. Rothberg, Corporate Strategy and Product Innovation, Second Edition, The Free Press, 1981, p. 191.

| PRODUCT EFFECT | NO TECHNOLOGICAL CHANGE<br>Does not require additional laboratory effort. | IMPROVED TECHNOLOGY<br>Requires laboratory effort utilizing technology presently employed, known, or related to that used in existing company products. | NEW TECHNOLOGY<br>Requires laboratory effort utilizing technology not presently employed in company products. |
|---|---|---|---|
| NO MARKET CHANGE<br>Does not affect marketing programs. | | *Reformulation* | *Replacement* |
| STRENGTHENED MARKET<br>Affects marketing programs to present classes of consumers. | *Remerchandising* | *Improved Product* | *Product Line Extension* |
| NEW MARKET<br>Requires marketing programs for classes of consumers not now served. | *New Use* | *Market Extension* | *Diversification* |

Key: Research and Development Department; Marketing Department; Joint Responsibility of R&D and Marketing Departments

**Figure 5.17** Relationship of New-Product Responsibilities by Department. *Source*: Robert R. Rothberg, *Corporate Strategy and Product Innovation*, 2nd Edition, The Free Press, 1981, p. 192.

Frohman and Bitondo have indicated several ways that technical strategy can be coupled to business strategy:[44]

- positioning the R&D strategy from defensive to offensive, depending on the market attractiveness and business position (Figure 5.18)
- posturing of the R&D effort with the spectrum from state-of-the-art research (technology invention) to prototype development (minor application of existing technology), depending on product-line need and market share strategy (Figure 5.19)
- R&D meeting objectives ranging from eliminating products to developing new products to new specifications (Figure 5.20)
- matching the needs of the product, depending where it is in the life cycle requiring R&D from product innovation to cost reduction (Figure 5.21)

After the investment and product-line needs have been defined, the functional responsibility for reaching the goals and the role of R&D must be determined.[45] Note that from Figure 5.20, for a product strategy relying on existing products, a market strategy is mainly required. For improved or new products, the emphasis is placed on the technology strategy for each product. The function responsible for leading and developing the specific strategy for each product will depend on the emphasis of the strategy. The implications of the investment strategy for the R&D strategy is shown in Figure 5.22. This chart is intended for the purpose of general positioning and getting correlation and agreement on the R&D strategy as it relates to market share and sales growth rate.

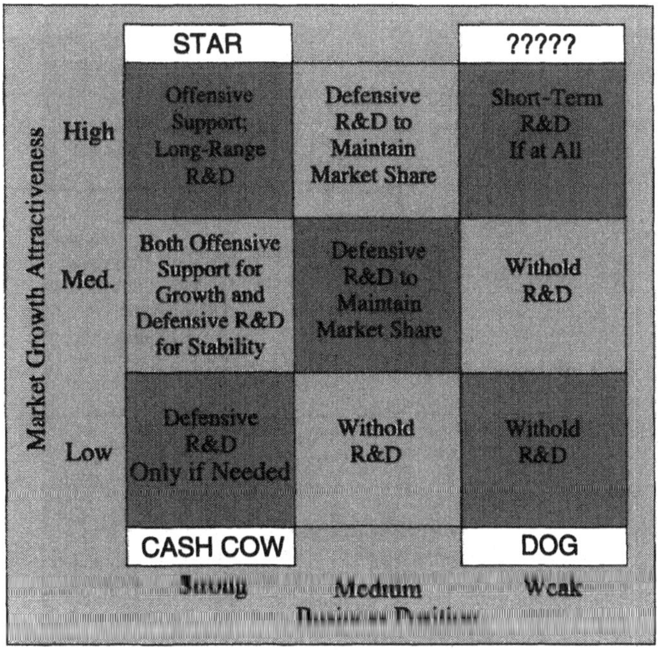

**Figure 5.18**
Positioning the R&D Strategy

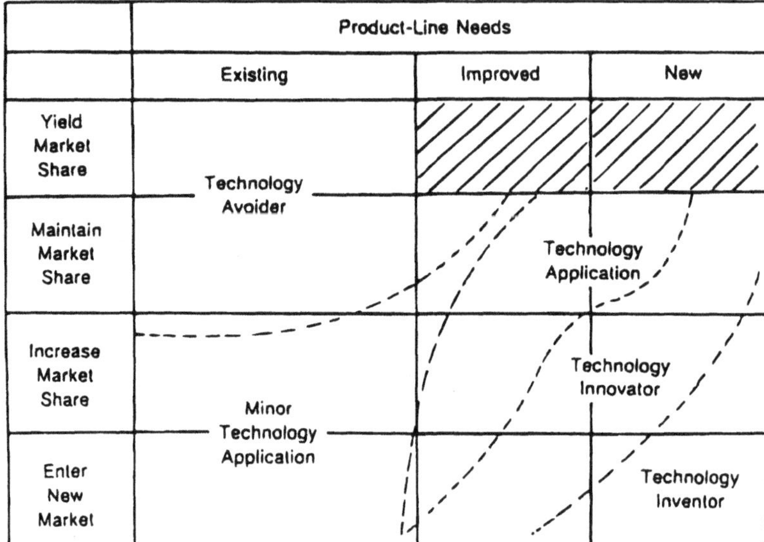


**Figure 5.19**
Posturing of R&D Effort.

| Market Share Strategy | | Product-Line Needs: Existing | Improved | New |
|---|---|---|---|---|
| | Yield Market Share | Reduce Products | | |
| | Maintain Market Share | Consolidate Products | Minor Product Improvement (if required) | New Product Existing Specifications |
| | Increase Market Share | Reduce Cost of Products | Product Improvement | New Product Improved Specifications |
| | Enter New Market | Apply Products to New Uses | Product Re-Design and Improvement | Diversification |
| | Functional Responsibility | ↑ Marketing: Market Strategy | ↑ Engineering: Product Development | ↑ Research: Basic and Applied R&D |

**Figure 5.20**
R&D Meeting Objectives.

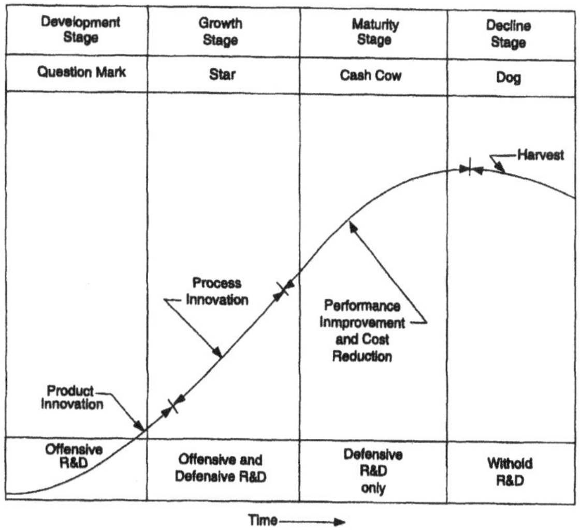

**Figure 5.21** Matching the Needs of the Product.

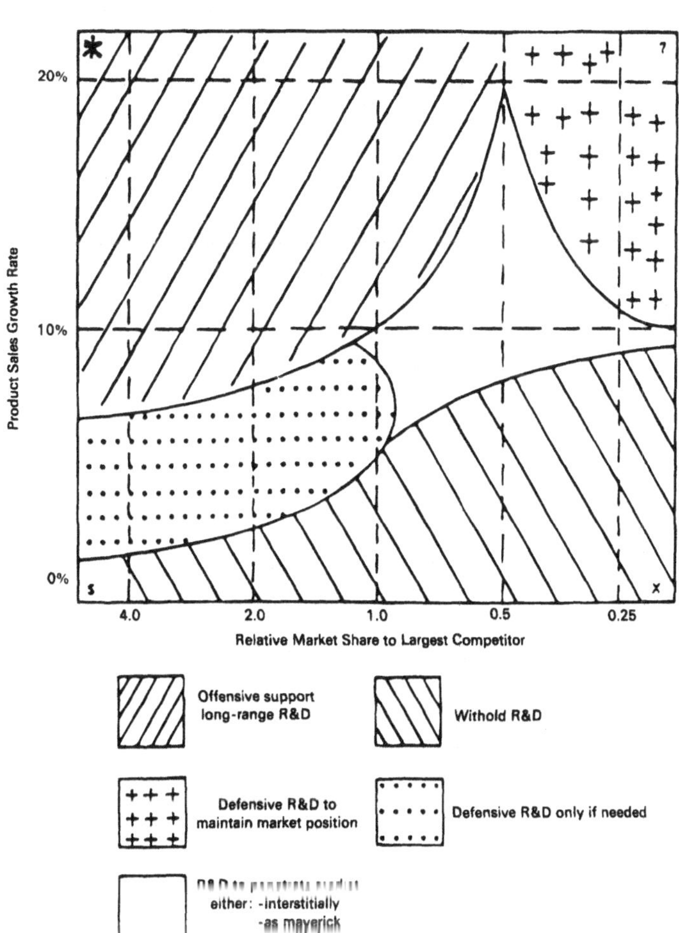


**Figure 5.22** Implications of the Investment Strategy [illegible]

# NOTES


1. Philip Kotler, *Marketing Management*, 4th ed. (New Jersey: Prentice Hall, 1980), p. 314.
2. D. G. Marquis, "The Anatomy of Successful Innovations," *Managing Advancing Technology*, American Management Associations, Inc., 1972, Vol. 1, pp. 35–48.
3. Booz, Allen, and Hamilton, *Management of New Products*, 1968, pp. 7–12.
4. E. Mansfield and S. Wagner, "Organizational and Strategic Factors Associated with Probabilities of Success in Industrial R&D," *The Journal of Business*, No. 48, April 1978, pp. 179–196.
5. Robert H. Hayes and William J. Abernathy, "Managing Our Way to Economic Decline," *Harvard Business Review*, July–Aug. 1980, pp. 67–77.
6. Adapted from Alan L. Frohman and Domenic Bitondo, "Coordinating Business Strategy and Technical Planning," *Long Range Planning*, Vol. 14, No. 6, Dec. 1981, pp. 58–67.
7. J. G. Wisseman, "Industrial R&D Prepares for the Eighties," *Research Management*, Vol. 22, No. 5, Sept. 1979, pp. 22–26.
8. Alan J. Frohman and Domenic Bitondo, "Coordinating Business Strategy and Technical Planning," *Long Range Planning*, Vol. 14, No. 6, Dec. 1981, p. 64.
9. H. Igor Ansoff and John M. Stewart, "Strategies for a Technology-Based Business," *Harvard Business Review*, Nov.–Dec. 1967. Also *R&D Management: Part II*, No: 8.032. Reprints from *Harvard Business Review*, p. 12. Copyright 1967 by the President and Fellows of Harvard University; all rights reserved. Reproduced by permission.
10. *The New York Times*, Thursday, December 13, 1984, p. D1.
11. James Brian Quinn and Robert M. Cavanaugh, "Fundamental Research Can Be Planned," *Harvard Business Review*, Jan.–Feb. 1964. Also, *R&D Management: Part I*, No. 8.031, p. 106, Reprints from *Harvard Business Review*. Copyright 1964 by the President and Fellows of Harvard University; all rights reserved. Reproduced by permission.
12. James Brian Quinn and James A. Mueller, "Transferring Research Results to Operations," *Harvard Business Review*, Jan.–Feb. 1963. Also, *R&D Management: Part I*, Reprints from *Harvard Business Review*, No: 8.031, p. 32, Copyright 1963 by the President and Fellows of Harvard University; all rights reserved. Reproduced by permission.
13. Ibid.
14. D. N. Foster, "Organizing for Successful Research and Development," unpublished paper, McKinsey and Co., Inc., New York, 1983.
15. Donald K. Clifford, Jr., "Managing the Product Life Cycle," *The Arts of Top Management: A McKinsey Anthology*, Roland Mann, editor, pp. 216–226. Copyright 1971 by McGraw Hill Book Co., used by permission of McGraw Hill Book Company.
16. David A. Curtis, *Strategic Planning for Smaller Businesses* (New York: Lexington Books, 1983), p. 75.
17. The remainder of this section has been taken from Robert A. Lunn, "A Sectoral Approach to Strategic Planning for R&D," *Research Management*, Jan.–Feb. 1983, pp. 33–36.
18. D. Warner and S. Strong, "Out of the Lab and into the Market," *Industrial Marketing*, 56 (December 1971), p. 20.
19. W. T. Hanson and H. K. Nason, "Funding and Budgeting Corporate Research Programs," *Research Management* (March 1980), p. 38.
20. Ibid, p. 39.

21. Philip Kotler, *Marketing Management*, 5th ed. (New Jersey: Prentice Hall, 1984), pp. 729–731.
22. E. M. Kipp, "How to Contract an Effective Corporate R&D Budget," *Research Management*, May 1978, pp. 14–17.
23. Matthew J. Liberatore, "An Incremental Approach for R&D Project Planning and Budgeting," *Research Management*, pp. 17, 18, 20.
24. Hughes Aircraft Company, *R&D Productivity* (Culver City, California: Hughes Aircraft Company, 1978), pp. 14–15.
25. James Brian Quinn and Robert M. Cavanaugh, "Fundamental Research Can Be Planned," *Harvard Business Review*, Jan.–Feb. 1964. Also *R&D Management: Part I*, No 8.031; Reprints from *Harvard Business* Review articles, p. 108. Copyright 1964 by the President and Fellows of Harvard University, all right reserved. Reprinted by permission.
26. Ibid.
27. James Brian Quinn and James A. Mueller, "Transferring Research Results to Operations," *Harvard Business Review*, Jan.–Feb. 1963. Also *R&D Management: Part I*, No. 8.031; Reprints from selected Harvard Business Review articles, p. 23. Copyright 1964 by the President and Fellows of Harvard University; all rights reserved. Reproduced by permission.
28. Lionel S. Goldring, "Defensive R&D as a Management Strategy," *Research Management*, May 1974, pp. 25–28.
29. Ibid.
30. William E. Souder, *Project Selection and Economic Appraisal* (New York: Van Nostrand Publishers, 1984), p. 6.
31. Ibid.
32. Samuel C. Johnson and Conrad Jones, "How to Organize for New Products," *Harvard Business Review*, 35, May–June 1957, pp. 49–63. Copyright 1957 by the President and Fellows of Harvard University; all rights reserved. Reproduced by permission.
33. Philip A. Roussel, "Cutting Down the Guesswork in R&D," *Harvard Business Review*, Sept.–Oct. 1983, pp. 154–160. copyright 1983 by the President and Fellow of Harvard University; all rights reserved. Reproduced by permission.
34. Adapted from D. Bruce Merrifield, "Selecting Projects for Commercial Success," *Research Management*, November 1981, p. 15.
35. Source unknown.
36. William E. Souder, *Project Selection and Economic Appraisal* (New York: Van Nostrand Publishers, 1984), p. 44.
37. David B. Montgomery and Glen L. Urban, *Management Science in Marketing* (New Jersey: Prentice Hall, 1969), pp. 303–312.
38. William E. Souder, *Project Selection and Economic Appraisal*, p. 43.
39. Ibid.
40. Edwin Mansfield, "How Economists See R&D," *Research Management*, July 1982, pp. 23–27.
41. Adapted from Walter A. Bunge, *Managerial Budgeting for Profit Improvement*, (New York: McGraw Hill Book Company, 1968).
42. James Brian Quinn and James A. Mueller, "Transferring Research Results to Operations," *Harvard Business Review*, Jan.–Feb. 1963; Also *R&D Management: Part I*, No: 8.031, p. 31. Copyright 1963 by the President and Fellows of Harvard University, all rights reserved. Reproduced by permission.
43. Ibid, p. 26.

44. Alan L. Frohman and Domenic Bitonda, "Coordinating Business Strategy and Technical Planning," *Long Range Planning*, Vol. 14, No. 6, 1981, pp. 58–67.
45. Ibid, pp. 60–61.

## ESSAY QUESTIONS

1. An oil company invests $5.2 million in an R&D project to improve the efficiency in refining heavy crude oil. The objective of the R&D project is to improve refinery efficiency by 10%. The oil company achieves its goal of improving efficiency by 10%, but at a cost of $8.75 million rather than $5.2 million. Under what conditions would this project still be considered as a success? As a failure?
2. Suppose the oil company discussed in Question 1 completes the project for $5.2 million but the efficiency improvement is only 2%. Under what conditions would this project still be considered as a success? As a failure?
3. During the unfavorable economic times, companies tend to cut back funding for training and R&D first. Either funding for R&D is reduced or the R&D staff is downsized. What is the rationalization behind this?
4. What types of R&D strategies (i.e., types of R&D) would a company pursue during a recession?
5. What types of R&D strategies (i.e., types of R&D) would a company pursue during unfavorable economic conditions other than a recession?
6. Under what conditions would the payback period be a critical parameter used in the selection of R&D projects?
7. Should an R&D group have its own budget to explore R&D projects other than those requested by marketing? Under what conditions is this mandatory?
8. A Fortune 500 company restructured into Strategic Business Units. Each SBU had the responsibility for its own R&D. The approval of R&D projects was based upon the grid shown below:

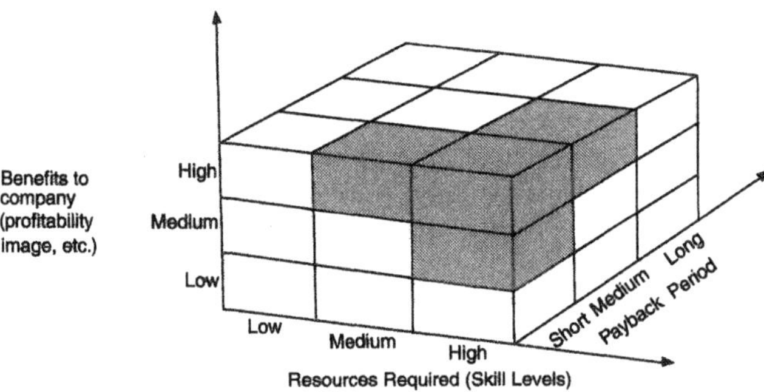


   a. Before the company restructured to SBUs, the grid was two-dimensional, including only "Benefits to Company" and "Resources Required." Why was "Payback Period" added after the restructuring?

b. The SBU would tend to authorize funding only for those grid boxes that were shaded in. These projects would be assigned a high priority. What can be concluded about the SBU's strategic plan, possible life cycle of its products, philosophy of management, etc.?

9. Under what conditions would R&D rather than marketing dominate the strategic-planning process?

10. Companies can grow internally or externally (i.e., by acquisitions or mergers). From an R&D perspective, what are the advantages and disadvantages or internal growth? Growth by acquisition?

11. Your company submits a "hostile" tender offer to buy out another firm, mainly for its R&D capability. The takeover attempt is hostile because the targeted firm wishes to retain its independence. From an R&D perspective, what are the risks of a hostile takeover?

12. Does a balanced product portfolio make it easier or more difficult to target R&D activities? Explain your answer.

13. Marketing identifies a market niche for a new product. R&D develops the product and submits the drawings to manufacturing for full-scale production. While manufacturing prepares its plans, R&D comes up with an ideal to enhance the value of the product. This will dictate a major change in the manufacturing plans *if* the change can be made at all.
   a. At what point should the design be frozen?
   b. Who determines whether the change will be made now or withheld until the next generation of the product?
   c. Could this affect the strategic plan?

## MULTIPLE CHOICE QUESTIONS

1. The primary reason(s) why a company performs R&D include:
   a. new product development
   b. enhancements to existing products
   c. improve the state of the art
   d. all the above
   e. a and b only

2. The weakest R&D link in most organizations is the result of a poor ___________.
   a. project selection criteria
   b. objective setting process
   c. information system
   d. competitor intelligence system
   e. involvement by senior management

3. Most companies perform R&D competitive intelligence functions through ___________.
   a. marketing

b. R&D
c. engineering
d. literature surveys
e. senior management

4. Typical stages of innovation include:
   a. product improvement, process improvement, and quality improvement
   b. systems innovation, product improvement, and process improvement
   c. systems innovation, state-of-the-art innovation, and product enhancement
   d. major systems, operational systems, and functional systems
   e. state-of-the-art changes, product improvement, and process improvement
5. History has shown that to develop one commercially successful new product may take ___________ new ideas.
   a. 10 or more
   b. 20 or more
   c. 30 or more
   d. 40 or more
   e. 60 or more
6. The new-product development process can be characterized as a decay curve where each state is ___________.
   a. progressively more expensive in terms of time and money
   b. progressively less expensive in terms of time and money
   c. progressively full of more ideas for product development
   d. progressively identified by more senior management involvement
   e. progressively more dependent upon marketing intelligence studies
7. R&D on a product line that competes in a mature and declining market would most likely focus on ___________.
   a. subcontracted R&D
   b. new-customer orientation
   c. production enhancements
   d. cost reduction
   e. none of the above
8. The federal government can influence industrial R&D through:
   a. technology transfer restrictions
   b. fiscal and monetary policy
   c. taxes
   d. all the above
   e. a and c only
9. Which of the following is *not* one of the four variables used to explain the differences between research and development?
   a. specifications
   b. resource skills
   c. scheduling
   d. engineering changes
   e. funding levels
10. Internal growth in R&D can be obtained:
    a. with existing resources that are technically qualified
    b. with existing resources that undergo internal technical training
    c. through newly hired employees

d. through consultants
e. all the above

11. External growth in R&D can be obtained:
a. by acquiring a company with the required skills
b. by joint ventures
c. by purchasing the technology through a licensing agreement
d. all the above
e. a and b only

12. The strongest "coupling" within an organization is usually between R&D and ____________.
a. production
b. marketing
c. human resources
d. prototyping
e. accounting and finance

13. The strength of the coupling between R&D and other functions is most frequently dependent upon ____________.
a. the product mix
b. the degree of executive involvement
c. the technical complexity of the project
d. the payback period
e. the length of the product life cycle

14. Small companies that wish to compete in markets characterized by short product life cycles must adopt which of the following marketing strategies?
a. first to market
b. follow the leader
c. applications engineering
d. "me-too"
e. b and c only

15. Which marketing strategy requires that R&D continuously recruit and retain outstanding R&D personnel?
a. first to market
b. follow the leader
c. applications engineering
d. "me-too"
e. b and c only

16. Which marketing strategy requires very little R&D?
a. first to market
b. follow the leader
c. applications engineering
d. "me-too"
e. b and c only

17. Which marketing strategy requires exceptionally quick response time by R&D personnel?
a. first to market
b. follow the leader
c. applications engineering

- **d.** "me-too"
- **e.** none of the above

**18.** Line extension, "flanker" products or cheap imitations are an indication of:
- **a.** the amount of R&D risk the company is willing to take
- **b.** the maturity of the product
- **c.** the competitive position of the firm
- **d.** a first-to-market strategy
- **e.** a company on the verge of bankruptcy

**19.** The pressure of short-term profitability will:
- **a.** increase R&D expenditures
- **b.** decrease R&D expenditures
- **c.** increase marketing expenditures
- **d.** decrease marketing expenditures
- **e.** a and c only

**20.** Product lines that are viewed as either stars or cash cows usually stress:
- **a.** offensive R&D
- **b.** subcontracted R&D
- **c.** defensive R&D
- **d.** a reduction in R&D expenditures
- **e.** none of the above

**21.** An R&D group is given instructions to look for product line spin-offs. The corresponding marketing strategy would most likely be:
- **a.** maintain market share
- **b.** build market share
- **c.** harvest market share
- **d.** withdraw market share
- **e.** none of the above

**22.** Scarce R&D resources are often diverted from R&D activities to address legislation and regulation problems with respect to:
- **a.** product liability
- **b.** health
- **c.** safety
- **d.** environmental factors
- **e.** all the above

**23.** Which type of R&D project generally requires the least funding or no funding at all?
- **a.** grass roots
- **b.** bootlegged
- **c.** basic research
- **d.** applied research
- **e.** production support

**24.** A company needs to develop a new product, but the highly talented R&D personnel are committed to higher-priority projects. The best option would be:
- **a.** cancel the project
- **b.** place the project on the back burner
- **c.** subcontract the project
- **d.** assign the project to unskilled workers
- **e.** none of the above

25. The R&D selection process is the responsibility of:
    a. the R&D employees
    b. R&D management
    c. marketing departments
    d. senior management
    e. all the above

# CASE STUDY: Garcia Sciences Corporation

In 1985, Dr. Roy Garcia retired as vice president for R&D from a small pharmaceutical company. Having been in R&D for more than 30 years, Dr. Garcia was confident that he could start up his own R&D company to produce medical equipment rather than drugs.

By 1995, Garcia Sciences Corporation employed 120 people and was generating $65 million in revenue. The R&D group had developed a family of new products that were well accepted by the medical community. The manufacturing groups were utilizing state-of-the-art manufacturing techniques and were producing high-quality, low-cost products.

Financially, Garcia Sciences Corporation was doing quite well. Internally, detrimental cultural issues and problems were coming to the surface. Dr. Garcia was now having second thoughts about whether the culture that he had created in the late 1980s was still acceptable.

Since a large percentage of the employee population had advanced degrees in engineering and science, an overabundance of freedom was given to these employees in order to keep them motivated. Dr. Garcia strongly believed that scientists wanted the "freedom" to be creative. Executive project sponsorship did not exist and R&D teams were empowered to set their own objectives for the projects.

Almost every R&D project was carried through to completion. Cancelling projects was unacceptable. Status reporting was infrequent and management often had to meddle in projects to find out what was happening.

Within the last six months, Dr. Garcia and several senior officers were cancelling projects because either the objectives were not acceptable to senior management, or the marketplace had changed. In either event, the morale of the organization was weakening because the team members were extremely unhappy when their R&D projects were cancelled in midstream.

Dr. Garcia realized that what motivated project personnel is the ability to see a project through from beginning to end. Through the grapevine, Dr. Garcia was informed that the employees felt that projects were being cancelled because of the personal whims of management rather than based upon sound business decisions.

## QUESTIONS

1. Describe the culture that Dr. Garcia instituted.
2. Can this culture be effective, and if so, under what conditions?
3. Were the R&D project teams given "too much" freedom? Explain.
4. Why was senior management cancelling R&D projects?
5. What was the real cause of the problems at Garcia Sciences Corporation and what can be done to minimize the recurrence of these issues?

# CASE STUDY: Corwin Corporation

By June 1983, Corwin Corporation had grown into a $150 million per year corporation with an international reputation for manufacturing low-cost, high-quality rubber components. Corwin maintained more than a dozen different product lines, all of which were sold as off-the-shelf items in department stores, hardware stores, and automotive parts distributors. The name "Corwin" was now synonymous with "quality." This provided management with the luxury of having products that maintained extremely long life cycles.

Organizationally, Corwin had maintained the same structure for more than fifteen years (see Exhibit CS5.1). The top management of Corwin Corporation was highly conservative and believed in a marketing approach to find new markets for existing product lines rather than to explore for new products. Under this philosophy, Corwin maintained a small R&D group whose mission was simply to evaluate state-of-the-art technology and its application to existing product lines.

Corwin's reputation was so good that it continually received inquiries about the manufacturing of specialty products. Unfortunately, the conservative nature of Corwin's management created a "do not rock the boat" atmosphere opposed to taking any type of risks. A management policy was established to evaluate all specialty-product requests. The policy required the answering of the following questions:

- Will the specialty product provide the same profit margin (20%) as existing product lines?
- What is the total projected profitability to the company in terms of follow-on contracts?
- Can the speciality product be developed into a product line?
- Can the specialty product be produced with minimum disruption to existing product lines and manufacturing operations?

These stringent requirements forced Corwin to no-bid more than 90% of all specialty-product inquiries.

Corwin Corporation was a marketing-driven organization, although manufacturing often had different ideas. Almost all decisions were made by marketing with the exception of product pricing and estimating, which was a joint undertaking between manufacturing and marketing. Engineering was considered as merely a support group to marketing and manufacturing.

**Exhibit CS5-1 Organizational Chart for Corwin Corporation.**

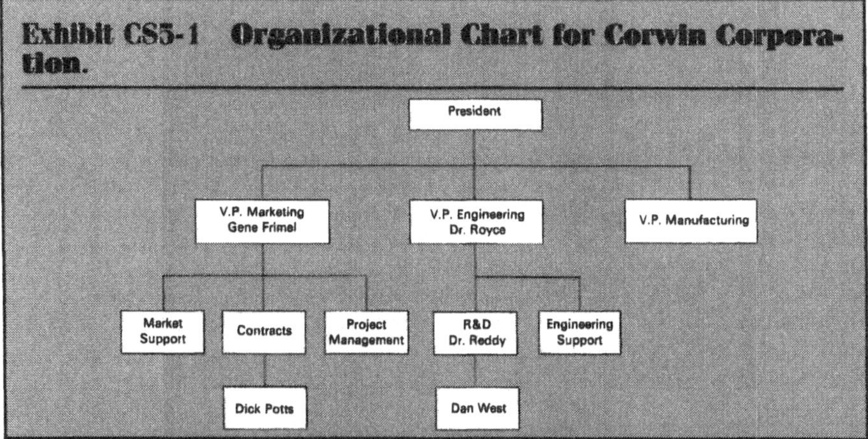


For specialty products, the project managers would always come out of marketing even during the R&D phase of development. The company's approach was that if the specialty product should mature into a full product line, then there should be a product line manager assigned right at the onset.

## The Peters Company Project.

In 1980, Corwin accepted a specialty-product assignment from Peters Company because of the potential for follow-on work. In 1981 and 1982, and again in 1983, profitable follow-on contracts were received, and a good working relationship developed, despite Peters' reputation for being a difficult customer to work with.

On December 7, 1982, Gene Frimel, the vice president of marketing at Corwin, received a rather unusual phone call from Dr. Frank Delia, the marketing vice president at Peters Company.

*Delia:* "Gene, I have a rather strange problem on my hands. Our R&D group has $250,000 committed for research toward development of a new rubber product material, and we simply do not have the available personnel or talent to undertake the project. We have to go outside. We'd like your company to do the work. Our testing and R&D facilities are already overburdened."

*Frimel:* "Well, as you know, Frank, we are not a research group even though we've done this once before for you. And furthermore, I would never able to sell our management on such an undertaking. Let some other company to the R&D work and then we'll take over on the production end."

*Delia:* "Let me explain our position on this. We've been 'burned' several times in the past. Projects like this generate several patents, and the R&D company almost always requires that our contracts give them royalties or first refusal for manufacturing rights."

*Frimel:* "I understand your problem, but it's not within our capabilities. This project, if undertaken, could disrupt parts of our organization. We're already operating lean in engineering."

*Delia:* "Look, Gene! The bottom line is this: We have complete confidence in your manufacturing ability to such a point that we're willing to commit to a five-year production contract if the product can be developed. That makes it extremely profitable for you."

*Frimel*: "You've just gotten me interested. What additional details can you give me?"

*Delia*: "All I can give you is a rough set of performance specifications that we'd like to meet. Obviously, some trade-offs are possible."

*Frimel*: "When can you get the specification sheet to me?"

*Delia*: "You'll have it tomorrow morning. I'll ship it overnight express."

*Frimel*: "Good! I'll have my people look at it, but we won't be able to get you an answer until after the first of the year. As you know, our plant is closed down for the last two weeks in December, and most of our people have already left for extended vacations."

*Delia*: "That's not acceptable! My management wants a signed, sealed, and delivered contract by the end of this month. If this is not done, corporate will reduce our budget for 1983 by $250,000, thinking that we've 'bitten off more than we can chew.' Actually, I need you answer within forty-eight hours so that I'll have some time to find another source."

*Frimel*: "You know, Frank, today is December 7, Pearl Harbor Day. Why do I feel as though the sky is about to fall in?"

*Delia*: "Don't worry, Gene! I'm not going to drop any bombs on you. Just remember,
all that we have available is $250,000, and the contract must be a firm-fixed-price effort. We anticipate a six-month project with $125,000 paid on contract signing and the balance at project termination."

*Frimel*: "I still have that ominous feeling, but I'll talk to my people. You'll hear from us with a go or no-go decision within forty-eight hours. I'm scheduled to go on a cruise in the Caribbean, and my wife and I are leaving this evening. One of my people will get back to you on this matter."

Gene Frimel had a problem. All bid and no-bid decisions were made by a four-man committee composed of the president and the three vice presidents. The president and the vice president for manufacturing were on vacation. Frimel met with Dr. Royce, the vice president of engineering, and explained the situation.

*Royce*: "You know, Gene, I totally support projects like this because it would help our technical people grow intellectually. Unfortunately, my vote never appears to carry any weight."

*Frimel*: "The profitability potential as well as the development of good customer relations makes this attractive, but I'm not sure we want to accept such a risk. A failure could easily destroy our good working relationship with Peters Company."

*Royce*: "I'd have to look at the specification sheets before assessing the risks, but I would like to give it a shot."

*Frimel*: "I'll try to reach our president by phone."

By late afternoon, Frimel was fortunate enough to be able to contact the president and received a reluctant authorization to proceed. The problem now was how to prepare a proposal within the next two to three days and be prepared to make an oral presentation to Peters Company.

*Frimel*: "The boss gave his blessing, Royce, and the ball is in your hands. I'm leaving for vacation, and you'll have total responsibility for the proposal and presentation. Delia wants the presentation this weekend. You should have his specification sheets tomorrow morning."

*Royce:* "Our R&D director, Dr. Reddy, left for vacation this morning. I wish he were here to help me price out the work and select the project manager. I assume that, in this case, the project manager will come out of engineering rather than marketing."

*Frimel:* "Yes, I agree. Marketing should not have any role in this effort. It's your baby all the way. And as for the pricing effort, you know our bid will be for $250,000. Just work backwards to justify the numbers. I'll assign one of our contracting people to assist you in the pricing. I hope I can find someone who has experience in this type of effort. I'll call Delia and tell him we'll bid it with an unsolicited proposal."

Royce selected Dan West, one of the R&D scientists, to act as the project leader. Royce had severe reservations about doing this without the R&D director, Dr. Reddy, being actively involved. With Reddy on vacation, Royce had to make an immediate decision.

On the following morning, the specification sheets arrived and Royce, West, and Dick Potts, a contracts man, began preparing the proposal. West prepared the direct labor man-hours, and Royce provided the costing data and pricing rates. Potts, being completely unfamiliar with this type of effort, simply acted as an observer and provided legal advice when necessary. Potts allowed Royce to make all decisions even though the contracts man was considered the official representative of the president.

Finally completed two days later, the proposal was actually a ten-page letter that simply contained the cost summaries (see Exhibit CS5-2) and the engineering intent. West estimated that thirty tests would be required. The test matrix described only the test conditions for the first five tests. The remaining twenty-five test conditions would be determined at a later date, jointly by Peters and Corwin personnel.

On Sunday morning, a meeting was held at Peters Company, and the proposal was accepted. Delia gave Royce a letter of intent authorizing Corwin Corporation to begin working on the project immediately. The final contract would not be available for signing until late January, and the letter of intent simply stated that Peters Company would assume all costs until such time that the contract was signed or the effort terminated.

West was truly excited about being selected as the project manager and being able to interface with the customer, a luxury that was usually given only to the marketing personnel. Although Corwin Corporation was closed for two weeks over Christmas, West still went into the office to prepare the project schedules and to identify the support he would need in the other areas, thinking that if he presented this information to management on the first day back to work, they would be convinced that he had everything under control.

## The Work Begins . . .

On the first working day in January 1983, a meeting was held with the three vice presidents and Dr. Reddy to discuss the support needed for the project. (West was not in attendance at this meeting, although all participants had a copy of his memo.)

*Reddy:* "I think we're heading for trouble in accepting this project. I've worked with Peters Company previously on R&D efforts, and they're tough to get along with. West is a good man, but I would never have assigned him as the project leader. His expertise is in managing internal rather than external projects. But, no matter what happens, I'll support West the best I can."

**Exhibit CS5-2 Proposal Cost Summaries**

| | |
|---|---|
| Direct labor and support | $ 30,000 |
| Testing (30 tests at $2,000 each) | 60,000 |
| Overhead at 100% | 90,000 |
| Materials | 30,000 |
| G&A (general and administrative, 10%) | 21,000 |
| Total | $231,000 |
| Profit | 19,000 |
| Total | $250,000 |

*Royce:* "You're too pessimistic. You had good people in your group and I'm sure you'll be able to give him the support he needs. I'll try to look in on the project every so often. West will still be reporting to you for this project. Try not to burden him too much with other work. This project is important to the company."

West spent the first few days after vacation soliciting the support that he needed from the other line groups. Many of the other groups were upset that they had not been informed earlier and were unsure as to what support they could provide. West met with Reddy to discuss the final schedules.

*Reddy:* "Your schedules look pretty good, Dan. I think you have a good grasp of the problem. You won't need very much help from me. I have a lot of work to do on other activities, so I'm just going to be in the background on this project. Just drop me a note every once in a while telling me what's going on. I don't need anything formal. Just a paragraph or two will suffice."

By the end of the third week, all of the raw materials had been purchased, and initial formulations and testing were ready to begin. In addition, the contract was ready for signature. The contract contained a clause specifying that Peters Company had the right to send an in-house representative into Corwin Corporation for the duration of the project. Peters Company informed Corwin that Patrick Ray would be the in-house representative, reporting to Delia, and would assume his responsibilities on or about February 15.

By the time Pat Ray appeared at Corwin Corporation, West had completed the first three tests. The results were not what was expected, but gave promise that Corwin was heading in the right direction. Pat Ray's interpretation of the tests was completely opposite to that of West. Ray thought that Corwin was "way off base," and redirection was needed.

*Ray:* "Look, Dan! We have only six months to do this effort and we shouldn't waste our time on marginally acceptable data. These are the next five tests I'd like to see performed."

*West:* "Let me look over your request and review it with my people. That will take a couple of days, and, in the meanwhile, I'm going to run the other two tests as planned."

Ray's arrogant attitude bothered West. However, West decided that the project was too important to "knock heads" with Ray and simply decided to "cater" to Ray the best he could. This was not exactly the working relationship that West expected to have with the in-house representative.

West reviewed the test data and the new test matrix with engineering personnel, who felt that the test data were inconclusive as yet and preferred to withhold their opinion until the results of the fourth and fifth tests were made available. Although this displeased Ray, he agreed to wait a few more days if it meant getting Corwin Corporation "on the right track."

The fourth and fifth tests appeared to be marginally acceptable just as the first three were. Corwin's engineering people analyzed the data and made their recommendations.

*West:* "Pat, my people feel that we're going in the right direction and that our path has greater promise than your test matrix."

*Ray:* "As long as we're paying the bills, we're going to have a say in what tests are conducted. Your proposal stated that we would work together in developing the other test conditions. Let's go with my test matrix. I've already reported back to my boss that the first five tests were failures and that we're changing the direction of the project."

*West:* "I've already purchased $30,000 worth of raw materials. Your matrix uses other materials and will require additional expenditures of $12,000."

*Ray:* "That's your problem. Perhaps you shouldn't have purchased all of the raw materials until we agreed on the complete test matrix."

During the month of February, West conducted fifteen tests, all under Ray's direction. The tests were scattered over such a wide range that no valid conclusions could be drawn. Ray continued sending reports back to Delia confirming that Corwin was not producing beneficial results and there was no indication that the situation would reverse itself. Delia ordered Ray to take any steps necessary to ensure a successful completion of the project.

Ray and West met again as they had done for each of the past forty-five days to discuss the status and direction of the project.

*Ray:* "Dan, my boss is putting tremendous pressure on me for results, and thus far I've given him nothing. I'm up for promotion in a couple of months and I can't let this project stand in my way. It's time to completely redirect the project."

*West:* "Your redirection of the activities is playing havoc with my scheduling. I have people in other departments who just cannot commit to this continual rescheduling. They blame me for not communicating with them when, in fact, I'm embarrassed to."

*Ray:* "Everybody has their problems. We'll get this problem solved. I spent this morning working with some of your lab people in designing the next fifteen tests. Here are the test conditions."

*West:* "I certainly would have liked to be involved with this. After all, I thought I was the project manager. Shouldn't I have been at the meeting?"

*Ray:* "Look, Dan! I really like you, but I'm not sure that you can handle this project. We need some good results immediately, or my neck will be stuck out for the next four months. I don't want that. Just have your lab personnel start on these tests, and we'll get along fine. Also, I'm planning on spending a great deal of time in your lab area. I want to observe the testing personally and talk to your lab personnel."

**Exhibit CS5-3 Projected Cost Summary at the End of the Third Month.**

| | Original Proposal Cost Summary for Six-Month Project | Total Project Costs Projected at End of Third Month |
|---|---|---|
| Direct labor/support | $ 30,000 | $ 15,000 |
| Testing | 60,000 (30 tests) | 70,000 (35 tests) |
| Overhead | 90,000 (100%) | 92,000 (120%)* |
| Materials | 30,000 | 50,000 |
| G&A | 21,000 (10%) | 22,700 (10%) |
| Totals | $213,000 | $249,700 |

* Total engineering overhead was estimated at 100%, whereas the R&D overhead was 120%.

*West:* "We've already conducted twenty tests, and you're scheduling another fifteen tests. I priced out only thirty tests in the proposal. We're heading for a cost-overrun condition."

*Ray:* "Our contract is a firm-fixed-price effort. Therefore, the cost overrun is your problem."

West met with Dr. Reddy to discuss the new direction of the project and potential cost overruns. West brought along a memo projecting the costs through the end of the third month of the project (see Exhibit 5-3).

*Reddy:* "I'm already overburdened on other projects and won't be able to help you out. Royce picked you to be the project manager because he felt that you could do the job. Now, don't let him down. Send me a brief memo next month explaining the situation, and I'll see what I can do. Perhaps the situation will correct itself."

During the month of March, the third month of the project, West received almost daily phone calls from the people in the lab stating that Pat Ray was interfering with their job. In fact, one phone call stated that Ray had changed the test conditions from what was agreed on in the latest test matrix. When West confronted Ray on his meddling, Ray asserted that Corwin personnel were very unprofessional in their attitude and that he thought this was being carried down to the testing as well. Furthermore, Ray demanded that one of the functional employees be removed immediately from the project because of incompetence. West stated that he would talk to the employee's department manager. Ray, however, felt that this would be useless and said, "Remove him or else!" The functional employee was removed from the project.

By the end of the third month, most Corwin employees were becoming disenchanted with the project and were looking for other assignments. West attributed this to Ray's harassment of the employees. To aggravate the situation even further, Ray met with Royce and Reddy, and demanded that West be removed and a new project manager be assigned.

**Exhibit CS5-4 Estimate of Total Project Completion Costs**

| | |
|---|---|
| Direct labor/support | $ 47,000* |
| Testing (60 tests) | 120,000 |
| Overhead (120%) | 200,000 |
| Materials | 103,000 |
| G&A | 47,000 |
| | $517,000 |
| Peters contract | 250,000 |
| Overrun | $267,000 |

* Includes Dr. Reddy.

Royce refused to remove West as project manager, and ordered Reddy to take charge and help West get the project back on track.

*Reddy:* "You've kept me in the dark concerning this project, West. If you want me to help you, as Royce requested, I'll need all the information tomorrow, especially the cost data. I'll expect you in my office tomorrow morning at 8:00 A.M. I'll bail you out of this mess."

West prepared the projected cost data for the remainder of the work and presented the results to Dr. Reddy (see Exhibit CS5-4). Both West and Reddy agreed that the project was now out of control, and severe measures would be required to correct the situation, in addition to more than $250,000 in corporate funding.

*Reddy:* "Dan, I've called a meeting for 10:00 A.M. with several of our R&D people to completely construct a new test matrix. This is what we should have done right from the start."

*West:* "Shouldn't we invite Ray to attend this meeting? I'm sure he'd want to be involved in designing the new test matrix."

*Reddy:* "I'm running this show now, not Ray!! Tell Ray that I'm instituting new policies and procedures for in-house representatives. He's no longer authorized to visit the labs at his own discretion. He must be accompanied by either you or me. If he doesn't like these rules, he can get out. I'm not going to allow that guy to disrupt our organization. We're spending our money now, not his."

West met with Ray and informed him of the new test matrix as well as the new policies and procedures for in-house representatives. Ray was furious over the new turn of events and stated that he was returning to Peters Company for a meeting with Delia.

On the following Monday, Frimel received a letter from Delia stating that Peters Company was officially canceling the contract. The reasons given by Delia were as follows:

1. Corwin had produced absolutely no data that looked promising.
2. Corwin continually changed the direction of the project and did not appear to have a systematic plan of attack.
3. Corwin did not provide a project manager capable of handling such a project.

4. Corwin did not provide sufficient support for the in-house representative.
5. Corwin's top management did not appear to be sincerely interested in the project and did not provide sufficient executive-level support.

Royce and Frimel met to decide on a course of action in order to sustain good working relations with Peters Company. Frimel wrote a strong letter refuting all of the accusations in the Peters letter, but to no avail. Even the fact that Corwin was willing to spend $250,000 of its own funds had no bearing on Delia's decision. The damage was done. Frimel was now thoroughly convinced that a contract could not be accepted on Pearl Harbor Day.

# CHAPTER 6 Manufacturing Strategies

## Introduction

Both American and foreign corporations are surprised and concerned over the way that once powerful American businesses are now struggling for survival. Foreign corporations, especially in Europe and the Far East, have continually increased their American and international market shares by enjoying low-cost labor and manufacturing advantages. Hayes and Wheelwright have identified several causes for why the United States appears to be losing its vitality and capacity for organic growth.[1] The usual explanations included

1. the growth of governmental regulation, taxes, and other forms of intrusion into business affairs
2. A deterioration in the American work ethic which, combined with an adversary relationship between labor and business, had produced crippling strikes, inflexible work rules, and wage increases not justified by productivity increase
3. interruptions in the supply, and rapid increases in the prices, of various forms of energy since the first OPEC oil shock in 1973
4. teenagers, women, and minority groups—who had to be conditioned to work in an industrial environment and trained in new skills
5. the advent of unusually high capital costs brought on in part by high rates of inflation.

Perhaps the main cause for America's ills is the continuous pressure placed upon executives for quick decisions and near-term financial successes. As a result, more emphasis is placed upon marketing and R&D strategies than upon manufacturing strategies. The reason for this is self-evident: Manufacturing strategies may require substantially much more capital (for facilities, equipment, personnel, training, etc.) and may very well be irreversible. The results of the manufacturing strategy may not be measurable for three years or more and in the meanwhile, executives are being pressured for short-term profits.

Even under situations where R&D and marketing strategies are long term, manufacturing strategies may be short term and often expressed in terms of obtaining more efficient utilization of existing resources. Short-term manufacturing strategies incur little risk, whereas long-term strategies for manufacturing incur high risks in the development of new products and processes to generate lower-cost products with increased productivity.

These short-term strategies have existed for so many years that even many of our prime manufacturing industries are plagued by severely aging equipment. According to Roger Smith, Chairman and Chief Executive Officer of General Motors:[2]

> Most of the industrial base in this country is 30 to 60 years old. And too many of our business systems are really not systematic at all, they are a maze of disconnected, uncoordinated, and even competing systems. This is because most of our companies developed through rapid growth. And as they grew bigger, the small basic systems that originally brought them success were simply enlarged.
>
> And unless we want to play a perpetual game of catch-up, we in American business have to do more than just meet our competition on a day-to-day basis. We have to beat them with a long-term strategy. We have to anticipate their future competitive moves. We have to understand their ultimate strategies and outstrategize and outsmart them.

Long-term manufacturing strategies require a serious commitment to long-term capital investment. Although the United States appears to be spending more and more each year on capital investment, the actual expenditure, when adjusted for inflation, appears to be at a much lower rate than French, German, and Japanese corporations. As a result, while the foreign competition becomes capital intensive, American corporations remain labor intensive. And because capital-intensive companies maintain a long-term cost advantage over labor-intensive companies, the result will be that ultimately Americans will be able to meet the competition on quality but not on cost.

These trends are significant and have been criticized by economists and executives alike. Even as far back as 1979, the problem was evident:[3]

> Somehow or other, American business is losing confidence in itself, and especially confidence in its future. Instead of meeting the challenge of the changing world, American business today is making small, short-term adjustments by cutting costs and by turning to the government for temporary relief . . . Success in trade is the result of patient and meticulous preparations, with a long period of market preparation before the rewards are available . . . To undertake such commitments is hardly in the interest of a manager who is concerned with his or her next quarterly earnings report.

Management of many U.S. companies today are unwilling to commit wholeheartedly to available manufacturing concepts and technologies. According to Thomas Gunn, the reasons for this foot-dragging are eight-fold:[4]

> First, articles and discussions of high-technology factory automation often focus on technical features instead of the proven strategic benefits that such factory automation can deliver

Second, because most U.S. chief executive officers and board members come from financial, legal, or marketing backgrounds, they often lack knowledge and a true understanding of design and manufacturing as it was 10 years ago, as it is today, and, more important, as it will be in the next five to 10 years. In addition, few of them have the backgrounds or interest that allows them to understand the powerful role of today's computer systems in integrating business functions.

Third, with their traditional capital budgeting techniques, they (or their lower-level managers) haven't been able to justify investing in risky long-term factory automation programs. They have no base of experience to deal with factoring benefits other than direct labor reduction or increased capacity into their justification calculations.

Then, too, most top executives seldom adopt a truly corporate-wide outlook to planning their design and manufacturing strategy and capital improvements to increase their strategic effectiveness, as well as efficiency/productivity.

Fourth, many top managers simply don't know who to believe any more. They seldom have complete trust in their own managers, since they are well aware of vested departmental or functional interests and the political maneuvering that often accompanies requests for capital expenditures. Vendors often have even less credibility due to the inherent conflict of interest their recommendations represent, and especially due to the fact that each vendor seems to have a different solution to the problem.

Fifth, many executives simply don't have (and perhaps have never had) an objective picture of where their company currently stands with respect to competing by its ability to execute its design and manufacturing mission effectively. They also lack knowledge of their competitor's design and manufacturing capability. Thus, they have difficulty planning or implementing change because they lack any frame of reference about their current position vis-à-vis their competitors or the state-of-the-art in their industry, in addition to what they will have to accomplish to be competitive as a manufacturer for world markets in the future.

Sixth, many companies lack an explicit manufacturing strategy that firmly supports that company's business strategy. Often, we find companies whose so-called "manufacturing strategy" is a vague motherhood statement espousing that they will be the high-quality, low-cost producer that will strive to increase its inventory turns. While these goals are all desirable, they are the strategies of every manufacturing company.

What will separate winners from losers is a process that will transfer these vague manufacturing strategies into an implementable action plant that achieves concrete measurable results against standards established by the competitive business world.

Seventh, top managers often lack an understanding of how factory automation and the increased permeation of the business environment by computing technology will affect their company's organizational structure and policies or their human resources, education, and training requirements.

Finally, top managers do not understand the consequences of not investing in factory automation or reviewing their design and manufacturing competitiveness. History teaches us that change and technological innovation are inevitable and inexorable, yet for many companies, even if they reversed field and made the financial and management commitment to implement "the factory of the future" in their company today with unlimited funds, it is too late for them. If management is to attack these problems head on, then the starting point must be a shift in corporate thinking. A reasonable set of criteria might include:

- focusing on and measuring results in the long-term, rather than the short-term
- developing a strategic plan which integrates marketing, R&D, and financial goals with manufacturing goals, rather than at the expense of manufacturing goals
- developing a new breed of manager with encouragement for hands-on experience

There are two critical issues that influence the planning for today's and tomorrow's manufacturing function. In the past, it was possible to develop strategic planning groups that would meet periodically. These groups might not have been headed up by an executive. Today, with a constantly changing environment, manufacturing technology breakthroughs can occur at any time and, therefore, without continuous monitoring and involvement by top management, strategic windows and opportunities may be missed.

Second, manufacturing today is highly innovative and manufacturing executives must foster a climate conducive to creativity and new-idea development. To take advantage of this creativity, management must consider the total manufacturing function, rather than the automation of small islands. This step requires a genuine and total commitment by senior management to depart from the static environmental thinking of the past three decades and to encourage an atmosphere of creativity.

Strategic planning in the United States appears to be dominated by financial considerations, especially in the calculation for return on investment (ROI). If the strategic goal is to improve ROI, then it can be obtained by either increasing the numerator (profits) or decreasing the denominator (investment). Obviously, the latter is easier to accomplish. Reducing investment can be achieved by either delaying the replacement of aging equipment, reducing preventive maintenance to as-needed maintenance, or replacing worn-out equipment with equipment encompassing the same technology, rather than looking for newer technology. In any event, the facilities continue to age to the point where the construction of a completely new and more costly facility may be the only solution.

If manufacturing strategies are not properly integrated with other strategies the result is like a two-legged stool. Marketing, R&D, and financial strategies are designed for compression, whereas manufacturing strategies stress expansion. To illustrate this, marketing has assessed a market need for a new product. The financial people, being optimistic, prophesize a substantial profit and market share. The project is then turned over to the R&D group, who are asked to create the impossible in an unbelievably short time frame. Marketing executives pressure R&D to work faster to achieve a first-to-market position. Financial executives pressure R&D to cut corners and use low-cost, readily available materials. By the time the product gets to manufacturing, the manufacturing personnel are asked to mass-produce a product that they have never seen or have seen but that has undergone numerous design changes so as to shorten their schedule. And, as is often the case, manufacturing is now told to "fast-track" the job by going into production without complete manufacturing plans, without proper quality control, without proper time to evaluate sources for raw material and subcontracts, without proper facilities and equipment, without properly trained personnel, and without any consideration that what is developed on an R&D bench may not be able to be mass-produced with the same quality. Finally, if the product does not meet up to specifications, let's simply blame manufacturing.

If integration is to be successful, then it must be based upon a total systems approach. Roger Smith stated that:[5]

> To develop a total systems approach, each business must create an integrated, coordinated, decision-making way of functioning which comprehends business plans, budgets, product programs, and everything else that helps run the business. It must build an integrated worldwide database that brings all parts of the business together. Such a database finally marries those two great singles, the manufacturing systems and the business systems, with no chance of divorce.
>
> The bottom-line benefit of such a wedding is that it allows businesspeople to understand their total business in a comprehensive way that was not possible before. They can actually see those cases where two can live more cheaply than one. They can simultaneously review all parts of the business—as well as the linkages which hold them together. And this newfound ability enables them to make more informed, more timely, and shrewder business decisions—decisions that can give a company a long-term competitive edge.

An important criterion today involves the development of a new breed of executive. The job description of an executive is to develop strategic and long-term plans so as to assure the growth and survivability of the corporation over the next five to 10 years. But every Christmas, the executive receives a bonus based upon 12-month profitability, rather than the results of the strategic-planning process. Executive compensation must be married to the strategic-planning process, rather than short-term profitability.

Employees climbing the corporate ladder must be given sufficient time in any given assignment to obtain hands-on experience. All too often, managers move from job to job and company to company without a chance to gain in-depth experience. The result is that they never stay in one job long enough to see the long-term impact of their decisions.

Many companies develop corporate cultures for allowing talented employees to climb the corporate ladder to success. All too often, the ladder to success avoids positions that require hands-on experience. As discussed by Hayes and Wheelwright:[6]

> American companies increasingly turned to people with financial, accounting, and legal backgrounds to fill their top positions. By the later 1970s, the percentage of newly appointed CEOs with such backgrounds in the 100 largest U.S. corporations was up 50% from its level 30 years earlier. As a result, correspondingly there was fewer hands-on experience in the more competitively oriented functions such as marketing, production, and engineering. The absolute change in numbers has not been as important as the change in attitude precipitated by this trend. Young managers searching for ways to get ahead tended to choose jobs and career paths that they perceived to be on the road to the top. If this road appeared to emphasize staff assignments, the best were attracted to staff positions.

Properly developed executives with an insight toward long-term strategic planning may very well be the starting point to meet the competition head on.

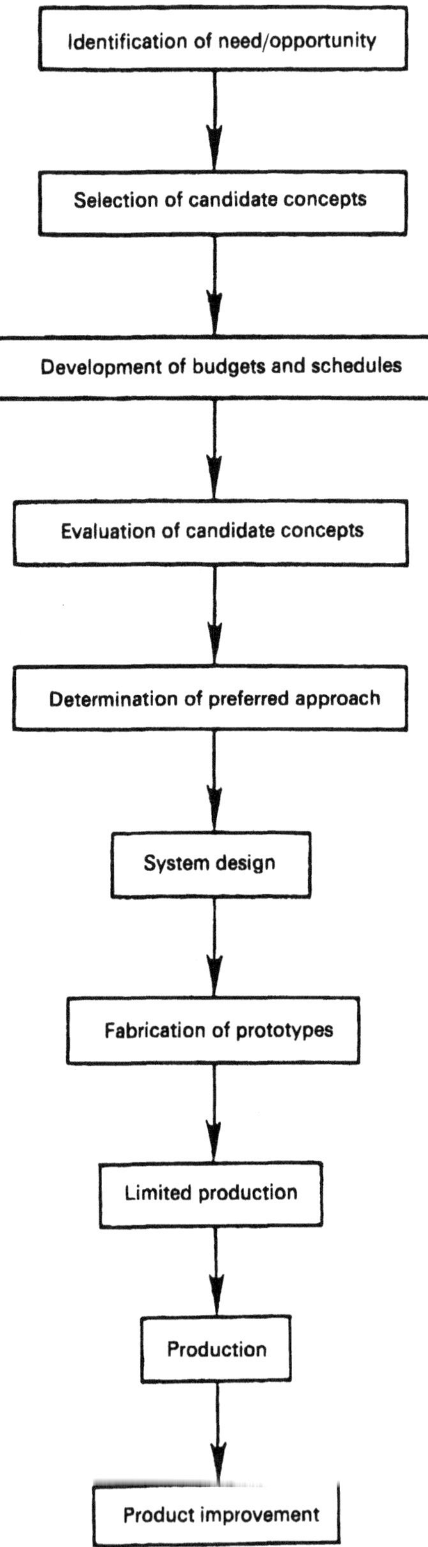


**Figure 6.1**
The Generic Product Development Process.

# Critical Issues

The long-term objective of any business entity is the generation of profits for the shareholders. In achieving profitability, a manufacturing enterprise must assure the effective application of the production resources to the task of building and delivering the product. Other pressures also exist that dictate the need for carefully defined plans. The pressure to control manufacturing costs and the need to meet schedules demand a carefully planned application of manufacturing resources and proper strategy planning.

Strategic planning for manufacturing falls into four categories.

- more efficient utilization of existing resources (process development)
- increasing/decreasing demand for existing products (product development)
- resource planning for new products (product development)
- a combination of the above

Based upon the product manufacturing demands, a manufacturing framework can be developed, such as shown in Figure 6.1, for a new product development process. This framework should define the specific elements of the organization that will be involved in the program and the amount and types of subcontractors and vendors that may be required. The decision regarding subcontractors and vendors should be made from the standpoint of contractor and vendor capability as well as capacity. Within the context of the defined business structure, there should be an identification of the specific resources required. Personnel should be identified in terms of both quantity and specific skill types required, time-phased over the planning horizon.

# Understanding Manufacturing Operations

Manufacturing (production) is the conversion of raw materials into products and/or components, through a series of manufacturing procedures and processes. It includes such major functions as manufacturing, planning, and scheduling; manufacturing engineering; fabrication and assembly; installation and checkouts; demonstration and testing; product assurance; and determination of resource requirements.

Manufacturing management is the technique of planning, organizing, directing, and controlling the use of people, money, materials, equipment, and facilities to accomplish the manufacturing task economically. A manufacturing management system is composed essentially of three phases: planning, analysis, and control.

During the planning phase, consideration must be given to such factors as material acquisition, an adequate workforce, engineering design, and provisions for subcontractor support. Production feasibility and producibility of the engineering design are critical factors that must be considered early in a program. This consideration must include planning, new processes, facilities, tools and test equipment, and cost control during design.

During the analysis phase, answers must be provided to such questions as: Is the manufacturing process working? Is it efficient? Is manufacturing being accomplished by the most economical method? Is the manufacturing plan being followed and are the established goals being met? During system design and development, these questions need to be projected into the future manufacturing effort to identify required preparatory actions and to assess risks.

During the control phase, the manufacturing effort must be monitored to ensure that the manufacturing management function is performing within the constraints and limits that have been established.

These three phases of a manufacturing management system can also be redefined as the three phases for strategic manufacturing planning. The objectives or strategic manufacturing planning are:

- to ensure that proper manufacturing planning has been accomplished early in product development so that the manufacturing effort will be performed smoothly
- to ensure that the system design will lead to efficient and economical quantity manufacture
- to assess the status of the product at any point during the production phase to determine if schedule, costs, and quality standards are being met, and whether changes must be made to the strategic and operational plans
- to conduct assessment and reviews of the manufacturing effort required to meet decision points at each phase in the life cycle of a product

To achieve these objectives, strategic manufacturing planning must begin in the product-design phase, well before the product ever reaches manufacturing. There are significant costs associated with the manufacturing effort. The current view is that those costs, to a great degree, are inherent in the design phase. As a design evolves and comes off the drawing board, certain costs are essentially fixed. Given the objective of minimizing cost and the existence of forward projections that indicate that limited dollars may be available for future manufacturing effort, it is necessary to identify costs at the point in time when they are being fixed.

## CUSTOMERS/CONTRACTORS/SUPPLIERS

Numerous reasons have caused the reduction in the size for the supplier base. The primary reasons include economic conditions, material shortages, foreign competition, and government regulations. The impact is fewer companies in the marketplace, some loss of competition (with all that entails), and a possible increase in lead times. The implications are obvious as numerous demands are placed upon a few suppliers.

To further complicate these problems, some companies prefer to limit their growth and customer base so as not to invest in additional facilities and equipment. As an example, the machine tool industry is characterized by a large number of small companies, most of which are selective of their customer base.

## CAPACITY AND INVESTMENT DECISIONS

Capacity can be defined as the maximum rate of productive or conversion capability of an organization's operations. Capacity is normally constrained by physical facilities, available productive equipment, tooling and/or test equipment. The portion of this capacity actually utilized is determined by the demand on the plant for current and known future workload. Firms must be particularly aware of a need for excess capacity, because customer demand tends to be somewhat unstable over time.

Operational and investment decisions each could increase capacity and are influenced by return on investment or profit in relation to the risk perceived and the potential return from other opportunities. Since the early 1970s, there are indications that a majority of industrial facilities have been growing older and new investment has not been keeping pace with equipment obsolescence or the advances in manufacturing technology which could lead to higher productivity and lower costs. During this period of time, thousands of suppliers have closed their plants and many others have been reluctant to increase capital investment. This has led to an industrial bottleneck, where certain limited suppliers are taxed to capacity. Lead times for the items produced at these facilities tend to be extremely volatile and subject to the demand lead time syndrome described previously.

## FEASIBILITY AND CAPABILITY

The issues of manufacturing feasibility and capability must be addressed in the initial phases of the strategic manufacturing planning. The evaluation of manufacturing feasibility and capability are directed toward analysis of the compatibility of the demands of the manufacturing task and the manufacturing facility and equipment required to accomplish it. The capability of a firm to successfully execute the manufacturing effort depends upon that firm having:

- complete understanding of the manufacturing task
- adequate qualitative production skills
- sufficient personnel (on hand or available)
- equipment in satisfactory condition
- adequate, operable test equipment
- assured, capable suppliers
- management capability
- plan to coordinate all resources

## MANUFACTURING RESOURCES

Manufacturing management can be defined as "the effective use of resources to produce on schedule the required number of end items that meet specified quality, performance, and cost." A few comments can be made about this definition to serve as a basis for consideration of the manufacturing planning issue. The first significant word is "effective." The question is: "Measured against what baseline?" How does something that has to be defined on a specific program in terms

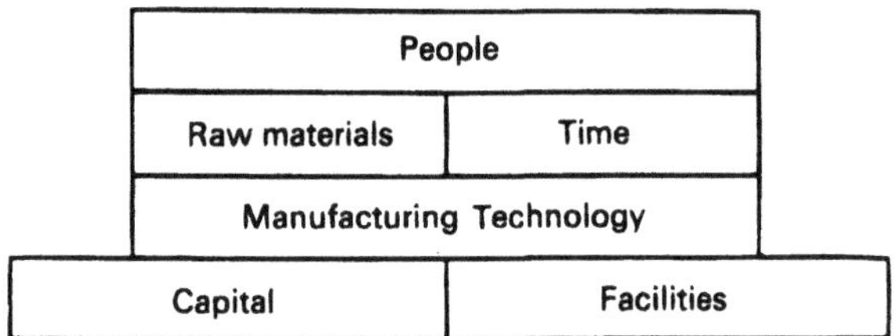


**Figure 6.2** Manufacturing Resources.

like relative or absolute cost, compare to other similar programs or performance within resource constraints?

The classic manufacturing resources required are: people, facilities, manufacturing technology, raw materials, capital, and time (Figure 6.2).

1. People. People include those in management, design engineering, manufacturing engineering, and (probably the most important) factory operations—the direct labor personnel and the indirect person personnel who support them.
2. Facilities. Facilities are the real property in the factory; the environment in which the products are built. The term includes the industrial equipment, the machine tools, and the shop aids to manufacturing.
3. Manufacturing Technology. Manufacturing technology is that set of efforts undertaken to improve the manufacturing process, techniques, or equipment required to support current and projected requirements. This area involves advancements in the way things are done in the factory, including the processes that are available to take raw material, enter it into a productive process, and transform it into something useful.
4. Raw Materials. Raw materials are the basic materials used in the manufacturing process. The focus of the effort should be on the most efficient utilization of the required raw materials.
5. Capital. Capital represents the monetary assets that are available. Capital can be used to finance ongoing work, as an investment to improve capacity or capability, to broaden the market base, or any of a large number of competing uses within the organization.
6. Time. Time is a resource available to all. It provides a constraint on the firm, since performance and delivery commitments are related to specific dates.

## MANUFACTURING RISK ASSESSMENT

Manufacturing risk assessment is a supporting tool for the decision-making process. It seeks to estimate the probabilities to success or failure associated with the manufacturing alternatives available. These risk assessments may reflect alternative manufacturing approaches to a given design or may be part of the evaluation of design alternatives, each of which has an associated manufacturing approach.

Manufacturing processes and materials may be divided into three broad groups: state of the practice, state of the art, and experimental.

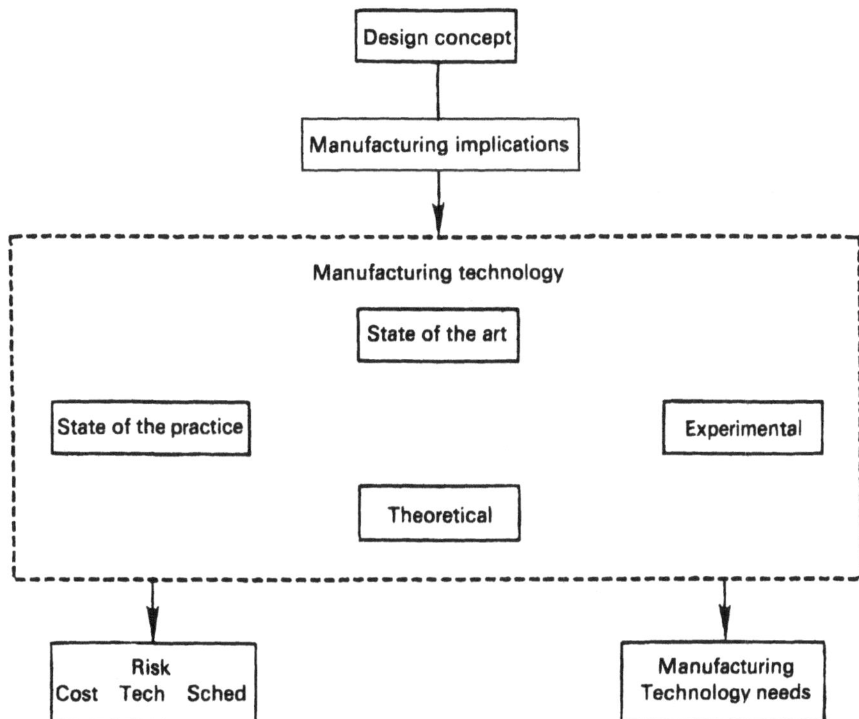


**Figure 6.3**
Manufacturing Risk Assessment.

*State of the practice* implies that the material or process is in general use in industry, is well understood, and has a long usage record. These processes and materials generally represent low-risk approaches.

*State of the art* implies that a material or process has had some factory usage, but was recently developed and is available from only one or a limited number of sources. These types of processes often provide the potential for cost or time savings but may introduce risk if they have not been used in the particular application or by the producer.

*Experimental* processes or materials have been demonstrated in the laboratory, but not in the factory environment. These processes and materials often hold great promise in terms of reduced cost, improved material properties, and better performance. Their use should be demonstrated in the factory environment prior to use in a manufacturing program.

As the design of a new product or process evolves, the manufacturing implications of various design options should be evaluated as part of the ongoing review process, as shown in Figure 6.3. The appropriate manufacturing concepts should be identified by the manufacturing engineers so that the risk levels associated with those approaches can be evaluated. This is a critical procedure if the selected system design alternative requires the use of an experimental material or process. If it does, or if a state-of-the-art material or process is to be used, two actions should be taken:

- Establish a plan to prove out the material or process prior to initiation of manufacturing.
- Identify a fallback approach if the material or process cannot be used successfully in manufacturing.

## PERSONNEL PLANNING

In developing a personnel plan, the company needs to consider the number of personnel, the specific skill types, the time phasing of the requirements, and the ability of the organization to absorb the additional personnel. The ability to meet the personnel demands will be a function of the labor pool currently available within the organization as well as the ability of the local area to provide the quantity and types of people required.

There needs to be a clearly defined profile of the required workforce and a plan for the acquisition and training of new hires. Although on-the-job training (OJT) may be an effective mechanism for providing required knowledge, its effectiveness is limited. Where the skills involved are relatively complex, there should be some form of formal training provided and planned for as part of the strategic-planning process.

Management should review the adequacy of the planned personnel hirings to ensure that adequate numbers of the required skill types can be made available. When a large personnel increase is planned, the sources of those personnel should be determined and evidence for their potential availability should be clearly indicated in the plan.

## FACILITY PLANNING

The facility includes the plant and productive equipment that is to be made available to accomplish the production task. In developing the facility plan, both the quantitative and qualitative demands of the product must be considered. The qualitative analysis determines the types of processes required. The firm then has the option of utilizing currently existing facilities, acquiring new facilities, requesting customer-furnished facilities, or subcontracting a portion of the effort. The quantitative analysis determines the size of the various processing departments within the facility. This requires consideration of the number of units to be delivered and the rate of delivery. The information collected in these analyses will provide a measure of the number of workstations and the floor space required.

After determination of the facility requirements, the next concern is layout and flow planning. In most cases, the layout is constrained by the existing facility; however, it may be possible to revise the layout for a new strategic product where future products can use some of the existing flow plan.

## STRATEGIC DECISIONS

Products that are thought up by manufacturing and designed by engineering have to be manufactured. Strategies developed by marketing, R&D, and engineering have to integrated with the manufacturing strategy. Therefore, it is useful to try to classify the strategic variables into categories. Hayes and Wheelwright identify the following eight categories:[7]

1. *capacity*—amount, timing, type
2. *facilities*—size, location, specialization
3. *technology*—equipment, automation, linkages
4. *vertical integration*—direction, extent, balance
5. *workforce*—skill level, wage policies, employment, security
6. *quality*—defect prevention, monitoring, intervention
7. *production planning/materials control*—sourcing policies, centralization, decision rules
8. *organization*—structure, control/reward systems, role of staff groups

Hayes and Wheelwright categorized the first four decision categories as long-term, structural decisions, whereas the last four are tactical decisions to support the ongoing business. There are, of course, other factors that are important to the business in general and have an impact upon the manufacturing strategies. According to Schmenner, they can be summarized as:[8]

- access to markets/distribution centers
- access to suppliers and resources
- community and government aspects
- competitive considerations
- environmental considerations
- interaction with the rest of the corporation
- labor
- site attractiveness
- taxes and financing
- transportation
- utilities and services

For simplicity sake, the six strategic areas identified in Figure 6.4 will be discussed in this text. Each of the strategic areas may or may not be impacted by strategic decisions outside of manufacturing.

**COMPETITIVE POSITIONING** Competitive positioning refers to the market segments in which the firm wishes to compete and how the firm wishes to compete. The decision usually embodies two ranges: (1) high quality to low quality, and (2) high cost to low cost. The ideal situation is to manufacture high-quality/low-cost products. Unfortunately, this is not always feasible. A competitive strategy must be established and this, in turn, may very well dictate the manpower skill levels, type and cost of manufacturing equipment, and degree of computerization.

Figure 6.5 shows a typical map that a firm can develop to help it make strategic manufacturing decisions. Each firm will develop its own strategic decision-making categories based upon its internal strengths and weaknesses and external opportunities and threats.

**PHYSICAL PLANT LOCATION** The decision where to locate a manufacturing plant is a complex problem. The ideal situation is to locate the plant in an area that

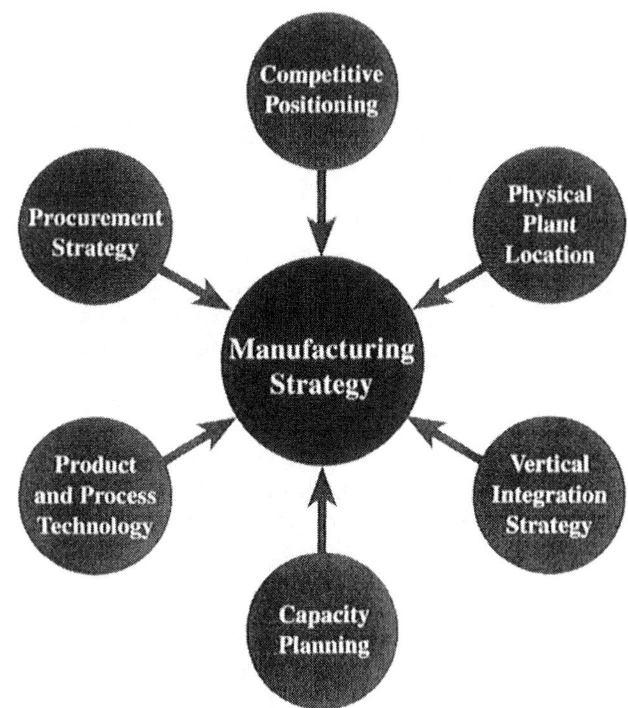


**Figure 6.4**
Components of a Manufacturing Strategy.

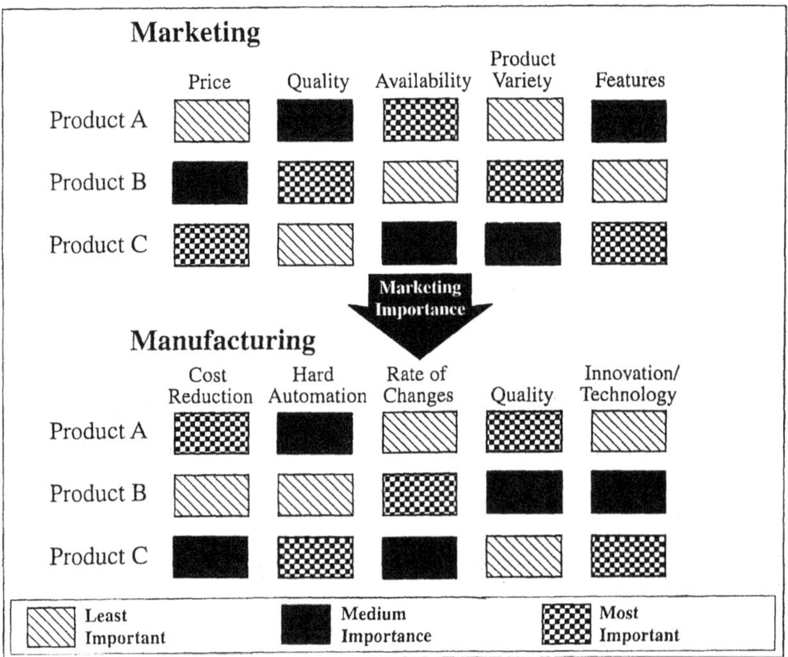


**Figure 6.5**
Differences in Strategic Importance.

has ample skilled labor, low-cost labor, a low tax base, and far enough away from highly populated areas such that problems with noise, toxic material, and pollution are not major problems. Unfortunately, being far away from highly populated areas can increase shipping costs.

Perhaps the most critical problem in plant location is the proximity to raw-material suppliers and finished-goods distributors. Easy access to railroads, airports, major transportation firms, and possible harbors also plays an important role.

**VERTICAL INTEGRATION STRATEGY** The decision on whether to integrate vertically, especially backwards, plays an important role in developing a manufacturing strategy. Backwards integration requires large manufacturing facilities and highly skilled labor that may have to be capable of working on several functions within the manufacturing process. With vertical integration, management must be highly trained in risk analysis and work integration.

**CAPACITY PLANNING** The majority of the capital resources in a firm are under the control of manufacturing. Since the cost of design, construction, operations, and support can be very expensive, extreme care must be taken in capacity planning. Having large excess capacity can be very expensive to maintain. Having demand exceed capacity can be equally bad, resulting in lost customers and a large loss of goodwill costs. Increasing manufacturing capacity may allow firms to take advantage of economies of scale, thus lowering unit cost. But excess capacity, which is underutilized, could have a detrimental effect. Capacity strategies are based upon an understanding of the following:

- predicted demand for product
- life cycle of product
- behavior of competitors (domestic and international)
- rate of change of technology
- cost of construction and operation for additional capacity

Not all companies are fortunate enough to be able to predict capacity requirements. The simplest solution is to assume linear capacity increase increments. Figure 6.6 shows the predicted linear capacity requirements for a manufacturing firm that assumes that in each of the next eight years, production capacity will have to increase by 10,000 units per year. Assuming a steady growth rate, the company has the luxury of deciding how and when the added capacity will be provided. In Figure 6.6 capacity leads demand. This would be representative of a firm that is afraid of running short and desires to maintain a capacity cushion or buffer zone. Although unused capacity is expensive, the firm may benefit through faster response to an increased demand (without overtime expenses), and a "goodwill" environment with customers by avoiding shortages.

In Figure 6.6, the added capacity is provided each year in increment of 10,000 units per year. In Figure 6.7, added capacity is provided every other year, in increments of 20,000 units per increment. In both cases, the capacity is added in advance with the expectation that future demand will meet the supply. In either case, there will exist slack capacity until demand catches up to supply.

Adding capacity can be risky if there exists a downturn in the economy or if the firm's competitive position changes. In such a case, the firm may not want to

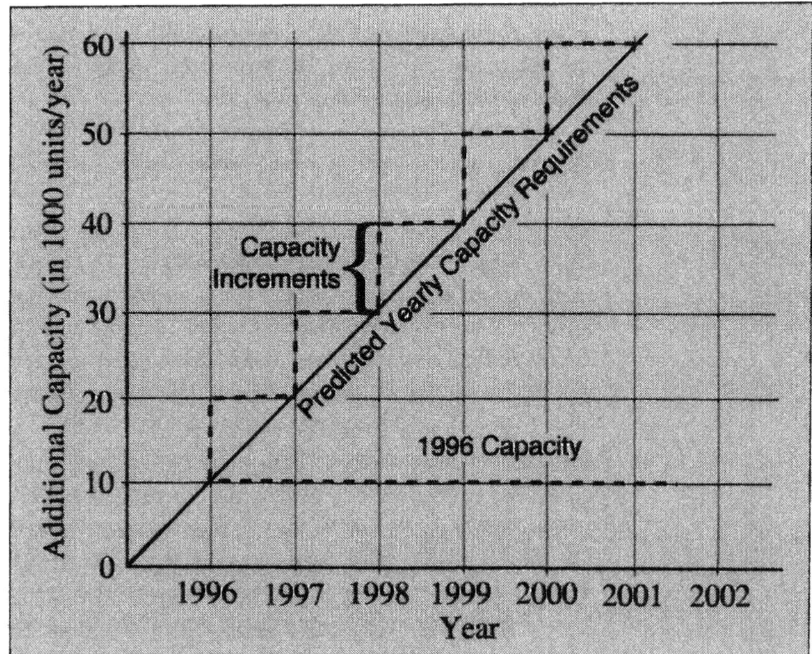


**Figure 6.6**
Capacity Increments to Meet Requirements (10,000 Units Every Year).

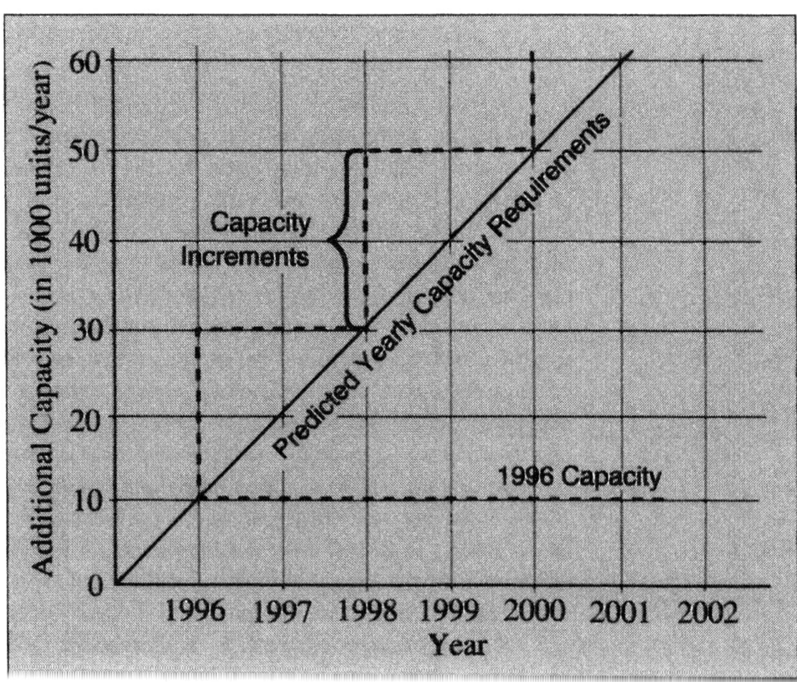


**Figure 6.7**
Capacity Increments to Meet Requirements (20,000 Units Every 2 Years).

risk added capacity yet. This problem can be overcome by using alternative sources or capacity such as:

- using overtime
- working multiple shifts
- subcontracting out some of the production
- purchasing parts from a competitor to fill excess demand

Figure 6.8 shows the use of alternate sources of capacity. In Figure 6.8, the firm allows capacity extenders to be used for a short period of time before increasing capacity. The minor or major advantage of using capacity extenders is cost savings. Overtime and multiple shifts are generally cheaper than adding capacity. However, there exist the disadvantages that excessive overtime will result in poor morale and lower quality. Multiple shifts may require changes in the wage and salary administration program, as well as possibly a renegotiation of union contracts. Subcontracting always puts a firm at the mercy of the supplier on both price and quality. Therefore, cost-benefit analyses are required before a final decision can be made. All these problems take on a completely new perspective if future demand is non-predictable.

In Figure 6.8, capacity and demand are in equilibrium. This case is dangerous because not only does it permit shortages to exist, but it assumes that capacity can be added as needed. In Figure 6.9, shortages can be large, because the firm may fear that demand will be reduced in the future. The firm will consider capacity expansion only when backlogged orders approach a certain critical point.

Unused capacity has both positive and negative considerations. On the positive side, it acts as a barrier to entry. On the negative side, the company may have

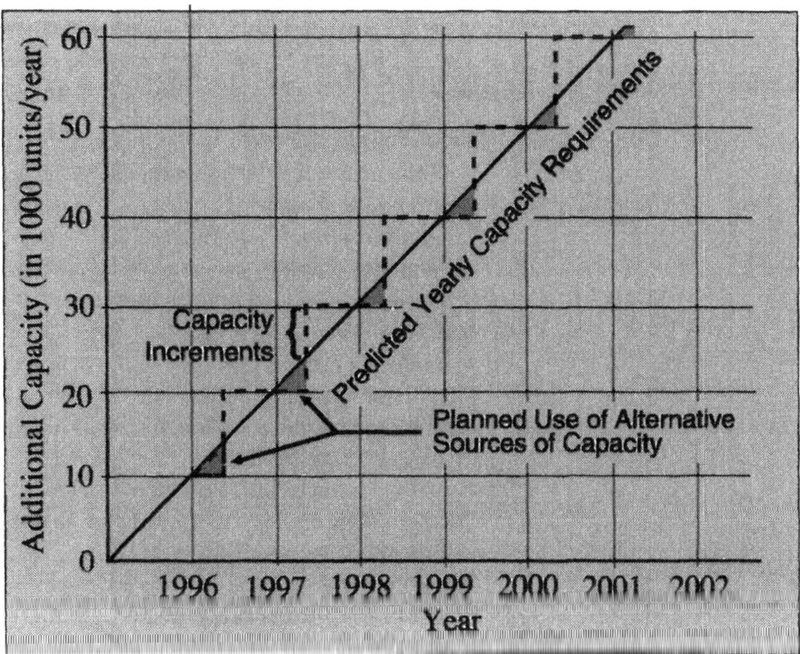


**Figure 6.8**
Using Alternate Sources of Capacity.

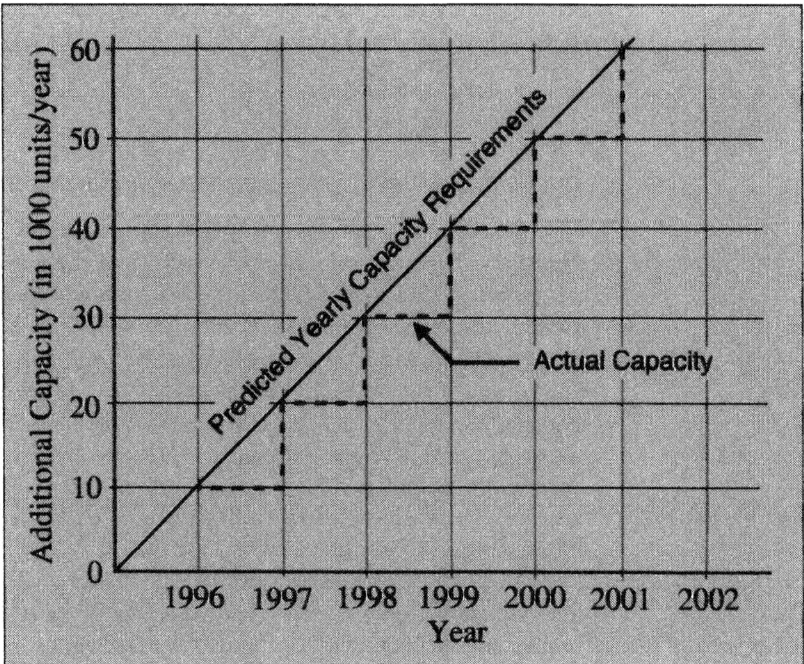


**Figure 6.9** Capacity Lagging Demand.

to change the manufacturing processes to handle increased capacity, and must plan for an adequate workforce, properly trained, to handle the increased workload. In addition, the changeover costs from one product line to another may create additional complexities.

Long-term excessive capacity can push a company well below the break-even levels. Porter has prepared a list identifying the causes for overbuilding manufacturing capacity:[9]

1. **technological factors**
   - adding capacity in large increments
   - economies of scale
   - long lead times in adding capacity
   - minimum efficient scale increasing over time
   - changes in production technology
2. **structural factors**
   - significant exit barriers
   - motivation from suppliers
   - building credibility with customers
   - integrated competitors
   - effect of capacity share on market share
   - effect of age and type of capacity on demand
3. **competitive factors**
   - large number of firms
   - lack of credible market leaders
   - entry of new competitors
   - advantages of being an early mover

4. **information-flow factors**
   - inflation of future expectations
   - divergent assumptions or perceptions
   - breakdown of market signaling
   - structural change
   - financial community pressures
5. **managerial factors**
   - management background and industry experience
   - attitude toward different types of risk
6. **governmental factors**
   - perverse tax incentives
   - desire for indigenous industry
   - pressures to increase or maintain employment

The geographical area plays an important part of any capacity decision. Consider the following:

- Will the required workforce become too big in relation to the population in the immediate area?
- Is the population skilled, or will the employees require training?
- How will the training be provided?
- Will the economies of scale offset the possible increased freight charges to other locations?
- How vulnerable are we if a natural disaster occurs (i.e., flood, earthquake, etc.)?

When the industry begins to mature, firms tend to prefer smaller facilities in order to minimize confusion, maintain better control, and avoid becoming too dominant a force in the local community.

**PRODUCT AND PROCESS TECHNOLOGY** Product and process technology refers to the knowledge base required to support existing and future products. Included in this area are CAD/CAM technologies, robotics, computer-integrated manufacturing, numerically controlled equipment, a quality assurance program, and concurrent engineering. Concurrent engineering is the ability to work with engineering and marketing in the early stages of product development such that product development includes manufacturability. Any engineer can design a product that cannot be manufactured, at least easily.

**PROCUREMENT STRATEGY** Simply because a component can be purchased more cheaply than it can be manufactured does not mean that it will be purchased. Likewise, having the capacity to produce a unit does not mean it is strategically a good choice to do so. The following questions need to be considered in evaluating the make-or-buy strategy:

**MAKE**

- Will it be less expensive?
- Is it easy to integrate this product into our existing production?
- Will it help us utilize idle capacity?

- Will we be able to maintain direct control over all aspects of production?
- Can we maintain design secrecy?
- Will making the product allow us to avoid unreliable suppliers?
- Will we be able to stabilize our workforce?

**BUY**

- Can we purchase it at a lower cost than our manufacturing cost?
- Do our suppliers have the skills to produce the item? Do we have the skills?
- Will this be a small- or large-volume procurement?
- Do we have limited capacity for production?
- Will the supplier augment our labor force?
- Can we maintain multiple sources of supply?
- Are we willing to accept indirect control?
- Are the suppliers of such quality that we can make use of just-in-time (JIT) inventory management?

It is highly unlikely that strategic manufacturing decisions will be black or white. In almost every situation, trade-offs are required. Skinner has identified several of the important trade-off decisions in Table 6.1.[10]

On the international scene, the list of typical decisions can be much more complicated. According to Skinner, typical decisions might include:

- how to deal with vendors who are habitually late in delivery and marginal in performance but are nevertheless the best vendors available
- how to minimize investment in inventory and yet prevent stockouts when replacement of a missing item may require four to six months and the cost of local working capital is 12% to 20% per year, and when it is difficult to hire stock clerks who can keep accurate records
- how to maintain a fair, motivation wage and salary rate in the midst of inflation, secrecy regarding practices of other companies, and traditional patterns of compensation such as automatic annual increments and "dearness allowances"
- how to select and train employees in the face of (a) language differences and often a low general-education level; (b) difficulties in testing applicants' potential; (c) the necessity of relying on new or weak lower-level supervision for the bulk of recommendations and training; and (d) high penalties for mistakes made (such as heavy compulsory severance pay to employees discharged)
- how to choose between (a) equipment or processes characterized by high initial cost, automated features, high maintenance, and low labor costs; and (b) alternatives with lower initial cost that may require more direct labor and tighter control in terms of quality and supervision. Such decisions are often complicated by unpredictable future costs and markets.

**Table 6.1 Some Important Trade-Off Decisions in Manufacturing—or "You Can't Have It Both Ways."**

| Decision area | Decision | Alternatives |
|---|---|---|
| Plant and Equipment | Span of process | Make or buy |
| | Plant size | One big plant or several smaller ones |
| | Plant location | Locate near markets or locate near materials |
| | Investment decisions | Invest mainly in buildings or equipment or inventories or research |
| | Choice of equipment | General-purpose or special-purpose equipment |
| | Kind of tooling | Temporary, minimum tooling or "production tooling" |
| Production Planning and Control | Frequency of inventory taking | Few or many breaks in production for buffer stocks |
| | Inventory size | High inventory or a lower inventory |
| | Degree of inventory control | Control in great detail or in lesser detail |
| | What to control | Controls designed to minimize machine downtime or labor cost or time in process, or to maximize output of particular products or material usage |
| | Quality control | High reliability and quality or low costs |
| | Use of standards | Formal or informal or none at all |
| Labor and Staffing | Job specialization | Highly specialized or not highly specialized |
| | Supervision | Technically trained first-line supervisors or nontechnically trained supervisors |
| | Wage system | Many job grades or few job grades, incentive wages or hourly wages |
| | Supervision | Close supervision or loose supervision |
| | Industrial engineers | Many or few such people |
| Product Design/ Engineering | Size of product line | Many customer specials or few specials or none at all |
| | Design stability | Frozen design or many engineering change orders |
| | Technological risk | Use of new processes unproved by competitors or follow-the-leader policy |
| | Engineering | Complete packaged design or design-as-you-go approach |
| | Use of manufacturing engineering | Few or many manufacturing engineers |
| Organization and Management | Kind of organization | Functional or product focus or geographical or other |
| | Executive use of time | High involvement in investment or production planning or cost control or quality control or other activities |
| | Degree of risk assumed | Decisions based on much or little information |
| | Use of staff | Large or small staff group |
| | Executive style | Much or little involvement in detail, authorization of nondirective style; much or little contact with organization |

# Personnel Availability

In deciding where to locate a new facility, there are two critical issues associated with personnel availability: the size of the population and community expectations. If a plant becomes a major community employer, then the community becomes heavily dependent upon the plant. In such cases, the community may become actively involved in the activities of the plant (as well as the parent corporation) and a hostile environment can develop. Some companies limit plant size (employment ceilings) to 5% of the population within a 50-mile radius. (There are other reasons for wanting low employment ceilings such as to keep the plant too small to be a union organization target.)

The second critical issue involves the social concerns of the corporation in regards to employee training and development. If the employment community is unskilled, then the community may have high expectations that the company will develop training programs to convert personnel from unskilled to skilled or semi-skilled workers. From a social perspective, the idea has merit, but from a financial point of view, large-scale training may not be cost-effective.

If a company converts a large portion of its workforce from unskilled to skilled, then the increased salary demands could cut into profits. In small communities, the turnover of personnel may be so small that each year, the average age of the workforce increases, thus driving up the fringe benefits costs and the adjoining overhead rates. If the community is large, then a high employee turnover rate could force the company to reassess whether it is getting a return on investment for its training dollars. Finally, if a company does, in fact, provide training programs for employee upgrading together with salary increases, then the most logical benefit to the company would be to take advantage of learning-curve effects on production quantities.

# Productivity

Productivity enhancement is an important part of strategic planning, because productivity growth leads to lower costs and provides an opportunity for lower-priced products and/or higher profits. It also makes possible increased compensatory benefits for employees. Productivity growth helps to ensure that production will meet cost and schedule targets, thus providing more resources for other manufacturing activities.

The productivity of any firm is a measure of how well the resources in that firm are brought together and used to accomplish a set of results. Productivity isn't just an increase in the volume of shipments, although this is one element. Traditionally, productivity has been defined as the acceptable output per labor hour. Using this definition, we would quickly discover that in a firm with many employees and little automation, productivity depends principally upon human achievement. On the other hand, in a firm where automation predominates, the human contributions to productivity play a lesser role.

Productivity is more than output over input. It is the relationship of the quantity and quality of products, goods, and services produced to the quantity of resources (personnel, capital facilities, machine tools and equipment, materials, and information) required to produce them. In order to improve productivity, both the output (performance achieved) and the input (resources consumed) must be capable of measurement.

Although several productivity ratio formulas exist, the preferred productivity ratio for endeavor is the one that best fits the purpose and resources of the organization involved. Practice, comparative use, and historic validation are some of the methods for giving productivity ratios meaning and/or validity.

# Trends in Productivity Growth

In recent years, both the United States and Europe have been losing their dominance in many different industries to the Japanese. The recent studies of Japanese improvements in productivity, product quality, and management have become the basis for changes in industrial practices worldwide.

During the 1950s and 1960s, the United States maintained a relatively high productivity growth rate. During the 1970s to the 1990s, the growth rate declined, but the United States is still ahead of the rest of the world. The challenge to the United States from other countries is a real one. It will take more commitment to increase innovation and this requires a commitment to strong leadership.

## FACTORS THAT INFLUENCE PRODUCTIVITY

The factors that influence productivity growth are the workforce, management, capital investment, and new technology.

**WORKFORCE** The members of the workforce represent an integral part of the productivity picture. This is portrayed in Figure 6.10. Referring to this figure, you can see that each of the three categories—workforce, process, and product—is composed of subordinate elements, any one of which can impact productivity growth. Productivity growth occurs when the cumulative effect of the interdependent elements is imposed.

**Figure 6.10** Productivity Results from Effective Interaction of the Workforce, the Processes, and the Product

The quality of the workforce affects productivity. As the quality increases or decreases, the productivity increases or decreases. There has been a decline in the quality of the workforce in the United States during the past few years. This decline can be attributed to a rise in the proportion of young and inexperienced workers in the workforce and the decrease in the average work effort. Also, the lack of motivation of many young workers has had an adverse affect on productivity.

**MANAGEMENT** One of the keys to productivity enhancement within any organization is management. The attitudes, actions, and personal examples of management pervade the organization and directly affect the attitudes, actions, and motivation of the workforce. It is from management that the workers generally take their cues. Accordingly, astute managers must convey clearly the importance they place on productivity and their desire to enhance productivity throughout the organization. Unfortunately, actions that management takes to improve productivity in one organization may not work out well when applied to another. Therefore, it is important for managers to assess the situation within their organization before taking specific actions to enhance productivity.

**CAPITAL INVESTMENT** Capital investment is absolutely necessary if productivity is to be enhanced. At the start of the 1980s, the picture was firm. The cumulative U.S. capital investment requirement for the 1980s was about $5 trillion. This figure exceeds the sum total of all capital investments made between 1900 and 1980. It averaged $350 billion more per year than was spent in the last 20 years.

According to some surveys, capital investment—after adjustment for inflation—may not show much growth. What caused a decline in capital investment? Inflation. In the early 1990s, when we needed more capital than ever before in our history, industry earnings were low, interest rates were high, equity financing was low, profits had eroded, and bond ratings were down. The portion of U.S. capital stock (technology, equipment, and facilities) that was five years old or younger had been declining steadily and the share of our total investment identified for building technological capital was declining at an alarming rate.

Inflation has an uncontrollable effect on productivity. Inflation tends to shed a negative light on productivity and capital investment. The volatile rates of inflation over the past 20 years, with its attendant negative impact on economic activity, has discouraged investment because of the perceived risks. It is very difficult for any business to plan adequately when accurate forecasts of inflation rates are difficult to obtain.

Productivity is influenced by the dollars industrial firms are able to set aside for investment in new technology, equipment, and facilities. If the United States is looking for a way to improve productivity, it needs to stimulate capital spending.

**NEW TECHNOLOGY** A well-managed industrial firm is one in which there is an effective integration of the workforce and advanced technology. The genesis of such an organization is an implementation plan that includes education of the workforce for factory automation, early identification of new manufacturing processes that will lend themselves to automation, manpower/workload forecasting that takes into account factory automation, and a mechanism for worker feedback.

United States industry and the government must foster more widespread use of industrial robots. The application of robots was one of the keys to the remarkably high levels of productivity achieved by the Japanese. The Robot Institute of America (RIA) suggests that U.S. industry assign high priority to the installation of robots, especially in dangerous, dirty, and dull jobs, "recognizing that robots are one of the quickest and cheapest ways to increase productivity." Also, industry must accept the responsibility for retraining workers who are displaced by robots. Industry managers will have to communicate with the workforce and help the workers to understand the advantages of using robots. Further, industrial managers will have to develop plans so workers will share in the benefits of increased productivity.

Someone has said that "if robots are becoming the tireless arms and eyes of production, then computers are their minds." The versatility of the computer has made it one of the principal elements leading to the automation of the factory. According to the center for Productivity for the National Science Foundation, computer-aided design (CAD), commuter-aided manufacturing (CAM), and computer-aided test (CAT) have more potential to radically increased productivity than any development since electricity.

New flexible manufacturing systems, in which several numerically controlled production machines are grouped along with a transport system, under a control of a main computer, are impacting productivity substantially. Using this type of manufacturing system, machine-tool utilization has increased as much as 45% in some companies.

# Facility Life Cycles

For years, marketing students were taught that products go through various life-cycle stages from R&D to ultimate death. These same concepts can be used to show that every factory has a life cycle. The life-cycle approach to facility decisions, just as in marketing/product decisions, allows companies to plan for the use of the facility during each evolutionary stage. The more thoroughly a company plans for the long-term use of its plants, the more efficient will be resources utilization, productivity planning, and contingency planning.

A facility's life cycle can be defined in three stages: initial planning and start-up, growth and maturity, and deterioration. Companies expect the new facility to be up and running as quickly as possible so that revenue and profitability can be planned for. Schmenner has identified several critical issues that should be considered in the initial planning and start-up phase:[11]

- the definition of the products to be manufactured and their desired output levels
- the plant's capacity and technological capabilities
- the specific process technology to be used, and the work-flow pattern to be followed within the plant

- the number of workers and the mix of their skills
- the recruiting, training, and other human-resource policies to be adopted in pursuit of the workforce goals
- the production scheduling and control systems to be employed
- the interrelationship between this facility and other facilities, as well as with suppliers, the distribution system, and ultimate customers
- the overhead functions and support staff to be provided—both those contained within the facility and those "borrowed" from outside sources
- a provision for the subsequent expansion and development of the facility and its human resources
- the capabilities and tasks that will not be required of the plant (at least during early stages)
- the events that would cause a change in the basic plan for the facility

During the growth and maturity stage, emphasis should be placed upon maintaining or improving productivity and preparing for possibly a new role. Included in this phase are:

- searching for ways to maintain or improve productivity of the plant
- investigating state-of-the-art technology, such as computer-integrated manufacturing techniques
- investigating better ways for production planning and materials control
- reassessing employee skill levels and accompanying salary levels
- searching for better ways to improve quality
- investigating the possibility for plant expansion to new product lines
- evaluating the potential advantages/disadvantages of vertical integration
- looking for ways for the plant to "stay alive" even as it ages

Every life cycle has a termination point, and termination must be planned for with the same accuracy as initiation planning. Planning for termination, the closing of a plant, is one of the most difficult decisions facing any manager. Schmenner has identified several signs of a failing plant that indicate that the distasteful contingency of plant closing must be planned for:[12]

- obsolescence reflected in technology deterring plant layout, poor materials handling, or problems with other physical aspects of the plant
- severe and unremitting sales declines
- substantial cost increases in labor, transportation, or raw materials
- militant union or other personnel problems
- needless duplication of operations of other plants

In preparing for the closing of a plant the company must consider:

- disposition of human and nonhuman resources
- financial and tax considerations
- reaction by suppliers and customers
- reaction by community
- reaction by other organizational units
- impact on other plants, product lines, services

# Environmental Protection

Restrictions imposed on manufacturing plants by regulations enforced by the Environmental Protection Agency (EPA) have had a severe effect on many industries in the United States. Pollution-control regulations have diverted capital and R&D funds into meeting these requirements. Many companies have ceased operations entirely, because the costs of compliance would make their profit margin so low that the resulting return on investment would not be acceptable. Funds have been diverted from R&D, plant-modernization programs, and start-up of new operations by many companies in order to stay in business and be competitive. The net effect has been the loss of innovation and a stagnant or even negative productivity rate.

EPA regulations have limited exploration and development of critical minerals in the United States and caused our dependence on foreign suppliers for strategic materials to be intensified. Mining of certain strategic materials is limited.

Easing of certain regulations as they now exist would do much to alleviate the curtailments that have been outlined. Legislative reform may be needed to repeal or amend some of the existing laws pertaining to environmental restrictions.

# Producibility

In the previous sections, we have emphasized the fact that manufacturing strategic planning must be coupled with R&D and engineering design. The purpose of this coupling is to develop and manufacture an item that is "producible." Specifically, producibility is a measure of the relative ease of producing a product. Producibility is the coordinated effort by design engineering and manufacturing engineering to create a functional design than can be easily and economically manufactured. The product must be designed in such a manner that manufacturing methods and processes have flexibility in producing the product at the lowest cost without sacrificing function, performance, or quality.

Producibility limitations must be recognized and addressed in each of the life-cycle phases of manufacturing strategic planning. Broad producibility considerations might include the selection of materials and manufacturing processes. The iterative design process mapped in Figure 6.11 is filled with decision points, each of which permits a potential trade-off against some other requirement. However, all demands upon the system such as reliability, availability, maintainability, safety, or producibility heavily interact with each other throughout the foreign process, creating the need for trade-offs.

## PRODUCIBILITY OBJECTIVES AND DESIGN

Considerations should include but not be limited to these areas:

- **To maximize**:
  - simplicity of design
  - use of economical materials

- use of material choices and process alternatives
- use of economical manufacturing technology
- standardization of materials and components
- confirmation of design adequacy prior to the production phase
- process repeatability
- product inspectability

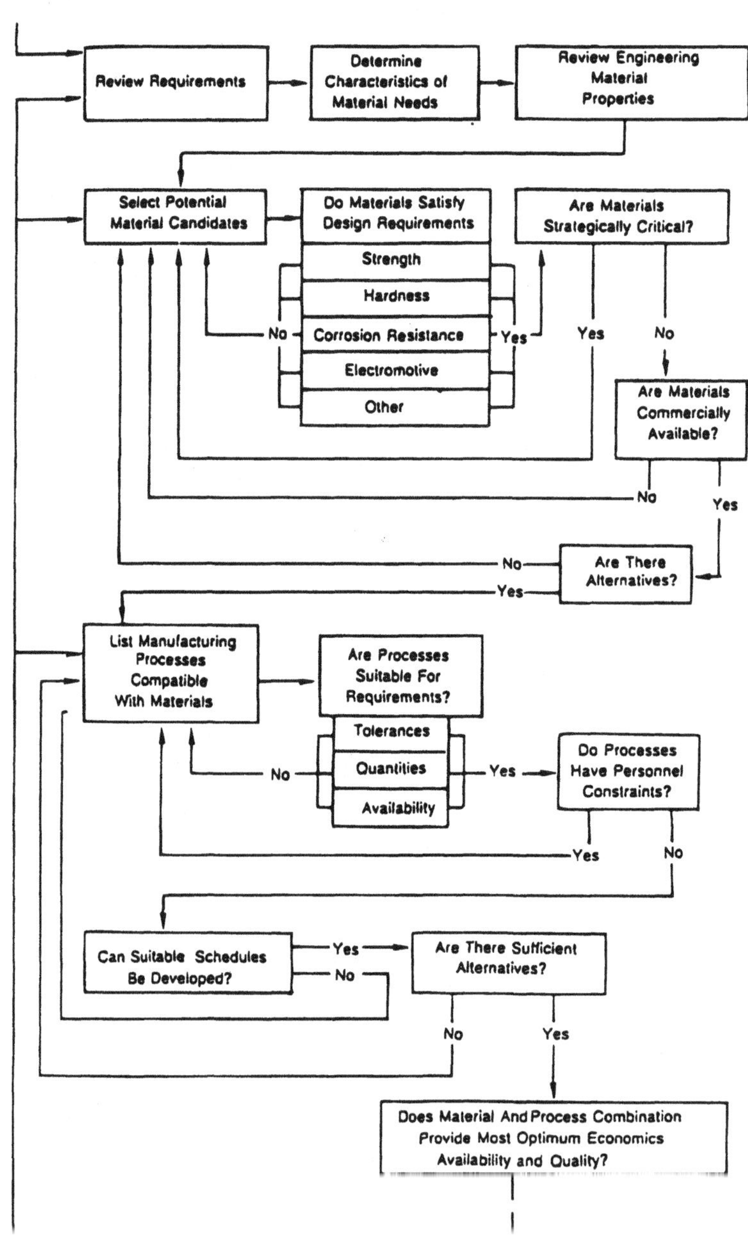


**Figure 6.11**
Producibility Considerations during the Iterative Design Process.

- **To minimize:**
  - procurement lead time
  - generation of scrap, chips, or waste
  - use of critical (strategic) materials
  - energy consumption
  - special manufacturing tests
  - special test systems
  - use of critical processes
  - pollution
  - skill levels of manufacturing personnel
  - unit costs
  - design changes during manufacture
  - use of limited availability items and processes
  - use of proprietary items without "production right" release

Too often, it is assumed that designing for the use of existing tooling is the most economical approach, without giving due consideration to new, more economical materials and processes. Further, designers also tend to design around their existing processes, without due consideration to ongoing manufacturing technology developments. This can have detrimental effects on producibility and future purchases, which may result in excessive engineering change orders. The producibility plan should identify the system of reviews of engineering designs to assure that the composite of characteristics that, when applied to equipment design and manufacturing planning, leads to the most effective and economic manufacturing approach.

# Manufacturing Problem Areas

When strategic manufacturing planning is performed, it should also include the development of policies, procedures, rules, and guidelines to overcome recurring problems. A list of major manufacturing problem areas might include:

- Inventory investment is excessive, yet there are shortages of needed material.
- Crash programs to reduce inventory to some arbitrary level occur frequently and are based on edicts.
- Delivery dates are often missed and overtime is used to meet new must-have dates.
- Production control, purchasing, plant supervisory personnel, and others are in a constant mode of expediting.
- Many manufacturing and purchase orders are past due but are needed to fill current shortages.
- Work in progress is clogging the shop floor and manufacturing orders are sometimes lost, albeit temporarily.
- Rejected material accumulates, and its disposal is usually made when a part is short on the assembly floor.

- There is a lack of rapport and communication among production-control, inventory-control, purchasing, sales, engineering, data-processing, accounting, and shop-floor personnel.
- Bills of material and routing and inventory records are inaccurate or incomplete.
- Overhead cost levels are excessive because current planning and control systems are not timely.
- Productivity is low because of excessive shortages, causing idle time and frequent equipment changeovers.
- Dates on which engineering changes become effective are not highly visible to everyone and configuration control is lost.
- The majority of shipments are made during the last week of the month.
- Lower output is achieved from a given amount of resources.
- Higher unit costs are incurred at all levels of manufacturing.
- Amount of waste is increasing in performing operations.
- Extra operations and equipment are increasingly needed to perform these operations.
- No improvements in the budgeting process are made, thus providing a poor basis for price estimating.
- No improvements in manufacturing-control activities and delivery-time estimation are made.
- Not enough attention is focused on cost reduction and cost control.

Needless to say, these areas must be accounted for in the strategic-planning process.

# Robotics

It is important to recognize today's manufacturing environment. Figure 6.12 presents a breakdown of typical manufacturing costs, by percentage. This breakdown is representative of the situation in defense, aerospace, electronics, and heavy

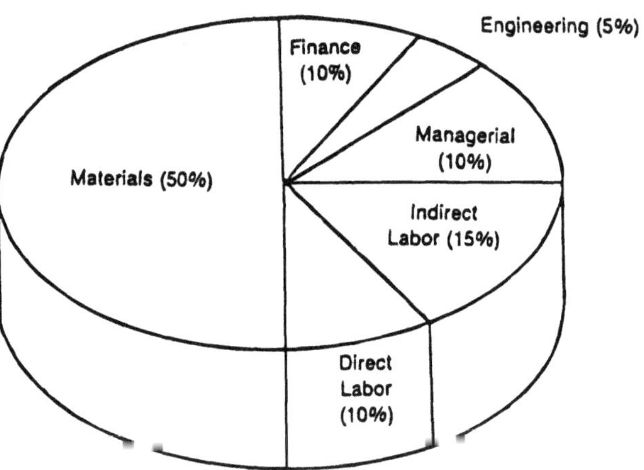


**Figure 6.12**
Manufacturing Cost Distribution

industries in the United States. Materials account for the biggest "slice of the pie."

The opportunity for reducing manufacturing costs by introducing robots has generally been in the area of direct and indirect labor tasks. With costs distributed as shown in Figure 6.12, the first inclination is to consider replacing direct and indirect labor with a robot, due to the similarity of robot motions to human arm movements. However, the potential for cost savings is greater if ways are also found to use robots to save materials.

For many years, robots were marketed as the answer to many of the problems faced by industry in the United States. U.S. industry was beset by rising direct labor costs; pressures to improve productivity; challenges posed by environmental and occupational health and safety authorities, based upon unpleasant and hazardous working conditions; and the need for better product quality. A modest, but increasing number of products have not only been able to solve these problems, but have been able to save materials and provide a manufacturing flexibility not available previously.

Robots are justified within the production-volume ranges shown in Figure 6.13. When fewer than 200 parts are to be manufactured per year, manual labor is usually less costly. Above 20,000 parts per year, hard automation is generally more cost effective.

Today, about 80% of the U.S. industrial robots are being applied to welding, material handling, and machine loading/unloading. The remainder of the

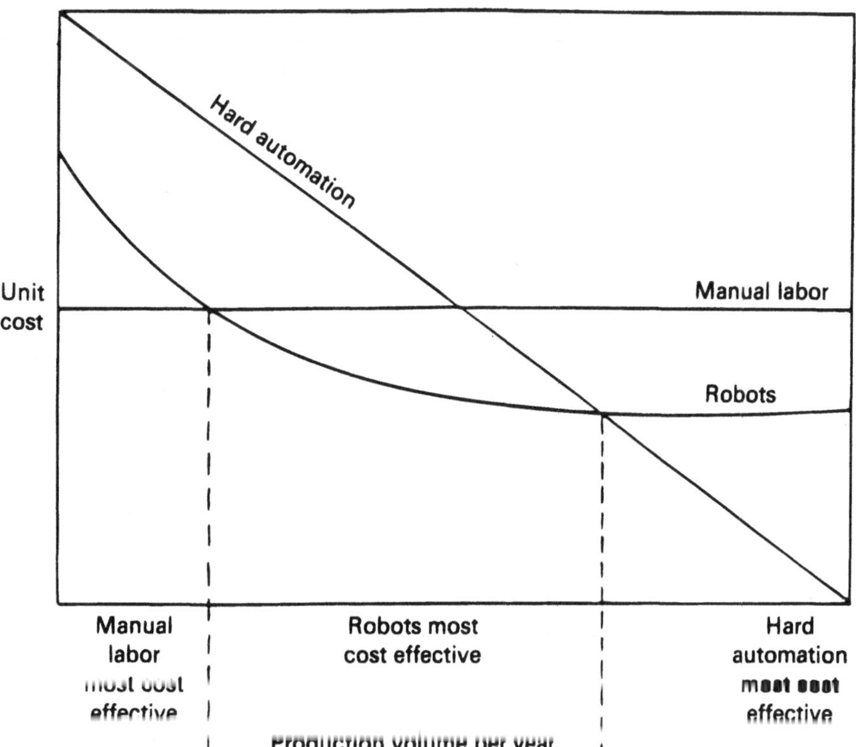


**Figure 6.13**
Robotics justification.

robots are being used in such activities as spray painting, machining, assembling, and pelletizing. About 40% is divided almost equally between foundries and the light-manufacturing industry that is producing nonmetal products. The remainder of the applications are in the heavy-equipment, electrical/electronics, and aerospace industries.

Over the years, the capabilities of robots have continued to increase. Much of the current robot technology was unknown just a decade ago—particularly control technology and programming. Now robot manufacturers have discovered electronic logic and computer software. These technologies are making robots adaptable to an increasing variety of complex tasks. Therefore, it is very important that each proposed application be carefully considered and the robot selected be properly engineered to endure success. Such a robot will inherently increase manufacturing flexibility and improve product quality and productivity.

Labor and other production costs continue to rise, but robot manufacturers have generally held the line on the price of robot installations in recent years. Thus, we can expect many more manufacturing companies to give serious consideration to purchasing robots. When they do so, they may find themselves on their own. Although the number of applications will increase, each application will be unique in some respects. Robot technology is still relatively new, and there is, therefore, little in-depth experience to call upon. As a consequence, the experience of most robot users is being guarded jealously, because they believe this experience gives them a competitive edge. It is quite possible that the "wheel" is being reinvented many times over by industry in developing robots for new applications.

Although robots are used to save workers from health hazards and fatigue, reduction in labor cost is still the most popular reason for employing robots in manufacturing operations. Let's examine this finding in more detail.

In 1981, the true cost of an hourly employee in the metal-working industry (except automobiles) was about \$15/hour. In the automobile industry it was about \$20/hour. At the same time the "all-included" cost of applying a medium-price robot was about \$6/hour. The hourly opening cost of a robot has only risen \$2 since 1967. GMC Chairman Roger B. Smith once said, "every time the cost of labor goes up \$1/hour, 1,000 more robots become economical."

In the design or redesign of every manufacturing system, management has the opportunity to explore options concerning the relationships between people, technology, and cost. Managers, normally concerned with technological improvements and reduction in cost, can ill afford to neglect the changes that will be wrought on the social system in the workplace by robots.

# Computer-Integrated Manufacturing (CIM)

CIM advocates that all functions in a manufacturing plant can be integrated by a computer system with strong communications channels. The manufacturing plant then becomes responsive as an organized unit. The best way to define CIM is to quote individuals from various industries:

From the management consulting business, Ray L. Discasali, Vice President of Management Science of America, says:

> This host of new technology is beginning to be collectively referred to as computer-integrated manufacturing (CIM). CIM is the umbrella under which all the independent pieces—CAD, CAM, GT, robotics and others—are organized to work together. We're still in the process of defining what it is, but we're at a point, I believe, where we can see several of the major pieces that will comprise CIM.
>
> Certainly, CIM is computer-based. It is hardware. It is also software. At the core, CIM is a view of the manufacturing plant layout from an information-processing perspective. It is a way of managing information as much as machinery and manpower.
>
> CIM is also firmware–dedicated pieces of automation, be they robotic, CAD/CAM, or automated storage and retrieval systems for material handling. These three components, as well as pieces not yet envisioned, comprise a powerful new tool for manufacturing.

From the computer-hardware industry, Stephen J. Gondert, Manager of Industry and Product Promotion for Computervision Corporation, says:[13]

> Computer-integrated manufacturing is not a 'thing.' It is rather an evolutionary process that has been going on in the manufacturing community ever since the advent of the computer. CIM is a global concept that includes far more than the traditional manufacturing processes found in the factory. CIM is truly a technological imperative that can help to ensure economic survival in an increasingly competitive international marketplace. CIM integrates all data-processing functions within the company, including financial accounting, purchasing, inventory, distribution, payroll engineering, and management, as well as the traditional manufacturing operations. Calling it a computer-integrated business functional system might be more appropriate.

From the plastics industry, Agostino von Hassell, Associate Editor of *Plastics Technology*, says:[14–17]

> Fundamentally, CIM means transforming a manufacturing operations that today consists of an assemblage of systems and subsystems operating more or less independent of each other into a single organism with an electronic "nervous system" of sensors and controllers. Everything that happens in the plant—from receiving a customer's order to shipping the finished product—is known to a central computer and can be controlled by it. The three fundamental phases of manufacturing—product design, production planning, and manufacturing—are integrated and accomplished without direct human effort, by the utilization of intelligent distributed control and effective machine intercommunications.

The details of each industry's definition of CIM will focus on different aspects of the general concept because the specific needs of each industry differ to some extent.

As with any advanced technology, it is easy to begin to think of CIM as an end in itself; but the real reason for investing in computer-integrated manufacturing is productivity. The pressures for increased productivity are very clearly explained by James A. Baker, Executive Vice President of General Electric Company, in the following:[18]

> Any manufacturing operation of any size that is not actively pursuing automation is on death row. It's a factory—and a business—with no future. Failure to automate will lead to the death of a business. But economic times and low capital funds are not

> argument against automation. The wait-until-good-times approach is custom-made for losers. The winners are begging, borrowing, betting everything on smart automation, using the leverage of technology to fight back. The losers are frozen like deer in the Japanese headlights, hoping for some outside force to save them. It won't. But automation can. We're running out of time. It is not only the rich companies that are spending on automation. The hardest-hit industries are doing it as well. Chrysler's going in hock up to its ears to automate. Iacocca knows, as do Ford and GM, that automation is the last, best hope for American industry and must be pursued no matter what the cost. The choice is between biting the bullet or biting the dust.

Rasy L. Discasali, Vice President of Management Science of America, makes the same point as Baker when he says:[16]

> With all the excitement surrounding CIM and what it will mean for U.S. manufacturing, we must keep in mind that CIM is not the goal. The goal is competitive survival. We must shorten development time, reduce costs, and improve quality. We must be both responsive to the market and more profitable.

Computer-integrated manufacturing is not a quick fix. CIM is basically a way to put computer power to use in manufacturing. Although it may be relatively easy to conceptualize what CIM should be, it is much more difficult to implement CIM technology in an organization. Implementation takes careful planning and step-by-step strategy, but a company that is willing to put forth the effort can realize the benefits.

## NOTES

1. Robert H. Hayes and Steven C. Wheelwright, *Restoring Our Competitive Edge* (New York: John Wiley & Sons, Inc, 1984), p. 2.
2. Roger B. Smith, Chairman and Chief Executive Officer, General Motors Corporation, "The 21st Century Corporation," delivered before the Economic Club of Detroit, Cobo Hall, Detroit, MI, September 9, 1985.
3. Ryohei Suzuki, "Worldwide Expansion of U.S. Exports—a Japanese View," *Sloan Management Review*, Spring 1979, pp. 67–70.
4. Thomas G. Gunn, "CIM Must Start at the Top," *Production Magazine*, March 1985, pp. 43–44.
5. Roger B. Smith, speech before the Economic Club of Detroit, September 9, 1985.
6. Robert H. Hayes and Steven C. Wheelwright, *Restoring Our Competitive Edge*, p. 10.
7. Robert H. Hayes and Steven C. Wheelwright, *Restoring Our Competitive Edge*, p. 31.
8. Roger Schmenner, *Making Business Location Decisions*, (New Jersey: Prentice Hall Publishers, 1982), pp. 33–36.
9. Adapted form Michael Porter, *Competitive Strategy* (New York: Free Press, a Division of Macmillan Publishers, 1980), pp. 324–339.
10. Wickham Skinner, "Manufacturing—Missing Link in Corporate Strategy," *Harvard Business Review*, May–June, 1969. Also reprints from *Harvard Business Review* reprints, *Production Management*, *Part III*, p. 33; © 1969 by the President and Fellows of Harvard College; all rights reserved. Reproduced by permission.
11. Roger Schmenner, *Making Business Location Decisions*, p. 28.
12. Roger Schmenner, "Every Factory Has a Life Cycle," *Harvard Business Review*, March–April 1983 by the President and Fellows for Harvard University; all rights [illegible]

13. Stephen J. Gondert, "Understanding the Impact of Computer-Integrated Manufacturing," *Manufacturing Engineering*, 93 September 1984, p. 67–69.
14. Agostino von Hassell, "Computer Integrated Manufacturing: Here's How to Plan for It," *Plastics Technology* 29, November 1983, p. 54–69.
15. Agostino von Hassell, "CIM Guidelines on Buying Hardware, Software," *Plastics Technology* 29, December 1983, pp. 59–69.
16. Agostino von Hassell, "New Controls Technology Aids Complete Plant Automation," *Plastics Technology* 30, July 1984, pp. 20–27.
17. Agostino von Hassell, "Computer Integrated Manufacturing: Coming Sooner Than You Think," *Plastics Technology* 29, May 1983, pp. 37–42.
18. James A. Baker, "Winning Your Case for Autcmation," *Manufacturing Engineering*, 93, July 1984, pp. 72–73.

## ESSAY QUESTIONS

1. As it relates to manufacturing, why has the United States lost its competitive edge?
2. Why is it necessary for R&D and marketing strategies to be "married" to the manufacturing strategy?
3. Why are manufacturing strategies usually expressed in terms of a long-term capital investment?
4. Why do plant managers often find it difficult to perform strategic planning? Could it be related to how long the individual expects to stay in the position of plant manager?
5. You have been asked to head up a team to design the factory of the future. What are the critical questions that must be asked? Assume that construction on the factory is to begin five years from now.
6. Explain the impact that Porter's five-forces model can have on developing a manufacturing strategy.
7. Is there a relationship between manufacturing strategies and exit strategies? If so, explain.
8. Explain how vertical integration can impact a manufacturing strategy.
9. Why do some firms avoid opening up manufacturing plants in small communities?
10. What are the critical factors in performing manufacturing risk assessment?

## MULTIPLE CHOICE QUESTIONS

1. Long-term manufacturing strategies require a serious commitment to ___________.
   - **a.** long-term capital investment
   - **b.** short-term capital investment
   - **c.** reducing capital costs
   - **d.** all the above
   - **e.** b and c only
2. Most strategists believe that America will be able to meet the competition on ___________ but not on ___________.
   - **a.** capital expenditure; quality
   - **b.** cost; quality
   - **c.** quality; cost
   - **d.** productivity; quality
   - **e.** quality; market share
3. To meet the competition we must:
   - **a.** focus on the long term
   - **b.** develop an integrated strategic plan incorporating marketing, engineering, and manufacturing

c. develop managers with hands-on experience
d. all the above
e. a and c only

4. Improving return an investment (ROI) can be achieved by either increasing profits or ____________.
   a. increasing capital expenditures
   b. reduce preventive maintenance
   c. reduce capital expenditures
   d. all the above
   e. b and c only
5. Strategies are based upon either an expansion or contraction philosophy. Which of the following would be an expansion strategy?
   a. marketing
   b. R&D
   c. engineering
   d. manufacturing
   e. finance
6. Strategic planning for manufacturing stresses:
   a. more efficient utilization of existing resources
   b. increasing demand for existing products
   c. resources planning for new products
   d. all the above
   e. a and b only
7. A manufacturing management system has the following three phases:
   a. strategic planning; execution; quality assurance
   b. planning; control; follow-up
   c. planning; documentation; control
   d. execution; documentation; control
   e. planning; analysis; control
8. Most companies in the marketplace are affected by:
   a. material shortages
   b. foreign competition
   c. government regulations
   d. economic conditions
   e. all the above
9. The maximum rate of productive or conversion capability of an organization's operations is called ____________.
   a. capacity
   b. investment decision making
   c. restrictions
   d. manufacturing constraints
   e. none of the above
10. Which factor(s) has/have a bearing on the firm's ability to execute the manufacturing effort?
    a. management capability
    b. sufficient floor space
    c. capable suppliers
    d. adequate production skills
    e. all the above
11. Materials or processes in general use are called.
    a. state-of-the art

   b. state-of-practice
   c. theoretical
   d. experimental
   e. none of the above

12. Competitive positioning, as it refers to in manufacturing is most often defined by:
   a. cost and quality of the products
   b. breadth of product line
   c. features offered
   d. enhancement capability
   e. quality of skilled labor
13. Which of the following is not one of the authors' six components of a manufacturing strategy?
   a. process and product technology
   b. vertical-integration strategy
   c. physical plant location
   d. government regulations
   e. capacity planning
14. Capacity strategies are based upon:
   a. predicted demand for product
   b. product life cycle
   c. competitors' behavior patterns
   d. rate of change of technology
   e. all the above
15. When capacity and demand are in equilibrium, then ___________.
   a. shortages are permitted to exist
   b. market demand is constant
   c. it is assumed that capacity can be added as needed
   d. all the above
   e. a and c only
16. Advantages of making a product rather than purchasing it outside include:
   a. indirect control
   b. lack of vertical-integration opportunity
   c. maintaining design secrecy
   d. creating excess capacity
   e. all the above
17. Advantages of buying rather than producing a component include:
   a. utilizing idle capacity
   b. not having to hire expensive, skilled labor
   c. direct control
   d. all the above
   e. a and c only
18. In deciding where to locate a new facility, the two critical issues are:
   a. personnel availability and tax abatements
   b. availability of skilled labor and proximity to transportation outlets
   c. personnel availability and community expectations
   d. ratio of skilled to unskilled labor and cost of training
   e. tax incentives and cost per square foot of space
19. The factor(s) influencing manufacturing productivity is/are:
   a. the workforce
   b. management
   [illegible]

d. technology
e. all the above

20. Which of the following is not considered in a strategic decision to close a plant?
a. disposition of human and nonhuman resources
b. financial and tax considerations
c. reaction by suppliers and customers
d. reaction by the community
c. reaction by competitors

## CASE STUDY: LTV Corporation's Joint Venture

LTV Corporation is a fully integrated steel producer that is ranked the third-largest steel operation in the United States and the second domestic producer of flat-rolled steel. LTV currently supplies about 20% of flat-rolled steel purchased by the U.S. automotive, appliance, and electrical equipment industry. LTV is a leading supplier to demanding markets for quality-critical steel.

A majority of LTV's 1994 revenues (93%) resulted from the sale of hot-rolled, cold-rolled, and coated-steel sheet as well as tubular and tin mill products. These products were produced at two integrated steel mills (Cleveland Works and Indiana Harbor Works) and various finishing and processing facilities. The remaining sales were provided by Continental Emsco Company, a wholly owned subsidiary and one of the largest suppliers of oil-field equipment and supplies in North America.

In December 1994, LTV announced a joint venture with Sumitomo Metal Industries, Ltd. and British Steel plc. to build a hot-strip minimill with an annual capacity of 2.2 million tons in the southeastern United States (Alabama). LTV would own 50% of the new minimill company, Trico Steel. Sumitomo and British Steel each would own 25% of Trico. The project is expected to cost $450 million and create roughly 300 jobs.

Trico Steel will have an electric furnace and a state-of-the-art thin-slab caster connected to a hot-strip mill. The mill will produce commercial and higher-quality grades of hot-rolled sheet, including light-gage hot-rolls that LTV believes will compete with some cold-rolled sheet products.

According to David H. Hoag, Chairman and Chief Executive Officer of LTV Corporation, "Trico Steel Company is the first major steelmaking joint venture in the U.S.A., with partners from three different continents. Combining the technical, financial, and management resources of these three high-quality steel companies will enable Trico Steel Company to introduce new competitive products to the market using the latest know-how in steel-making and rolling technology." Sumitomo and LTV have had two previous successful electrogalvanizing joint ventures. Both companies have benefited greatly from this high level of technical exchange.

Trico Steel Company has met with much opposition. United Steelworkers Union put together a list of proposals for the new plant, including asking LTV to build it in an existing plant and giving laid-off workers first preference for employment. These proposals were rejected by LTV. LTV employees believe that LTV should not jump on the bandwagon of minimills, but use their excess cash, $225 million, to fund the pension plans, which are only 65% funded, or even invest in expansion of present plants. LTV Corporation believes the best interest of the employees are being considered. The joint venture will give LTV Corporation another revenue stream and provide growth in a new marketplace. Expanding their market with technical advancements will also open the door to new product development, while taking on only a portion of the financial responsibilities.

The Southeast was considered due to the rapid demand for steel in this region during the past 15 years. The Southeast was also considered since LTV currently operates three facilities in the Midwest. LTV management believed that for external growth, the company has to expand its market area. The choice for Trico and future sites will be driven by the marketplace.

Trico will cause tremendous pressure on two of Alabama's oldest steelmakers, U.S. Steel and Gulf States Steel, which are benefiting from the hottest market in 15 years. Currently, these companies' mills are located near Decatur, Alabama, which is the proposed site for Trico. Opposition exists because of the incentives being offered to Trico, which include a competitive package of job training, infrastructure grants, tax credits, and tax construction and development. Initially, the incentives had not been approved because the Mercedes Law did not cover limited-liability partnerships, which includes Trico Steel Company. These incentives had to be approved by legislation to include limited-liability partnerships by Governor Fob James. Although various lawsuits from steel competitors stalled the incentive package, the package was eventually approved, and allowed new and expanding industries state income tax breaks for up to 20 years. These companies will also be allowed to deduct 5% of their construction costs from their income taxes each year.

The other steelmakers feel that they are being put at a disadvantage because Sumitomo and British Steel are subsidized by their respective countries, while most American steel companies are not. Additionally, the incentive package given to Trico creates in uneven tax advantage for Trico Steel to underprice the older companies. The incentive package would mean a break of at least $3 per ton of steel produced by Trico compared with the other steel companies in the region.

To these steel producers, the danger of the incentive package is clear: When the presently surging highly cyclical steel industry hits the next down market, companies will be stuck with excess. New lower-cost plants, such as Trico, could then snatch customers from older operations, by providing a cost-efficient product due to the incentives given.

Trico plans to focus on new, low-cost production technologies and operating practices. Trico will create external growth for LTV Corporation through new distribution channels, in the Southeast and globally, advancing to a new market area and creating future opportunities to increase their product lines. Taking on a partnership will lessen the barrier of capital requirements to expanding their market area, while achieving a cost-effective quality product, high-cost, nonefficient companies will be entering the minimill market, which will create competition for Trico. Some higher cost producers may not make it in the growing industry of steelmaking.

Besides this joint venture with Sumitomo and British Steel, LTV Corporation has changed its marketing strategy to identify and target orders that are a profitable mix of products within the market they already exist in. Currently, LTV Corporation has been identifying opportunities for performance breakthroughs, including redesigning function, which will reduce costs, improve productivity, and enhance the quality and speed of customer service.

## QUESTIONS

1. Does LTV's joint venture seem like a strategically sound decision? Who are the winners and who are the losers?

2. What impact do government subsidies have on the development of a strategic plan?
3. What rights, if any, does a union have in changing a corporation's strategic plan?
4. What are LTV's objectives for the joint venture and what are the union's objectives?
5. Can a "clash" in objectives transform internal strengths into internal weaknesses?

# CHAPTER 7 Small-Business Strategies

## Introduction

Small firms that are growth intensive have to develop a marketing posture that strategically balances sales and new-product development. The essential areas with which marketing is concerned are:

- understanding goals of the business
- growth objectives
- product marketing
- advertising and promotion
- sales and distribution

One major difference between a growth-oriented company and its competitors is the amount of income spent on marketing. If, for example, the industry average marketing expenditure is 10% of new sales, a growth company may spend 20% to 30%. Of course, the trick is to be successful, which means marketing must use its budget wisely.

The goals of the business, when clearly defined, provide a beginning point from which the marketing strategy must be developed. The strategic market plan may be thought of as involving four sets of related decisions:

- **defining the business**[1,2]—The CEO and top-level managers must decide, "What business are we in?" The definition must state:
  - **scope**—the product and markets: customers to be served, needs that can be satisfied; what ways (technologies) are to be used.
  - **product and market segmentation**—a definition of how a firm groups customers with respect to needs and how they are satisfied.
- **determining the mission of the business**—Performance expectations in terms of sales growth, market share, return to investors, net income, and cash flow must be determined. Short-term expectations should be balanced with long-term alternatives.
- **formulating functional strategies**—The costs and benefits of various alternatives functionally determine how marketing, manufacturing, R&D, service, and physical distribution interact.

- **budgeting**—The planning cycle produces a resource-allocation plan. At this stage, specific financing decisions are made and operating budgets are determined.

This should work quite well for a large company with enough staff and the time required. The smaller company has limited resources and so many pressing daily problems that it may be difficult for them to plan. But successful growth companies have to develop goals to achieve.

The marketing strategy defines what will be offered to buyers, which market will be targeted, and how. The market definition evolves from what has been sold and to whom. The starting point for small-business strategic planning is industry posture, whether fragmented or not. Research has to be conducted to determine the company's present market share, growth average for all competitors in that industry, and the size of the market the company may serve. The customer list can be checked to determine common markets, number of successful applications, and why the client decides to buy. This information may be gathered from field-sales feedback.

# Product Marketing

Every company has to consider its customers' needs. The mission and definition of the business define the general market and what types of customer needs will be served. Following that, products and services are the responsibility of the marketing team.

Growth-oriented small companies spend a major portion of their resources developing new products. Ideas for new products come from many sources including:

- sales feedback from customers
- CEO and marketing brainstorming sessions
- customer surveys
- competitive pressures
- defensive R&D for product and productivity improvements

Products have a life cycle, beginning at introduction to the market and ending as the market moves on to another preference. Each stage of the product life cycle has to be estimated and managed in conjunction with the company's goals and objectives, external environmental, and competitive pressures. The sales history of most products follows a pattern of:

- **introduction**—a period of slow sales growth as the product is introduced in the market. Profits are low and cash flow is high in this stage due to the initial costs.
- **growth**—a period of rapid market acceptance and substantial profit improvement.
- **maturity**—a period of slowdown in sales growth because the product has reached acceptance by most of the potential buyers. Profits begin to decline as costs to compete increase.

- **decline**—the period when sales show a strong decline and profits erode.

Small companies very often struggle with acceptance of product life-cycle strategies because of severely limited resources and poor management. New-product strategies are the most important growth element for small businesses. Unfortunately, the products/services of small businesses may have a much shorter life cycle than those of larger companies, and the cost and resources necessary for life-cycle phase analysis may not be beneficial.

# Marketing Strategies

All companies, large and small, have competitors, need to grow in sales and profits, and need many market opportunities. To decide how small company will grow requires one of the following market strategies, regardless of whether the company management knows and accepts it. Firms in industry pursue different competitive strategies and enjoy different positions in the market. Arthur D. Little, a consulting organization, rates firms in one of five competitive positions:

- **dominant**—This firm controls the behavior of other firms and has a wide choice of options.
- **strong**—This firm can take independent action without endangering its long-term position, regardless of competitors' actions.
- **favorable**—This firm has a strength that is exploitable in particular strategies and can improve its position.
- **tenable**—This firm is performing at a level to warrant continuing in business.
- **weak**—This firm has unsatisfactory performance and no opportunity for improvement.

Growth-oriented small companies must assess their competitive position. If the markets being served are growing, then growth companies may be satisfied to be favorable or tenable if the strategy is a developing one. In stagnant or declining markets, growth companies have to be strong or dominant to sustain growth.

Market leadership strategy is well-suited to small growth-oriented firms that must create ways to expand total demand. The firm must protect its current market share through solid defensive and offensive actions. The firm can try to expand its market share further as the market rate slows.

Market-challenger strategies are used by smaller firms that are new in a market or have acquired a company or product line gaining access to a market. Challengers are generally more successful if their means is to improve market share. An aggressor can choose to attack one of three types of firms:

- *Attack the market leader*. The risk is high, but the payoff is greatest if the market leader is not serving the market well.
- *Attack other firms of similar size*. Works best if the competitive firm's resources are limited.
- *Attack smaller firms that are underfinanced*. Works well to displace entrepreneurial firms in start-up mode.

Market-follower strategies fit smaller growth companies if the market is expanding rapidly and enough business is available to suit the growth goals of the firm. Challenging the industry leader can weaken the firm if the leader has sufficient defenses. The follower defines a growth path but one that does not invoke retaliation from the leaders. Three strategies can work for followers:

- **close follower**—Here, the follower lives off the market expansion of the leader and is basically a copy of the leader.
- **distant follower**—The company differentiates in some ways from the leader but follows similar pricing and distribution channels.
- **selective follower**—The firm picks key areas to follow, but this company is innovative and may become a challenger if the market slows in growth.

One major goal of followers is relatively high profits, perhaps in a short time.

Market-niche strategies are excellent for small growth-oriented companies. These firms try to find a market niche that is safe and profitable. The difficulty is finding a niche market that will grow steadily. An ideal market niche has the following characteristics:

- sufficient size and purchasing power to be profitable
- growth potential
- negligible interest to major competitors
- required skills and resources available to serve the niche effectively
- the firm can defend itself against an attacking competitor

Niche marketing requires the firm to specialize in a particular market with specific customers along a narrow product line. Notably, the firm will act as a specialist in one of several categories including:

- end-use
- application orientation
- specific customer type
- geographic area—this may by anywhere in the world
- product or product line
- product feature specialist
- one-of-a-kind specials
- quality/price
- service

The risks are high that the niche will evaporate. Small firms in the growth phase must consider diversification to ensure growth and long term success.

# Successful Marketing Plans

Once a strategy has been selected, the marketing plan must be developed. The initial planning requires that the following questions be asked:

- Where does the company stand now?
- What will the future be like for the firm?

- Where should the company be heading?
- How can the firm get there?
- Who is going to do it and when?
- How much will it cost, and what do these costs cover?
- What are the results?
- What changes need to be made?

**Table 7.1 Situation-Analysis Planning Tool.**

| Issues to Be Addressed | Purpose | Sources and Techniques to Use in the Analysis |
|---|---|---|
| 1. Product sales | To track trends in business sales | Company sales records |
| 2. Product sales by market | To examine trends in product sales by market | Management Information System (MIS) segregating sales by market, industry, or SIC* |
| 3. Product sales by market by geographic area | To examine strengths of products and markets by location | MIS |
| 4. Sales by method of distribution | To determine volume of sales by direct and indirect methods | Company sales records |
| 5. Sales by size of customer | To evaluate quality of sales provided by large, medium, and small accounts | Company sales records augmented by data on customer output or number of employees |
| 6. Key-customer sales | To identify most important customers | Listing of customers in descending order of sales volume |
| 7. Key-customer economic-power factors | To evaluate key customers' ability to dictate marketing terms | Survey of their impact on your business; fraction of their purchases of your product; possible backward integration (to produce your product) |
| 8. Total market size | To track trends in market share by product and to determine degree of market saturation | Survey of salesforce; general survey of sample customers and extrapolation of results |
| 9. Growth of markets | To determine product growth trends in existing markets | Survey of literature; data from survey in issue 8 |
| 10. Market development opportunity | To determine underdeveloped sales opportunity in unexploited markets | Survey of sample of suspected markets and extrapolation of results |
| 11. Product attributes | To develop data on customer likes and dislikes | Survey of customers in issue 8 |

* [illegible]

**Table 7.2 Forecast Problems and Opportunities Based on STEEP Factors—Acme Machine Tool Co.**

| STEEP Factors | Marketing | Research and Development | Manufacturing | Others (Financial, Legal, Human Resources, Materials Management, Product Reliability) |
|---|---|---|---|---|
| **Sociological**<br>• Toolmaker shortage<br>• Sunbelt migration<br>• Extended work career | • Point out time-saving aspects to management<br>• Sell on ease of use and simplicity of design | • Design for use by less-experienced worker<br>• Use computer-assisted design (CAD)<br>• Institute training sessions for customers | • Use computer-assisted manufacture (CAM)<br>• Recruit older, experienced craftspeople | • Assist in picking attractive areas for expansion (human resources)*<br>• Train and retrain employees |
| **Technological**<br>• Direct numerical control (DNC)<br>• Computer-assisted design (CAD)<br>• Computer-assisted manufacture (CAM)<br>• Robotics | • Sell virtues of DNC, CAD, CAM, and built-in automatic features as value/price purchase incentives<br>• Sell advantage of low reject rate | • Design state-of-the-art products for productivity improvement<br>• Improve internal production processes to reduce costs constantly<br>• Do not overdesign | • Use latest cost-effective methods to stay competitive | • Make sure new equipment purchased for production is cost effective (finance)<br>• Assist marketing in developing ROI justifications for customers (finance) |
| **Economic**<br>• Inflation<br>• Productivity<br>• Depreciation<br>• Interest rate levels<br>• Devaluation/revaluation<br>• GNP growth<br>• Funds availability | • Institute purchase plans<br>• Sell productivity improvement aspects<br>• Point out faster write-off possibilities<br>• Sell to low-profit as well as high-growth industries<br>• Take advantage of high relative value of dollar overseas | • In high-growth periods, use outside assistance to keep permanent staff low<br>• Design modular units that can be purchased piecemeal | • Use outside vendors if cash flow and funds availability are tight<br>• Make sure capacity is not outstripped by forecast demand<br>• Keep work-in-process inventory low | • Keep all inventory levels as low as possible to minimize interest expenses for working capital (materials management)<br>• Work out advantageous lease-purchase plans (financial, legal)<br>• Consider last-in, first-out, (LIFO) accounting controls (finance)<br>• Evaluate new distribution methods (materials management) |
| **Environmental**<br>• Energy costs<br>• OSHA requirements<br>• Nonproductive capital expenditures | • Point out safety features<br>• Branch out into environmental protection | • Develop designed-in safety features<br>• Design for lowest energy consumption possible | • Adhere to OSHA regulations<br>• Reduce energy consumption | • Examine new products for safety (product reliability)<br>• Train employees to work safely |
| **Political**<br>• Imports to less-developed countries (LDCs)<br>• Tariff negotiations<br>• Antitrust regulations | • Work to eliminate restrictions | • Design products with specific country markets in mind | • Consider plants or joint ventures inside growing LDCs | • Use hedging procedures to minimize exchange losses (finance)<br>• Check potential acquisitions or mergers for antitrust implications |

* Source unknown.

For any business, the implementation of a growth-strategy concept begins with marketing issues. For small companies, one fact is always true: "Nothing happens until a sale is made."

The first two questions above, when answered, produce what large-company planners refer to as a "situation analysis." A detailed look at the products or services that are offered by the business is necessary to understand the dynamics of customer needs, market growth, and product-line demand. The major input for the situation analysis comes from company sales records. These records are generally available by product, market, geographic location, price channel of distribution, and even end-use application within the industry. Table 7.1 identifies what information (and the respective issues) should be analyzed using the situation-analysis planning tool.

The second logical market tool that will help the small company develop growth strategies is consideration of the STEEP factors. The evaluation of sociological, technical, economic, environmental, and political (STEEP) factors help put the data developed from the situation analysis into perspective. Consideration of how the company fits into the world situation identifies the opportunities and threats the firm faces. An example of this analysis for a growth-oriented company is presented in Table 7.2.

Previous discussion introduced the product life-cycle concept. During the introduction phase, small quantities are produced that must absorb fixed costs. Prices can be adjusted to reflect cost reductions. Thus, as the firm moves forward on the experience-curve, the relationship leads directly to the idea that the market-share level is critical for business success, because it is achieved by economies of scale and learned expertise. This holds true for both large and small companies. Some growth-oriented companies can often develop economies of scale quicker than large firms.

# The Integrated Strategy

"Strategy" is the term we use to define what the business will be and in which direction the company resources will be applied to sustain growth. Strategy development begins with a situation analysis for the business. Next comes the definition of why the company is in business. From these two steps, a purpose for the company can be clarified. Following these two steps comes an analysis of possible resource-development moves. Competitive moves in the market can be anticipated at this point, and marketing-resource deployment can be assessed, together with the financial state of the company.

After these factors are known, several alternative strategies are compared. From this analysis, a strategic business plan is written to direct the company either forward on a growth program or possibly to a retrenchment position. The strategic plan identifies the most effective means of deploying corporate resources in relation to the changing characteristics of the business environment. More directly slated, strategic planning is the process by which a business prepares to maintain or change its competitiveness in the marketplace. Strategic plans are dynamic and must change to ensure business continuity. The frequency of change is small firms may be more often than in larger firms.

# Defining the Business

Strategy formation begins with an analysis of what the company is doing presently. To get started, one must first define the boundaries of the business. The major boundaries of a business include:[3]

- geography served
- products and services
  - currently offered
  - planned
- customers served
  - by geography
  - buying patterns
  - industry
  - distribution

These boundaries must be compared with the results obtained with expanded boundaries that may result from penetration of related businesses or unserved market sectors.

Next, the main company operations must be examined for resource definition. The following outline can be used as a guide:

- staff
  - skills
  - experience
- technology
  - product
  - process
  - operation
- cost structure
  - value added
  - experience curve
  - inventories and accounts receivable
- financial aspect
  - cash-flow sources and uses
  - profit and loss
  - balance sheet
- strengths and weaknesses
- historical performance
  - reason for changes
  - original strategies

As the analysis proceeds, a definition of what the firm is and does will unfold.

Timing issues are extremely important to small businesses. All plans involve both achievement and schedules. Industries and companies have natural rhythms that have to be planned for. For example, one major growth strategy may be as simple as changing the timing of new-product introductions. To change requires knowledge of the present conditions so that the timing of the following can be identified:

- product development
- manufacturing
- product life cycle
- technology life cycle
- order-completion cycle
- capital purchasing
- acquisition of staff
- acquisition of capital

At this time, the firm may have identified many problem areas. A typical list of the problems that are presently common to the small business includes:[4]

- standards of costing/pricing
- irrational competitors
- product life cycles
- situation dynamics
- R&D funding
- lack of data
- no apparent strategy

The last important area necessary to define the business is the firm's environment. For small firms intent on growth, this is the weakness-analysis area. The present environment is always changing. Successful-growth companies read these changes quickly and capitalize on the opportunities presented. The environment can be characterized by the following elements:

- economic environment
  - government regulation
  - inflation
  - interest rates
  - GNP
- technical environment
  - trends
  - other technologies available
  - life cycle
- ecological social/political environment
  - new processes
  - modernization vs. new plant and equipment
  - changes in inventories served

# Strategy Formulation

There are several steps that can be taken to reduce the complexity of the planning process. The most common, which is usually available to small businesses, is to merge strategies. Most small companies should develop a corporate strategy. Market and product strategies need not be separated and developed on their own. For a small growth-oriented company, the corporate strategy will lead to the appropriate action plans when concentration on objectives is stressed.

The next task in the strategic-planning process is to identify discrepancies between the conditions revealed in the situation analysis and the desirable conditions. Three areas should be stressed at this point:

- comparison and contrasts of the firm's capabilities in each identified key success factor
- competitive strengths and weaknesses
- current situation compared with corporate objectives

There may be discrepancies in each area, and adjustments must be made in order to point the strategic plan toward the elimination of the variances. The strategic plan will involve risks, and the strategy planner has to make the distinctions between avoidable and unavoidable risks that can be successfully dealt with.

Creativity in studying the discrepancies is important. The company may not be strong enough in a key area for success for example, the numbers of engineers in R&D. But the firm may recognize that a computer-aided design system will leverage the design team and improve the competition position. The strategic plan should consider whether the acquisition of a computer-aided design system will improve the company's competitive position or whether other changes are necessary. If the value added from marketing, sales, and service is increasing rapidly, perhaps part of engineering can be subcontracted without sacrificing quality or margins.

Similarly, the impact of weakness in comparison to competitors may be minimized by strategies that hasten changes in the industry or change the importance of key success factors. Improving product reliability to reduce service calls is a strong selling point against a competitor with a strong service organization.

Formulating strategies is not a cookbook process. The following ideas are suggested as a framework from which a successful strategy can be developed. No guarantees are available in defining the one best strategy. The firm will evolve into the best strategy by practice, careful analysis of competitive moves, and periodic planning updates.

Describing the business after the situation analysis is complete will differ from the original analysis, but it should be consistent with the owners'/CEO's personal objectives, strategic logic, and corporate objectives. It is the description of what the business should be after the strategic plan is implemented. The business activities included in the description must be aimed at exploiting the firm's strengths. As far as possible, the description should be consistent with long-term defensive goals.

Several possible strategies should be examined. Examples of one-dimensional strategies that can be used as patterns for formulating custom-growth strategies are presented below:[5]

- **technology-strategy options**
  create a new technology

  - exploit advanced technology
  - follow up on technology development
  - apply technology in product, processes, or services
  - improve firm's share of available technology
  - protect critical technologies
  - ensure security of technology base
- **product-strategy options**
  - product offering by type
  - differentiated products from competition
  - product breadth
  - product plus limited service
  - product plus application expertise
  - product plus full line service
- **product-pricing strategy**
  - high—sell on performance, quality, and specification
  - equal to competition—sell on substitution or system-cost criteria
  - low—sell on limited substitution criteria

This is not exhaustive but is intended to focus on those strategies that will promote growth for the small industrial manufacturing firms.

Two-dimensional strategies are more sophisticated than those already discussed, but a simple graphical technique shown in Figure 7.1 adds clarification.[6] The figure depicts a way of describing alternative strategies, recognizing that markets and technologies are interrelated. The figure shows, in a two-dimensional format, a company's current position and future opportunities in both technology and markets.

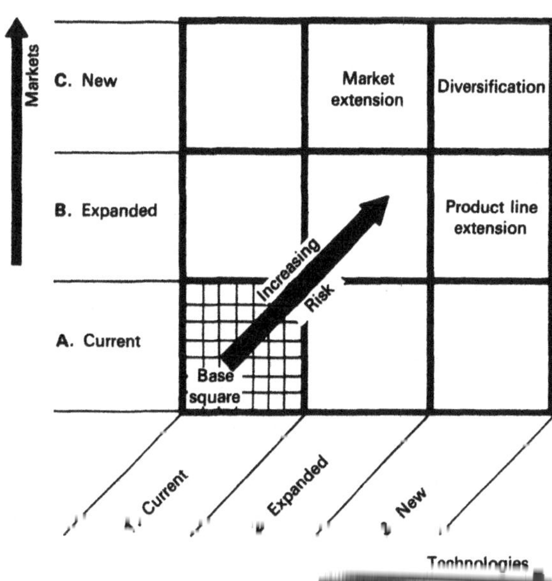


**Figure 7.1**
The Basis for Discussing Alternative Two-dimensional Strategies.

| | Maintain Status Quo | Create New Base Squares | Insure Markets | Maintain Markets via Technology Changes | Maintain Technology via Market Changes | Improve Market/ Technology Position |
|---|---|---|---|---|---|---|
| Caution | | | | | | |
| Risk Reduction | ● | | ● | | | ● |
| Risk Hedging | ● | | ● | ● | ● | ● |
| Risk Diversification | | ● | | | | ● |
| Risk Spreading | ● | ● | | | | ● |
| Evolution | | | | | | |
| Mandatory | | | ● | ● | ● | |
| Elective | | | ● | ● | ● | ● |
| Revolution | | ● | | | | ● |
| Aggression | | ● | | ● | ● | ● |

**Figure 7.2**
Strategic Planning for Smaller Businesses.

The six two-dimensional strategy alternatives are to:

- maintain the status quo
- create new base squares (A1)
- ensure markets
- maintain markets by technology changes
- maintain technology by market changes
- improve both market and technology position

Notice that as the company moves outside the base square, increasing risk is suggested.

However, maintaining the status quo will not proceed toward growth. Competitive strategies, changes in the environment, and the market work against this strategy. It can be shown that trying to keep the company products in square A1 will cause a decline in the company's competitiveness.

Formulated strategies have to account for experience and company-resource deployment to develop and achieve implementation of a strategic plan. Our illustration of a company's style of approach to developing strategies and plans is shown in Figure 7.2.[7] Coupled with the two-dimension strategy matrix, the firm can consider many strategies and plan implementation styles.

Unfortunately, intended strategies do not usually happen by plan. Unstructured considerations not planned for always have to be dealt with. Quite often, small-company business leaders fail to see that experience and its value can be overestimated. Changing the strategy results from a decision made outside of or without consideration for the strategic plan. The decision may correct, but it must be made weighing all the alternatives, and elements affected are a part of the formal strategic-planning process.

In summary, the main points to consider when developing a strategy for the firm are:[8]

- use a list of business discrepancies identified by the situation analysis
- consider the fact that the strategic plan will call for a change in the business
- strategies and the business are dynamic
- capitalize on strengths and understand weaknesses
- use strategies that share costs between activities
- consider costs, cash-flow, and growth alternatives
- develop contingency ideas for future planning

Following the development of several strategies, each should be tested for clarity and consistency with the goals of the CEO and owners. Further, each strategy should be compared with unexpected changes in the market and business environment.

# Evaluation and Selection

To select a strategy from several alternatives, the firm has to evaluate the research done in the strategy-formation process. Often, several strategy alternatives will not pass a cursory examination. But, for those alternative strategies that remain, a systematic process should be used. Techniques include:

- quantifying qualitative information
- handling the lack of data
- financial evaluation
- growth rate check
- nonfinancial criteria
- final selection

These techniques do not ensure that the ultimate strategy will be selected. Success is a painfully slow process when evaluation of much subjective data is involved. However, the alternative is not acceptable for growth-oriented companies.

Quantifying qualitative data is a precise way to present and evaluate information about which the firm can't be totally sure. Generally, a weighing method is used. Major activities performed or involved are listed for the company that are common to competitors, the market, the industry, and the environment. Justification of the weights is subjective but can be enhanced using past experience.

Handling the lack of data requires decision-making analysis and the knowledge of the associated cost to gain the information. Essentially, the task is to assess the probability that perfect information does not exist about competitors or cost of implementation in the future. For example, if the firm's competitor is entering a new market and information is desired, the company may have to pay a consultant to study the market. Suppose it is enough to know the competitor is entering this market. Then the cost of additional "better" information is prohibitive. A computer software package can estimate the cost of perfect information and further increase confidence by probability analysis. These techniques include Monte Carlo analysis, histogram probabilities, and various "what if" analysis techniques.

The financial evaluation has to emphasize the time value of money. Present value and discounted cash-flow analysis should be applied to relate the cost involved of strategy alternatives. If capital investments are called for, the net present value, internal rate of return, and payback period have to be considered. For growth-oriented small businesses, the main concern is how much cash is required before the program starts to generate revenue.

The direct cash-flow calculation method should be employed to check the discounted cash-flow method. Often, a small business does not have the necessary month-to-month cash flow, even though an investment passes all other tests.

Next, a breakeven analysis should be applied if the strategy calls for financial investment. Breakeven analyses can be generated graphically to help determine whether the rate of return from the activity is acceptable. The breakeven calculation shows the point at which revenues equal the total of fixed and variable costs.

Return on investment made in a new program can be deceiving in a small business. Calculating profit from the investment does not account for cash flow. The issue is that of establishing a figure for profit and a suitable investment time frame without examining the fluctuations in cash flow that occur on a daily basis over the period.

The question of growth rate for a small business is quite serious. Rapidly growing businesses are most often derailed due to undercapitalization. In other words, the growing concern can't bring in enough cash from operations, loans, and equity to cover the short-term needs. Aggressive growth strategies require a sanity check, because a firm has to balance debt and equity financing with short-term cash flows. The formula given here is useful to measure the capability of the business to grow.[9]

$$G = P[R + (D/E) \times R - I]$$

where

$G$ = sustainable growth rate/year
$P$ = percent of earnings retained
$R$ = return on net assets
$D/E$ = debt-to-equity ratio
$I$ = effective interest rate on debt after allowing for income tax

Caution has to be used when applying this formula, because debt has to be repaid from earnings. It would be better to use the ratio of extra debt to be incurred for the strategic plan under consideration to the incremental equity available to calculate the program's sustainable growth rate.

The final quantitative evaluation comes from generating pro-0forma operating statements. These statements do not provide the same precision as the cash-flow test, but the time horizon is extended over several years. In this way, alternative strategies can be assessed over the longer term.

Nonfinancial criteria include the evaluation of contingency plans and a description of the risk involved. The action plans called for by the strategic plan have to be backed up with alternative plans to satisfy the strategy. The problem is to isolate what caused missed sales targets so a correction plan can be implemented. Early feedback is the key to using contingency plans successfully.

Classification of risks is again a judgmental process. However, if the results of the previous planning period have been recorded, then risks can be compared from experience. The final analysis rests with the CEO, whose decisions are the final strategy criterion.

To make the final decision on selecting the growth strategy for the firm requires a choice of trade-offs between sustaining cash flow and maintaining the growth objectives. If no strategy can be selected after this process, then modifications to do the strategy must be considered. In some cases, a combined strategy will work. More likely, the successful firm will implement the simplest strategy that receives the highest evaluation. The surviving strategy is reduced to action plans, and the results measured for success.

## NOTES


1. Bernard A. Rousch, *Strategic Marketing Planning* (Boston: Amacom, A Division of American Management Associations, 1982).
2. Dereck F. Abel, *Strategic Market Planning* (New Jersey: Prentice Hall, 1979).
3. David A. Curtis, *Strategic Planning for Smaller Businesses* (Lexington: D.C. Heath & Co., 1983), p. 94.
4. *Ibid*, p. 96.
5. *Ibid*, p. 121 (adaptation).
6. *Ibid*, p. 124.
7. *Ibid*, p. 134.
8. *Ibid*, p. 135.
9. *Ibid*, pp. 154–155.


## ESSAY QUESTIONS

1. What are the fundamental differences between strategic planning in the large company and strategic planning in the small company?
2. What fundamental differences exist in the human-resource management function between large and small companies?
3. What are common types of competitive positions for small firms?
4. What types of strategies are available for small firms that opt to be followers?
5. What are the [illegible] of a market niche?
6. What is the best way for a small firm to perform a situation analysis?

## MULTIPLE-CHOICE QUESTIONS

1. Most small business strategies tend to be:
   **a.** marketing oriented
   **b.** production oriented
   **c.** engineering oriented
   **d.** all the above
2. The interaction of marketing, sales, production and R&D is called a ____________ strategy.
   **a.** global
   **b.** functional
   **c.** small business
   **d.** strategic
3. Ideas for new products generally come from:
   **a.** sales feedback from customers
   **b.** customer surveys
   **c.** CEO and marketing brainstorming sessions
   **d.** all the above
4. Small companies very often struggle with acceptance of product life-cycle strategies of ____________ and ____________.
   **a.** limited resources; poor management
   **b.** not enough customers; poor financing
   **c.** poor sales staff; subpar products/services
   **d.** all the above
5. Challenger strategies are generally more successful if they focus on ____________.
   **a.** market domination
   **b.** carving out a niche
   **c.** new product development
   **d.** improving market share
6. Firms that pick key areas to follow are called:
   **a.** distant followers
   **b.** selective followers
   **c.** dominant followers
   **d.** none of the above
7. Small firms that adopt a niche strategy must be willing to ____________ to ensure growth.
   **a.** retrench
   **b.** reduce manpower
   **c.** diversify
   **d.** cultivate existing products
8. The STEEP factors for situational analysis are sociological, technical, economic, environmental and ____________.
   **a.** production
   **b.** people
   **c.** political
   **d.** promotional
9. Small-business strategies and large-business strategies both rely on the use of learning curves.
   **a.** true
   **b.** false
10. Techniques looked at for the final evaluation and selection of a strategy include
   **a.** quantifying qualitative data

**b.** financial evaluation
**c.** nonfinancial criteria evaluation
**d.** all the above.

# CASE STUDY: Victoria's Secret

What is Victoria's Secret? Victoria's Secret is one of the most successful marketing phenomena of the decade. All around the country, Victoria's Secret boutiques and bath shops are becoming as ubiquitous as McDonalds, and currently number over 600. Victoria's Secret takes a softer, more feminine approach to selling women's underwear. Tastefully decorated, the stores create a relaxed, unfrenzied shopping experience in very desirable boudoir-like atmosphere. Merchandise is removed from hangers and shelves and tucked into drawers, soft music is gently piped in the air, and an ever-present fragrance of potpourri fills the air. The once low-margin business called "foundations," usually designated to a remote corner of a high floor of a department store, has exploded to a new high and lingerie is now proudly and openly displayed in most department and discount stores.

## History

Roy Raymond, a Stanford MBA graduate, started Victoria's Secret in 1977. After studying the market for eight years, Raymond opened the first of many stores in a shopping mall with $40,000 and the help of his parents. His mother did the books, his father helped with the inventory, and his wife manned the counter. Raymond's concept was simplicity itself: Men were embarrassed to buy lingerie for their wives or girlfriends. He wanted to make them feel comfortable. The only outlets at that time were "corsetière" salons in department stores, often secluded, hidden, and considered forbidden places to men. With this in mind, special attention was paid to even the smallest of detail—the creation of a "friendly" atmosphere, one to help men feel at ease. The shops were designed and arranged by Raymond himself. The decor was done in dusty rose and dark wood, private, fanciful, and a little bit sexy. He further insisted that every purchase, no matter how small, be wrapped in tissue and sealed with a gold foil sticker. (The stickers cost fifty cents apiece.) He wanted every customer to feel as if she were opening a present. That was part of "the secret" to make women feel good about themselves, and in turn, desire to make more purchases from Victoria's Secret.

Raymond had been a catalog buff since he was 10 years old and had produced a catalog, not unlike Victoria Secret's current one. The main difference was that Raymond was now selling high-quality, rather expensive lingerie—Lejaby, Dior, Hanro—considerably more upmarket than what is usually found today and decidedly more so than Frederick's of Hollywood.[1] Raymond was very careful to set his stores apart from Frederick's, which had the only other lingerie catalog. Raymond hired top photographers, stylists, and models from New York and Paris and changed the whole concept of marketing and retailing of intimate apparel. Victoria's Secret catalogs are well known, and the models have become incredibly popular. The catalog targets women 18–49 years of age and has the highest profitability and fastest growth rate of any catalog in the U.S. In 1990, catalog sales alone reached over $250 million.[2]

Victoria's Secret did well under Raymond and by 1982 had five stores and annual sales of $6 million.[3] Soon, rapid growth became a problem and Raymond needed backing since expansion was ahead of capital. Because Victoria's Secret was becoming [illegible] Raymond sought venture capital. Leslie Wexner,

CEO of The Limited, a Columbus, Ohio–based company, had brand identification and The Limited had a proven retail track record and money. Raymond accepted Wexner's offer.

## Original Plan

Wexner's plan was to take the business up to 700–1,000 stores. Since Raymond did not want to be part of that big an operation, he sold the boutiques, the concept, and the name for a million dollars worth of Limited stock. Raymond was assured that he would keep his job and had every intention of staying involved with the business. Raymond saw it as an opportunity to learn from Wexner, "a tuition-free supplement to business school." But Raymond never received any income from future grosses. He received payment in stock and terminated his involvement with Wexner. Raymond spent every penny he had—$4 million—trying to duplicate the success of Victoria's Secret. He lost it all in the process. Raymond never really got over giving up his business and many times openly stated he felt that he failed and should have been able to obtain the necessary financing to save it.[4] On August 26, 1993 Roy Raymond committed suicide by jumping off the Golden Gate Bridge.

## Wexner's Secret

The growth of Victoria's Secret under Wexner has been astonishing. In 1990, sales rocketed to $900 million and Wexner's goal was to hit $1.5 billion by the mid-1990s. The stores and catalogs were two separate yet connected divisions. The President of Victoria's Secret stores, Grace Nichols, says while the target market originally was directed toward men, this has changed. Her current mission is the 30–40-something woman. Both the catalog and store divisions of Victoria's Secret are headed by women.

Grace Nichols and Cynthia Fedus, president of the catalog sector, are both very quality oriented, with a strong emphasis on attacking a problem head-on. They both share the philosophy that "quality is not a place you get to, because the goal always gets higher."[5] There have been new developments as well as some new problems. Issues of poor quality and out-of-stock on many items are two of the biggest complaints and problems facing Victoria's Secret in both the catalog and store divisions.

Specifically, the panties sold at Victoria's Secret have been scrutinized as lower quality—they fail to hold up to repeated washings and the lingerie, in general, has been criticized as poor as well. At a recent board meeting, Ms. Nichols introduced a "new and improved" panty, which is guaranteed to stand up to 40 washings, with improved stitching and material. An indicator of persistent quality problems is the 5% decline in same-store sales for the first quarter of 1993.[6]

Inventory control and reordering are two technical components being targeted for improvement, as well as the adoption of a new calendar for its test marketing to ensure an adequate supply. In addition, a linkup with big suppliers like Vanity Fair and Haynes via a computerized reorder system, which would generate an order on its own when supplies in the distribution get low, is in the works. After much convincing and proven sales, Victoria's Secret obtained its own private-label goods with guaranteed exclusivity and better profit margins. This was a strategic move that paid dividends. Today, Victoria's Secret is Vanity Fair's biggest customer, buying $75 million worth of lingerie every year.[7]

A few years ago, Victoria's Secret customers started asking if they could buy recordings of the foreground music they heard in the shops. Ever alert to an incremental sale, Wexner produced the first album. His latest move is the packaged five-album boxed set that is available via the catalog and in the stores. The albums are so popular that five out of 10 of the classical music albums that have ever gone platinum (meaning a million or more) are sold by Victoria's Secret.[8] Wexner started out by offering the first album on cassette as a free gift with a purchase of $50 or more . . . the rest is history.

Despite the fact that Leslie Wexner attempted to support U.S. textile manufacturers when shopping for material, he was not very successful. He searched for a specific velour-type terry cloth to fill an order and wanted to "buy American." Wexner approached many U.S. mills only to find that no one made the terry cloth, nor were any of them willing to do a special run. Wexner has been criticized for importing fabric from other countries.[9]

Victoria's Secret had estimated sales of $950 million in 1992 with a 18.4% margin. But same-store sales only rose 5% in 1991 after four years of double-digit growth. Wexner's new strategy was to expand more into the perfume and fine toiletries sector. Perfumeries were installed in 50 stores by Christmas 1993 with the hopes of building fragrance into a $500 billion business by the year 2000.[10]

## Background on The Limited

The Limited, based in Columbus, Ohio, runs several separate divisions: Limited, Express, Lerner, Lane Bryant, and Victoria's Secret. The Limited and Lerner have a combined 1,700 stores and almost $2.3 billion in sales for 1991, representing 37% of the parent company's total.

In 1992 Howard Gross, who had been in charge of Victoria's Secret stores through the five years of great growth, was handed the presidency of Limited Stores, Inc. He was told to "do whatever it takes to turn around the business" and fix the failing stores. During his first year in charge, sales in stores open for a year or more fell 5% and profits went down 56% to $102 million with total sales of $1.2 billion. Part of his overall strategy was to turn around the image of The Limited from fashion-oriented "throwaway clothes" to one of high-quality clothing. He fired 70% of the prior merchandising team and hired top merchants from Sak's 5th Avenue and R. H. Macy & Co. He found factories in Italy and Asia that manufactured clothes for upscale designers. However, this strategy and Gross's efforts were not fruitful. Both Lerner and Limited have suffered. His buying team was in turmoil, and four of his top buyers resigned after less than a year with Gross. The new image of attracting women with taste for better quality and less "glitz" was slow but Gross was convinced that with time, this would turn around.

## Current Plan

In March 1995, Wexner announced that he was considering a split of most of the operations into two public companies—one for the apparel stores and the other for the faster-growing lingerie and toiletries units. This was an attempt to pump up undervalued stock. The stock had been depressed by a prolonged slump at Limited's women's apparel units, which last year accounted for almost 60% of the company's $7.32 billion in sales. Hopefully, the split would encourage investors to value Limited's "parts" more highly than the "whole."[11]

With this announcement, Limited's stock immediately went up to 12% in heavy trading, closing at $22, up $2.38. The split would put Limited, Express, Lerner, New York, and Lane Bryant under one company. The other company would include Victoria's Secret and Cacique lingerie units as well as the Bath & Body Works and Penhligon's toiletries chains. Limited plans to keep control of both companies and will offer 10–15% stock in each one to the public (see Figure 7.3).

Wexner is looking for "strategic financial and marketing partners" for its proprietary credit-card operations with receivables of more than $1.3 billion. They may [illegible] in the operations. Cash proceeds from such a sale and from the two stock offerings would be distributed to Limited's shareholders. The offerings alone could raise more than $1.2 billion, resulting in a special dividend of $5–8 per share. Standard & Poor's Ratings Group and Moody's Investor Service both cited concern that The Limited's plan will "affect a large majority of its earnings and cash flow" and could diminish its credit quality. About $650 million in senior debt and commercial paper is affected.

The plan puts the spotlight on the Victoria's Secret chain, which contributed $1.18 billion (25% of total revenue, 37% operating profit) in store sales and $569 million in catalog sales for the fiscal year ending January 28, 1994, representative of a 23% increase.[12]

## Future Plans

Plans for Victoria's Secret include expanding into furnishing, primarily bed and bath, towels, gifts, and accessories. Also under consideration is a second catalog and separate retail stores. Wexner said "a company that values names and access to customers could bring in marketing and sales and create an opportunity for it to grow, which is something we're not capable of. Selling the operations outright would not be a very attractive option".[13]

## QUESTIONS

1. Was Victoria's Secret created with a focused strategy? A target market in mind?
2. Did a niche exist in the market?
3. What opportunities and threats exist for Victoria's Secret before the split up and afterwards?
4. What internal strengths must exist for Victoria's Secret to keep growing?

Limited would remain a public company, with 85% to 90% stakes in two new public companies composed, respectively, of a lingerie and personal-care unit and a women's apparel unit. Limited would retain 100% ownership of other ventures.

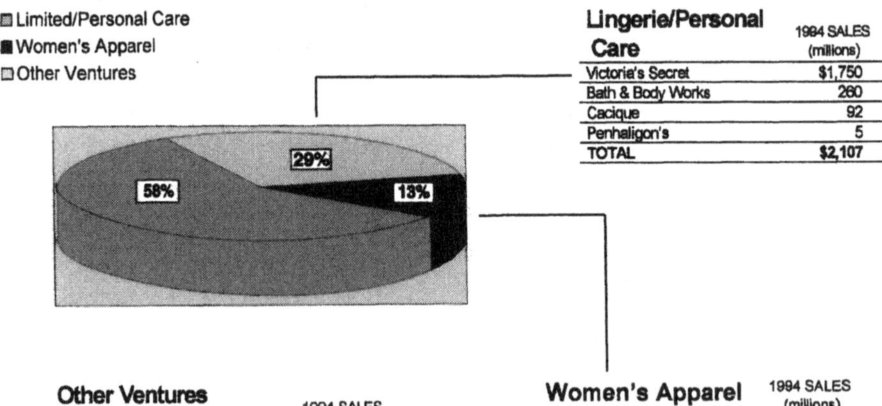


**Lingerie/Personal Care**

| | 1994 SALES (millions) |
|---|---|
| Victoria's Secret | $1,750 |
| Bath & Body Works | 260 |
| Cacique | 92 |
| Penhaligon's | 5 |
| TOTAL | $2,107 |

**Other Ventures**
Limited retains 100% ownership

| | 1994 SALES (millions) |
|---|---|
| Structure | $555 |
| Limited Too | 174 |
| Abercrombie & Fitch | 165 |
| Henri Bendel | 84 |
| TOTAL | [illegible] |

[illegible] fiscal year ended Jan. 28, 1995

**Women's Apparel**

| | 1994 SALES (millions) |
|---|---|
| Express | $1,387 |
| Lerner New York | 1,018 |
| Lane Bryant | 959 |
| Limited | 869 |
| TOTAL | [illegible] |

[illegible]

**Figure 7.3**
How the New Limited [illegible] Would Look

## NOTES

1. "When Victoria's Secret Faltered, She Was Quick To Fix It," *The New York Times*, November 21, 1993, Section F-10, Col. I–III.
2. Holly Brubach, "Mail Order America," *The New York Times Magazine*, November 21, 1993, p. 54, Col. 1.
3. Dodie Kazanjian, "Vogue's View," *Vogue*, April 1992, p. 218.
4. Johanna Schneller, "Death of a Dream Merchant," *Gentleman's Quarterly*, September 1994, p. 194.
5. Dodie Kazanjian, "Vogue's View," *Vogue*, April 1992, p. 218.
6. Laura Zinn, "No Off-The-Rack Solutions Here," *Business Week*, May 25, 1992, p. 116.
7. Amy Feldman, "Leslie Wexner's Classical Act," *Forbes*, December 20, 1993, p. 20.
8. Ibid.
9. Walecia Konrad, "Why Leslie Wexner Shops Overseas," *Business Week*, February 3, 1992, p. 30.
10. Holly Brubach, "Mail Order America," *The New York Times*, November 21, 1993.
11. Laura Bird, "Limited Is Weighing Splitting Operations Into Two Companies," *The Wall Street Journal*, March 29, 1995, Section A-3, Col. II.
12. Ibid.
13. Ibid.

# CHAPTER 8 Multinational Strategies

## Introduction

Multinational enterprises that manage global systems of trade, production, technology, and finance demonstrate the highest degree of multinational involvement and foreign-market penetration. Although most of these companies tend to be large (they include almost all the Fortune 500), several medium-size companies have also become multinational enterprises and are impressive in the international sophistication of their management. They did not start that way. The actual historical experience of U.S. manufacturers indicates that the process of internationalization is likely to be a gradual evolution over time.

## Why Go International?

Ultimately, the answer to this question is specific to each company. In general terms, however, it can be said that companies go international when they can no longer achieve their strategic objectives by remaining at home. They may go abroad to:

- achieve profitable growth that is blocked at home by saturated or slow-growing markets
- keep up with domestic competitors, the so-called bandwagon effect
- follow their domestic customers who are going international
- earn additional income on existing technology
- take advantage of faster-growing foreign economies
- spread fixed manufacturing and development costs over larger sales volume
- compete more effectively with foreign companies invading their home markets
- achieve other objectives

For the most part, however, these objectives become explicit only after a company has made its first, tentative venture into foreign markets. The impulse behind that first entry—almost always as an exporter—is simply the prospect of obtaining profits on immediate sales. Only later, after some success in casual exporting, do companies begin to design strategies for a sustained buildup of international business over the long run. To do so, their management must cast off popular misconceptions about international business.

# Misconceptions about International Business

Several misconceptions about international business have prevented U.S. manufacturer from taking the first step into foreign markets. The following are some of that more prominent ones.

**MISCONCEPTION #1:** *The skills needed to manage international payments (handling foreign exchange, financing sales, ensuring payment, etc.) or the are beyond the capabilities of our managers, who have only domestic experience.* Most certainly, the management of international payments appears mysterious and often threatening to the domestic executive; however, these fears are unwarranted, because the executive can easily obtain the assistance of banks that specialize in international payments arrangements. Furthermore, because most U.S. export shipments are payable in dollars, the risk of adverse fluctuations in exchange rates is usually borne by the foreign importer.[1] The executive with an open mind will find that he or she can learn about international payments in an intense, but short, learning experience.

**MISCONCEPTION #2:** *Export sales are just too complicated, with all sorts of documentary requirements, like special price quotations, involved transportation arrangements, foreign custom clearance, and so on.* It certainly is true that the requirements of export shipments are more demanding than domestic shipments. However, once again, the manufacturer can easily obtain the assistance of specialists, such as international forwarders, who will take care of most of the details of export shipments. Because shipment is intimately linked with financing and payments, banks also offer assistance in meeting documentary requirements.

**MISCONCEPTION #3:** *We just don't know anything about foreign markets, and it's hard to find out anything about them.* As a matter of fact, a great deal of information about foreign markets may be acquired quickly, and at little cost, from a variety of secondary sources: the U.S. and State governments, foreign governments, international and regional organizations, banks, trade associations, and other agencies, as well as from numerous publications.

**MISCONCEPTION #4:** *Risks are far higher in international business than in domestic business.* This statement is inapplicable unless both the risk and the foreign country are identified. Once this is done, it becomes evident that risks vary within the same country or between countries. More fundamentally, the international economy should not be viewed as a jungle. For example, the major trading countries are committed to observe certain rules in their treatment of foreign [illegible] participants in the General Agreement on Tariff and Trade (GATT). Furthermore, the United States has scores of bilateral agreements with foreign countries covering trade, investment, industrial property rights, taxation, and other subjects of concern to international business. Beyond these formal agreements, national governments are unlikely to introduce radical changes in their treatment of foreign trade and investment because they fear retaliation, to say nothing of other economic costs. For the most part, therefore, the international economy can be considered as a regulated environment.

All this is not to deny that political risks (the risks that rise from government actions adverse to foreign business interest) may be much higher in some countries than in the United States (where they are by no means entirely absent). However, it is possible for the U.S. company to manage political risks in the same objective way it manages the usual business risks. There is no basis, therefore, for describing international business as generally riskier than domestic business. Indeed, for some risks in some foreign countries, business may be less risky than business at home!

**MISCONCEPTION #5:** *International business demands a great deal of capital and careful management.* This misconception derives from ignorance about the many modes of foreign entry, ranging from indirect exporting to full-scale foreign manufacturing. At one extreme, indirect exporting requires zero or only modest commitments of capital and management because the export job is undertaken by an intermediary located in the United States. At the other extreme, full-scale manufacturing abroad may involve substantial capital investment and specialized management teams at both the parent company and the subsidiary. The important point here is that international business is open to small and big companies alike, as long as they offer distinctive products and skills to the market.

The foregoing misconceptions reduce to a general misconception that international business is totally different from domestic business. Certainly, business environments in foreign countries differ from the U.S. business environment, but the principles of good management are the same everywhere. Less common is an opposing general misconception that international business is the same as domestic business. This misconception springs from narrow attitudes that predispose U.S. managers to believe that what works best for their companies in the United States will also work best abroad. This misconception (ordinarily implicit rather than explicit) has caused many blunders and unfortunately encourages U.S. companies to undertake foreign ventures that are ill-designed for success.[2]

# Three-Stage Evolution

The transition from domestic to multinational enterprise may be described as an evolution in three stages: the export stage, the foreign production stage, and the multinational-enterprise stage.

## THE EXPORT STAGE

The export stage ordinarily starts with an unsolicited inquiry about a company's products from a domestic-export intermediary or direct from a prospective foreign buyer. When the inquiry results in a profitable sale, the manufacturer follows up subsequent inquiries and makes sales to other foreign buyers, probably through domestic export middlemen. At some point, however, the manufacturer decides that his or her export business should be actively developed, and to that end, he or she appoints an export manager with a small staff. If the manufacturer experiences a continuing growth of export sales, the inadequacy of a small, built-in export department becomes evident. The next step, then, is to establish a full-service export department at the same level as the domestic sales department. Further growth of export sales may justify the establishment of sales branches overseas to replace foreign agents and distributors and even assembly operations to obtain lower transportation and/or tariff costs.

The manufacturer has now evolved toward a systematic export program supported by market research, advertising, and other forms of promotion. The company may be selling full-product lines in many of the foreign markets, and its other export sales may be 10% or more of total company sales. However, the manufacturer still depends entirely on exports (including assembly operations) to penetrate foreign markets.

For a comparatively small number of high-technology firms, licensing may be the mode of the first entry into international business. Licensing does not require capital investment and poses few risks to the newcomer. The manufacturer simply licenses the use of its patents, production know-how, or trademarks to an independent foreign producer in return for royalty payments. A pure licensing agreement means that the manufacturer can substitute an export of someone else's technology for the export of its own products.

The first stage in the evolution of a multinational company ends when the manufacturer decides to enter foreign markets by means of foreign production under one or more arrangements.

## THE FOREIGN PRODUCTION STAGE

Most exporting manufacturers prefer to stay out of foreign production. Exports and licensing, however, are not always sufficient to achieve a manufacturer's objectives in foreign markets. The most common explanations of this situation are high tariffs or other import barriers imposed by governments, and more intense competition within a foreign market. Consequently, the motivation behind the first entry into production is usually a defensive step taken to maintain an existing export market. Nevertheless, the first direct investment by a manufacturing company in foreign-production facilities marks a critical step in its evolution as an international company. (Because most U.S. manufacturers are inclined to view investment in Canada as domestic rather than foreign, it is their first investment outside the United States and Canada that becomes the critical step.) For the first time, the manufacturer commits substantial financial, managerial, and technical resources to an international venture. It now becomes exposed to risks (such as expropriation) that go far beyond the risks associated with exporting or licensing. To a far greater extent than before, the entry into foreign production most often involves top management of a company in decisions relating to international business.

The first investment abroad traditionally paves the way for later investments. Eventually, plants may be established in several countries to produce all or part of the manufacturer's product lines. At the same time, the manufacturer will continue to export domestic products to other countries and, increasingly, to its own foreign subsidiaries. The manufacturer also continues to license technology abroad, but mostly to its own affiliates rather than to independent foreign manufacturers. At the end of the foreign-production stage, the U.S. manufacturers will be penetrating markets throughout the world by means of several foreign-production bases, in conjunction with exports from the United States. The management of these diverse far-flung operations places new strains on the planning, organizing, and controlling functions of the parent company. To accommodate those strains, management moves toward global concept of a single-enterprise system that marks the beginning of the multinational-enterprise stage.

## THE MULTINATIONAL-ENTERPRISE STAGE

A company becomes multinational when its management starts to plan, organize, and control its total operations on a worldwide scale. Such a company both poses and answers questions such as:

- Where in the world are our best markets?
- Where in the world should we manufacturer products for these markets?
- Where in the world should we obtain financing for our capital investments and current operations?
- Where in the world should we recruit people to staff our global system?

During the foreign-production stage, a manufacturer tends to follow a binational strategy with respect to foreign markets. It may perceive each foreign market as unique and separate from other national markets, thereby ignoring potential relations among them and among its manufacturing affiliates located in different countries. However, at the multinational stage, the manufacturer replaces binational strategy with global strategy. National markets are now viewed as segments of broader regional and world markets. As a consequence, managers must concentrate their energies on building intra-enterprise flows of products, technology, capital, and personnel among their many affiliates in order to take advantage of international specialization and economies of scale.

Only a minority of international companies have reached the multinational stage.[3] Although their numbers will almost certainly grow both in the United States and in other advanced countries, the majority of U.S. manufacturers that engage in international business will probably remain in the exporting stage, and other manufacturers will probably not move beyond the foreign-production stage. Of course, the great majority of U.S. manufacturers will remain wholly domestic in their orientation. Thus, there is no inevitable progression to the multinational stage. Nor should one consider multinational strategy necessarily superior to exporting strategy. Limitations of size will prevent many U.S. manufacturers from entering foreign production or will permit entry only on a modest scale. The important point is that manufacturers should choose those entry strategies that promise to be most effective in attaining company objectives. For some, a succession of entry strategies over time will bring an evolution to a multinational enterprise and, for others, an evolution to more and more sophisticated export management and operations.

# Designing Entry Strategies

A company may choose as its corporate strategy one or more paths to long-run profitable growth:

- greater penetration of old markets at home with old products (increased market share)
- the development of new markets at home for old products (adding market segments)
- the introduction of new products to serve old markets (product replacement)
- the introduction of new products to serve new markets at home (product diversification)
- the entry into foreign markets with old and/or new products (international business)

It follows that foreign-growth strategies should be assessed against domestic-growth strategies if a company intends to allocate its resources rationally over the long-term future. For the purpose of this analysis, it is assumed that such an assessment has been made in favor of foreign market entry. The next section is directed at how a company should plan that entry.

# A Planning Model

The foreign market entry strategy of a company is a comprehensive plan that determines the objectives and policies that will guide growth of its international business over a period of time long enough to encompass economic, political, and other factors critical to success in foreign markets. For most companies, the entry-strategy period probably runs from three to five years. For some companies, it may be only a year; for other companies, a decade or more. The important point is that the planning period should be long enough to compel managers to raise and answer fundamental questions about the future direction and scope of their company's international business operations. Also, the planning period should encompass the effects of decisions that are taken in accordance with the plan. For the convenience of this analysis, it is assumed that the entry-strategy period is on the order of from three to five years.

Although one may speak of a company's foreign-entry strategy as if it were a single plan, it is actually the end result of many individual product market plans

Basically, managers should plan the entry (or reentry) of each product in each foreign market. The individual plans should then be brought together and reconciled to form the overall foreign market-entry strategy of the company. The constituent product-market plans often involve:

- the choice of a target market
- the choice of a market objectives
- the choice of a market-entry mode or modes
- the monitoring of market performance that may lead to a subsequent revision of market objectives and entry modes

Thus, each product-market plan defines a course of action over the next three to five years to achieve defined objectives in a target foreign market. When we speak of exporting, licensing, and production abroad as foreign market entry strategies, we are speaking, therefore, of the complete strategic plans.

Some managers in small and medium-size companies may believe that only big companies can afford strategic planning for foreign market entry. They often identify such planning as using elaborate analytical techniques applied by expert planners to a large body of quantitative data. This approach, however, is unlikely to succeed. Fundamentally, market-entry planning is an effort to chart the future course of a company's international operations by using reason and facts rather than depending on hunch or day-to-day decisions. What is important is the idea of planning a foreign market entry, irrespective of how limited its resources may be. The very activity of systematically thinking about where a company's international business should be five years from now, and what will be needed to get there, can instill a creative spirit in managers. To say that a company cannot afford a foreign market entry strategy is to say that it cannot afford to think systematically about its future.

The elements of the entry-strategy planning process for a specific target market are shown in Figure 8.1. Although these elements are presented as a logical sequence of activities and decisions, this sequence is not unidirectional. Quite the

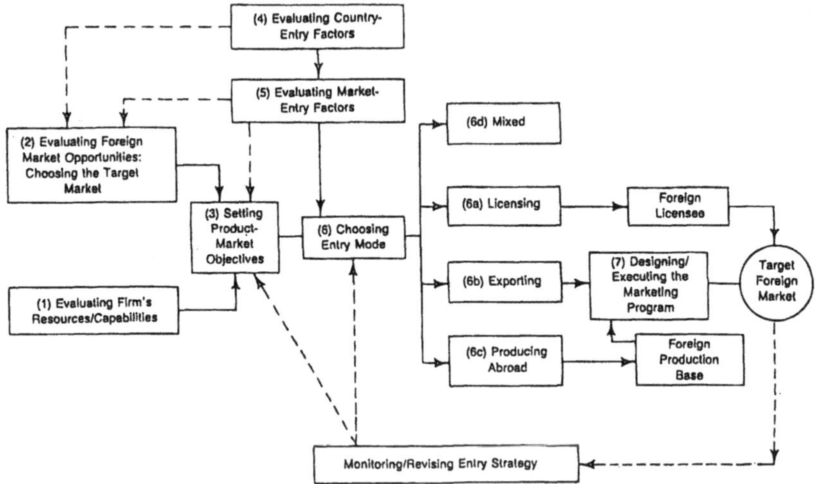


**Figure 8.1**
Entry-Strategy Planning.

opposite, the planning process is iterative through time and has many feedback loops (only some of them are shown in Figure 8.1). Evaluation of alternative market-entry modes, for instance, may cause a revision of market objectives or initiate a reassessment of the firm's resources and capabilities. Planning the foreign market entry usually begins with an evaluation of a firm's resources and capabilities. For example, what are the firm's resources in personnel, materials, technology, and capital? Does the firm have distinctive products that can gain a competitive niche in foreign markets? If the firm is already in some foreign markets, what are the strengths and weaknesses of its international business performance? In brief, what are the driving and restraining forces within the firm with respect to foreign market entry? Such questions need to be raised and answered by managers if they are to establish reasonable objectives for a market-entry strategy.

# Choosing Target Markets

Step 2 in Figure 8.1 is the evaluation of foreign market opportunities to choose the best target for the company. Listed below are some questions that must be answered in the evaluation:

- Which countries are prospective target markets for the company's product type?
- Of these prospective targets, which countries offer high market potentials?
- Of the high-potential countries, which country offers the highest sales potential for the company's own products?
- Which market segment, or mix of segments, is optimal in this target market?

The analytical steps by which managers can get answers to these questions are shown in Figure 8.2.

The first step—preliminary screening—identifies foreign markets that warrant further investigation. Because of the large number of national markets, preliminary screening should be done quickly and economically, using readily available information and simple techniques. At the same time, it should be sufficiently discriminating to select prospective target markets from a heterogeneous set of markets. Because the screening is preliminary, it should be comprehensive. Otherwise, managers may ignore countries that offer good prospects for their product types and leave them to more discerning competitors.

Although there is no single best set of screening criteria, they may be classified as general criteria that relate to a particular country and criteria that relate directly to the generic product. Country-specific criteria include population, gross national (or domestic) product, geography, manufacturing as a percentage of national product, per capita income, energy consumption, total imports, imports from the United States, and other significant features of the country. In contrast, product-specific criteria vary from company to company. Based on their experi-

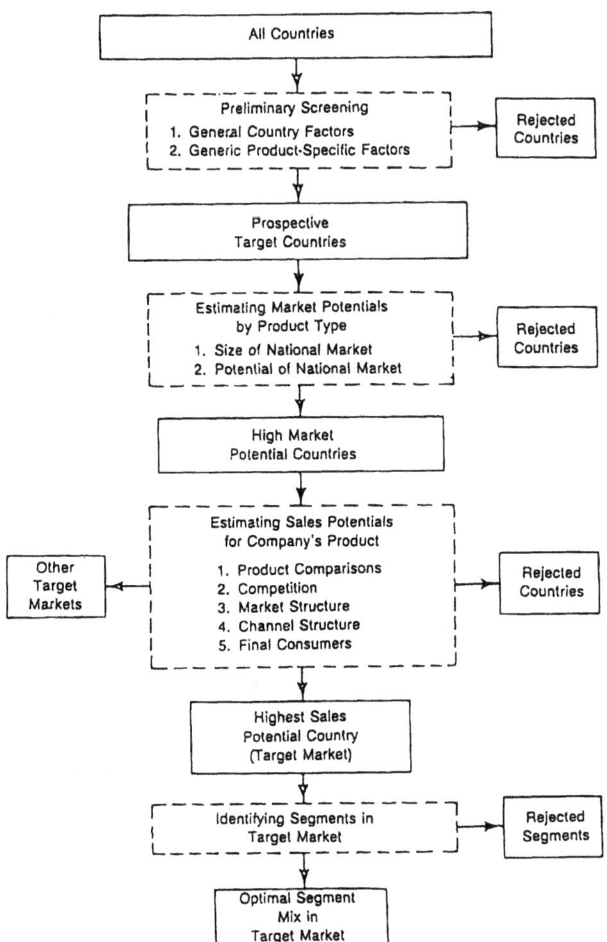


**Figure 8.2** Screening Target Markets.

ence at home or elsewhere, managers should decide what criteria will discriminate among countries with respect to market opportunities for their product. For example, manufacturers of industrial products may use criteria that measure the size and growth of industries they serve; manufacturers of consumer products may use criteria that measure significant household-consumer characteristics. When a country exceeds the minimum (or threshold) values of the criteria employed by a company, it becomes a prospective target country.

The second task is to estimate market potential of a prospective target country. Market potential can be described as the most probable total future sales of a product by all sellers in the designated country over the company's planning period. Several techniques are unavailable to estimate market potentials, such as trend analysis, correlation, and survey methods. However, it is always important to know current and past sales of the product in the market under study. When a generic product is wholly new to a foreign market, then experience in other markets, comparison with older products serving the same market needs, surveys of consumer attitudes, and so on, may prove useful. If actual sales data are not available, managers may be able to estimate apparent consumption from local production, import, and export data. The estimate of a country's market potential provides a quantitative measure of a market in which the manufacturer must find a place if entry is to be successful. It can tell him how big the market is, and how it is most likely to grow over the next three to five years.

The third step is the estimation of the sales potential of a company's own products in a high-market potential country. Sales potential can be described as the maximum sales that a company can reasonably plan for in the foreign market. Alternatively, sales potential is the projection of a company's maximum share of the market potential over the next three to five years. The sales potential is not the same as a sales forecast, which determines the sales goals of current operations; rather, it is usually considered the basis of a market-entry strategy.

To estimate a company's sales potential in a foreign market, managers should evaluate and measure (when feasible) several factors. Probably the first area of investigation should be an appraisal of any entry restriction imposed by the foreign government on inflows of products, technology, and equity investment. This is indicated in Figure 8.1 by the dashed line connecting Box 4 and Box 2. Consideration of country-entry factors together present a key element: The sales potential in a given foreign market will ordinarily depend on the mode of entry chosen by the company. At this stage in planning market-entry strategy, however, country-entry factors are usually evaluated only to the degree necessary to answer the question, Is there an acceptable way the company can enter the market? Full evaluation of these factors is usually undertaken only after the selection of the target market. Thus, sales potential estimates at this stage are tentative, becoming definite for the target market only after the entry mode is decided by management. Although tentative, sales potential estimates should be firm enough to identify with an acceptable degree of confidence the country with the highest sales potential, which becomes the company's target market.

Next, a series of comparisons can be made between the manufacturer's product line and those competitors in the foreign market. The comparisons should go beyond price to encompass quality, design, and other aspects of product differentiation. Nor should the comparisons be confined to the tangible product alone; comparisons also need to be made for before- and after-sales services provided to customers. Finally, comparisons should be made among all products—whether or not in the same industry—that satisfy the same function or need. In the final analysis, the U.S. manufacturer is competing not against other products, but for the favor of potential customers. Other areas of investigation include competition, market structure, channel structure, and the behavior of the final consumers or users of the manufacturer's product line.

The target country market may be heterogeneous, consisting of several submarkets (market segments) that differ significantly in sales potential and in their responses to marketing variables such as price, quality, promotion, and so on. It is desirable, therefore, for the manufacturer to undertake segment analysis of the target market, using criteria that influence sales potential, such as age, sex, income, lifestyle (for a consumer product) or industry, firm, size, and geographical location (for an industrial product). Market-segment analysis can be an important input into the design of the marketing program, apart from its bearing on the choice of market-entry mode.

# Choosing Entry Modes

Once the U.S. manufacturer has selected a foreign target market and has determined its objectives in that market over the planning period, it must decide on the most appropriate mode of entry for its product or product line. A logical entry-decision process requires awareness of the different entry modes available to the company and a comparison of the benefits and costs associated with alternative entry modes for a particular combination of product and market. There are several reasons why the entry-decision process cannot be reduced to a formula or even to a complex quantitative model that is manipulated by a computer. In this regard, it is the same as any other strategy decision.[4]

One reason is the multiplicity of entry modes. Although there are only three primary modes for foreign market—entry-exporting, licensing, and producing abroad—there are many secondary modes within each primary mode. The number of entry modes is further magnified by the possibility of mixed modes of entry that combine two or all three primary modes. Thus, a search for alternative entry modes is an indispensable element of a rational entry-decision process.

Several other reasons make it difficult to compare alternative entry modes. The benefits and costs of each mode must be evaluated in terms of the company's multiple objectives, which are sometimes in conflict. An entry mode that scores highly on one objective (rate of growth in sales) may score low on another objective (profitability). Therefore, managers must decide on the trade-offs between conflicting objectives. In addition, some of the benefits and costs associated with a particular entry mode may be difficult to identify and/or measure. For example, the use of licensing precludes the opportunity to enter a target market with a new mode later on or the licensee's emergence as a competitor in export markets.

Another reason why entry decisions are so complex is that comparisons are made between projected benefits and costs over a future planning period. Managers are, therefore, comparing expected benefits and costs under conditions of partial ignorance. Because a company new to international business is often aware of its ignorance, it is inclined to choose an entry mode that appears to require less experience than other modes. Also, the different entry modes are subject to different sets of risks, with different amounts of company assets exposed to those risks. Therefore, it is management's responsibility to adjust benefits and costs for both market and political risks.

The complexity of the foreign market entry decision makes all the more desirable an analytical framework that facilitates systematic comparisons among alternative entry modes. The framework presented here assumes that one of the few objectives (if not the overriding one) of management is profitability over the planning period. Even though management may not choose that entry mode with the highest profitability because of other objectives, internal constraints, or risk preference, it remains important to know the sacrifice in profitability resulting from an alternative. Furthermore, profitability analysis may rule out certain entry

| | Projected Cash Inflow[1] | Projected Cash Outflow[2] | Net Cash Inflow[3] | Time Adjusted Cash Inflow[4] | Other Criteria | Recommended Entry Mode |
|---|---|---|---|---|---|---|
| Indirect Export | | | | | | |
| Direct Export | | | | | | |
| Foreign Assembly | | | | | | |
| Licensing | | | | | | |
| Foreign Contract Manufacturing | | | | | | |
| Joint Venture | | | | | | |
| Wholly Owned Manufacturing Subsidiary | | | | | | |
| Mixed | | | | | | |

[1] Based on unit sale and price projections and/or any other projected cash inflows (royalties, management fees, dividends, and so on), net after foreign, and U.S. taxes, and repatriable in U.S. dollars.

[2] Based on projections of the U.S. company's foreign investment base and operating costs borne by the U.S. company.

[3] Projected cash inflow less projected cash outflow.

[4] Net present value.

**Figure 8.3** Financial Analysis of Entry-Model Alternatives.

modes because they do not satisfy a company's profitability threshold (internal rate of return).

Profitability analysis regards the entry decision as an investment decision. As used here, investment includes not only capital, but the allocation of any of a company's resources with the purpose of generating income over a lengthy future period. Thus, "start-up costs" to enter a new business environment—hiring new skills, negotiating with the host government and local business people, conducting market research, planning product adaptation, and so on—are just as much a part of a company's "entry-investment base" as a cash investment in a new foreign plant.

Major steps that are applied by a company in preparing a profitability analysis are:

- Identify, measure, and project over the planning period all incremental revenues (net after foreign and U.S. taxes) that will be received by the company as a direct or indirect result of each entry mode (including mixed modes).
- Do the same for all costs.
- Using the projections from the first two steps, calculate the incremental net cash flow of each entry mode over the planning period.

- Adjust the net cash flow for the time value of money (the cost of capital to the company) by calculating the net present value of each net cash flow.
- Rank-order the alternative entry modes by their net present values.

Once the profitability analysis is completed, management needs to evaluate each entry mode with other criteria it considers significant, such as other objective, risk, control, the exchange rate, and internal constraints. Therefore, the entry mode chosen by management may not be the mode with the highest net present value. Figure 8.3 summarizes this approach to the foreign-entry decision with a comparison matrix.

# Monitoring and Revising Entry Strategy

The discussion, thus far, of foreign market entry strategy has been for a single planning period. However, the entry strategy that is optimal for a company in a given target market at one time may not be optimal at a subsequent time. To maintain optimal entry strategy over time, therefore, managers need to monitor and evaluate changes continually in factors that bear on the direction and effectiveness of the current entry strategy. These factors include changes in the target market (such as country- and market-entry conditions, competition, buyer preferences), changes in company objectives, changes in company resources and capabilities, and changes in the company's actual performance in the target market.

The evolution of international companies may be described as a sequence of entry strategies, adopted to sustain and strengthen their positions in foreign markets over time. It is a cumulative process: Entry strategies today prepare the way for new entry strategies in the future. This interdependence among entry strategies becomes evident when we further examine the three primary market-entry vehicles: exporting, licensing, and production abroad. Interdependence is revealed by Behrman's study of the investment-export relation of 53 companies.[5] Twenty-two percent of the companies reported situations where changes in import tariffs and quotas led to a shift from exporting to foreign production in order to preserve or develop the market.[6] Twenty percent reported a similar shift after the appearance of local and third-country competitors in the foreign market.[7] Twenty-seven percent indicated situations where export products were displaced by foreign investment but where new and different export products were induced by the investment, or where foreign investment opened up export opportunities for new finished products.[8] Other situations of interdependence were also cited by the companies.

## NOTES

1. S. L. Srinivasulu, "Strategic Response to Foreign Exchange Risks," *Columbia Journal of World Business*, Spring 1981, p. 127.
2. David Ricks, *International Business Blunders* (Columbus, OH: Grid, Inc., 1974).
3. William A. Dymsza, *Multinational Business Strategy* (New York: McGraw-Hill, 1972), p. 257.

4. Igor H. Ansoff, *Corporate Strategy* (New York: McGraw-Hill, 1965) p. 116.
5. Jack N. Behrman, *Direct Manufacturing Investment, Exports, and the Balance of Payments* (New York: National Foreign Trade Council, Inc., 1968).
6. *Ibid*, p. 41.
7. *Ibid*, p. 41.
8. *Ibid*, p. 41.

## ESSAY QUESTIONS

1. Why do some companies want to become multinational while others prefer to stay domestic?
2. How can a firm become multinational without a heavy financial investment?
3. What critical factors should be considered in deciding which countries should be targeted first for multinational expansion?
4. What impact would a foreign country's monetary policy have upon your decision to expand globally?
5. What are the advantages and disadvantages of licensing, producing abroad, and exporting?

## MULTIPLE-CHOICE QUESTIONS

1. Reasons for going multinational include:
   a. following domestic customers who are going multinational
   b. earning additional income on existing products
   c. penetrating other fast-growing markets
   d. all the above
2. Most companies believe that domestic managers are not qualified to manage multinational activities.
   a. true
   b. false
3. The risks in managing multinational activities versus domestic activities ________.
   a. are the same
   b. are greater
   c. are less
   d. cannot be determined without additional information
4. The three stages of evolution from domestic to multinational activities are:
   a. export, foreign production, and multinational
   b. conceptual, multinational, and implementation
   c. domestic, planning, multinational
   d. none of the above
5. For most small companies, especially high-tech firms, the first step in going multinational is:
   a. licensing
   b. joint ventures
   c. purchasing technology
   d. all the above
6. Exporting and licensing do not always satisfy multinational objectives because of:
   a. incapable management
   b. tariffs and import barriers
   c. [illegible]
   d. all the above

7. The number of U.S. companies that are international and have achieved multinational status is:
   a. small
   b. average
   c. large
8. Which of the following is NOT part of a firm's entry-strategy planning?
   a. evaluating firm's resources/capabilities
   b. evaluating entry factors
   c. choosing the entry mode
   d. none of the above

## CASE STUDY: Bhopal—A Case of Corporate Negligence

Who bears responsibility when the capitalistic endeavors of a corporate giant result in the death and maiming of thousands of innocent poor? Such a tragedy occurred, shortly after midnight, outside the Union Carbide plant on December 3, 1984 in Bhopal, India. On a night when over 8,000 people were killed and over 300,000 suffered serious injury, who among the corporate leaders of Union Carbide was willing to accept responsibility for the worst industrial accident in history? The answer is, apparently no one.

The company consistently ruled out the possibility of negligence by claiming that the accident was due to the deliberate introduction of water into a chemical storage tank in an act of sabotage by a disgruntled worker. According to a statement issued by a Union Carbide investigating team, "The accident started when a large amount of water (100–200 gallons) was introduced into a MIC (methyl isocyanate) storage tank. When the water reacted with the MIC, heat was released while the temperature inside the container rose rapidly until the situation was out of control." As a result, approximately 80,000 pounds of MIC was released into the densely populated neighborhood surrounding the Bhopal plant.

As indicated above, company officials contented that the accident was a result of sabotage. However, several documented facts leave the disturbing impression that wholesale negligence existed in the areas of safety, training, and maintenance.

Consider the following:

1. The shift engineer (a 26-year-old, non-degreed native Indian) during that tragic evening would normally have had at least one year of MIC handling training. However, because the plant had been incurring large monetary losses, MIC recruits were rushed through crash four-month courses.
2. Additionally, once the training was over, according to the shift engineer, trainees were often turned loose to work on their own, but with only a trainee's pay (approximately $30/month).
3. By late 1984 only six operators, per shift, were working with MIC together with only one supervisor, as opposed to an original 12 operators and three supervisors per shift. Also, the night shift no longer had a maintenance supervisor.

As a result of the reduction of manpower per shift, indicator readings for MIC monitoring equipment were logged [illegible] hours, instead of once every hour. MIC samples were checked for impurities only once per shift, rather than twice every eight hours.

There was also, according to many workers, a complacent attitude toward safety by management, as evidenced by limited safety warnings issued by shift supervisors. Safety equipment was also not being used by the employees. There were claims made by the workers that disciplinary action was initiated against them, in the form of wage docking, when complaints were voiced concerning safety violations. Plant officials, however, responded to these allegations by indicating that grievances were exaggerated or fabricated, and training was, in fact, thorough. However, when asked to give details, officials declined, claiming that pending litigation prevented them from disclosing any more information.

Workers also contended that alarms and gauges monitoring the MIC tanks were often inoperable, antiquated, ill designed, and unsupported by modern backup systems. (The tank that was to eventually burst had alarms, which, according to workers, had not been working for years.) Workers further contended that only eight shutdown devices serviced the MIC unit, while safety engineers called for three times that number of safety devices.

The fears of the workers became a reality when at approximately 12:40 A.M. on December 3, 1984, the pressure on tank #610 escalated past 45 pounds per square inch. The temperature reached an astonishing 107.6° Fahrenheit (about twice the recommended ceiling).

What occurred during the next eight hours or so would shock the world. When final statistics were tabulated, 8,000 innocent men, women, and children died, with hundreds of thousands injured and maimed.

Further tragedy has resulted from the fact that, although the Indian government is now disbursing a $470 million award it obtained from Union Carbide, half of the claims now submitted are being rejected due to a lack of documentation to prove death or injury. As one local advocate states: "The government represented the victims. Now it says 'Prove your injury to me'" (*Scientific American*, June 1996).

There is also the added risk that soil and groundwater may still be contaminated. However, the National Environmental Engineering Research Institute concluded that there was no contamination during its study in 1989.

The question is asked then, Could Union Carbide wash its hands of this tragedy by claiming sabotage and deliberate violations of company procedures by its workers? The bottom line is that mega U.S. corporations, like Union Carbide, can never cleanse their failure to consistently and diligently maintain safety standards and training when operating dangerous industrial plants abroad. If proper training standards had been adhered to, along with proper maintenance and monitoring of the MIC equipment, an accident could still have occurred through sabotage, but Union Carbide could have convincingly proven its earnest efforts in maintaining satisfactory safety standards.

When the arms of an industrial giant reach across foreign lands, it does not absolve itself of an obligation to maintain the same standards of safety that it adheres to in its own backyard. Union Carbide may have placated a third-world country with blood money, but the legacy of Bhopal will serve as a disgraceful epitaph for capitalism and a painful memory for generations of innocent Indian citizens.

## QUESTIONS

1. Why did the problem occur?
2. Could the same problem have occurred in a U.S.-based manufacturing plant?
3. Who should be held accountable?
4. [illegible] of the "grand" strategy or the functional strategy?

5. What would be a reasonable approach for implementing a manufacturing functional strategy that involves a joint venture with foreign government?

## REFERENCES

Dan Kurzman, *A Killing Wind*. (New York: McGraw-Hill, 1987).
Turk & Turk, *Environmental Science*, 4th ed. (San Diego: Saunders, 1988).
*Scientific American*, June 1995, V. 272, p. 416.
*Business and Society Review*, May 1993, pp. 26–28.

# Index

**T**



**U**



**V**



**W**

9 780471 29197